SOUTHERN BIOGRAPHY SERIES

Mr. Crump of Memphis

MR. CRUMP

Baton Rouge, 1964

OF MEMPHIS

WILLIAM D. MILLER

LOUISIANA STATE UNIVERSITY PRESS

To the memory of my father

ACKNOWLEDGMENTS

FOREMOST among those who in many ways have helped me is Professor Forrest McDonald. It was he who provided the impetus for me actually to begin this work, and in its course he gave me friendly advice and encouragement. Such is my respect for his judgment and ability that his comments always meant much to me.

My friend Professor Lee N. Newcomer read the manuscript and made good suggestions for its improvement. In addition to his critical faculties, he had his own firsthand knowledge of Memphis to bring to bear on the subject.

I would like to thank all those persons in Memphis and Holly Springs, Mississippi, who, with traditional hospitality, took me into their homes and offices to tell me what they knew about Mr. Crump. Their names are found in the footnotes.

I received very important help from two gracious ladies who worked closely with Mr. Crump during his lifetime—Miss Clara Muller and Mrs. Evelyn Humphreys, who spent much time in pulling together Mr. Crump's papers for my use. Mrs. Humphreys accompanied me to Holly Springs and showed me landmarks associated with the Crump family history and introduced me to persons who had known Mr. Crump when he was a boy. Miss Muller repeatedly, and with unfailing kindness, helped me locate information necessary to bridge gaps in my knowledge of the subject.

Mr. Thomas Phillips of Memphis gave me many hours of his time, reliving the experiences that he had shared over the years with the subject. It was from the many discussions with Mr. Phillips that I was able to put together some of the basic elements that provided the insight needed to understand the subject. The time Mr. Phillips spent with me was, I am sure, a labor of love on his part, for he greatly admired Mr. Crump. Yet above his affection for Mr. Crump was his respect for the truth, a fact that time made clear to me.

In the preparation of this biography it was necessary to seek and to utilize to the maximum advantage the cooperation of the Crump family. The family's overriding expressed interest, stated at the outset, was to see that the project was reasonably performed, and beyond that it would have nothing to say. I am grateful to Mr. E. H. Crump, Jr., the principal representative of the family, for having faithfully followed this formula. In my initial contact with Mr. Crump, Jr., he stated that no evidence would be withheld, and all that he in turn asked of me was that I relate it truthfully. Over the several years of research and writing Mr. Crump scrupulously followed this initial prescription. In dealing with a subject of this kind it is good to feel fully free from the pressure of special family interest, and in this sense I could not have been less inhibited.

Three grants provided financial assistance toward the execution of this work. Some nine years ago, when I was working on a history of Memphis, I received a grant from the Henry M. and Lena Meyer Kahn Trust Fund through the good offices of Mr. Abe D. Waldauer. Since much information in this work was drawn from my Memphis study, it would not be amiss to express again my appreciation to Mr. Waldauer and the Kahn Trust Fund. A grant from the American Philosophical Society of Philadelphia enabled me to bear the expense of the first year of research. Later, when the prospect of writing became imminent, a grant from the then American History Research Center of the Wisconsin State Historical Society enabled me to take a year off from teaching. Marquette University provided time and financial assistance.

In the latter hurried days of getting the manuscript ready for press review I sent it to my sister-in-law Bertha Heeth Bond for proof-reading. I thank her for this work.

W. D. M.

CONTENTS

ILLUSTRATIONS

Mr. Crump of Memphis

⊠ ☐

HOLLY SPRINGS

IT WAS one of those days when Memphis was at its best, a bright April morning with cool, soft air and a mockingbird piercing the Sunday quiet. In front of 1962 Peabody Avenue motorists slowed their cars to look at the profusion of azaleas blooming in the yard. To the rear of the two-story brick home a Negro chauffeur rolled open the door of an old-fashioned carriage house and backed out a gleaming 1933 Lincoln sedan. A tall, elegantly dressed man, cane in hand, came out of the house and looked with satisfaction at his yard. A moment later his wife appeared, and he turned to assist her into the car. Driving south on McLean Boulevard for several blocks, the car angled into Lamar Avenue, Highway 72. Forty-five miles down the road was Holly Springs, Mississippi. Edward Hull Crump, the Memphis political leader, was off for his traditional Sunday visit to his mother.

They were scarcely out of Memphis when they crossed the state line into Mississippi—unkempt roadside establishments and red clay gullies. After passing through the town of Byhalia, the halfway mark, the land became rolling, and the scenery improved. Ten minutes more, and they were in Redbanks—a few houses and a roadside filling station. Then, from atop a high hill, they could see the clock tower of the Holly Springs courthouse. Entering the town, they passed

3

the buildings of Rust College for Negroes, and then made a short ascent to the town square where the courthouse stood. Across the square they drove into a street where old homes, many built before the Civil War, sat discreetly back from the street beneath the shade of magnolias and oaks. The Crump house, one of the oldest in Holly Springs, was two blocks off the square. When they arrived, Mollie Nelms Crump, tall and erect in the doorway, greeted her son and daughter-in-law affectionately.

Later, Crump's sons and their families arrived, and all had Sunday dinner together. In the afternoon more relatives came, among whom were his cousins, Frank and Dabney Crump; they, like himself, had migrated from Holly Springs to Memphis as young men. Crump was especially fond of them; he had lived with them in his early years in Memphis. He regarded both as "the salt of the earth," and Dabney, he said, came closer to being a "100% Christian" than any man he knew.[1] They spent the afternoon in relaxed talk, calling up memories of their youth. The next day in Memphis, Crump noted the visit in his memorandum pad. "My personal affection for the Crumps grows with the years. The pleasant afternoon with so many pleasant good people is like reading the Sermon on the Mt." [2]

The emphasis on family was one of the cornerstones on which his structure of principles was erected. It was an important part of the tradition in which he had been reared, and he maintained throughout his life a close contact with all members of the family, even distant ones. "Father possessed a sense of extreme duty with respect to maintaining family unity," observed E. H. Crump, Jr.[3] "He tried to inculcate those thoughts in all of us." [4] A gathering of the family in Holly Springs was always a gracious moment for him, and as his life passed into its middle years, his feeling for such an occasion became reverential.

By nature a traditionalist, Crump could scarcely have found a society better suited to his temperament than the one into which he was born. In the Reconstruction era Marshall County, Mississippi,

1 From notes made by Crump's secretaries. Hereinafter cited as Secretaries' notes.
2 Memorandum, undated Crump Papers.
3 Crump himself was also junior, but since he never referred to himself as such, his son was called E. H. Crump, Jr., rather than E. H. Crump, III.
4 Interview with E. H. Crump, Jr., January 7, 1958.

was one of the most "Southern" spots in the South. To a high degree, the values of its inhabitants were solidly rooted in the planting heritage of the Old South. Tradition was an important part of their birthright, and it operated powerfully in their lives.

Marshall County had fertile soil and natural beauty. One of its earliest residents declared that in its native state it had been a "most lovely region, and no one could look on its beautiful prairies and its forest lands covered with variegated flowers without longing to make it his home." "No wonder," he mused, "that the Indians chanted their almost funeral dirge when they bade their last farewell to its lovely vistas." [5]

When the county was opened in 1837, Southerners with their slaves were ready to take possession. In 1840 the county had eleven hundred persons, leading all others in the state in population. By 1858 it was claimed that more cotton was grown in Marshall County than in any other in Mississippi, and that in acreage production a world record had been set.[6] On the eve of the Civil War the county was accounted one of the three wealthiest among the state's sixty.[7]

Springing up shortly after the area was opened were several small towns—Old Salem, Hudsonville, Chulahoma, and Holly Springs—all seeking to become the county seat. Holly Springs, obviously in the ascendant, was the choice. Incorporated in 1837, it immediately experienced a remarkable prosperity. Imposing homes were built and filled with all the luxuries the time afforded. One year after its incorporation it had fourteen law offices, six physicians, two banks, five churches, three hotels, and several private schools.

An important concern of the town's residents was that their life exemplify the highest degree of Southern planting culture. Sherwood Bonner, a writer whose knowledge of the townspeople was derived from having lived among them throughout her youth, described them thus:

5 A. M. Clayton, *Centennial Address on the History of Marshall County, delivered at Holly Springs, Mississippi, August 12th, 1876* (Washington, 1880), 5. Crump Papers.
6 These and subsequent facts on the history of Marshall County have been taken from a brief unsigned "History of Marshall County." Crump Papers.
7 U. S. Bureau of the Census, *Agriculture of the United States in 1860, Compiled From the Original Returns of the Eighth Census* (Washington, 1864), 232.

They have the immense dignity of those who lived in inherited homes, with the simplicity of manner that comes of an assured social position. They were handsome, healthy, full of physical force, as all people must be who ride horseback . . . and do not lie awake at night to wonder why they were born. That they were Southerners was, of course, their first cause of congratulation. After a Northern tour they were glad to come home and tell how they were recognized as Southerners everywhere. . . . They felt their Southern accent a grace and distinction, separating them from a people who walked fast, talked through their noses, and built railroads.[8]

The Southern idyl in Marshall County was short-lived, for the Civil War destroyed the foundation on which it was built. The county that had been named for John Marshall backed its stake in a slaveholding society by contributing eleven generals to the conflict.[9]

One of the young officers from Holly Springs was Lieutenant Edward H. Crump. One of Crump's principal regrets was that he had not known his father, for he had died before his son was old enough to remember him. His father had not left him much in a material way, but there had been adventure in his life, and the spirited way in which he had moved through it charged his son's imagination. He had been a brave man; his bravery was almost legendary in Marshall County. An old Civil War captain, C. Q. Withers, who had led Holly Springs troops in battle, once remarked that Lieutenant Crump was "one of the bravest men I ever knew." "John," he said to Judge John Martin, one of Crump's cousins, "you've heard the expression that a brave man under fire can hold a glass of water without spilling a drop? Ed Crump actually could." [10]

Like many other Mississippians of the early period, the senior Crump was not a native of the state. He was born February 26, 1838, in Fredericksburg, Virginia, of a planting family.[11] Sometime during

8 Quoted in "History of Marshall County," (n.p., n.d.).
9 They were Major General Edward Carey Walthall, Brigadier General Winfield Scott Featherston, Brigadier General James R. Chalmers, Brigadier General A. J. Vaughn, Brigadier General Claudius Sears, Brigadier General Henry E. Williamson, General Alex M. Bradford, General Thomas Polk, General George M. Govan, General Daniel C. Govan, and General Christopher Mott.
10 Interview with Judge John Martin, September 16, 1957.
11 Crump's Virginia forebears were substantial people. An inventory of the estate of one of his father's uncles, Brodie S. Hull, made out September 3, 1825, listed holdings of 1,774 acres of land, forty slaves, stocks and bonds, and a sizable library.

his boyhood, he moved to Marshall County with four brothers. Economic considerations prompted the move. Prospects in Virginia were not good. Decades of tobacco planting had worn the land, and the Crump boys, an adventuresome lot, decided to move to Marshall County where there were relatives to receive them.

In his mature years Crump spent much time collecting information about his father and his background, visiting cemeteries in Virginia, looking up family records, and corresponding with persons who had known him. In 1912, when Crump was mayor of Memphis, he wrote to one of his father's comrades in the Civil War, seeking more information about his father's role in the conflict. His correspondent, W. C. Hamm, of Coldwater, Mississippi, answered his queries in considerable detail and commended him "most highly" for his interest in his father's service.[12]

"Ed, and all of his brothers," wrote Hamm, "were my schoolmates at old 'St. Thomas Hall': He was the big boy and I was the little boy, who always looked to him for protection, and he never failed me." Hamm had lost sight of his friend sometime before the Civil War, hearing that Crump had gone to Texas and had joined the Texas Rangers. Whatever the case, when the war began, the first E. H. Crump had just entered the United States Naval Academy as a cadet.

What he did the first year of the war is not clear. According to Hamm, he was not among the members of the two companies initially formed at Holly Springs—although three of his brothers were. "Billy [Crump] was Orderly Sergeant in the Company with myself, under Captain Kitt Mott." These two companies, combined as the Ninth Mississippi Regiment, returned to Holly Springs in February, 1862, after the expiration of the year's enlistment period. Out of them was formed a new company in which the senior Crump was a member—"a body of the finest boys I ever saw, grand men: young, brave and active, with the creed 'Be true to your country, be true to each other' and many, many times, have I seen them risk their lives to the limit to save a fallen comrade or retrieve a prisoner."

After the battle of Shiloh in April, 1862, the Holly Springs group wired Colonel John H. Morgan, asking if he would accept a company, mounted and equipped. "Yes: come on," was the response, and the company joined Morgan at Chattanooga where a raid was initiated into Kentucky. "Morgan's raid," as it is called, was of questionable

12 W. C. Hamm to Crump, July 20, 1912. Crump Papers.

military value, but it furnished some of the legendary exploits that contributed to the war's dramatic aspect.

In his letter to Crump, Hamm went into great detail concerning the activities of Company F, the Holly Springs group. "It would be impossible for me to give details of the service of individual actions in this great drama: but one thing, My Dear Sir: you may rest assured, there was never a blur on the escutcheon of Lieut. E. H. Crump." As an officer, "he was always just and attentive to the boys, and with him it was always 'Come on boys' and not 'Go on.' " Whenever someone under Lieutenant Crump took exception to his orders, there was an attempt to reason through the difficulty, but if this failed, the young officer would "jump up and jerk off his little-worn jacket, with a scarce discernible stripe on the collar, throw it on the ground, saying 'there's the Officer and here's Ed Crump, the man' and they would proceed to fight it out, there and then, and if he got the worst of it, he would so acknowledge, and, holding out his hand to the man, say: 'we are as good freinds [*sic*] as ever, and this must end right here.' "

One incident of the war stuck in Hamm's memory. "It was in the winter of '63 (if my memory is correct), Federal General Streight made a raid through East Tennessee and Southern Virginia, to strike the Kanawa Salt Works . . . and thirty men of Company 'F' . . . under command of Lieut. E. H. Crump, were dispatched to hang on their flank, harry them, and send reports of their movements to head-quarters. They stopped in Abingdon, Va., on the retreat; we were close behind them, and each of us with a Yankee overcoat on, and as we stood there cold and hungry . . . one after another of the 'Boys' would ride around to Ed and say 'Lieut.: take us into Abingdon.' " But Crump would "kuss," then say, "No, do you want to get me cashiered?" "Then," continued Hamm, "I sauntered up to him and said: 'Lieut. these boys want to go in and you want to go in too; take us in.' I remember now, his look on that occasion; he replied 'You too, d—— you' and then continued—'Billy, it is a temptation and I won't resist it.' He called the boys around him and said—'I will take you in on two conditions; first, not a word to be spoken by any one of you; second, not a shot to be fired until you can lift the cape of a Yankee overcoat with the muzzle of your pistol.' We moved in close together, until we were fully in their ranks, and then Ed. yelled—'Here's Morgan's men' and commenced firing, in which all joined, and in two minutes, the town was clear. The Company immediately formed, and Ed. rode up and down the line, as calm as May Day, asking if there was anybody hurt: all answered 'No.' "

Lieutenant Crump stayed with Company F until the war ended. In the final year of conflict the Holly Springs group was little more than a guerrilla outfit following Union armies, seizing stragglers, and interrupting supplies.

When he returned from the war, he was twenty-seven years old. It was time to settle down and make a home. The problem was difficult, for starting anew required improvisation in the face of the most discouraging circumstances. He owned good land; he would farm. He met the problem of a labor supply in a manner characteristic of the times. On December 28, 1865, an "agreement" was made between Edward H. Crump and "Phoebe, Admire and Logan and Ellison, Frances, Mary Anne and Asbury and four small children," for "one fourth part of the cotton and corn made by them." The freedmen were to be furnished their bread and meat at "the cost price . . . and the amount thus furnished is to be deducted from what may be earned by Logan, Ellison, Mary Anne and Asbury and it is understood and agreed that the said Freedmen are to conform to such reasonable regulations in regard to their conduct as the customs of the County and the laws thereof may dictate, and are to obey all orders given them by the proprietor." [13]

With the question of his livelihood settled, he took the next appropriate step—he got married. The wedding was announced with an engraved card: "Christ Church, Holly Springs, Tuesday, October 2, 1866, 12 o'clock M." With this card were two smaller ones: "Mary C. Nelms" and "Edward H. Crump." Another card announced that on October 24, a complimentary party would be given to "Capt. Ed. H. Crump & Lady" at Franklin Hall in Holly Springs.

The marriage could not have been the result of a romance of sudden inspiration. Holly Springs was too small for that. Crump had known Mary Nelms, whom everyone called "Mollie," from the time of his youth, and their marriage was largely the consequence of the arranging force of tradition, since a similarity of position and family background determined their mutual suitability. The romantic element was also present. Crump had an adventuresome and im-

13 Crump Papers.

pulsive spirit that could have appealed to Mollie Nelms, for her life
had been sheltered, and she gave way to no impulse but sternly
conformed to the demands of principle and duty. In Mollie Nelms,
Crump saw order and strength.

Mollie Nelms was of a planting family that had migrated into
northern Mississippi in the early 1850's. She was born in Anson
County, North Carolina, March 24, 1843. The Nelmses were wealthy
slaveholders, but the decline in the fortunes of the Southern seaboard
states and the promise of the new land to the west induced the Nelms
brothers—Charles G., Dr. J. P., and Eben—to sell their land and
with their families, slaves, and household goods, make the long
journey to Mississippi.

Eben Nelms went first. Accompanied by a neighbor, the two
families traveled together. When Sunday came, the neighbor insisted
that they continue on, but the pious Nelms refused to be led into
desecrating the Sabbath. Virtue was rewarded; he reached Mississippi
two days ahead of his Sunday traveling acquaintance.

Charles G. Nelms built a great home on the Mississippi called
"Norfolk," the lumber for which had been floated down the Mississippi from Cincinnati. When the war broke out, he organized the
"DeSoto Rebels" and led them to battle at Shiloh. Wounded at a
place called "Hornet's Nest," he was carried to Holly Springs where
he died. It is said that before General Albert Sidney Johnston's death,
he had recommended to the Confederate War Department the promotion of Colonel Nelms to brigadier general and that Jefferson
Davis had signed the commission.[14]

Dr. J. P. Nelms, Mollie Crump's father, settled in De Soto County
where he built a "castle-like house of hewn logs," and quickly became
one of the leading and respected citizens. He served as a physician in
the war, and when Memphis was devastated by the fever epidemic
in 1878, he went to aid the sufferers. Later he died of the disease
in Louisiana.

Mollie was quite young when her mother died, and much of her
education was entrusted to private boarding schools. She was first
sent to the Nazareth School, near Bardstown, Kentucky, described
in its 1860 catalogue as "a Public Boarding School for Ladies." She
attended the school in 1858 and 1859, promenaded with her friends

14 George M. Moreland, "Norfolk: Where Old-Time Memories Linger,"
Memphis *Commercial Appeal*, July 14, 1929.

about the pleasantly shaded campus, and applied herself diligently to her studies. Reviewing Mollie's record, the present sister superior writes that "throughout the years that Mollie Nelms was at Nazareth, she distinguished herself in Grammar, Reading, History, Arithmetic, Composition, piano, guitar, voice, dressmaking and Embroidery and Needlework. I notice she also received an award for Parsing in Poetry." [15]

After the Nazareth School she attended a finishing school for girls in Philadelphia known as "Madame Chagarey's French School." It is difficult to know the ultimate effect of these schools in fashioning her mind and character, but the nuns at Nazareth, if they did no more, probably reinforced the decided Nelms trait of living life in terms of objective principles, and Madame Chagarey, whose brother was an "original Frenchman" and a one-time mayor of New Orleans, did teach the young lady how to speak some French phrases.[16]

Mollie and Edward began their married life on a farm near Hudsonville, a small settlement seven miles northeast of Holly Springs. The house was a one-story frame building, with four large rooms, two on each side of a wide hall. Later when the children came, the hall was curtained off, and the front served as a parlor.[17] A long porch ran across the front, and close by the road stood a summer kitchen. Further to the rear were two whitewashed pine log structures, once slave quarters but now used for the tenant freedmen. Back of the cabins was a rail fence, over which one could cross into the fields by using a stile of upended logs. From the rear door a path ran down through a grove of trees to a spring.

The first child, John, was born in 1868. A year and a half later there was a girl, Kate, and finally a second boy, Edward Hull, Jr., born on October 2, 1874.

The years of Edward's infancy must have been difficult ones for his parents. The hope of creating a good life from the land in the post–Civil War South was largely futile. The Southern economy was

15 Sister Rose Catherine, Nazareth Academy, to the author, October 30, 1961.
16 The comments on Madame Chagarey's brother were made by Crump in a memorandum. Crump was always impressed by what he presumed to be his mother's fluency in the language, and he once proudly declared that even in old age she could still "speak it like a native."
17 Interview with Dora Boone, April 28, 1956. Miss Boone remembered the Crump house as it had been in the 1880's.

placed at a greater disadvantage by the rising tide of industrialism than it had ever been before the war, and to this was added all of the social and economic disabilities that came with defeat. The thing that Crump remembered above all else from his childhood was poverty.

He had but one recollection of his father. He had been standing on a gate, and his father led a horse through it, then mounted and rode away.[18] When the boy was four years old, his father died, a victim of yellow fever. The disease ravaged the lower Mississippi Valley in 1878 and 1879. In the early phase of the epidemic, it was assumed by the Holly Springs authorities that the town was immune since its altitude of over six hundred feet relieved it from the noxious effects of the "miasma" that clung to areas of lower altitude and which, it was thought, harbored yellow fever. Consequently, the city officials opened the town to refugees from other areas only to have the disease spread rapidly through its own population.

In his late years, Crump wrote to a cousin in Mississippi relating a part of what had happened within his own family circle during the epidemic: "My father moved my mother and his three children to Uncle William Hull's plantation in the adjoining county of Benton." [19] Then the father, aware of the risk, went to Holly Springs where his brother William and cousin Brodie lay ill with the disease. Taking them to the Hudsonville farm, he nursed them as best he could. Brodie, who had been the first president of the Bank of Holly Springs, died September 7, 1878, and William, in the mercantile business with Brodie, died three days later. On October 4, the brother who had tried to save them died. Listing the dead in column after column, the Holly Springs *Reporter* said, "If there are dregs in the cup of sorrow, we who live here, have well nigh drunk them all." [20]

When her husband died, Mollie Crump put on mourning and wore it for the rest of her life. It was not solely a symbol of personal grief. It was a reminder of the loss the family had suffered with his death, and it was the ultimate steadfastness of her nature that his loss would be remembered as long as she lived—and to remember, too, that her husband's role was now hers. She decided against living with relatives. When the epidemic was over, she and the children

18 Interview with Clara Muller, August 6, 1957.
19 Crump to Brodie Crump, May 18, 1950. Crump Papers.
20 Holly Springs *Reporter*, September 20, 1878.

returned to Hudsonville and to the new grave where her husband lay in a grove of cedars, the center of desolation that spread to all parts of the land.[21] The cotton remained unpicked in the fields, for the tenants had fled before the plague. The livestock was gone, and chickens wandered through the house.

Mollie had the strength to begin anew. Physically, she possessed little of the delicate and fragile femininity that was held by romantic legend to be the unfailing mark of the Southern woman of quality. She was tall and big-boned, with large hands and red hair. Her energy was inexhaustible, and she remained in good health for ninety-seven years, active and clear-minded. Even in old age, she carried herself with a ramrod posture, and when guests came to her home, she stood until they had all been received. Her grandson, E. H. Crump, Jr., thought of her as a "Spartan woman" who had "austerity in her character." When principle was involved, she could be stern and inflexibly willful, but she also had "a wonderful sense of humor." Crump's second cousin, Judge John Martin, recorded her "as remarkable a lady as I ever knew in my life. Ed inherited from her his remarkable memory. She could remember way back with perfect accuracy. That was one of Ed Crump's predominant characteristics."

In her later years she lived an almost secluded life in her Holly Springs home, taking great pleasure in raising flowers. On summer mornings she could be seen in her yard working with the Negro boy who helped her, for she wanted things done precisely. When a neighbor was asked what she had done with herself in the years that she lived alone, the answer was: "What did she do with herself?—she sat up there in state. She was stately and charming—a lovely person —a gracious hostess." [22]

When not attending her yard, she read on a wide range of subjects. She entertained infrequently but, when she did, she insisted on a strict observance of all the amenities that she had been taught to regard as marks of good breeding. An Episcopalian, she accepted religion and the moral precepts that it offered as "true." The subject required neither introspection nor external marks of fervor. She read her Bible "adequately" and attended services at the Episcopal church in Holly Springs only occasionally. To shun public gatherings, even

21 The body was later reinterred in the Holly Springs cemetery.
22 Interview with Mrs. Matt J. Coffey, June 24, 1957.

church attendance, was in part an acceptance of the seclusion she
chose at her husband's death. Throughout her years she remained
totally a woman of the Old South. The changing customs and ways
that came with modernity did not touch her. The Civil War was a
tragedy that she was never able to forget, and the feeling of partisan-
ship that she had absorbed as a young woman never left her.

Young Edward was like his mother. He resembled her physically
—his flowing red hair, his height, facial features, large hands, and
erect posture. In character he was even more like her. He inherited
her willfulness and her passion for order; and like her, he revered
the tradition in which he had been reared. What he did not inherit,
he consciously tried to imitate, for he profoundly respected her. And
where Mollie Crump was concerned, her feeling for her son was
expressed in the phrase she invariably used when speaking of him
to others—"my son Edward," never just "Edward."

When Mollie Crump began the task of running the Hudsonville
farm, the boy was just beginning to store impressions in his mind.
What he remembered most was the family's constant battle with
poverty. He often alluded to it when trying to impress upon his
own sons the virtue of thrift and industry. His frequent references
to this theme, and his conviction that there were lessons to be
learned from living under such rigorous conditions would sometimes
draw from his wife the amused remark that his chief regret in life
surely must be that his mother had not taken in washing. He remembered that money was so acutely scarce that everything the
family ate or wore was raised on the farm. He recalled that they
would lay fruit on the roof of the house to dry, and that what little
money the family got came from his mother's churning butter and
selling it to a wholesale house.

At Christmas time the children got only an orange and some nuts
in their stockings, and their principal excitement of the day came
from popping hog bladders that had been saved from the fall butcher-
ing. Crump recalled the chores that fell to him at an early age: riding
a mule to the mill with a full sack of corn to be ground; sometimes
falling off when the animal shied, and then, with great labor, hoisting
himself and the corn back on. He remembered with strong distaste
that he had been obliged to watch that the hogs did not eat the
cottonseed which had been thrown into the gullies to prevent further
erosion; nor did he like mending a gap in the fence to keep the cows

from getting out or having to turn a grindstone to sharpen a meat ax or reaper's scythe.[23]

He had other memories—experiences once common to rural Southern boys which left upon them a permanent mark of their Southernness. There had been the mile-long walk in winters over roads that were rutted and bogged with water to the one-room frame schoolhouse where the girls swept and dusted and the boys chopped wood for the stove. There were the summer days—scuffling barefooted on the hot clay road to Hudsonville to get something his mother needed from the store; jumping to the shady patches in the road to cool his feet; stopping to pick blackberries that grew along the roadside; exchanging greetings with some Negroes he knew who were loading pine logs on a flatcar; and reaching the store to delight in the dark coolness and musty fragrance of its interior. He returned home in the hot somnolence of noon, nearly silent except for a crescendo of cricket chirping when the sun passed behind a cloud. Reaching finally the haven of the porch, he paused to cool his burning feet. He was tired, but he was also hungry with the great open appetite of youth. The family meal was about ready and looking into the hallway, he could see his sister placing food on the table: smoked meat, garden vegetables, and milk cooled in the spring.

He remembered nights when, lying awake from some childhood sickness, he had heard the timeless sounds of the rural South: distant barking dogs, the whistle of a train, and rich laughter from Negroes making their way home from a social gathering. He remembered going to Duck Pond to fish and swim and breaking in a calf to pull a cart made from the wheels of a discarded cultivator.

He remembered these things because he frequently talked about them in later life. Sometimes, then, he would return to Hudsonville to give a barbecue down by the spring for the few residents who remained, like Mrs. Alma Law, with whom he had walked to school as a child.[24] Like the land, they declined in spirit and fortune, and a few drifted into a poverty-stricken old age. These Crump helped with his checks. As one of them observed after his death, "He loved his Marshall friends; he always came back to us."

In 1883 when the boy was nine, his mother took the family from Hudsonville to Holly Springs. Several factors influenced her to move.

23 Secretaries' notes.
24 Memorandum, undated, written by Mrs. Law. Crump Papers.

It was becoming apparent that farming would never afford a respectable livelihood for the family. In town advantages would be offered to the children that they could not get in their present circumstances. It was about this time that she inherited some land in Tunica County and a part of the Norfolk plantation that had belonged to her uncle. With the income the property gave her, the move was feasible.

As the family moved into Holly Springs, a six-year-old boy watched the procession come down the street and stop in front of a house across from the vacant lot where he stood. He was Mason Jones, the son of a storekeeper, and the friendship that developed between him and young Ed Crump was to last throughout their lives. Jones recalled the day on which they had moved in. The household goods had been transported on a large wagon pulled by a four-horse team. They had arrived around noon. Leading the procession was young Ed driving "Bally" the bull, hitched to his cart. Crump later recalled that they had passed the Holly Springs public school and that the spectacle of a wagon piled high with furniture and a boy driving a bull yearling had upset the deportment of the students. No doubt as the boy drove past, his commands to the bull became louder and more imperious.

For two years, the Crumps did not live in the house that later became their home, possibly because Mollie Crump had not yet inherited it. When they did occupy it, they moved into an historic building—one of the earliest homes in Marshall County. It had been built in the 1830's by Samuel McCorkle, Mollie Crump's great-uncle, the county's first banker and the first Indian commissioner in the area. Through the years the home was kept continuously in the same family, and its original portraits, furnishings, silver, and china remained in daily use.

Holly Springs in the eighties had lost the bustling character it had possessed in the fifties. The misfortunes that afflicted the rural South after the war caused the town's population to decline, a factor that had much to do with producing inbred character. Throughout Crump's political career the people of Holly Springs accounted him as a member of the family-like community, and they unanimously refused to believe that his detractors were motivated by anything except willful malice or ignorance. "We know him," they would say.

Although the town was small, it provided opportunities for the boy that he had not had in the country. It still served in the eighties as a center of commerce for the outlying rural areas, with three drug stores, four hotels, and several mercantile stores. Here a young man might begin an apprenticeship in business, or he might avail himself of the educational opportunities that were at hand. As a self-conscious seat of plantation culture, the town in its early years had chartered "The University of Holly Springs," but the "university" never came up to the expectation held out by its title. As the town's centennial orator admitted, it had "a capacity scarcely equal to that of a good grammar school, [and] its performance fell so far short of its promise as to inflict serious injury on the place." [25] The town did, however, sustain a number of private schools (a holdover from the antebellum period when the planting aristocracy supported such institutions) and a free public school.

Young Edward was placed in the public school, where he was taught by "Uncle" Albert Anderson, "one of the best men that ever lived." [26] The few remaining people who were able to testify first-hand to the boy's scholarly qualities affirmed that he was industrious and quick to learn, but the subject soon induced a reminiscent mood in which his pranks figured as largely as his scholarship. Mason Jones recounted one incident with great relish. "Uncle Ally," as the boys called the schoolmaster, had been wounded in the Civil War, leaving him with a stiff right arm. However else it handicapped him, it was useful for taking roundhouse swings at students needing discipline. One year, Jones recalled, the classroom was so overcrowded that Edward was assigned to a stool behind Uncle Ally's desk. Once, as the teacher pursued a subject with the class, the boy quietly moved his stool by the blackboard and began to draw pictures, attracting more attention to his artistry than Uncle Ally got for his teaching. Sensing that something was wrong, the master turned, and tiptoeing up behind the artist, swung at him, intending to unseat him from his perch. But the boy, seeing the blow coming, ducked quickly, and Uncle Ally's great swing knocked down the chimney to the stove. The room was filled with so much smoke and soot that school had to be dismissed.

As Jones related this tale, the vision of Uncle Ally's fist crashing into the stove pipe came again into his mind, and he laughed for some time. In the late years of Crump's life, these two sometimes

25 Clayton, *Centennial Address,* 3.
26 Interview with Mason Jones, July 11, 1957.

sat together in Crump's side yard and reminisced about the old days. Certainly this story passed between them more than once.

In his thirteenth year, Ed began to grow tall. By the time he was fifteen, he was over six feet. He was a slim, raw-boned boy, fair-skinned and freckled, with a cleft in his chin and bright red hair that grew in such curly abundance that it was almost impossible to manage. "I used to work hours trying to prepare this red, hard-headed hair of mine for the girls," he once said, adding that "it had a habit of trying to stand on end." Never one to introspect over anything, he apparently thought of his hair as a favorably distinguishing mark. In his scrapbook there is a clipping, preserved from youth, which stated that "the greatest men . . . of this world were red-headed, from bold adventurers to kings and queens." They were the most energetic, they made the most cheerful companions, and they seemed "to keep their brains alert and active under conditions which make men of other complexions dull and despondent."

His nature was outgoing, affectionate, and assured. His cousin recalled that he was "most attractive with his dare-devil ways." [27] Jones remembered occasions when the Holly Springs boys would swim at Lumpkin's Mill Pond, and when "Ed would duck a boy, you could hear him laugh a mile." He was not quarrelsome. Jones remembered that of the Crump boys it was John who got into fights, but not Ed as a rule. He recalled that whenever the boys planned a hunting or swimming expedition, his mother would let him go only if Ed Crump were going, since she felt he would be kept from ill-advised adventures. When some of the others planned a petty piece of vandalism, Ed would refuse to join them. "He always led a clean life," said Jones.

Every fall the circus stopped at Holly Springs, sometimes the great Barnum and Bailey show, or Peck and Furman's Daniel Boone Company of "30 people, 5 acting horses, 18 real Indians," whose show was climaxed with the "reknowned" presentation of "Chas. Gaylord's border drama, entitled 'On the Trail; or Daniel Boone the Pioneer.' " Invariably, the boy found the means to attend. The high degree of precision that was displayed in erecting and dismantling tents fascinated him, and in later years he would allude to the example when trying to effect better organization in the Memphis government.

27   Interview with Mrs. Helen Craft, June 24, 1957.

Usually, the period immediately after the departure of a circus was a critical one for young Crump, for he could not watch daring feats by bare-back riders without trying them himself. Once he acquired a wrenched back while somersaulting, an indiscretion that he paid for with occasional twinges throughout his life. He became expert at marbles, vying with Frank Rand for the town championship. Later Frank and his brother Edgar went to St. Louis to become the heads of one of the country's leading shoe manufacturing firms.

Every summer the boy would ride horseback to adjoining Benton County to visit his Aunt Mary Hull, who would knit all of his woolen stockings for the approaching school season. She always asked him what color he wanted and his answer was always "any color will do so long as it's red."

The year 1889 brought changes in the Crump household. In January, Kate married Jasper Butler, a Holly Springs merchant. Kate Butler's married life was short, for she died in 1902. She left three daughters to be reared by Mollie Crump. Later, when they were young women, they went to Memphis and lived for three years in Crump's home.

The year Kate was married, Ed left school. He had exhausted the opportunities which the Holly Springs public school offered. The time had come to get a job. Working for money was not a new experience for him, since customarily he earned what he spent. He picked up odd jobs; during the summer he made money by going around the town to see whose orchards had the best fruit, and then he would sell it to passengers on the Illinois Central Railroad when the train stopped in town. During the weeks before Christmas he managed a concession selling apples and oranges on the street.

His first full-time job after leaving school was setting type for the Holly Springs *South Reporter,* a town newspaper owned by his second cousin, John Mickle. Crump was fond of his cousin, but he left the job after a year. Quite likely, he could see no future in it, and one suspects that being perpetually smeared with ink was too much for his fastidious nature. Yet in his mature years he liked to recall that he had once been a "printer's devil," an occupation that suggested a parallel between his life and Benjamin Franklin's. Once, when John Mickle was confined to a Memphis hospital, he provided an inquiring reporter with some recollections of his youthful cousin's work as a newspaperman. As a typesetter, he "never was very proficient at it. He didn't stay in it long enough—just about a year, I think." [28] He had been "mischievous and full of life. They called him 'Skinny'—he was such a lean skinny boy. He fattened as he grew older."

After leaving the newspaper office, there seems to have been in the succession of the youth's activities the design of a plan that would culminate with his going to Memphis. His cousins Frank and Dabney Crump had become successfully established in the city, and they urged him to look for employment there. To the young and ambitious, Memphis offered opportunity. In the eighties its economy had begun a spectacular expansion, and it was generally assumed in Holly Springs that any young man worth his salt would try his mettle in the city. Memphis represented more than just economic opportunity: it provided a metropolitan atmosphere that the young man savored. While throughout his life he scrupulously avoided the kind of sins for which Memphis was noted, he was young and human enough to be attracted by the glamor that emanated from the city.

Memphis also had men of wealth, fabulous characters in the imagination of the youth. In the last year of his life, Crump wrote a letter to Dave Halle, a merchant of the city, thanking him for a birthday card and recalling with humorous fancy his youthful memories of Halle's father. When the senior Halle had come to Holly Springs, "he came in luxury with his valet and he told us of the fine horses he had in Memphis and the liveried coachman to handle them. And he provoked our envy further by asserting that when he didn't spend his summers in Switzerland, he was gambling on Lookout Mountain. In those days I believed that if there were three persons in America who really had money, they were Dave Halle, Tobe Leidy and Orlando Hammond." [29]

The Mississippi River held a great fascination for boys of the era, and this figured in the lure of Memphis. Crump once recalled a boyhood river adventure:

Some of us boys at Holly Springs came to Memphis in the years of the Anchor line steamboats. All of us knew Memphis well. Of course, Main Street was the attraction. We paraded it from one end of its busi-

28 Scrapbook news clipping.
29 Crump to Dave Halle, October 8, 1953. Crump Papers. Tobe Leidy and Orlando Hammond were Memphis merchants.

ness houses to the other, stopped down about Gayoso Street to get a mess of fried catfish. Then we sauntered up Front Street to the upper elevator, where the City of Hickman was landed to take on and discharge freight. We went on board, looked her over from stem to stern, talked with some of her crew and was told she would stop at the foot of Beale or the lower elevator, to take on more freight.

"Can we ride her down to that point?" I asked one of the men. He said "yes." We went up to her cabin and sat down. I suppose there wasn't a boat on the Mississippi River we hadn't heard about or seen, so we talked of them. Finally the Hickman backed away from the landing, out into the middle of the river and headed downstream. I saw she wasn't going to land at the lower elevator and got busy. Finding the captain, I told him we were to ride to the elevator and get off.

"We're headed for New Orleans," the captain answered gruffly. "Who told you we'd stop at Beale?"

I explained about one of the crew giving us this information. Well, the captain said a few words that wouldn't look nice in a Sunday school lesson, but he went in at the lower landing and let us off. [30]

In the spring of 1891, when he was sixteen, Crump began to put his plan into effect. He decided to farm for a season in the hope of raising enough cash to take a short course in bookkeeping. It was probably his intention to plant cotton on some of his mother's property, or farm with one of his uncles on a share basis. Miss Dora Boone, his Hudsonville neighbor, thought he had gone to Sledge, Mississippi, to work with an uncle and that he had made money by picking cotton at the rate of forty to fifty cents a hundred pounds.

The bookkeeping course was completed by the spring of 1892, and the youth immediately took a job as a bookkeeper and clerk in a country store at Lula, Mississippi. He needed experience before trying the big city. Lula was a small mercantile center situated at the junction of the Yazoo and Mississippi Valley Railroad and a narrow gauge road that ran from the Mississippi River southeastward to Jonestown, Mississippi. The main street was clay, and along its length were six mercantile houses, as many saloons, and a railroad siding for freight handling. It was a tough town, and nearly all the male inhabitants went armed.

In after years Crump recalled his days at Lula as "healthy and happy ones," but age sometimes assigns to youth a perpetual joyousness it did not always possess. Rooming and boarding is ordi-

30 *Commercial Appeal,* October 6, 1944.

narily a monotonous experience, and it would have been very much so in a place like Lula. Moreover, he developed stomach trouble that lapsed into a chronic condition, plaguing him periodically for the rest of his life.

Despite his tedious existence, he found opportunities to enjoy himself. Even the routine of boarding was relieved by the practice of "eating out" bad debts, a subject that he was fond of reminiscing about in later years. This practice, which was a product of the scarce money economy in the postwar South, partially compensated the young clerk by room and board provided by individuals who owed the store money. In this manner a bad debt was salvaged and a customer retained, although there was inherent in the system the danger of losing a clerk. Crump likely did not get the nutritious meals he needed at this period of his life, and his health suffered from a too steady diet of fatback, grits, and beans.

While at Lula, the young man began formally to call on girls. An awareness on the part of some village wags that the youth was a novice at courtship led to some bucolic horseplay. One evening as he was calling on the local schoolmistress, a neighbor invaded the parlor where they sat, and with a show of much agitation declared that a burglar was in her house. If the young man would go over and confront the prowler, the neighbor woman would hold a lantern for him to see. Crump agreed to the mission immediately, welcoming the occasion to impress the lady with a demonstration of cool courage. On reaching the neighbor's home, the light from the lantern did indeed illuminate a figure in one of the rooms. As the young man approached, the "burgler's" arm arose menacingly, whereupon Crump delivered a fusillade of pistol shots into the object. When the light was shown on the victim, it was seen that it was a cleverly contrived dummy, moved with wires from an adjoining room.

A phase of the young man's maturing interest in women was seen in his enthusiasm for attending dances. Occasionally on weekends and holidays he would return to Holly Springs to see his mother and attend a dance or party. The Holly Springs *Reporter* of January 7, 1892, noted that "our time honored friend, Mr. Ed. H. Crump," was as "handsome and pleasant as ever," and had been "one of the most gallant beaux" at the New Year's Eve ball held in the Holly Springs Masonic Hall. The ball had been attended "not only by the youth and beauty of Holly Springs but also a large number of visitors from neighboring cities and towns." An orchestra from Memphis had furnished the music.

Crump recalled that part of the excitement of going to a dance was "the arrival of a dress suit from Memphis that was rented. It had probably been worn the night before by some headwaiter, but its glory overshadowed that in my mind. After the dance I would hurry to the station to ship it back to Memphis. Delay would mean another dollar rental." [31]

There were less formal affairs, parties that were sometimes held in the surrounding country areas. Ed would mount a mule behind his brother and with the others of the party would make their way along rural roads so dark that they had to pin white handkerchiefs on their backs so as not to become separated. If they were lucky, a thunderstorm would so fill the streams that a return home would be made inadvisable until daybreak.

In May, 1893, the young man took leave from his clerking job and returned to Holly Springs. His stomach trouble had worsened, and business in Lula would be dull until the fall cotton crop was harvested. He hoped that something would present itself in Memphis before he had to return. It was a good summer—rest, parties, and baseball. Shortly the Holly Springs newspaper was printing accounts of the fortunes of the "Nine Diamonds," the town's baseball team, captained by Ed Crump, first-baseman. "The baseball games were great sport," he once recalled. "I was a long, lanky kid and was known around my section as bow tie because of my build. . . . I thought I was pretty good in those days. Once when we beat Water Valley we celebrated by forcing a bull onto the second floor of the hotel." [32]

Jones remembered that Holly Springs was "a real baseball town" and that rivalry with the surrounding towns was intense. It was so strong that the Holly Springs club was sometimes hard pressed to get a winning team. Brodie Finley, another of Crump's cousins who preceded him to Memphis, occasionally brought one of the city's professional baseball players to Holly Springs for a weekend game. When the team played away from home, it traveled in a wagon with a twenty-foot bed, pulled by four mules—a conveyance furnished by one of the town's baseball enthusiasts. Mercer Mickle, another cousin, in later years recalled Crump's organizing ability as a team

31 Scrapbook news clipping.   32 *Ibid.*

captain. "Even then," he exclaimed, "he gave evidence of what he was going to be by the way he handled boys. . . . When he'd leave a town, he'd carry away the best player the other team had. Why, he became invincible; nobody could beat him!" [33]

The team that Crump captained in the summer of 1893 was a strong one, but the season had its blemishes. The *Reporter* recorded on June 22: "The Holly Springs Base Ball Team played a game with the University Club of Oxford. The Oxford boys were victorious . . . the score standing 32 to 10." Again, on August 18, the *Reporter* mentioned a game between the "Kid nine with Jas. Bennett as captain and the Nine Diamonds with Ed Crump as captain." Up to the sixth inning "the situation of the Kids looked gloomy, but through the skillful management of their fearless captain they rallied to a man, when they whitewashed the Diamonds in the last three innings winning the laurels in a close combat—9 to 8."

The summer of 1893 was unusually hot and dry for northern Mississippi: sweat came readily and red clay dust hung on the drooping leaves of trees that lined the roadsides. When the Nine Diamonds played a weekend game in a neighboring town, they tried to leave Holly Springs early to avoid too long traveling in the afternoon heat. Throughout the morning they jolted along clay roads that ran through fields of bright green cotton plants, down hills to the cool of bottomlands where their rig splashed through a stream, and through pine thickets where a country church stood. At noon they stopped to eat their lunch near a spring or in the yard of a farmhouse where they could draw up a bucket of water from the well. After lunch they "warmed up," mightily impressing the young boys on the premises. Reaching their destination, the boys jolted across a railroad track in their wagon and into town. Passing in front of the stores, they were barraged with good-humored jeering and predictions of defeat by the Saturday groups of rural people who stood or sat wherever they could find shade.

As the wagon moved to the pasture that served as the playing field, a mood of destiny settled on the Nine Diamonds and their faces became stern. Captain Crump stood among them, revealing new refinements of strategy. Then, as the word got around town that the team had arrived, the boys would go through their preliminary warm-up on the field. The game was the climax of tension

33 *Ibid.*

and drama: heroes that were real played with a fierce determination to win. Afterwards the begrimed and weary contestants were taken to the homes of the townspeople, and frequently later in the evening they attended a dance or a party held for the visiting team.

The Nine Diamonds played their last game of the 1893 season in Senatobia. The town newspaper, *The Democrat,* spoke well of them. "The Holly Springs boys are a jolly, good-humored set and play ball like young professionals. They made a fine impression by their skill and enthusiasm on the diamond and their uniform deportment as gentlemen and clever fellows." [34]

When Ed Crump returned to Holly Springs from the Senatobia game, a phase of his life was ending. The friends that rode on the wagon with him—the Rand boys, Henry Levy, Earl McKie, Minor Mickle, and others—would remain friends, but the days of warm uncomplicated association which only youth can have were over. He was going to Memphis—to what he did not know, but he was not worried, for he possessed an assurance that came from an invincible determination to overcome all the barriers that lay between him and success.

Behind the young man's studied determination "to amount to something" was his great pride. He had always had a horror of inadequacy and dependency. He had never been a burden to his mother. He had to be captain of the baseball team because he knew he could run it better than anyone else. And because he was the captain, his team had to be the best. His pride was his strength, and in those areas where human frailty asserted itself he erected a wall to keep others from seeing his innermost self. There would be few times in his life when his guard was down. His pride was that of a Nelms, but it was also a part of his Southern heritage—an almost exaggerated sensitivity concerning the inviolability of self. Another factor drove his ambition further: the Crumps and Nelmses had been important people, leaders in their society, beholden to no one. Reconstruction and the economic blight on the land had brought hardships to his family and especially to his mother. He would change that.

The *Reporter* of Holly Springs announced on September 21, 1893, that "Mr. Ed Crump left Tuesday for Memphis to accept a situation in a business house." The "business house" was the objective of

34 Holly Springs *Reporter,* September 7, 1893.

many enterprising young men leaving rural towns for the city, and Ed was joining their number. But the *Reporter* was a little premature. Crump was not "accepting" a situation—he was looking for one. Naturally the editor knew this, and everybody else did too, but a kindly sentiment would not have him depart without receiving the typical small town journalistic flourish.

Very likely he did go to Memphis, but apparently he found nothing suitable, for he spent the fall working for his old employer at Lula. At Christmastime he returned to Holly Springs, determined that at the end of the holiday season he would go to Memphis again. In January, 1894, Crump went to Memphis again, and this time he remained.

⊠ ☐

Chapter II

MEMPHIS

HERODOTUS wrote that in ancient times there stood at the apex of the Nile delta a splendid city founded by the first king of Egypt. It was called "Men-ofer," or "Memphis," which meant "good abode." In 1819, when Andrew Jackson, James Winchester, a general in the War of 1812, and John Overton, retired chief justice of the Tennessee supreme court, planted a town on their tract on the fourth Chickasaw bluff, they christened their undertaking with the same name.

In its early years the river town was a "tough and uninviting place, overrun by the scum of the river." [1] But the commercial potential of Memphis was such that by the eve of the Civil War it had a population of over twenty thousand. A prosperous mercantile class had emerged that provided economic and social stability in the town's affairs, while over four thousand Irish and fourteen hundred Germans provided cultural variation in the city's character.

The Civil War left the South facing the necessity of reordering its life and outlook. The stress and change that marked the era of the New South intimately affected Memphis and disorganized its society. Lawlessness and political and physical disorder became so apparent

1 Gerald Capers, *The Biography of a River Town, Memphis, Its Heroic Age* (Chapel Hill, 1939), 44.

that the city seemed to take on again the wild character of its early river town days.

There was first Reconstruction, producing the familiar problem of corruption. Urban services deteriorated, and crime, vice, and filth flourished as never before. A Negro population which numbered 2,882 in 1860 increased to 15,000 in 1870, creating the profound problem of its integration into the city's life. "I wonder why they gave it such a name of old renoun, this dreary, dismal, muddy, melancholy town," sang an English news correspondent who visited Memphis in this era.[2]

Then Memphis suffered an almost mortal blow. In May, 1878, yellow fever broke out in the West Indian Islands. By July it was in New Orleans, and then like a noxious fog it drifted up the Mississippi Valley. The disease claimed its first life in Memphis on August 13. Ten days later it was epidemic. There was nothing to do but flee, and those who could, deserted the city in a panic-stricken exodus. Twenty-five thousand departed, many of whom did not return. With the first October frost the plague ended, leaving over five thousand dead.

Before this catastrophe struck, the city of Memphis owed six million dollars to New York bondholders. After the epidemic, it could pay nothing to its creditors. To escape a governmental paralysis brought on by the suits of creditors, Memphis was dissolved. On January 31, 1879, the Tennessee legislature repealed the city's charter and enacted the Taxing District Act to provide for the administration of city business. Governing powers were given to a board of commissioners responsible to the state. It was not until after the turn of the century that Memphis regained its rights of self-government.

Down and nearly out, the city revived almost miraculously. The thrust of industrialization accounted for the change. In 1880 Memphis had slightly over two million dollars invested in manufacturing establishments. Ten years later it had nine million.[3] During the decade its industrial growth was greater than any other major Southern

---

2   J. P. Young, *Standard History of Memphis, Tennessee* (Knoxville, 1912), 141.
3   U. S. Bureau of the Census, *Report on Manufacturing Industries in the United States at the Eleventh Census: 1890* (Washington, 1895), II, part 2, p. 4.

city.[4] The backbone of this growth was cottonseed oil and lumber; the latter industry had been attracted to the area by the relatively untouched stands of hardwood timber in the lower Mississippi valley.

With industrialization came a phenomenal population growth. From 33,000 in 1880, Memphis more than tripled, growing to 102,320 by 1900. Among Southern cities only New Orleans and St. Louis had more people at the turn of the century.[5] There were probably few cities in America that so completely embraced a new population at the time as did Memphis. In the two decades following the epidemic, approximately 68,000 newcomers arrived.[6] The majority were rural people from the depressed areas of north Mississippi and west Tennessee. For the most part they were sober and industrious—Calvinists, who liked their religion periodically seasoned with the spice of a revival meeting. Not a few were physically enervated by improper diet and chronic disease. They were "bilious," had "spring humors," and relied on bromide-laden tonics to make life bearable.

Almost as many Negroes came into the city as whites, but it was a white man's world, and they lived on the white man's terms. Out of sight of the white man, the Negro had a life of his own. It was one filled with the affairs of fraternal organizations and churches—and Beale Street. During the day Beale was somnolent. Loafers dozed in chairs tipped back against store fronts, and the air hung heavy with the odor of burnt grease and fried "chitlings." But at night it awakened. Prostitutes and glittering dandies with diamond stick pins sallied into the streets, and gambling dens became alive. In Pee-Wee's Saloon at 317 Beale, W. C. Handy thumped his piano and looked at a large painting on the wall that depicted a scene from *Othello*. Now and again a "Fancy gal with shadowed eyes and a wedding-ring waist glanced through the doorway" or ventured inside to "see if anybody had set eyes on her sweet good man." [7] Beneath it all there was sadness, and Handy wrote the blues.

Violence was common on Beale, so common that the police scarcely investigated the murders that took place in the saloons and bordellos. Sudden death was an integral part of the Beale Street saga.

4   *Ibid.*, 3–5.
5   U. S. Bureau of the Census, *Thirteenth Census, Population*, I, 82–83.
6   Capers, *Biography of a River Town*, 226.
7   W. C. Handy, *Father of the Blues* (New York, 1941), 92.

It provided the tension, and it lurked in the background as the final excitement. It was the line that one crossed irrevocably. At night Beale pressed against that line, and the tension showed itself in the way the actors affected to disdain it—drinking, gambling, whoring, and perhaps killing or being killed. A man could not flinch.

Whites, too, drank, gambled, whored, and killed. "Killing is now the most thriving industry in this part of the country," declared the Memphis *Commercial Appeal*. "They kill them next door to the city hall and shoot them in the parks." Newsboys should cease crying about the "big murder," since "every day is murder day." [8]

The *Commercial Appeal's* outcry was, unfortunately, fully substantiated by statistics. The city's high murder rate was first brought to public attention in 1912, when the *Literary Digest* expressed concern over the rise in urban murder rates. It pointed out that during the decade ending with 1910, the national average for cities had been 7.2 homicides per 100,000 population. Memphis led with a shocking 47.1. In the single year 1911 the city reached 63.4. Altogether, it had 556 homicides in the period 1901–10. [9]

But that was not all. In 1918 Dr. Frederick L. Hoffman, a consulting statistician of the Prudential Insurance Company of America, published a series of pamphlets on comparative murder rates in the major cities of the United States. It was Hoffman who designated Memphis the "murder capital," backing his charge with a survey of murder rates among 31 large American cities. In 1916 Memphis had 134 homicides, giving it a rate of 89.9 per 100,000—more than twice as many as Atlanta, its nearest competitor. [10]

Memphis was a disorganized city. The disorganization came from its rivertown heritage of violence; it came from the new population— a people, both white and black, whose religion had no relationship to culture, but was almost totally subjective, a people whose rural values were out of place in industrial urban America, a people who had implanted in their minds the conviction that status was related to physical daring and the quickness with which one sensed and accepted a challenge.

8 *Commercial Appeal,* March 3, 1909.
9 "Explaining Our Homicide Record," *Literary Digest* (October 19, 1912), 656–57.
10 Andrew A. Bruce and Thomas S. Fitzgerald, "A Study of Crime in the City of Memphis, Tennessee," *Journal of the American Institute of Criminal Law and Criminology,* XIX (August, 1928), p. 14.

But Memphis also had its residents of settled culture, the older families who managed commerce and staffed the professions. They brought concert artists to town, attended plays at the Lyceum Theatre, and sent their sons and daughters to private schools. There was another group, a growing number of young businessmen, office workers and executives in the city's commercial and industrial expansion. They were interested in order and social progress, and as the new century progressed, they insisted on taking a more prominent position in the administration of the city's affairs.

The Memphis into which Crump came was a burgeoning city of expanding commerce and industry, and gentility had no significant part in its life. Memphis was willfully set in the mold of its easy-going sinful ways. The outcries of the clergymen or the serious concern of some reform-minded young businessmen could do little to correct its basic problems.

It was early on a cold January morning in 1894, when Ed Crump, nineteen years old, arose and lit the lamp on his dresser to dress for his trip to Memphis. As he ate breakfast, he discussed again with his mother what he would do when he reached Memphis and what he hoped to do thereafter. Then he kissed her good-bye, picked up an old valise, and walked in the first light of morning to the railroad station.

He arrived in Memphis at the Illinois Central station at the foot of Poplar Street. Leaving the coach, he walked south on Front Street toward the center of town. To his right the levee dropped precipitously to the mud flats that ran out to where the gray Mississippi coursed southward. Across the river the flat marshes of Arkansas were discernible through the morning haze. Further down the mud flats gave way to deep water where river steamers were moored. In the distance he could see the outlines of the railroad bridge that had been built two years earlier.

Front Street had just come alive with morning activity. Running north and south along the top of the bluff, it was a street of warehouses, saloons, and quick lunch establishments. It was a street of cotton, where most of the big factors had their offices. Cotton, roped into "snakes" for sampling and grading, was in the warehouses and on the sidewalks. It was a street of smell, sound, and motion. There was the stagnant odor of Wolf River, a small turgid stream that meandered from the interior country westward along the northern limits of the city to empty into the Mississippi. Mellow moist smells came from the saloons and hot rancid ones from the lunch counters. There was the smell of offal on the street and the delicate aroma of spices and fruits that lay in the warehouses. There was the perpetual cry of draymen ordering their beasts through the perils of a street pitted so deeply that axles were sometimes broken. Along the base of the bluff a switch engine whistled and puffed, and farther below from the decks of the steamers came the sound of shouting rousta-bouts and the banging of cargo.

Some aspects of the picture were soon to change. Trucks would replace wagons, and the new railroad bridge foreshadowed the end of the romantic era of river steamers. But there was still that grand moment on Front Street when a steamer arrived or departed; spectators were impressed by the deep rolling blasts from its whistle that reverberated along the river and by the powerful thrust of its wheel.

The busy scene quickened the young man's excitement. It was the impulse to be a part of the early morning action that prompted him to stop at a lunch counter for a cup of coffee. Accustomed to the familiarity of small town associations, he could now join in the ritual activities of morning cloaked with the dignity of anonymity. But Ed Crump was never the type to permit romantic fancy to trespass on reality, and he left the restaurant without getting his coffee. The waiter had on a dirty apron, an unsurmountable affront to Crump's fastidious standards. Turning east off Front onto Adams, he came shortly to the city's number one fire engine house. In front of it a fireman sat in a chair. The young man stopped to ask where he might get coffee in a more appetizing atmosphere. "Why, you just come on in here and I'll give you a cup," the fireman said. He led the young man into the station where a coffeepot sat on a coal stove. He offered to fry an egg, but Crump declined. He was never one to impose too much on another's good will. As he drank his coffee, he looked over the equipment, especially the steamer.[11]

The fireman's name was Richard Borner. Later when Crump was mayor, Borner drove the last horse-drawn steam pumper that the city owned—today housed in a glass-enclosed pavilion in Overton Park. The fireman's friendly gesture was the beginning of a lifelong acquaintance. Borner was the kind of man Crump thought well of,

11   Interview with Mrs. Nola Borner, June 7, 1957.

a simple, kindly person, happy with his lot in life. In later years Borner told of his first meeting with Crump and added, "Through all the years since, I've seen him time and time again, and let me tell you through all the years of his success he never forgot old Dick Borner." [12]

One day toward quitting time Crump sat in his office over the North Memphis branch of the Union Planters Bank and looked back a half century to the time he had come to Memphis to get a job. Someone, he said, had circulated a report that he had had thirty cents when he reached the city. He denied this. "As a matter of fact, I recall distinctly, I had only 25 cents. I was holding it like grim death for I debated the lunch bill of fare between a fried fish stand at the southeast corner of Gayoso and Main and a restaurant between Jefferson and Adams where the Lily Bakery and Lunchroom is now." He finally chose the latter place because it was accessible to the number one fire engine house where he had had coffee that morning with Dick Borner. He wanted to see the fire horses hitched up at noon. He thought of Borner a moment and of how fast the years had gone, for Borner was already in retirement. "He was always a courageous fireman," Crump said. He thought again of the events of the day he had come to Memphis. "That afternoon I was in Johnston and Vance, leading clothing merchants store, under the old Peabody Hotel, on Main Street where Lowenstein's now stands. A fire occurred in that vicinity. All the uptown fire equipment answered the call. Of course it was all horsedrawn. It was a cold day. The horses were snorting and bucking. . . . That sharpened my taste for metropolitan life." [13]

He mentioned other things that came into his mind. "Every Sunday morning you could see 10 to 12 Mississippi River boats tied up at the wharf." The city hall had been a dingy old building on Front Street, and the drinking water had come from the Wolf River. The county was run by magistrates, and it had no good roads and hardly a respectable school. "I spent my first night in Memphis at 588 Exchange Extended," Crump mused.

He thought of his first years in Memphis. It had been a difficult period, but he had never doubted that he would win success. "Plan your work and work your plan." That was his favorite adage. The

12 *Commercial Appeal,* October 18, 1959.
13 Scrapbook news clipping.

plan took into account initial adversity, and initial adversity there was. The year 1894 was not an auspicious one for young men seeking their fortune in the city. The panic of 1893 had produced a slack in the economy that made jobs difficult to get, and Crump's first weeks were spent seeking work. Eventually he found a temporary clerical position with Walter Goodman Cotton Company on Front Street. With spring, cotton trading fell off, and the job hunting began again. During the summer he worked for the Galbreath Real Estate Company, and when fall came he went again to the cotton company. In the spring of 1896, he found a permanent job as a bookkeeper for the Woods Company, one of the city's established firms in the carriage and saddlery business.

In that era, before the advent of bookkeeping machines and automatic calculators, a bookkeeper's job was an important one, and the young man was happy to have it. But as one of his secretaries later wrote, "it was merely a means to an end, and he was not satisfied to settle down on that stool and remain there any longer than was necessary to qualify for something higher up the line." [14] He worked at it for two years, and there were many times when a late evening passerby who happened to peer through the dusty show window of the Woods Company on south Second Street would apprehend in its darkened interior a solitary light suspended from a high ceiling, beneath which sat young Crump, coatless, wearing a green eyeshade, putting the accounts in order.

In the spring of 1898, the Woods Company consolidated with the Chickasaw Saddlery Company, forming the Woods-Chickasaw Manufacturing Company. In the new organization, Edward H. Crump was named cashier. It was a distinct promotion for the young businessman, one, which his secretaries say in their collection of notes on Crump's life, was made over the expectations of several older employees. "Had they but known it," say the notes, "this red-head was destined to keep right on up the middle of the road and the day was not very far distant when he would win the business and have all of them eating out of his hand." "But," they prudently add, "let's not get ahead of our story."

As Crump moved to his cashier's cage, national affairs were moving into dramatic channels. The struggle for freedom in Cuba was demanding national attention. Memphis, finding its own problems

14 Secretaries' notes.

too immediate to be romantic, was all heart when it considered the plight of Cuba. On a warm August evening the elite of Memphis society assembled in the Lyceum Theatre to witness the presentation of a regimental flag to the Fourth Tennessee Regiment. The press account of the affair glowed. The flag was accepted by Major Eldridge Wright, whose speech was "exquisite." In his "superbly eloquent" conclusion he sent a deep thrill into the hearts of his listeners by advising the mothers and sweethearts that the honor of the regiment was more important than life and that the flag presented would never be lowered in surrender.

Following the speech some of the young ladies staged a "tableau vivant" which featured "America"—Ruth Martin—holding the flag of the regiment, with "Cuba"—Estelle Wolf—at her feet. Miss Martin sang "There's Room for One More Star," in a "clear sweet voice," and Miss Wolf performed a Cuban dance. And "then while Grace Lewellyn recited 'Our Defenders' Miss Wolf stood close by supporting the flag with the folds wrapped around her." [15] Crump may have attended this affair, but there is no evidence that he ever gave thought to military adventure in Cuba.

The young man's tenure as cashier was not a long one. Within a year he took another long jump into the executive circle of the new company through his election as treasurer. In 1900 he was made secretary and treasurer, a position that offered him the opportunity to advance his own ideas concerning the management of the business.

During these years he lived on the south side of the city on Polk Street with his uncle James, the father of his cousins Frank and Dabney. He joined the Business Men's Club and the Fashionable Tennessee Club, and he sometimes dined and drank beer with his friends at Luehrman's Restaurant. His social appearances were frequent enough to make him generally known among the city's younger set, but he was not noted for his enthusiasm as a partygoer. "He was always too busy with his work," explained an acquaintance who had known him in those early years.[16]

He was well liked. His somewhat flamboyant red hair, his height and erect bearing, and the confident way in which he carried himself gave him an arresting appearance. His friends were among the city's rising young business and professional men. He met Tom Phillips

15 *Commercial Appeal,* August 6, 1898.
16 Interview with Mrs. Edward Fontaine, January 10, 1958.

about this time in Luehrman's Restaurant. Phillips was beginning a career in journalism as a reporter with the *Evening Scimitar*. Later, when Crump was mayor, he served as Crump's secretary for several years and was thereafter closely associated with him for the rest of his life. Frank Rice was another associate and later became widely known for his supervision of the organizational details of the Crump machine. Another friend was Galen Tate, son of the Shelby County sheriff. Afterwards Tate developed political aspirations that ran counter to Crump's, and when they were thwarted, he pushed himself into the foremost circle of Crump's detractors. Crump returned the favor by placing Tate's name in his "red book," a special list of persons who had grievously wronged him.

Older people invariably found him the model young man. He was instinctively courteous and most considerate. They liked his serious-minded side and his ambition. He had few of the traditional vices that were supposed to typify young men. His moral deportment was above reproach. He did not frequent any of the low dives and gambling resorts around the city, and his conduct toward women was so strongly anchored in the canons of propriety that he could never have given cause for offense.

With all his propriety, he had a streak of showmanship that led him into youthful escapades. Tom Phillips recounted two instances of deviltry that a Memphis patrolman, Mike Kehoe, had related to him. One evening Kehoe came upon a group of young men watching another at the top of a tall lamppost. It was Ed Crump, and Kehoe ordered him down. When Crump alighted he explained that he had just won a five-dollar bet. On another occasion Kehoe was attracted by laughter to where a group of young men were gathered. Crump had just won another bet by hitting the chimney of the Peabody Hotel with a watch that belonged to Mike Tate. (Shortly afterwards, Tate received a fine new watch from Crump.)

An episode Phillips personally witnessed occurred one late fall day when Crump walked into the Chickasaw Club on the fifteenth floor of the Exchange Building. Although there had been a heavy frost, the stiff straw hats of three members were on the rack. Going to a desk he wrote three notes stating, "Winter is here," and enclosed with each an order on a Memphis hat store for "the best winter hat." Then going to a window he tossed the hats out and was engrossed in reading when their owners picked up the orders.

With the Woods-Chickasaw Company, the young executive was all business. When the company did not fare well, he came forward to advocate policies calculated to shake off its lethargy. The secretaries' notes describe Crump's wish to rehabilitate the business along "progressive lines" contrary to that of "reactionary officials" who would have the company follow the "path of least resistance."

The main issue concerned the automobile. In the first years of the century the Woods-Chickasaw Company seemed content to rely on urban clients who customarily purchased expensive lines—phaetons, broughams, and the family carriage. These models were the first to feel the competition of the automobile. Crump was confident that it would be a number of years before the automobile would make serious inroads into the company's rural trade, and he therefore thought that the major sales effort should be directed at the rural buyer. But his "every effort in that direction . . . met with a chilly rebuff from the older heads who mistook his consuming desire for success to be nothing more or less than youthful impertinence." [17] He was "passing through the darkness that precedes the dawn."

Yet all was not darkness. Sometime early in 1901, Crump began seriously to court Miss Bessie Byrd McLean. Although he had seen her at social functions for a year or more, he did not try to advance his cause directly. Rather, he spoke to others of his high regard for her beauty and charm, and these remarks, by clever design no doubt, were repeated to Miss McLean. Once as she listened to an account of judgments that Crump had made of her, she exclaimed quite positively, "I wish he would tell me that." [18] In later years she told a friend of this incident and confessed that she on her part had been interested in Edward. She thought him a very attractive man but had met him only infrequently since "he was always busy." Yet this was a point in his favor, for even as a young girl she had said that she wanted to marry someone who "could get things done." To her daughter-in-law she once said, "I knew he was the kind of man I wanted the minute I laid eyes on him." [19]

Perhaps Crump got the word. In matters of the heart an exchange of sentiment can be elaborately contrived. Late one afternoon Betty McLean sat on the front porch of her parent's home at 211 Monroe

17 Secretaries' notes.
18 Interview with Clara Muller, August 6, 1957.
19 Interview with Mrs. E. H. Crump, Jr., January 10, 1958.

playing with a pet monkey and Crump walked by. It was a pastime unusual enough to permit him a reasonable excuse to linger and observe. The invitation that he had hoped would arise was graciously offered: "Won't you come in?" she asked.[20] After that he came to see her every night, and late that summer when the McLeans were vacationing at a mountain resort, he took time off from his work to visit them and to give their daughter an engagement ring.

They were married at Calvary Episcopal Church on January 22, 1902. Frank Rice, William Bruce, and Dabney Crump were among the groomsmen, and Brodie Finley, a friend from Holly Springs days, Galen Tate, and Edward Fontaine served as ushers. Before Crump entered the picture, Edward Fontaine had been one of the bride's most attentive admirers.

The wedding was given generous coverage in the society pages of the newspapers. The bride was described as "one of the most popular of the young ladies who have given Memphis social circles a wide fame for beauty," while the groom was "equally well known in business and social circles. His popularity extends all over the South. His energy makes him a leader in whatever he undertakes." After the wedding they took a boat trip to Nassau.[21]

Crump's life thus far had a storybook quality. Within eight years, through hard work and seriousness of purpose, he had made a remarkable rise in the business field, climaxed by his marriage to one of the city's most beautiful and sought-after women. One of the remarkable aspects of his life was the serene and idyllic character of his married life. In Bessie McLean he found his ideal mate.

The McLeans were Scotch. In the early days of the Republic they had lived in North Carolina, and one McLean signed the Mecklenberg Declaration of Independence. Bessie's father Robert had lived for a while in Murfreesboro, Tennessee, but had later moved to Memphis to become vice-president of his uncle's firm, the William R. Moore Dry Goods Company, one of the largest mercantile firms in the South. In Memphis Robert McLean married the daughter of William S. Bruce, the organizer of the W. S. Bruce Company, dealers in iron, stable hardware, carriages, and wagons. The Bruce Company building was the first five-story building in Tennessee, located where the National Bank of Commerce stands today.

20 Interview with Clara Muller, August 6, 1957.
21 Scrapbook news clipping.

Bessie was born September 13, 1877. She was an only child. As a girl she went to the fashionable schools kept by Miss Clara Conway and Miss Jennie Higbee, and after the completion of her formal education she made her debut. The years before her marriage were like the era in which she lived them—unclouded and fun-filled. She kept a scrapbook of the happy occasions she had known. There are faded pictures of vacations at the seashore and a flower, brittle with age, pressed in the fold of yellow pages. Calling cards, announcements, and the stubs of theater tickets are pasted to pages, and beneath them are noted the event and the name of the person who escorted her.

Perhaps it was a young girl's vanity that prompted her to keep certain letters. They tell of the hopeless, yet hopeful, love of young men who had been overwhelmed with her beauty and gentle disposition. "Please pardon me for the liberty I take in addressing you without your permission," began one letter. "Several days have passed since you left. . . . Words are powerless to express to you my unhappiness. . . . Pity me Miss McLean. . . . My object in writing you . . . is quickly told. I love you. Please pardon me. I met you accidentally and saw you but a single day. But I repeat it. I love you with all my heart and soul." Another letter ran on for twenty pages and concluded with an outpouring of feeling: "If you only knew how the memory of you is associated with my every act and word, you would wonder that I could write of anything other than my love for you. . . . You could object to my loving you, but will you? Your objection would be respected but by no means sustained. The matter stands now, I love you."

Bessie McLean was an ideal wife for Crump. Like him, she had few hidden recesses in her nature to harbor moods of introspection. Bright and vivacious, she liked to laugh and tell funny stories. She was "so cute in the way she told things," a friend recalled. "Her eyes were very expressive while she talked." She was without affectation or social ambition. Although she liked to have friends visit her and she enjoyed playing bridge, she tempered her interests to her husband's. "Father did very little socially," E. H. Crump, Jr., explained. "He worked on something practically every night of the year. Mother just adjusted to his wishes."

To Betty Crump it seemed inconceivable that her husband should ever be a controversial figure. When anyone said anything against him she would exclaim, "I know it is wicked to hate, but I detest that man." [22] Sometime in the early years of their marriage she began calling him "Rudy," because he reminded her of Rudolph Rassyndale, the hero of Anthony Hope's *A Prisoner of Zenda.* The name was first applied as a bit of affectionate teasing, but it stuck.

In the first years of their marriage they lived with the McLeans. It is said that Crump's wedding was scarcely over before he assured Mrs. McLean of his wish that she be a part of the family circle. And she was, for thirty years later when he was in Congress, Crump wrote to her on the occasion of his wedding anniversary:

We have all heard, since childhood, the threadbare "Mother-in-law joke," where husbands and wives have spoken contemptuously of the mother-in-law as an obstacle in the way of marital felicity. Of course, it has been exploded in thousands upon thousands of instances, and particularly in my own case, for I have loved you very dearly since the day Betty and I were married, thirty-two years ago today. You have made the pathway much brighter all along the way for us and I hope you will help us to commemorate many, many more anniversaries. [23]

Marriage was a happy opposite to the frustration Crump experienced in his business affairs. His insistence on a change of policy increased the tension between him and the older members of the firm, and his proposals were rejected more emphatically than they had ever been. Matters went from bad to worse, and in the fall of 1902 he resigned. The occasion was characterized by high drama.

There is no doubt that the president of the company was provoked. Once Crump had decided that a course was wrong, it was impossible for him to concur in it silently. The grain of his nature was so solidly set that whatever ran contrary to it produced a considerable stress reaction. His continuous criticism gradually brought the president's nerves to the breaking point. In the midst of a particularly stormy session, the president drew a pistol, apparently intending to rid himself of the offending member or to precipitate an on-the-spot resignation. The resignation was offered, but "in disgust" rather than from intimidation, for "the alert . . . Secretary-Treasurer promptly took the pistol away from him and gave him a sound thrashing with the weapons with which nature had endowed him, a pair of brawny fists." [24]

22 Interview with Mrs. E. H. Crump, Jr., January 10, 1958.
23 Crump to Mrs. Robert McLean, January 22, 1934. Crump Papers.
24 Secretaries' notes.

Behind this exciting affair was the company's steadily worsening financial condition. On December 17, 1902, the Woods-Chickasaw Manufacturing Company filed a petition of bankruptcy in the chancery court, listing its assets as $138,000 and its liabilities at $126,000. The action was precipitated by its inability to cover an overdraft of $800 at a Memphis bank. In a statement to the press the president attributed the failure to "friction between stockholders and officers of the corporation regarding policy." [25]

The receiver's sale was held on January 28, 1903. With security put up by his wife's parents, Crump borrowed $50,000 from the old Memphis National Bank, and his high bid of 71 5/8 cents on the dollar put him in possession of the company that had formerly employed him. After the sale, an unsuccessful bidder, Eugene Rehkopf, sought out Crump and proposed a partnership, which was immediately accepted.

The new organization did well from the beginning. By 1905 it had become the leading establishment of its type in Memphis, occupying six floors of the then modern building known as "22 South Second Street." It had a large warehouse with railroad facilities, pictured on the Crump Company stationery to give the impression of tremendous size, with flags flying from its roof and toy-like freight trains at its sidings.

As a young executive, Crump on one occasion acted like his father, who had been one of Morgan's Raiders. In the midst of an argument a company salesman observed that were it not for the difference in their positions, he would not have permitted Crump to berate him. Thereupon Crump took off his coat and "turning to his business force, he said: 'If anyone interferes here in this little argument, they'll have to find another job!' " [26] The fight lasted until "both were about all in." Later the man returned and asked for his job, stating that he liked Crump's style. "He's still working for Crump," the account concluded.

Crump frequently sought advice and sometimes took it, but he did not like to share authority, and this may have had something to do with the purchase of his partner's share of the business in 1906. After that, the firm was called the "E. H. Crump Buggy Company." It was sold in 1910 when Crump became mayor of Memphis.

Business success was matched by other triumphs. In 1905 Crump

25 *Ibid.*   26 Scrapbook news clipping.

was elected director of the Business Men's Club, the organizational forerunner of the Memphis Chamber of Commerce. The election was usually preceded by energetic campaigning, and from the time the candidates were announced until the polls were closed there was much logrolling and buttonholing. Crump's election reflected his popularity, for most of the candidates on the "Blue Ticket," which he headed, were defeated. The campaign was managed by Frank Rice, and his work was so effective that the question of who should manage future political campaigns was settled.

As a consequence of his election, Crump's picture appeared for the first time in Memphis newspapers on February 11. It was this picture that was reprinted from time to time during the early years of his career. According to the notes made by his secretaries it was "one of the very few" photographs for which he ever posed. He had an aversion to formal portraits, and in later life when news photographers took his picture, he would react with self-conscious mugging.

On May 8, 1903, a son was born to the Crumps—Edward Hull, Jr.—and on December 29, 1905, another—Robert McLean. With a growing family and a successful business he still had time for politics. He was once asked how he started in politics and he replied, "Frankly, I don't know," but added that his interest was an "aggressive one from the day I cast my first ballot when I was twenty-one years old." [27] He was initiated into politics in the old fourth ward, one of the toughest sections of the city, where notorious George Honan and Mike Haggerty operated the Turf Saloon. Crump's first job was poll watching—one that was neither genteel nor pacific. His secretaries state that he fought with the "gang" in the streets and around the polling places on elections, and once, when a notorious safeblower and murderer "wearing green glasses" came in to vote a second time, Crump recognized him and "politely, but also firmly and positively," ordered him to leave. The desperado retired without protest.

In 1902 Crump was elected from the fourth ward to the local Democratic legislative convention, his first elective position. He was heading toward the political leadership of his ward, but as he later confided, his political activity was prompted by business reasons:

27　Jonathan Daniels, "He Suits Memphis," *Saturday Evening Post*, CCXI, (June 10, 1939), 48.

he was as concerned with registering sales for his firm as he was with registering voters.

The business angle was shortly superseded by another. The combination of Crump and Memphis set up an interactive response that made politics inevitable for him. His nature required an almost total response to a challenge that tested his capacity to bring order out of disorder. Slackness, ineffectual action, and confusion brought him to test his mettle against them. He insisted on an orderly arrangement of the smallest particulars in whatever goal he sought. Even the business on his desk was ordered to the last detail. No one ever saw his desk cluttered. Visitors in his office would observe papers on his desk placed together in neat classified piles held down by paperweights of polished brass or colored glass. He also kept his bedroom in order. His wife once related to a friend that in the early days of her marriage she was awestruck at the way her husband kept his personal effects: everything down to the last button was kept in its place. Crump's chauffeur, Clint Cleaves, recalled how insistent Crump had been that everything be kept clean and in its place in the garage and how it was periodically inspected and suggestions made to improve order.

Behind his passion for order was rigid implacable self-discipline. Discipline began with himself, and he applied it so inflexibly that most men would be made uneasy by it. An episode that occurred three years after he arrived in Memphis illustrates this point. Exhausted by overwork, he went to Hot Springs, Arkansas, to take a treatment in one of the spas and to consult a renowned physician. The physician told him to give up cigarettes, coffee, and drink. At the time Crump was a heavy smoker and drank a lot of coffee. As for alcohol, he apparently indulged himself adequately on social occasions. It was smoking that made him hesitate to accept the prescription, and he asked the doctor if he might not "taper off." The doctor, a "very stern man," would not hear of the proposition. Crump should adhere uncompromisingly to the treatment or get another physician. The patient refused to commit himself but told the doctor he would have the answer before the day was over. He left the office and walked directly across the street to the old Arlington Hotel where he spent an entire hour "wrestling with the question." Returning to the physician's office he agreed to the treatment. For the remainder of his life he never touched tobacco or drank another cup of coffee. In later life he did drink an occasional bottle of beer, but this itself was the result of medical advice.[28]

In the years to come, Crump would tell of his visit to Hot Springs. After leaving the doctor's office, he went to a baseball game played by two Negro teams—one representing Hot Springs and the other, the "Yellow Jackets" of Waco, Texas. While watching the game, and "dying for a smoke," he was asked for a cigarette. His response was, "I haven't got one and what's more, I never will have one."

If such lifelong consistency had been exclusively a dietary matter, Crump could have been dismissed as a health faddist. Faddist he was, especially after he began his junkets to Battle Creek, Michigan, in the twenties, but he imbued his life with principle not only in his diet, but at every point. He liked his principles in epigrammatic form, and his papers contain page after page of quotations offering rules for living. They are found in abundance penciled in his scratch-pads. "One of the most comfortable places to live is just inside your income." "Read, listen and ask." "Observe, remember and compare." "Never put a sponge on the end of a hammer if you expect to drive a nail." "Nothing worth while is easy and easy things are not worthwhile." "Everybody must work." There are many more. Whether he found them of such inspiration that he was able to persevere with a single-minded purpose in his conduct, or whether he delighted in them because they simply struck a responsive note in his nature, there was remarkable agreement between the values expressed in his axioms and the ones that operated in his life.

One of his most frequently repeated statements was "Observe, remember and compare." The extremes to which he went to employ this principle became legendary in Memphis. On his desk was a little black loose-leaf notebook that bulged so with notes that he had to keep it shut with a stout rubber band. Notes and pads accompanied him everywhere. On the reading table by his bed there were always a note pad and pencil to record some reflection that might enter his mind during the night. When he traveled, his note

28 There is an interesting sequel to young Crump's visit to Hot Springs. The daughter-in-law of the physician who treated Crump became his colleague in Congress in the early thirties. The physician, a Dr. Greenway, had a son John, a Rough Rider with Roosevelt and later a prominent figure in the development of Arizona. After John Greenway's death the state honored his memory by placing his statue in the Hall of Fame in Washington. His widow, Charlotte Greenway, served in Congress.

pad was with him; it went with him on his Sunday visits to his mother, and it even went on pleasure trips. Once on a fishing trip someone playfully hid the note pad and produced it only to avoid having the whole party retrace its steps.[29]

The note pads that were gathered up at the time of Crump's death filled several large cardboard cartons. They were mostly simple jottings: a phrase that resulted in censuring a political opponent in one of his advertisements, occasionally a statement "for the record" of an event in which he had participated and which he apparently thought had significance. But usually they were simply memoranda—repairs, needed on his mother's home and always those things that would further improve Memphis.

His extraordinary capacity for order, and above all his implacable self-discipline, made Crump unique. He fashioned an image of himself compounded of a schoolboy's axioms and the values of a Horatio Alger hero; then he lived by this image so completely that those who knew him were awed by the spectacle of it. Memphis, disorganized and unruly, represented the foil for Crump, organized and disciplined, and the interaction of the two was to produce an unusual kind of bossism in American city government. E. H. Crump, Jr., caught the substance of the matter when he observed that his father was a "willful enough man" to do something that appealed to him. "Memphis was a problem worthy of his mettle."

The events that brought Crump actively into politics took place in January, 1903. For a year or more the clergy of Memphis had been railing against widespread commercialized gambling and the Sunday opening of saloons. Although the people of Memphis were zealous churchgoers and relished fiery sermons full of sensation, they were not moved to a sustained attack against the evils that had been dramatically described to them. The authoritative *Commercial Appeal* stated that the Sunday closing law could not be enforced by the "spasmodic ebullition of the church element in one of its periodical fits of high pressure morality," if that element "forgets to register, forgets to vote, forgets to pay poll tax, and forgets that we have any public question at other times." There was a more serious problem at hand—the "general and growing practice of sending children to saloons and corner groceries for beer."[30]

29 *Commercial Appeal,* October 17, 1958.
30 *Ibid.,* March 12, 1903.

Reform appealed to another group—the business community—for practical reasons. City services were expensive and inadequate. The fire department was so ill-equipped and so badly administered that in the spring of 1902, Memphis policyholders received word in their premium notices that they were being charged an additional 25 per cent "by reason of inefficient and inadequate fire protection for a city the size of Memphis." [31] It required the purchase of considerable additional equipment before the insurance companies restored the old rate.

Memphis streets offered the most obvious subject for complaint. In 1900 there were about 175 miles of them, only twelve of which were variously paved with stone, brick, and wooden blocks. There was much discussion about the problem but no action. In 1903 after a survey of the situation, the city engineer estimated that unless about four million dollars were spent for repairs, the city would have only eight miles of serviceable pavement within three years. Mayor John Joseph Williams pressed for action, inviting prominent citizens to join with him in planning improvements, but by 1905 Memphis had only twenty-two miles of paved streets. In Nashville, with its lesser population, there were nearly two hundred miles of pavement.[32]

House numbering was without system. In 1900 the legislative council decreed that all houses in the city should systematically be renumbered, the cost to be borne by a fifty-cent assessment against the owners. Perhaps some owners found it difficult to finance the change, and others, perhaps, held a sentimental attachment for their old numbers, for the change was slow in being effected. After several months the *Commercial Appeal* remarked that "As we expected, the project of numbering the city has fallen through. We gave the city engineer's office until the middle of the twentieth century to renumber Memphis, and we see no reason why we should change the forecast." [33] Finally, in 1905, the postmaster declared that he would cease delivering the mail to improperly numbered houses, and with that threat the reform was finally brought about.

These aspects of the city's disorganized character were not as

---

31 Secretaries' notes.
32 U. S. Bureau of the Census. *Statistics of Cities Having a Population of Over 30,000: 1905* (Washington, 1907), 199.
33 *Commercial Appeal*, July 28, 1900.

significant nor as darkly tragic as murders and other acts of violence, but they were matters that annoyed the business class. The misery of people who lived in areas of the city they seldom saw did not touch them directly, but things like insurance rates, poor streets, and a confused house numbering system took money out of their pockets and interfered with the smooth flow of commerce.

More pertinent to the interests of the business class was the tax rate. In 1903 it was $2.85 per one hundred dollars of assessed property valuation—the highest rate in the city's history. In January, 1903, when Mayor Williams informed a select group of prominent citizens that four million dollars was needed to improve the streets, Walker Wellford, a distant cousin of Crump's and a successful cooperate manufacturer, was dismayed. Although he had "always supported Mayor Williams, [he] like many others could not understand, with the high rate of taxation, why the city was in its deplorable condition." [34] Wellford then asked Mayor Williams "very pertinent" questions concerning the disposition of the city's money, and receiving what he considered inadequate answers, he demanded access to the city's books. "I thought," explained Wellford, "before heavier tax burdens were imposed . . . it was desirable to know the cause and suggest just such an examination as a business house would have made under the same conditions." [35]

When Williams refused the request, Wellford felt that he had good reason to press on with his investigation. Employing two attorneys, one of whom was young Kenneth McKellar (later to become senator), he secured an opinion that as a citizen and member of the corporation of the city of Memphis, he was entitled to examine the corporation's books. The issue was fought through the courts to the Tennessee supreme court, which in June, 1903, decreed that Wellford be given the permission he sought. Wellford immediately employed the National Audit Company of St. Louis to make an investigation.

Walker Wellford was not Horatio at the bridge to all of the people. Although the Memphis *Morning News* and *Evening Scimitar* supported the Wellford crusade, the *Commercial Appeal* was critical. It quickly dubbed him "Expert" Wellford, stating that before he

34 Walker Wellford, *Report to the Citizens of Memphis* (Memphis, 1904), 1–2.
35 *Ibid.*, 2.

made his request to examine the city's books he "was hardly known in this community." [36] The *Appeal* thought it was "very questionable" whether he was qualified to pass judgment on the city's financial administration. The audit report was published on October 10, 1903, and while it found no instances of misappropriation of funds, it did find a "general lack of system in the accounting methods of the city, each department apparently being managed according to the opinion of the officer in charge." [37]

The investigation put a new political force in motion in Memphis. It brought about a union of the reform interests of the clergy and local businessmen, and for a time Wellford served as a leader of this new movement. In 1904 elections were to be held for the city legislative council, a bicameral body composed of an upper board of commissioners called the fire and police commission, and a lower board called the board of public works. Wellford managed the selection of an antiadministration candidate and personally saw to it that more than a perfunctory campaign was made.

The election, conforming to established tradition, was a hot one, marked, as the *Morning News* stated, "by the use of torch and pistol in the hands of a lawless and riotous mob." [38] Memphis crime czars Mike Haggerty, George Honan, and Mike Shanley gave evidence of their zeal for the Williams administration by stealing the ballot box in the ninth ward.

Although administration men won most of the offices, the reformers, led by Wellford, continued the attack. Several days after the election a mass meeting was called to protest election frauds, and a committee was appointed to bring charges against the police chief for "indulging in profanity on election day" while in uniform—a violation of a city ordinance. Then a delegation from the committee called on Mayor Williams to demand that he enforce laws governing vice, gambling, and Sunday closing.

Williams, a "practical" politician, decided that the best way to discredit the reformers was to do what they demanded. On February 2 he ordered police to close all saloons at midnight, to shut up all the houses of prostitution, and to suppress gambling completely. The *Commercial Appeal* observed that Memphis was becoming a "Sun-

36 *Commercial Appeal,* August 7, 1903.
37 National Audit Company, "Report" (mimeographed), 8.
38 Memphis *Morning News,* January 8, 1904.

day school town," the "cleanest place this side of the river Styx." [39]
The day following the enforcement an editorial appeared in the
Commercial Appeal containing the thought and literary quality of
Colonel Michael Connelly, nonpareil as a writer of journalistic
whimsy:

> In very truth had the tenderloin been smothered in the robes of reform,
> and the blaze of lights did not invite to the gilded quarters of sin. The
> crimson lamp was extinguished at the stroke of 12 and the foolish virgins
> had no care to tend the wicks. Over all the pink precinct was stillness,
> stillness, stillness.
>
> The clink of the beer glasses could not be heard by the plainclothes
> man. . . . The noise of the piano was stilled. . . . It is said that the red
> lights will soon give place to blue, to be in harmony with the spirit of
> the crusade. [40]

Williams was thorough. He asked the members of the Tennessee
and Chickasaw clubs to refrain from poker playing and dispensing
liquor after midnight on Saturday. He pointed out that the consequences of these practices could be embarrassing, since many club
members were also on the "Committee of Fifty."

The clergy was certain that at last, in the long battle against sin
in Memphis, the tide had begun to turn. A committee of Protestant
pastors visited Williams to congratulate him on his determination
to enforce the law. The Reverend William E. Thompson, pastor of
the First Methodist Church, told Williams that he thought 90 per
cent of the people were behind him.[41]

In the matter of reform, Thompson and Wellford were closely
associated, and both seem to have been impelled by a puritanical
conscience that would remove all blemishes, or at least the external
ones, from the city. In April they went on the warpath again, swear-
ing out warrants against several prominent businessmen, charging
them with "conspiring to violate the Sabbath by . . . planning . . .
to conduct an exhibition of automobile races." [42] All of the accused
"positively disclaimed" the event, and one—the utility magnate Sam
Carnes—declared that he knew nothing about the supposed automobile race until he was brought into court.

The zeal of Wellford and Thompson finally reacted against them.

39 *Commercial Appeal*, February 8, 1904.
40 *Ibid.*, February 4, 1904.
41 *Ibid.*, February 12, 1904.
42 *Ibid.*, April 10, 1904.

The *Commercial Appeal's* comment that with a "few more Walker Wellfords in this town . . . Memphis would take to dismal swamps" was becoming a generally held opinion.[43] Press criticism of Thompson's role was so persistent that the Methodist churches of the city took a vote on the propriety of his action.

The reform of Wellford and the preachers seemed to have run its course. The Williams administration apparently faced no further disturbance on this score and might have continued in its old easygoing ways except for an extraordinary flouting of the law that tended to accentuate a developing mood of civic self-examination. On the night of July 1, 1904, a gambling den in full operation on DeSoto Street was raided by five deputy sheriffs, one a Negro. About forty men and women had been tied together to be taken to the police station, when crime leaders George Honan and Mike Haggerty and two associates came to their rescue. On entering the dive, Haggerty was reported to have said, "Go back and get shotguns and we will kill all the s——of-b's." [44] But the rest were not in a waiting mood: using their pistols, they disarmed and then shot three of the deputies and freed the prisoners. One deputy, the Negro, died immediately. One of the white deputies lived long enough to name George Honan as his murderer.

After the shootings the reformers were afire again. Three nights after the affair two "monster meetings" were called, out of which was formed a "committee for public safety" to call on Mayor Williams and demand that the law be enforced.[45] Williams shortly gave his reply to the committee. He pointed out that the city charter did not prohibit gambling and prostitution, but that the law respecting these issues read: "to regulate, control and suppress" them.[46] He stated that his policy had been inherited from that established by administrations running back to 1897, when the current charter had been adopted. He added that his predecessors had, with public connivance, collected revenues from the gambling elements of Memphis, revenues which had been used for public improvements. He had, he declared, terminated this practice in response to a sentiment coming from the press and pulpit. He did not believe that it was possible to

43   *Ibid.*   44   *Morning News,* July 12, 1904.
45   *Ibid.,* July 15, 1904.
46   *Memphis Digest,* 1902 (Memphis, 1903), 2–3.

suppress prostitution, Sunday liquor selling, and gambling in Memphis. But if it was clear that the people of Memphis wanted absolute suppression he would attempt it, warning that the law would have to be enforced fairly.[47]

Williams' reply was an honest appraisal of the situation, and his simple candor found favor with the *Commercial Appeal.* His answer should have confounded his political enemies, but "like Tennyson's brook," they "run on forever." [48] Run on they did, calling another mass meeting which labeled Williams' reply "unsatisfactory," whereupon the *Commercial Appeal* ran an historic editorial called "Tired But Not Satisfied." The committee on safety, it said, "was like the wife of one of the Caesars, who would slip out of her master's bed to spend the night dissolutely and return to her spouse in the morning murmuring 'lassata sed non satiata'—tired but not satisfied." [49]

When the *Morning News,* the voice of the clerical reformers, urged that action be taken against the *Commercial Appeal* for sending obscene literature through the mails, the latter journal replied: "The scholarly News cannot object to classical quotation" and that "quoting from the Sixth Satire [of Juvenal] which is frequently selected by divinity students as subject for their examination essays before professors and grave fathers of the church cannot be less than commendable."

The committee sputtered on for another week and died, but the issue of reform did not die. American cities of the industrial age were showing more significant signs of maturity as a younger generation began to take over leadership at the turn of the century. Urban reform was becoming a more serious business; the stage marked by a periodic and fruitless ebullition of clerical reformers was passing. Throughout America the issue was passing into the hands of young and professional men whose approach was less moralistic and more pragmatic.

In Memphis a group of young, politically ambitious, professional men found reform an inviting cause. A group of these led by young Kenneth McKellar in an organization called the Jackson Club sought to amend the city charter to provide for "home-rule against one-man power and political bossism." In electing members to the state legislature that fall, candidates supporting the program of the Jackson

47 *Commercial Appeal,* July 17, 1904.
48 *Ibid.*   49 *Ibid.,* July 19, 1904.

Club defeated administration men, and in March, 1905, the governor of the state signed the McKellar-inspired amendments to the Memphis charter.

The charter changes echoed a reform note that was being heard with increasing frequency in other American cities. The amended charter provided that no franchise could be granted or sold to a public service corporation except by ordinance and with the approval of the public in an election for that purpose. Accountants were to make a yearly examination of the city's books, and a civil service program was provided for. In the controversial section that dealt with gambling, the phrase "to regulate, control and suppress gaming houses" was amended to "to suppress." [50]

There were changes in the structure of the city government. Hitherto, the legislative council had been a unicameral body, its two boards—the fire and police commissioners and public works—sitting together with the mayor to enact laws. The amended charter made the legislative council into a bicameral body with the board of fire and police commissioners becoming an upper house and the board of public works the lower. Each of the boards was enlarged by two members.

On the issue of reform, the Memphis press was divided. In December, 1904, the *Morning News* and the *Evening Scimitar* were sold to a Memphis businessman of means, Gilbert D. Raine. Raine merged the two into an evening journal and called it the *News Scimitar*. The *News Scimitar* continued its predecessor's policy of supporting the reformers, but more loudly and persistently, and it also began to advocate the public ownership of utilities. The *Commercial Appeal* was suspicious of reform. "There isn't a man of adult intelligence in this city," it declared, "who does not know that the reform crusade was merely a movement to put the Outs into offices . . . and to provide a lot of hungry buzzards with a carcass to feed on." [51] The paper had had its fill of reform. "We have seen long nosed hypocrites trying to reestablish the Blue Laws of Connecticut in this city. We have seen a lot of Pharisees of the holier-than-thou vintage trying to improve the morals of everybody but themselves."

50   *Acts of the State of Tennessee, Fifty-Fourth General Assembly* (Nashville, 1905), 46.
51   *Commercial Appeal*, April 30, 1905.

For several years thereafter, the *Commercial Appeal* professed to oppose reform on the ground of its hypocritical character. Actually opposition to reform was premised on the connection between reform and the public ownership of utilities.

In January, 1904, Gilbert Raine, editor of the *News Scimitar* and member of the Shelby County delegation to the state legislature, sponsored a law that gave the city the privilege of building its own light plant. The act provided that the city might issue one million dollars in bonds to build the plant, but there were so many restrictions placed around their sale that no action was ever taken.

From the first, the *Commercial Appeal* opposed the project. While the 1905 law was pending, it urged that it not be adopted. The city could not go into debt another million dollars with the bonded indebtedness already over six million.[52] Throughout the next decade, with the public ownership of the light plant as a recurring theme in Memphis politics, the *Commercial Appeal* editorialized repeatedly against such action. The *News Scimitar* charged that the *Commercial Appeal* opposed public ownership of utilities because the paper was part of an interlocking directorate that included the gas and electric company. The charge was true. Although the *Commercial Appeal* did have reason to oppose the large amount of hypocritical cant that went with the early phase of the reform movement, after 1905 the reform issue was more probing and rational in character. When the *News Scimitar* accused the *Commercial Appeal* of opposing public ownership in order to protect its stockholder's investments, it was probably correct.

In September, 1905, the administration forces, with Mayor Williams heading the list, announced their ticket for the November city elections. On October 3 the "Independents" or reform faction called a meeting to name candidates to oppose the regular Democratic nominee. Kenneth McKellar was elected temporary chairman of the group. On October 9, the Independents held a public meeting in the Lyceum Theatre to announce their slate. James H. Malone, an upstanding lawyer, was named for mayor; and as a concession to the old-line forces, John T. Walsh, a political power representing the Irish wards of north Memphis, was chosen for vice-mayor. The platform contained planks calling for annual auditing of the city's books, removal of politics from the police and fire forces, and open

52 *Ibid.,* January 17, 1905.

bidding for franchise privileges. When the plank calling for the public ownership of utilities was read, there was "hearty and prolonged applause." [53]

Listed among the seven candidates for the board of public works —the lower board of the legislative council—was the name of E. H. Crump. He was a natural for the ticket—a clean-cut aggressive young businessman with new ideas, whose popularity had been demonstrated the preceding spring by his election as director of the Business Men's Club.

As in the case of Crump's candidacy for director of the Business Men's Club, the campaign was managed by Frank Rice. It was Rice's formal induction into a lifelong career dedicated to the organizational implementation of Crump's politics. Rice had a gift, even genius, for organization, and he loved the tension, excitement, and combativeness of politics. Beginning in 1905, he attended sessions of the Tennessee legislature for more than thirty years, but only once did he serve as an elected member of the body. "I was a complete failure as a Senator," he remarked in later years.[54] He was at his best working for the Shelby County legislative program in the corridors and hotel rooms rather than on the floor of the legislative chamber. His influence was far-reaching, for in his role as mentor and spokesman for the large Shelby delegation which traditionally voted as a unit, he possessed considerable power.

Rice was colorful. Once a neophyte worker in the Crump organization was ordered by a county magistrate to pay a fine for dumping some garbage in a neighboring lot. Feeling abused because the lot was ill-kept in the first place and because he had been willing to clean up the mess, he sought out Rice, who happened to be working in a neighborhood political organizing effort. He found him seated behind a table issuing directions to workers, vigorously gesticulating with his cane for emphasis. Hearing the doleful story, Rice sent a message to the offending magistrate. He was to drop his action against the new recruit. So the aggrieved one returned to the office of the magistrate, who was found taking his ease on a couch in the rear. On receiving Rice's order, the magistrate responded: "Frank Rice can go to hell." Again the new recruit went to Rice. The response was dramatic. Violently banging the tabletop with the length

53 Memphis *News Scimitar,* October 10, 1905.
54 "Senate Resolution Eulogizing Rice After His Death" (typed).

of his cane, Rice demanded of the startled workers: "Who does that bastard think he is?" Turning to a policeman, he ordered him to bring the magistrate to him. It was done and there followed a cringing abnegation on the magistrate's part.[55] By what authority this was done is not clear, but such shenanigans were mighty impressive at the ward level.

In his later years Rice suffered considerably from arthritis, a condition that disposed him to lean heavily on alcohol for its analgesic effect, and perhaps, too, for the consolation it gives to a man who wearies from the pace. But he never slackened. Almost to the end of his days he continued to go to Nashville when the legislature was in session, even though he was so ill at times that he had to do his work from his hotel bed.

Judge Lois Bejach, a lifelong stalwart in the Crump organization, thought of Rice as Crump's "field marshal," but to opponents of the organization Rice was the hatchet man, the instrument for effecting the detailed maneuvers and applying the sometimes harsh pressures that were required to maintain discipline and keep the organization invulnerable.

Hard and unyielding as an organization man, Rice possessed a broad streak of compassion and generosity in his nature. He was one of the most thoroughgoing liberals in the organization in the sense that his sympathy and interest was always with the underprivileged. When anyone in a predicament asked for his help he could never say no, although he was frequently imposed upon. More vital a requisite than anything else where Crump was concerned was honesty: Rice was scrupulously honest in the management of the organization's affairs, and he was honest in public statements relating to politics. By newsmen he was regarded as an unfailing source of accurate information. He never tried to mislead anyone. He possessed another invaluable trait so far as Crump was concerned: he never betrayed any restiveness under Crump's ultimate control of things. Crump was always the general and he, the lieutenant.

Crump's association with Rice must have begun shortly after Rice came to Memphis, for when Crump was married in 1902, Rice was on close enough terms to be selected as one of the groomsmen. After Rice married, he and his wife maintained some social contact with the Crumps, but this decreased with the passing years as Crump

55 Interview with John Gorman, September 22, 1957.

became increasingly preoccupied with his family and work. Time also progressively revealed the incongruity in the personalities of the two. Rice, profane and indelicate, plunged through life indifferent to all except the basic impulses of his nature, while Crump disciplined himself to a superhuman degree hoarding his physical resources and posting his life with the principles of his cherished maxims.

With Rice attending to organizational matters, Crump forcibly pushed his campaign for membership in the legislative council. "He was the most vigorous campaigner imaginable," E. H. Crump, Jr., remarked. He established a rapport with voters through personal relationships. He never made a campaign speech, and few speeches of any other kind for that matter. He addressed the voters face-to-face and won them with his charming manner, elegant dress, and his unfailing ability to remember a name. In time he became legendary because of his memory for names, but in 1905 he was still a relative newcomer to the Memphis political scene.

In the campaign the forces of the Williams administration attempted to present themselves to the people as a properly conservative businessmen's ticket for "thinking people." They charged that the Independents were working to register Negroes, an action abhorrent to self-respecting people. The *Commercial Appeal* was all for Williams—unmindful that it had once accused him of getting into office by the use of Negro votes—and charged the Independents with being "ready to break up the local Democracy, to destroy municipal harmony and make an alliance with the toughest negro element in the city to carry their point." [56]

The Independents struck the notes familiarly heard in those years throughout America as part of the reform impulse known as the Progressive movement. They charged Williams with being an advocate of "high assessments and high taxes for the poor and middle classes, and of low assessments for wealthy individuals and opulent corporations." [57] The election was to be a fight of the common man "against corporate influence and organized wealth."

On November 9 reform was victorious. James Malone was elected mayor, and Crump led the list of the fourteen candidates seeking the seven positions available on the city council. Of the results, the

56 *Commercial Appeal,* September 23, 1905.
57 *News Scimitar,* October 5, 1905.

News Scimitar sententiously observed that the "people can be trusted at all times to do the right thing at the right time," for the "people do not act against their own interests." [58] The *Commercial Appeal,* on the other hand, was bitter. "Reform" was the consequence of switched and stolen ballot boxes. There had been unprecedented frauds in the election. "Never . . . in our wildest dreams did we ever imagine that such a brazen attempt would be made to debauch the ballot box as was made yesterday." [59]

According to the 1905 charter amendment, Crump, as one of the additional members of the board of public works, was scheduled to be sworn in on November 20, but the arrival of that date found him seriously ill with typhoid fever. He had felt ill several days before the election but had kept going until the balloting started. During the phase of his illness when he was sickest, his wife had several wagonloads of sawdust spread on Monroe Street in front of their residence to deaden the noise of passing wagons.

Crump was sworn into office on January 4, 1906, the occasion of the inauguration of the new mayor. He was scarcely noticed. The attention was on Joe Williams, the old master politician who had not broken with the old ways. Urbane to the last, he smilingly handed over his gavel to Malone in the flower-filled council room of the old city hall, and an attendant group of reformers applauded, believing that a new kind of administration for Memphis was at hand.

Although the new mayor did make vigorous initial gestures at enforcing the law, matters went along pretty much as they always had. Police Chief George O'Haver was given formal orders to enforce the Sunday closing laws, and a little later Malone personally visited police headquarters, and while the whole force stood at attention, he sternly lectured on the necessity of enforcing the law. The weary policemen, accustomed to working twelve-hour shifts, heard him through, but the lecture to the troops did not alter the realities of law enforcement: the saloons remained open on Sunday, and gambling and prostitution received only a token harassment.

Otherwise, reform bore fruit. A uniform tax rate was effected throughout the city, and substantial progress was made in street paving and sidewalk construction. It was during Malone's four years in office that Memphis began to assume the appearance of a modern

58 *Ibid.,* November 10, 1905.
59 *Commercial Appeal,* November 19, 1905.

city. Two fifteen-story high buildings—the Memphis Trust Company Building and the Tennessee Trust Company Building—were constructed in the downtown area, while luxurious homes for newly rich industrialists sprang up along fashionable streets like Peabody and Central.

As Malone struggled to enforce the laws, Councilman Crump remained quiet. "Observe, remember, and compare," he doubtless was telling himself. He found a lot to observe. He discovered quite soon that the board to which he was elected had little to do with final decision-making in important matters. Councilmen tended to be regarded as useless appendages by the members of the Fire and Police Commission. This nettled Crump and provoked him to declare at a board meeting that "he personally (and he thought the other members felt the same) did not want members of the lower board placed in the attitude by the upper board of a parcel of school boys." [60] This outburst of feeling, which created a "mild sensation," was an expression of wounded pride. Crump himself knew that the lower board was largely pointless, and his brief experience there caused him to look with increasing favor on the commission form of government.[61]

Crump's record as a councilman showed that he was bent on reform. As chairman of the electric committee he was charged with the stimulating task of locating light and telephone poles. In this position, as the secretaries' notes state, Crump gained a knowledge "of the inner workings of the public utilities in general." He studied the work of other departments and came to the conclusion that the city was scarcely getting value received for any of its fund outlays. After close figuring he decided the city was paying too much for street lighting. At the council meeting of August 9, 1906, he advocated a reduction in the detective force from fifteen members to eight, which he said could be done without impairing its efficiency in the least and which would save the city $8,000 a year.[62]

In December he informed the council that there were 599 saloons in the city which paid sixty dollars annually for their licenses. As compared with the license fees in other cities, this was ridiculously low, and he proposed an increase to $250.[63] The ordinance was re-

60 Secretaries' notes.   61 *Ibid.*   62 *Ibid.*
63 *Commercial Appeal,* December 16 and 22, 1906.

jected by the upper board at the insistence of Vice-Mayor John Walsh, who was thinking about the many saloon owners among his constituents in north Memphis. Crump opposed the letting of contracts involving more than five hundred dollars without inviting competitive bidding, and he found fault with fourteen carloads of inferior gravel for street paving and persuaded the council to reject it. He released, in fact, a continuous stream of recommendations designed to effect more economical operations in all areas.

In one notable instance he turned his attention to legislation concerning a problem of the times. From 1900, when General Sam Carnes introduced the first automobile to Memphis, there had been an increasing number of machines on the streets, posing a mounting problem to life and limb for those who held to the old ways. The *Commercial Appeal* took frequent note of this "new danger." [64] To deal with the problem Crump introduced an ordinance in 1906 to limit the speed of automobiles to six miles per hour between blocks and two miles per hour at intersections. But allegedly because of the influence of automobile dealers and speed demons, the "antiscorching" ordinance was defeated.

Crump realized very quickly that in his efforts as a councilman to bring order and economy into city administration he was only a gadfly. The old easygoing ways were too deep-seated to be easily changed. Beneath the whole system—and what insured the perpetuation of the system—was a political factionalism that created disorder and then fed on it to sustain more factionalism. Crump was disgusted. He knew that he could change little in his role as councilman, and in September, 1907, he resigned his office. "The press of business," he explained to the newspapers.

64 *Ibid.*, August 27, 1902.

☒ ☐

Chapter III

COMMISSION GOVERNMENT

IT TOOK Crump three weeks to get his business affairs straight. On October 11 he announced that he would be a candidate for the fire and police commission to fill one of the two vacancies on the upper board that would exist beginning in January, 1908. He declined to enter the Democratic primary, already conspicuous by the presence of Memphis' elder statesman J. J. Williams, who was seeking to crowd out the incumbent commissioner. In the primary election it was assumed that he would have an easy time with Crump in the November election.

In announcing for office, Crump showed himself fully in the stream of the progressive current. Representing a new kind of thinking that was emerging at all levels of government in America, he believed that the days of unbridled *laissez-faire* should come to an end where corporate wealth impinged on public interest. The political machines gained comfort and security for themselves by granting profitable franchises to corporations without getting a fair payment for them in taxes, and Crump opposed their old easygoing ways. "I am determined," he declared in announcing his candidacy, "that the Cumberland Telephone company shall be brought to taw . . . I am going to keep up the fight on it until it capitulates, and the people obtain what they are demanding." The *News Scimitar,* which carried the announcement, went on to say that Crump had gotten fed up with the way the telephone company had given the people of Memphis a "merry ha-ha on their efforts to procure better services and cheaper rates."

The announcement alluded to another area in which Crump thought the public was not getting what it deserved. "In announcing my candidacy, I want to say that I am for a municipal light plant. . . . I will fight along this line . . . until the plant is an actuality." [1] A long time would pass before this promise could be fulfilled, providing his career with more tension and drama over the years than any other issue. Of all the manifold concerns with which he became involved in his public life, this was the one that he considered the most significant.

In 1907 Crump had no large body of assigned voters, but he won by 909 votes. He won because of his energetic campaigning, because of the support of the reformers, and because many voters apparently resented the Williams brand of old-fashioned machine politics. Finally, he had the support of one ward boss who gave Crump his bloc vote on the mistaken assumption that Crump was a passing phenomenon and that Joe Williams was ultimately the man to beat.

The election was held on Tuesday, November 5, and late that evening when it appeared certain that he had won, Crump went to his campaign headquarters where he was greeted with "a perfect roar of applause, and . . . was lifted bodily to the table by enthusiastic admirers." A speech was demanded and it was characteristically brief: "Gentlemen, I thank you from the very bottom of my heart. I assure you that I appreciate and will remember the work of every loyal friend today. This is the happiest moment of my life." [2] Then he was carried on the shoulders of his friends to the *News Scimitar* office "where the newly elected commissioner made a happy speech, expressing his gratitude at his election and his thanks to the *News Scimitar* for the support it had accorded him." Again he was placed on the shoulders of his friends and carried to the steps of the Cotton Exchange, presumably for another speech. But he was spared, for Tom Collier, an eccentric member of an old Memphis family, took over as master of ceremonies and, climbing the steps of the building where all could see him, shouted: "Here is our next mayor of Memphis, Ed. H. Crump." In later years Collier considered himself Crump's major

1 Scrapbook news clipping.
2 Memphis *Evening Scimitar,* November 6, 1907.

political opposition in Memphis and kept the electorate amused with his antics.

During the triumphal evening many were heard to congratulate Frank Rice for his skillful management of the campaign. That same evening Crump was summoned from his home to the police station to vouch for a supporter who was so exuberant after the election that police chief George O'Haver found it necessary to lock him up. The enthusiastic supporter was Huey Long, who liked the public-ownership-of-utilities plank in Crump's platform. At the time, Long was a Bible and socks salesman in Memphis.[3]

Crump was sworn into office on the morning of January 2, 1908. He began his administration "aggressively," asking that a meeting of the board be called for that afternoon. At the meeting he startled Mayor Malone, the commissioners, and Chief O'Haver when he "unequivocally asked that the police be instructed to see that every saloon of every class and character . . . be closed at midnight." Turning to Chief O'Haver, Crump declared that he was not going to depend on the police department but that he "personally" was going to see the order obeyed. "The language of the new commissioner was unmistakeable," said the *Commercial Appeal*.[4]

What was operating on the new commissioner to produce this demonstration? Probably Crump could not stand the duplicity of administration members who held that the laws were being obeyed. When he had been a member of the lower board, a councilman had once remarked that there was no gambling in Memphis. "Are you really in earnest about that?" asked Crump. Before a reply could be given, Mayor Malone and two other commissioners interjected that they understood there was "no gambling of any kind going on." When Crump accused them of joking and they denied it, he replied: "You are in error."[5]

There is another and quite fundamental explanation for Crump's startling activities during his early days as commissioner of the upper board. He possessed a theatrical sense for dramatizing issues. The struggle against wickedness must be made very real to the electorate. No tepid Sunday-school approach to a problem would do. Time and again, when the resolution of an issue involved a decision by the

3 Interview with Thomas Phillips, April 11, 1962.
4 *Commercial Appeal,* January 3, 1908.
5 Secretaries' notes.

electorate, Crump would move directly against the devil of the moment and impale him against the wall with thunderous execrations and flashes of lightning.

The mayor and the commissioners, Crump decided, must be shown that they were wrong and in a way that would produce reverberations powerful enough to reach every voter in the community. There was a preliminary buildup: at a meeting of the board on January 17. Crump adverted so frequently and forcibly to the remissions of Captain O'Haver and the police department in the matter of law enforcement that the *Commercial Appeal* described the session as "Mr. Crump's meeting" and said that the other four board members were "merely present." [6]

Then came the climax. "It remained for Ed Crump, youngest member of the fire and police commission . . . to demonstrate conclusively the absolute ridiculousness of the claims of the police, and of those higher up, that there is no gambling in Memphis." So wrote Tom Phillips, Crump's friend on the *News Scimitar,* when he described the event for his readers. "This he did Saturday night, when twenty men, nineteen of them special deputy sheriffs, raided three negro dives and found crap games in full blast, with crowds of negroes about the tables." Crump personally headed the raiding party, backed up by eighteen acquaintances of his youth recruited from the Holly Springs area. Just before the raid, the eighteen along with Crump had been specially deputized in Crump's business office by a friendly justice of the peace. Only one member of the party was a member of the Memphis police force.

The raiders swooped down suddenly on the well-known spots: Hammett Ashford's place on Beale, Jim Kinnane's at Front and Winchester, and Will McVey's resort on Rayburn Boulevard. As the raids progressed, continued Phillips' account, "the old police station presented a busier appearance than in many months. Wagon load after wagon load of prisoners were brought in, searched by the turnkey, their names docketed by the sergeant, and then led to their cells." For two hours the patrol wagon was kept busy bringing in prisoners, and as each wagon load reached the station, Crump would smile broadly. The haul at Jim Kinnane's place was mainly composed of women, who were subsequently released on money put up by the famous Memphis desperado, Mike Shanley. This chivalrous act was

6 *Commercial Appeal,* January 18, 1908.

the last account the Memphis public would have of Shanley, for soon afterwards he was killed by a policeman. After the raid Crump and his deputies went to a downtown restaurant and had dinner.

A sequel to the raid took place on the Monday night following Crump's Saturday night affair. Captain O'Haver, feeling perhaps that the police had been exposed as less than vigilant, had his men crack down on violators of the Sunday closing law. The following cases were disposed of in Monday's court:

Will Windler . . . a bartender employed at Doc Hottum's saloon, Madison avenue and Maiden Lane, was fined $50 for the city and bound over to the grand jury . . . on a charge of violating the Sunday ordinance. Windler was caught handing a pint of whiskey to a customer . . . by Detective Tom Shea. Despite the fact that Windler contended that he gave the whiskey to a stranger when he complained of being ill, Detective Shea testified that he saw the man hand 40 cents in payment. . . . Doc Hottum says the men were not in the saloon when the whiskey changed hands, but that Windler gave the bottle to a stranger as an act of kindness. . . .

The case against J. P. Rawlings, a saloon-keeper . . . was dismissed. . . . Rawlings contended that he heard a commotion in his barroom, adjoining his living apartments, and that when he went to investigate he found his pet bulldog fighting his cat. He opened the door to eject his dog and in that brief interval Patrolman Williams gained entrance and arrested him. [7]

This commendable zeal in enforcing the law was demonstrated too late. Crump was already pinning the blame for poor law enforcement on Chief O'Haver. The day following the raid the *Commercial Appeal* quoted Crump as saying that he "just wanted to show the police up" and "if Chief O'Haver and his men cannot suppress gambling in this town, I can." [8]

Under the 1905 charter provisions, the police chief might be suspended by the mayor on the formal filing of charges against him by a commissioner, the suspension to obtain until a trial could be held before the legislative council. Early Monday morning following the raid, Crump was at the city hall to file charges against O'Haver. "I think the time has come," said Crump, "for a change in the office of chief of police. If Mr. O'Haver claims that gambling was not going on when I have proved that it was, he is incompetent, and should be

7 *News Scimitar,* January 20, 1908.
8 *Commercial Appeal,* January 19, 1908.

removed. On the other hand, if he did allow it to proceed, he had violated his oath of office, and should be removed." [9] With Crump, things were simple.

But Mayor Malone was leaving town, and it was not until the morning of January 24 that the commissioners assembled for O'-Haver's hearing. A reporter from the *Commercial Appeal* was in the council room to note the proceedings. His attention was immediately drawn to Crump as the time approached for the opening of the meeting. He "was chafing at the bit. He was growing impatient. His young blood was beginning to pump a little faster than usual and there were barometrical signs of an approaching storm."

Suddenly the storm hit. The exchanges that occurred between Crump and O'Haver and between Crump and Commissioner B. G. Henning were given a verbatim reporting. They show Crump in his fighting pose, pushing directly to his objective, ignoring all premises but his own, and paying little attention to the sensibilities of those who were caught in the web of the circumstances:

Turning to Chief O'Haver, he opened up. He asked if it was not a fact that on January 2, he had stated to Mayor Malone and himself and the commissioners that gambling was going on and that if the commissioners wished it stopped, he could stop it. Chief O'Haver replied that this was true and he had no reason to retract what he said.

"Why didn't you stop it then?"

"I did wherever I located it. You see, it is an easy matter to start a game and an easy matter to hide it. My knowledge that it existed is the knowledge that we have that there will always be more or less gambling, for some people will take chances. Where such cases are located we apply the law. You will remember the next day you told me that there was gambling at the Climax. Chief Kehoe and myself broke in to find out. We asked you to accompany us, but you declined. There was no evidence of gambling in the Climax. . . . We asked you the source of the information, and you replied it came from strangers. We could do no more."

"But you admit that you did state on that date that gambling was going on and that you could stop it."

"Yes, I made that statement."

"And you didn't stop it, as our raid last Saturday showed. Well, chief, I say that you are absolutely incompetent to manage the affairs of the police department of this city, and I insist upon your suspension. Now, don't you know that you are incompetent?"

"That may be your opinion," replied Chief O'Haver in a quiet voice,

9 Scrapbook news clipping.

but growing very white. He was holding his temper under a desperate curb.

"But isn't it a fact?" urged Commissioner Crump, becoming more aggressive and rising from his place at the council table.

"That is for the gentlemen of the commission to say. I have been a member of this department for thirty years."

"Yes, I know you have, and that's too long," interrupted the junior member.

"Yes, for thirty years," continued the chief, "and this is the first time that I have ever been charged with incompetency. I served through two epidemics and through days when conditions were far worse than they are now, and it is the first time that such a charge has ever been made."

"I make it now," continued Commissioner Crump. "I know that you are incompetent. You are not the man for the place you hold, and I was surprised that Mayor Malone did not make the suspension on January 2. I did not say anything then. I wanted more facts. I imported men and got them. I proved to the public that you are incompetent. I have had you suspended and I think you should be dismissed."

At this point, Commissioner Henning began to speak, trying to ease the tension that had developed. He stated his opposition both to gambling and to the saloons being kept open after midnight and on Sunday. He spoke at some length, observing "that in political times, and especially during the days preceding an election, the laws were eased up a bit." Henning continued:

"The usual stringency relapses and the closed door swings open and," turning to Mr. Crump, "the last time it swung open, Mr. Crump, it was to let you enter this council."

"Who ordered it open, then," demanded Mr. Crump.

"Oh, well, it swung open, Mr. Crump, and you know as well as the rest of us that politics did it."

In conclusion Henning stated that he was going to recommend that the suspended officers be returned to their duty "with the understanding that if they do not close these places by February 6 they shall be dismissed, and I promise you to vote for a new department from patrol driver to chief; but if they fail let Mr. Crump send to Mississippi and fill the department."

But Crump was not appeased:

"Dr. Henning you don't stand for anything unless you suspend this man," he fairly shouted. "You are taking backwater. You announce with great emphasis that you would quit this council if you didn't stop gambling. I have given evidence that you haven't stopped it. If you vote not to suspend this man you shouldn't be in the council. No Commissioner with such evidence before him has a right to vote unless he suspends upon it. They should get out of the council. I mean this, and I tell you that you are not going to make any monkey out of me."

Henning's rejoinder was brief: "If Mr. Crump and Jim Malone think they can bully me into casting my vote for a measure I do not think just, I want to tell them they cannot do it."

Three times Mayor Malone ordered O'Haver dismissed, and three times a majority reinstated him. In the end, O'Haver remained.

Crump's performance was contrived. O'Haver was a pawn in a larger issue. In the summer of 1908, the subject of a commission government for Memphis was making the rounds. In July the City Club, a politically nonpartisan fact-finding group of more than three hundred members, endorsed the idea. On July 19 the *Commercial Appeal* carried a large two-column editorial advocating commission government. "The tendency in the development of municipal government has been against the bicameral council. . . . It is now recognized that the governing body of a city should be a business body and not a forum for a perpetual gabfest." The Memphis government as it stood was a "curse." It was "like a pig in a balloon. It will have to go." The *News Scimitar,* which had been advocating commission government since 1905, was undoubtedly warmed to find itself for once on the same side of an issue as the *Commercial Appeal.* It added a long-breathed and grammatically obtuse statement on its position: it did "not urge a commission form . . . merely to give more power and dignity to the occupants to [*sic*] such offices, or only for minor reforms in administration, but in line with its view of progress for the whole people and in order that such a business and compact government might safely take hold of more business or quasi-business enterprises that dealt in necessities for the people." [10] In other words, the *News Scimitar* saw commission government as an avenue to the public ownership of utilities.

Crump quickly allied himself with the cause, for he had seen the disruptive effects on government of too much political factionalism. He had also experienced first-hand the frustration of serving in a somewhat ineffectual position as a member of the lower board that had been created by the 1905 charter.

In supporting commission government Crump broke away from any alliance that seemed to be in the making between Mayor Malone

10 *News Scimitar,* August 23, 1909.

and himself. Neither Malone nor any of the commissioners supported the idea. Malone stood with the early reform group that had initiated the 1905 charter, and the vice-mayor, John Walsh, stood with Malone.

The issue received its first political test at a meeting of the county Democratic executive committee, held September 30. Crump was fully aware that, with the Walsh-Malone group in control, the committee would not endorse commission government as a campaign issue for the election of delegates to the state legislature the following month. Early on the morning that the committee was to meet, Crump, Frank Rice, and several others gathered in the office of Crump's business establishment for a strategy meeting. Crump laid out the plan: "Unless we can get the opposition to do something very foolish at its . . . meeting this morning," he said, "we haven't a chance to beat them. We must do a lot of foolish things ourselves, and if possible, make them mad, in the hope that their convention, composed of all the old standpatters, will adopt a Primary Plan recognizing only the voters in the old wards and disfranchising those in the recently annexed territory." [11]

The plan was this: Crump would deliberately goad the Walsh-Malone majority to anger, then introduce the issue of defining the voting districts for the Democratic primary, urging that a broad electorate be included which would enfranchise the newly annexed outlying residential areas where Crump had strength. The committee, he hoped, would district the city so as to put emphasis in the old downtown wards where it had its strength. What the committee did not know was that Crump, after his apparent defeat on the matter of the voting basis, would organize a slate of independent candidates for the legislature, pledged to commission government and armed with a charge that the Democrats had attempted to disfranchise progressive-minded citizens.

The *News Scimitar* published what happened at the meeting. "With their 'steam roller' well greased and in fine working order, the Walsh-Malone combination triumphed in the county democratic committee this morning. . . . Commission government advocates were their opponents." The committee "successively voted down amendments which called for the Patterson-Carmack primary vote of 1908 and the gubernatorial vote of 1906 as a basis, and finally passed the 1904 basis, giving a great advantage to uptown wards in convention repre-

11 Secretaries' notes.

sentation." Crump and his associates played their roles like seasoned actors, provoking a "wild scene." As the voting went against him, Crump "clamored for a roll call, demanding fair play and wanting to know if it was the purpose to choke off all chance to present the other side." In the midst of the argument over the basis of representation "the 'thriller' of the meeting was pulled off":

Mr. Crump mounted a table directly in front of the chairman and demanded a roll call. Mr. Roach refused to entertain it. Growing very white in the face, Mr. Crump faced the chairman, who also showed his rising anger by an equally pallid countenance. "I say you shall give us a roll call," declared the fire and police commissioner. "I say you will never get it," returned the chairman, "the motion on the table has been put and carried." There followed an exceedingly lively exchange between the two men, who faced each other with every evidence of intense, though suppressed anger. Followers of the steam roller hissed the militant commissioner.

On October 20 the supporters of commission government called a mass meeting at Germania Hall to nominate a "People's Democratic Ticket" of delegates to the state legislature pledged to commission government. A slogan was adopted: "The People Shall Rule." Crump took no prominent part in the proceedings, leaving the oratory for others. The election on November 4 resulted in a decisive victory for the Crump slate. "A Smashed Machine," was the *Commercial Appeal's* description of the Walsh-Malone faction.

Victory in Shelby County did not assure victory in the state legislature. The issue was clouded by the killing of former United States Senator Edward W. Carmack, then editor of the Nashville *Tennessean,* by Robin Cooper, son of Colonel Duncan B. Cooper, close personal friend and political adviser of Governor Malcolm Patterson. The tragedy occurred in the shadow of the state capitol on November 9, five days after the general election. The shooting was the climax to a long and bitter feud between Carmack and Colonel Cooper, with Carmack attacking Cooper in editorials in the *Tennessean.*

When the legislature convened in January, 1909, feeling was so intense over the Carmack murder that delegates were divided into Carmack and Patterson factions, with the Patterson men in the majority. Consequently, as Crump recognized, "a difficult task confronted anyone who hoped to have proposed legislation . . . considered on its merits." [12] The Memphis commission government bill pre-

12 *Ibid.*

sumably would be affected, because Patterson was a friend of former Mayor Williams and Commissioner Walsh, Crump's political opponents.

Another obstacle to the passage of the bill was the presence of a strong Memphis lobby to fight it. Headed by the Reverend William E. Thompson of the First Methodist Church and assisted by Luke Lea of Nashville, the group numbered most of those who had worked for the 1905 charter, among whom was Kenneth McKellar.

But Crump was there too, with Frank Rice, Charles Bryan, and others who had campaigned for the commission government ticket. Establishing headquarters at the old Maxwell House, Crump began the battle even before the legislature was organized. Long before the time came for a test vote on the measure, he had personally talked with every member of the legislature, and having done so, he made notes on how he might get every doubtful vote. His greatest gift as a politician was in the area of face-to-face persuasion. His manner was direct and unaffected, and his ability for remembering names was a great asset. Crump's capacity for detail was nowhere better shown than in the painstaking way he gathered information about those with whom he was to deal.

In the evenings he would hold long strategy sessions with the Shelby delegation, mapping out plans for the following day. When everyone else had gone to sleep, he would lie in bed propped up with pillows, jotting notes for the next day's action.

Opposition quickly melted. On January 21 the senate committee on municipal affairs unanimously approved Memphis charter bills calling for a commission government and providing for recall by the people of elected officials. When the bills were reported and a senator from Chattanooga interposed an objection, Crump called him a "hound." [13] There was no further excitement; the bills passed quickly and were signed by Governor Patterson on February 12.

The act establishing commission government provided for six administrative departments: public affairs and health; police; streets; bridges and sewers; accounts and finances; and public utilities, grounds, and buildings. The mayor, in addition to his function of presiding over commission meetings and integrating the work of the administrative departments, was also to have charge of the depart-

13 *Commercial Appeal,* January 22, 1909.

ment of public health. The success of the commission government act was due, said the *News Scimitar,* to "the splendid, organization of the forces behind . . . the bill. Fire and Police Commissioner E. H. Crump was general in command." [14]

As the commission government issue moved to its climax, the Crumps moved into their new home at 1962 Peabody Avenue. A two-story brick building with a glassed-in sun porch attached to its eastern side, it stood four or five feet above the street level, and was approached by a rise of steps and a walkway that ran briefly to the front porch. The porch with its Doric columns added a touch of adornment to the otherwise simple character of the structure.

East of the house was a large corner lot, which Crump filled over the years with a variety of shrubs and trees. In his notes are many references to the upkeep of his yard: "Holly tree in front of side porch, move to another place. Might put it out in front on west side of new cedar opposite the other Holly. . . . Small juniper in front bed just west of the new cedar on terrace. . . . Need 4 Azaleas. . . . Piece of shrubbery by first bird feeder. . . . Juniper on East side of front porch by the side porch," and so on. In later years spring would bring such a proliferation of color to the yard that Sunday church-goers would crowd Peabody Avenue to view the spectacle. In time the growth of thick shrubs around the corner lot produced a retreat that Crump would use on summer evenings. With his shirt unbuttoned at the collar, he would sit there to read, visit with his family, or in later years, reminisce with his friend from boyhood, Mason Jones.

The house was built during the summer of 1908. Tom Phillips recalled that frequently he would leave the *News Scimitar* office in the late afternoon, meet Crump at his business office, and together they would take the streetcar out Peabody Avenue to inspect the day's progress. "He inspected every brick that went into that house," Phillips said. "He lived there forty-five years." [15]

Willie Thomas, Crump's gardener, recalled that his employer was very concerned about his shrubs and flowers. When Crump would come back from one of his trips, he would go in and greet everybody, then go into the yard and walk around and inspect everything closely. He would call out: "Where's Willie?" and Willie would come to explain what had been done and what needed to be done. After that

14 Scrapbook news clipping.
15 Interview with Thomas Phillips, April 11, 1962.

Crump would walk down the street to get the long view. "He loved his home," Willie concluded.[16]

On August 22, 1909, Crump made a public announcement: "At this time . . . I think nothing more is needed than to say that I shall be a candidate for mayor in the November election." [17] It was a foregone conclusion that Joe Williams would attempt a political comeback, and five days after Crump's announcement, Williams declared that he too was in the race. In the meantime, two other candidates announced: Walter Talbert, a well-known member of the Memphis Chickasaw Guard drill team, and Cornelius Simon, a Socialist candidate.

As usual, Frank Rice managed Crump's campaign. Crump concentrated on establishing personal contact with the voters and left the oratory for others, notably William J. Bacon, Leo Goodman, and Charles M. Bryan. All three were young, intelligent, and dedicated adherents of the Crump crusade.

Bryan was the spellbinder of the group. A grandson of Raphael Semmes, the naval hero of the Confederacy, he graduated from the University of Notre Dame and then went on for a law degree at the University of Virginia. Later he served in the Crump organization as both city and county attorney, but time did not bring him to the front as an organization stalwart. He wrote poetry and differed from the rest in other ways. By erecting a wall around himself he eventually became something of a stranger to his associates. Yet he served Crump well as a substitute speaker. Years later the *Commercial Appeal* observed that for all the time that Crump had been in public life "nobody ever heard of his making an address. . . . Back in the days when Mr. Crump was mayor and it was the thing to do to put in the convention programs that the mayor would welcome the delegates and so on, nine times out of ten Charley Bryan . . . would show up." [18]

Crump used newspaper advertisements to state his position on current issues, a method of campaigning that had not been used much in Memphis. His appeal was directed to reform sentiment. He advocated the public ownership of utilities, and he stressed the need to force large corporations—especially the railroads and the street rail-

16 Interview with Willie Thomas, August 8, 1957.
17 Scrapbook news clipping.
18 *Commercial Appeal,* March 24, 1933.

way company—to contribute their fair share toward the support of the city. The theme of a "business government" had caught on practically everywhere in urban America during that era, and while all of the Memphis candidates assured the electorate they were for it and would bring it to pass, Crump sounded more convincing than the rest. He ran, too, as he declared in a large advertisement the day before the election, as "the foremost advocate of the commission form of government." [19]

While his friends spoke for him, Crump shook hands. Williams could make a good platform address, but he was not a "mixer." But, said the *News Scimitar,* "Crump knows everybody and he shakes hands with everybody. His handshake is so hearty that no man can doubt his sincerity. He can cover more territory and be in more places at the same time than any man that ever entered the political game." [20]

During the campaign the *News Scimitar* did a profile on each of the candidates. The interviewer was impressed: "Mr. Crump has the stamp of good fellowship all over him. . . . He is very approachable, cordial, considerate and obliging." But interviewing him was "as difficult as trying to squeeze water out of a bale of cotton; . . . before you realize it, you become the interviewed instead of the interviewer." When he did not want to answer a question, he could "say a whole lot without imparting any real information." Crump's appearance was described as "tall and rather spare for his height . . . and when he stands, the calves of his legs bow out backwards like a barrel stave." He was "all bone and muscle," and his "crowning glory" was a "luxuriant mop of . . . red hair." In the course of the interview Crump noticed a sketch of Joe Williams on a desk. "Mr. Williams is certainly a fine-looking man all right, I'll say that much for him," Crump remarked. "But," he added, "he's a fox!"

The political seers predicted a victory for Williams, who was known to have a hard-core following in the center of the city. Crump's strength lay in the suburban areas, but so did Talbert's, and although Talbert was not regarded as a serious contender, whatever votes he got would be largely drawn from Crump.

The prognosticators saw something else that indicated trouble for Crump. Memphis had witnessed an especially large registration, indi-

19 *Ibid.,* November 3, 1909.   20 *News Scimitar,* March 30, 1909.

cating that the Williams forces were lining up the Negro vote. Of the eighteen thousand registrants, it was estimated that twelve thousand would vote, and therefore the person elected would have to have six thousand or more votes. With upwards of two thousand Negroes voting, Crump had a serious disability to overcome.

On election day Crump helped with the poll watching. In the fifth ward, where the saloonkeepers had registered Negro voters in large numbers, he found the Negroes taking official ballots already marked into the polling place and then bringing out a ballot marked for the next man. When one Negro started in with a marked ballot, Crump stopped him, but the Negro objected and was backed in the argument by a white saloonkeeper. When the Negro insisted on voting, Crump struck him in the face, and then turning to the group, he threatened dire consequences to anyone using marked ballots. He spoke of the fracas later: "I should not have done so, but I was so outraged over the matter that I struck him." [21]

When the votes were counted, Crump's majority over Williams was 79. Williams immediately claimed fraud and demanded a recount of the ballots. "I had figured," he said, "that I would receive 6,100 votes." He attributed his shortage to Crump's election day activity, stating that "votes cast for me in several precincts were not counted, but were counted on the same complaint when cast for Mr. Crump." There was also a matter of poll tax receipts. "If I could have gotten all . . . I needed there would have been no question about my being elected. But I stuck to my agreement with Mr. Crump and Mr. Talbert not to issue any poll taxes from any place except headquarters. I know Mr. Crump had poll tax books at every ward. . . . We ran out of poll tax receipts before noon Thursday. Mr. Crump had them all day." Another thing that nettled Williams was that "Crump was backed by plenty of money. . . . If Mr. Crump is elected it has been done by a lavish outlay of money, something I never had." [22]

In the days immediately following the election, eleven different lawsuits were filed "prying into every possible crack in the armor of the new administration." [23] Crump quickly obtained court orders to counteract the stratagems of the Williams forces, who were trying to prevent his inauguration.

21   Scrapbook news clipping.
22   *Ibid.*
23   *Ibid.*

The validity of the vote count was challenged and a recount demanded. Aside from the uncertainty that this created for Crump, it produced a moratorium on the payment of election bets. "Election bets amounting to approximately $20,000 are tied up until the mayoralty contest is settled," the *Commercial Appeal* reported. "Will Overton is said to deny that $2,600 wagered by ex-Chief of Police Geo. T. O'Haver was his money. Aleck Utley, a Crump man representing a pool, covered most of it. Councilman Geo. Love won $500 from Councilman Sambucetti, and the latter also lost $25 to Utley, which he bet against $100 that Crump would finish third. In the fifteenth ward, several Crump men pooled $1,500 against the same man, said to have been a prominent banker." [24]

Fighting off attack after attack, Crump took office on January 1, 1910, and began business by rapping for order with a gavel given to him by his wife. Almost immediately F. T. Fitzhugh, a prominent Memphis lawyer representing the utilities, filed a suit with the courts attacking the constitutionality of the commission government. Ultimately the state supreme court declared the new charter constitutional, and finally on November 18, Williams' chief counsel asked the courts to dismiss the vote fraud case against Crump. It had been established beyond doubt, he said, that the election "was honest and that the count was not only accurate, but laboriously so." [25]

On the same day that Williams' attorney asked for the dismissal, Williams wrote Crump a letter as "a matter of simple justice":

After advising with my attorneys as to the law governing elections I accepted their conclusions, believing them to be correct, and well sustained by ample authority. Leaving questions of law to them, I undertook to fortify them with the facts. During my investigation I was honestly led to believe by many and urgent friends, who, I am now satisfied, were misled by statements made to them about irregularities and many cases of fraud perpetrated on elections in the count of ballots. . . .

Having secured an honest recount, I have found a totally different result from what I expected. The boxes have only disclosed the greatest ignorance and carelessness on the part of many voters, and the exposure of fraud has failed most utterly. I therefore take on myself the responsibility of the failure of my attorneys to carry my case against you to a successful conclusion.

24 *Ibid.*
25 *Commercial Appeal,* November 19, 1910.

I want the dead past to bury its dead, and in withdrawing my suit I wish to say I hope your administration will be a credit to yourself and friends, and of great benefit to the community. And I further wish to assure you that I leave this contest without animosity. [26]

26   J. J. Williams to Crump, November 18, 1910. Crump Papers.

⊠ ☐

Chapter IV

MAYOR

WHEN CRUMP became mayor of Memphis, the old riverboat town was in the process of yielding to new customs of the machine age. But the inhabitants were not passing from one era to another without signs of reluctance. In the year 1908, for example, a few Memphis women began to smoke cigarettes in public, provoking the *Commercial Appeal* to comment that "when a woman starts out to make a fool of herself she usually goes the limit." [1]

There were even more disquieting signs for those who cherished the womanly ideal of the Old South. In 1909 the Lyceum Theatre ran *The Blue Mouse,* a play that the *Commercial Appeal* thought was flagrantly indecent. When the producers declared that it was really "art," the paper replied that it was "as artistic as the nude painting that decorates the wall of a gin mill on the first floor of a panel house." [2]

New and disconcerting trends were developing in music and dancing. During the summer of 1911 a favorite in the park concert program was Mendelssohn's "Spring Song" played in ragtime, and the latest popular song was "a story of Mrs. Casey Jones' second mar-

1 *Commercial Appeal,* February 1, 1908.
2 *Ibid.,* March 30, 1909.

riage and her divorce." [3] How sad, thought the *Commercial Appeal,*
"when we listen back into the days of a generation ago and recall the
vogue of 'Nellie Gray,' 'My Old Kentucky Home,' 'Grandfather's
Clock,' 'Old Dog Tray' and the melodies of that generation." [4] As for
dancing, by 1912 Vernon and Irene Castle's "Grizzly Bear" and
"Turkey Trot" were finding favor with the younger members of the
social set. The *Commercial Appeal* had a sour word for this fad: it
had come "from the dance halls of the red light district of San Francisco." [5]

There were other signs of the times reflecting changes in the mode
of life. By 1910 Memphis had one thousand automobiles, and the
Sunday *Commercial Appeal* was devoting a full page to automobile
news, advising men on the care of their cars and women on what
they should wear when they ventured out in them. In 1910 the first
airplane flew over the town. It was still a novelty, like the motion pictures that were shown along with vaudeville acts at the Jefferson Theatre.

The face of the city had changed. The Memphis skyline of 1900,
as one viewed it from the Arkansas shore, was low and squat along
the top of the levee. By 1910 there were three "skyscrapers" of fifteen or more stories. Some of the city's most intimate links with the
past were lost during these years. In 1909 Luehrman's famous hotel
and restaurant on Main Street, symbol of a warm graciousness and
conviviality, was put up for auction. In 1911 the old city fire station
on Adams and Second was razed. Three years later the Bell Tavern
came down. In the 1820's it had enjoyed a degree of renown under
the proprietorship of Paddy Meagher. Patty's little daughter Sally was
a favorite of General Jackson and would sit on his knee when he
visited the tavern. Sally developed early into womanhood and was
reputed to have sat on many another knee. In 1824 the Bell Tavern
was visited by General Lafayette, accompanied by Fanny Wright,
and it was there too that Davy Crockett "pulled off one of the greatest drunks that ever happened on the Chickasaw Bluffs." [6] In the
forties the tavern deteriorated in tone and "became a den of thieves
and debauchery." It was finally condemned by a building inspector
who had no feeling for history.

3   *Ibid.,* July 11, 1911.
4   *Ibid.,* July 30, 1911.
5   *Ibid.,* December 15, 1912.
6   *Ibid.,* October 11, 1914.

With Crump's inauguration, the city government for the first time occupied offices in the new Shelby County Courthouse, which had been under construction for three years. Occupying a whole city block, the exterior was finished in white stone and adorned with rows of marble columns on all four sides.

But in January, 1910, nothing so exemplified the new in Memphis as its mayor. There were early indications that a revolutionary change was at hand. The basic challenge to Crump's administration was the city's crime record. On taking office Crump made a statement to the press in which he declared that the administration would do three things in dealing with the problem: it would rid the city of thieves and thugs, break up the practice of carrying pistols, and "clean up the dives which have flourished so long in this city." [7] To be sure, he was thirty years in accomplishing these objectives, yet he took vigorous action from the beginning. Periodic roundups of transients and vagrants were made, and for a while every Negro found on the streets after midnight was taken to the station house. Beggars were ordered off the streets, with the provision that worthy cases could take up residence in the county poorhouse. So aggravated was this condition that the *Commercial Appeal* observed that at times "Main Street has been infested by no less than half a hundred of the poor unfortunates, and pedestrians have found it a positive nuisance to run the gauntlet." [8]

Crump's secretaries, who gave much emphasis to the accomplishments of his mayoralty, claimed only a moderation of the crime problem. Open gambling became less conspicuous; slot machines were driven out entirely; dance halls were practically eliminated; and policy writing, a form of gambling operated principally among Negroes, became a lost art in Memphis. Houses of prostitution were confined to a definite district and "street-walking was greatly curtailed."

Crump made a strong effort to stop members of the administration from accepting favors. He set a good example. Four days after he took office, he wrote the general superintendent of the Yazoo and Mississippi Valley Railroad Company: "I am in receipt of your kind favor . . . an annual pass made out in my favor over the Illinois Central lines. . . . While appreciating the compliment . . . I return

7 *Ibid.*, January 12, 1910.   8 *Ibid.*, April 27, 1910.

the pass herewith as the new commission charter forbids the acceptance of such favors upon the part of those connected with the city
government." [9]

To Crump, of course, the return of the railroad pass was more
than compliance with the law. He always refused favors that put
him under obligation to others. At times he received gifts that were
so obviously the result of a merely generous impulse that it was
difficult to refuse them, but he always did. One letter begins, "Dear
Tony, I thank you for remembering me" (with a half cask of beer),
but "while I appreciate the courtesy, I would rather send you my
check to cover the shipment. It is indeed a rather delicate thing to
'look a gift horse in the mouth' but I am sure you will appreciate
my position." Crump added that while he had not drunk beer in
a long time, "I like to keep a little in my house so this came in very
nicely." [10]

In spite of his efforts, it was difficult to stop others from accepting
favors, and shortly after he became mayor there was a public display of the mutual esteem with which the Memphis police and the
criminal element traditionally regarded each other. In March, John
Persica, the overlord of gambling and purveyor of gaudy entertainment in his Garden Theater, held a banquet honoring the new chief
of police, W. J. Hayes. At the banquet Hayes was presented with
a star, "one of the handsomest that ever adorned the breast of a
police official." [11] The solid gold badge was set with seven diamonds
—one in each of the six points and a more prominent one in the
center. The presentation speech, to which Hayes responded, was
made by one of the highly respected members of the Memphis judi-
ciary, Judge P. Harry Kelly.

As soon as Crump learned that Persica had honored his chief in
such a splendid way, he sent for Hayes and reminded him that the
acceptance of the gift was in violation of the city charter and ordered
him to return it. In a statement to the *Commercial Appeal* Crump
said that while he harbored no dark suspicions that Persica's intention had been to subsidize the police department, he was not at all
certain that the public would take that view. The *Commercial Appeal*'s editorial on the subject was entitled "A Fallen Star."

9 Crump to W. S. King, January 5, 1910. Crump Papers.
10 Crump to Tony Brignardello, September 15, 1913. Crump Papers.
11 *Commercial Appeal*, March 15, 1910.

Some months later Crump enlisted the aid of the public to stop graft in the police department. He stated that he personally had secured the insertion of the article in the city charter prohibiting the acceptance of gifts by public officials and that he had had this section printed on the back of every check issued to city employees. He declared that in "every instance since this government came into power, whenever there was the slightest proof of graft, the offender has been promptly discharged." He invited the public to cooperate with the administration "in this matter, and if any man knows that grafting exists and will report it to me his name will be withheld if he so desires. I wish it understood, however, that I will entertain no anonymous charges, but in every instance must know who is making the allegations, even if I do not make his name public." [12]

The new era found the police department meeting new issues and doing it well. The automobile brought parking regulations into effect. Police officers began to direct traffic at busy intersections, and a motorcycle squad was created. After a year of commission government, the police department had "improved in appearance, in efficiency, and in courtesy. . . . The officers are smarter, are neater in appearance, and do not look as if their time was spent chiefly in loafing around saloons." [13]

With all the extreme measures taken to reduce the crime problem, there was little real change in the situation. Appearances were a little more refined, but the murder rate, the city's most fundamental crime problem, continued to rise. It reached its highest point in 1916 with eighty-nine murders per hundred thousand population: Memphis was called the nation's "murder capital."

That the murder rate had increased was not the mayor's fault. Some of the more ebullient of the clerical reformers assumed that all Crump had to do was to give the word, and the dives would be forever closed, saloons would keep the Sabbath, and murders would cease. Short of martial law, Crump did the best that could be done. Crime in Memphis was so chronic and so deeply rooted in the political power base that there could be no rapid or simple solution to the problem.

The Crump administration inherited an inefficient fire department whose equipment was so antiquated and badly worn that insurance

12 *News Scimitar*, September 23, 1910.
13 *Commercial Appeal*, March 11, 1911.

underwriters required rated policy payments. During the next several years new equipment was added; fire stations were repainted; and firemen were given new beds and bathtubs. Old horses with stiffening joints were sent to the gluepots and were replaced with engine-driven trucks. In 1913, the capstone was added in the way of technical modernization when the chief was provided with a new Cadillac in which to race to conflagrations. It was said "to be the most complete of its kind ever put into service by any city." [14] Equipped with a mighty fifty-horsepower engine, it could attain a speed of sixty-five miles per hour. The body was made entirely of aluminum, and all the fixtures, of solid nickel.

These improvements, together with an increase in efficiency and morale of departmental personnel, provided quick respite from the onerous burden of rated premiums. The Memphis fire department was on its way to the fame it won in the high Crump years of the forties, with its national awards for fire fighting efficiency.

There was progress in other areas. In 1909 by the provisions of the commission government charter act, the board of health underwent reorganization. The mayor became a commissioner of health, which gave him "general supervision over the officer of superintendent of health and matters relating thereto." [15] The charter provided for the appointment of a superintendent of health and for the creation of divisions of sanitary inspection, chemistry and bacteriology, contagious diseases, school inspection, and dairy inspection.

Of all the conditions in Memphis that adversely affected human welfare, poor health undoubtedly stood foremost. The pages of the newspapers were filled with advertisements of patent medicines, and numerous quack doctors capitalized on the credulity and chronic malarial infections of the great number of rural newcomers. As late as 1915 pellagra was listed as a leading cause of death, indicating that many people still clung to the diet of the rural poor white: fatback, dried corn, and beans.[16] The same source also cited tuberculosis as a leading killer, claiming that "there were not less than 1,000

14 W. M. Pope, "Memphis Commission Government" (mimeographed), I, No. 5, p. 6.
15 W. F. Walker and Dorothy F. Holland, *A Survey of Health Problems and Facilities in Memphis and Shelby County, Tennessee for the Year of 1929* (Memphis, 1930), 14.
16 *Associated Charities Fourth Annual Report, 1914–1915* (Memphis, n.d.), 5.

tubercular patients in Memphis," and that among children under fifteen, tuberculosis killed more than measles, scarlet fever, croup, and diphtheria combined.

The city's first public health office was established in 1838, but it was not until 1879, after the yellow fever epidemic, that provision was made for a public health program as one of the integral functions of the city government. Yet public health work remained largely ineffective because of the crude notions still prevailing concerning the cause of disease and because of public resistance to remedial programs. It was still thought that malaria was caused by miasmic vapors, and even the *Commercial Appeal* opposed vaccination against smallpox. In 1901, when the president of the board of health required vaccination as a condition to admission to school, the paper could not understand why "40,000 healthy children shall have injected into their veins poison from diseased kine" because "a few negroes who wallow in filth in the bottoms contact the disease and come into Memphis." The order had been issued out of "an idolatrous worship of a theory of which the best that can be said is like Rabelais' religion—'a great Perhaps.' " To make vaccination compulsory was "a species of tyranny unworthy of the age in which we live." [17]

Such conservative views did not affect the Crump administration. One of its most pressing health problems was securing a pure milk supply. Most of the milk was produced on the outskirts of the city by small "city dairies" that kept their cows in vacant lots and customarily milked them in a sea of filth. Much of the milk was ladled out to consumers—unrefrigerated—from cans that were carried on horse-drawn carts. In later years a Memphis physician recalled how he had once toured these dairies with a health inspector and, on emptying a milk can, had found an inch of filth deposited on the bottom.[18]

Crump's new superintendent of health was Dr. Max Goltman, a man of energy who made the milk problem his immediate concern. He instituted a policy of dairy inspection, requiring the maintenance of standards of sanitation which had already been defined and written into the statute books. The dairymen, accustomed to the old ways, were slow to conform, and some complained that Dr. Goltman's rigid inspection policy "was aimed at them with the view of

18 Interview with Dr. A. G. Hudson, September 12, 1956.
17 *Commercial Appeal*, August 22, 1901.

helping certain dairy interests. . . ." To this Dr. Goltman responded that the law was applied "irrespective of persons or interests other than the public health." [19] Particularly, the dairymen balked at the requirement that they rid themselves of cattle infected with tuberculosis. By the summer of 1911 only a few dairies could meet the city's standards. In his weekly health bulletin, Dr. Goltman warned that "this condition of furnishing unclean milk to the community" would have to stop. It had "brought about a great deal of sickness and this sickness to a large extent among babies." [20] Unless the dairies could produce milk that met health department requirements, the city would ban the use of their milk and import what was needed. Crump was probably behind this threat, for he was not one to let a problem drag on interminably. Three days later, on July 18, the dairymen's association was reorganized, and full cooperation with the health department was pledged.[21]

Other measures were taken to improve public health. In addition to his weekly health bulletin, Dr. Goltman distributed pamphlets that explained the cause and treatment of contagious diseases. An ordinance of 1910 regulated the practice of midwifery, widely used among the colored. A year later, the health department, assisted by a fund obtained from public subscription, established a free milk dispensary for needy mothers, supervised by nurses who gave instructions in the preparation of formulas. Four visiting nurses, one of whom was colored, were added to the health department staff in 1911, and in 1912 a system of medical inspection was inaugurated in the schools. A screening ordinance required owners of dwelling houses, restaurants, hotels, and factories to screen their buildings, an important step toward the eradication of the yellow fever menace. Large scale immunization against smallpox and typhoid fever was undertaken. In the summer of 1912, when the Mississippi River overflowed and contaminated a part of the Memphis water supply, thirty thousand persons were given free typhoid inoculations.

Crump's mayoralty marked the beginning of the development of Memphis into the large medical center that it is today. In 1911 the

---

19 *Commercial Appeal*, December 29, 1910.
20 *Ibid.*, July 16, 1911.
21 *Ibid.*, July 19, 1911. *One Year and Eight Months Under Commission Government* (Memphis, 1911), n.p.

University of Tennessee medical school was located in Memphis and became the nucleus of an expanding system of hospitals. Initially, the medical school operated in conjunction with the City Hospital, later renamed the John Gaston Hospital. On October 28 the Crump administration published its "Third Quarterly Report," which declared that the hospital had been "overhauled, repaired, and repainted" from "cellar to garret." [22]

The report also announced that "this administration has abolished private wards," believing "that the hospital should be devoted exclusively to the care of the poor and unfortunate . . . and has raised the price of those who are sent there from outside Shelby County by well-to-do corporations and individuals."

The strength of the public health program demonstrated administrative vigor, but it represented more than that. Crump himself prized health and pursued it throughout his life. Disease, deformity, and other forms of affliction of body and mind perpetually concerned him, as one gathers from his jottings about such matters and from the testimony of those who knew him. In his nocturnal tours of the city he was quick to spot those individuals suffering from some particularly depressing deformity and to plan some means for the alleviation of their plight. One suspects that his sensitivity to the matter of health came from the fact that his energy frequently pressed hard the reserves of his physical stamina. He needed no formal definition of the proposition that good health is necessary for creative and useful lives.

The principal contribution of the Crump administration to an already extensive park system was the purchase, in August, 1911, of old Montgomery Park. Once the scene of annual horse racing meets, it was made into a site for the annual tri-state fair.

Crump was also concerned about the lack of recreation areas for Negroes. In the early months of his administration he urged the park commission to provide a park for them. The *Commercial Appeal* had already given its support to the idea by declaring that "the decent negroes of Memphis want a park. By a common consent they have withdrawn from the public parks now used by the white people. . . .We believe it would be a good thing for Memphis and a good thing for negroes." [23]

22 *News Scimitar,* October 28, 1910.
23 *Commercial Appeal,* April 20, 1910.

It was the issue of a park for Negroes that produced one of the first "feuds" that marked Crump's public life. The chairman of the park commission in 1911 was Colonel Jacob Galloway, a charter member of the commission from the time of its inception in 1900. He was a man of large means with a proud family name, and through his years of work with the park program he came to look upon the subject of parks as his special area of competence. The idea of a park for Negroes produced in him no warm response, but in February, 1911, feeling that a gesture had to be made, suggested that a nearby island in the Mississippi would be a good site. There, he said "the negro park question is forever solved." [24] He recognized that the island was inundated by the high waters of spring, but this he considered an advantage, for when the water subsided it left "a rich alluvial deposit . . . which accounts for the rich luxuriant growth that covers the island. . . . The negro ought to be in his glory among all that tropical growth." He made no mention of how those who would enjoy this muddy, bushy, flat were to reach it—by swimming perhaps.

Crump was not taken with this plan, and several months later he supported the proposal of a commission member that the city purchase fifty acres of land several miles beyond the town's eastern limit as a park for Negroes. Galloway, at the time, was cruising on his yacht in the Caribbean, but when he returned to Memphis he "immediately donned his war clothes and . . . sent a letter to Mayor Crump notifying him that he . . . was ready at any time to appear before the board of city commissioners in opposition to the plan." [25] When the city commissioners voted in April on the proposal that Crump favored, they stood with Galloway, and the matter was momentarily dropped. But afterwards, the meetings of the park commission became increasingly tempestuous as Abe Goodman, Crump's agent on the commission, continually criticized Galloway's policy.

In February, 1913, Galloway was rebuffed on his own particular plans for the acquisition of park lands. For some time he had been recommending that the city purchase a relatively small site called Jackson Mound on the bank of the Mississippi. When the city commission refused to act on his recommendation, he concluded that Crump was meddling in the affairs of the park commission. Galloway

24   *Ibid.,* February 14, 1911.
25   *Ibid.,* March 4, 1911.

was against truckling to the mayor. "When the park commissioners put the purchase of Jackson Mound up to the city and the mayor said: 'Gentlemen, you are all wrong,' we should have had enough manhood about us . . . to say you can go to h——l with your park board and get a new commission. . . . I have spent twelve years trying to put my experience gleaned from all over the world into results here. My reward is a slap at my integrity." He then dared Crump to debate the issue, stating that he would pay for the theater and band and then "eat him up." [26]

Two months later Crump's plan for a Negro park was realized when the city purchased fifty acres out east of the city in what was called the Macon Road area. The new addition was called Douglass Park after the famous Negro emancipationist of pre–Civil War days, Frederick Douglass. A year after Douglass Park was acquired, the city purchased Jackson Mound and changed its name to De Soto Park to please the more historically minded citizens of the city, who were convinced that Hernando De Soto had crossed the Mississippi at that point. These developments spoke plainly of the impotence of Colonel Galloway's position as park commission chairman, and he shortly resigned the office. Where Crump was concerned, the issue was simply a matter of having things done his way. Undoubtedly he saw the Negro park matter as part of a larger plan that Galloway knew nothing about. Crump might have been thinking of Negro votes, but he could also just as well have considered it a matter of justice: he had a remarkable facility for tying abstract ideals to an immediate political objective.

Colonel Galloway's attempt to run the park commission as an autonomous agency brought him afoul of Crump's own views of the subject. When a personality intruded itself between Crump and a desired end, he would endeavor to remove the obstacle by diplomacy, but if he could not, he moved to the attack with the righteousness of an Old Testament prophet, for he thought persistent hostility to himself could be accounted for only by malicious perversity. Colonel Galloway was stung and perhaps a little bewildered by the way in which his deficiencies were aired in the park commission dispute, but others would follow who would be as badly stung and bewildered.

Crump's passion for neatness showed itself in the improved appearance of the city. Much closer attention was given to repairing

26 *News Scimitar*, February 11, 1913.

holes in the streets, and a concrete road-wide viaduct replaced a ramshackle wooden structure over the Frisco tracks on Madison Avenue, one of the main east–west arterials leading out of the city. The downtown business district was modernized. Along Main Street, for two miles, and on Madison Avenue, ornamental cluster lights were installed, providing night-promenading citizens a truly metropolitan sight—the "longest 'Great White Way' in the United States," they boasted, and "the envy of every city of comparable size in the country." [27] All electric lights, telephone, and telegraph wires in the business district were put underground, and in the residential sections the utility companies were forced to paint their poles green to harmonize with the foliage. An ordinance prohibited the posting of tin and cardboard signs on poles, and only ornamental illuminated signs were permitted in the business district. Another required the tearing down of all wooden awnings on Main, Beale, and Front streets. Crump made a personal war on old shacks around the city and gradually, using one expedient or another, caused many of them to be torn down. Most of the changes came at his suggestion. He spent hours at night riding about and making notes. When the mayor found something amiss, the commissioners would hear about it.

City employees found themselves under a new kind of tension. In the old days the mayor's ignorance of some of the more remote aspects of administrative detail could be capitalized upon by employees, but times had changed. After a night ride, Crump "would reach City Hall the next morning knowing more about needed street repairs than the street commissioner," and almost "any morning he was apt to show up at the city stables for a thorough check of the mules, carts and harness." [28] Old City Hall tales recount how many a garbage collector went without his breakfast in the dash to beat the mayor to the stables. A city foreman once remarked that "Crump could tell if the boxing were loose on any wheel of the city wagon—it seemed he could hear it rattling from South Memphis to Chelsea." [29]

The improper use of city time and material was summarily stopped. "It was back in the horse and buggy days," Crump recalled some years later. "City employees used to use city-owned horses and buggies in their work. However, we found that during

27   Secretaries' notes.
28   *Commercial Appeal*, October 17, 1958.
29   Marvin Pope, "Official Record" (mimeographed), 3. Crump Papers.

the baseball season all those horses and buggies were parked out in front of the ball park. So we painted city buggies yellow. After that they didn't park in front of the ball park. They were so conspicuous they kept moving and on the job." [30]

On the other hand, a cooperative and hardworking city employee could normally expect promotion. Marvin Pope in his "Official Record" states that "practically all vacancies during the Crump administration were filled with men from the ranks. . . . He was considerate, fair and just. . . . He never failed to stand by a city employee when he thought he was right in the discharge of his duty."

Efficiency in financial matters was a passion with Crump, and no phase of administration received more personal attention from him than this one. Shortly after taking office he found that the tax assessor, an elected official, was bungling his work. He reacted characteristically. The hapless assessor, who probably thought he was doing an adequate job, was struck by the Jovian bolt that Crump customarily used to brand high public servants as unworthy. The assessor received the following indictment:

The city will soon run short of money. We must make arrangements with some bank to carry us until the taxes come in. The first things the banks undoubtedly will want to know is just how much money will be needed, and for how long. . . .

The single request the commissioners make upon you is to give us the books on May 1, and report in writing each Monday morning, so that we may know how you are progressing. We ask this because the previous administration had trouble with you, the books always being held back, and in order to hurry them along a lump sum was given you to spend that the city might get the books earlier, thereby saving the taxpayers interest in the overdraft in bank. . . .

I . . . contend if you and your assistants would readily do a full day's work, as others connected with the city government are now doing, you could, on your own statement to the commission, get the books up much earlier than May 1.

If after one assessment is turned in you would begin preparing your notes for another year's work, get the transfers from the register's office and building permits from the building inspector's office, you could either make the changes daily upon your records or keep them on file and on Jan. 10 make them all at one time. Then on Jan. 10 you would be ready to go into the field for new property and new assessments. In the meantime you could mail out your personalty blanks and certainly by May 1,

30 *Press Scimitar,* February 1, 1941.

or earlier, your books could be written up by the machines and ready for the board of equalization. . . .

In conclusion, I will say that we may have to endure a certain amount of your style of doing business for a time, but I can not believe that we will have to contend with it throughout my entire administration. This city is too big to delegate that much power to one man, and we now notify you that we expect at the earliest possible date, to establish a new system of assessment, along the lines of our larger cities. [31]

Doubtless the tax assessor felt a little faint after reading this letter, and the thought of it would press on his mind for many days to come. Whatever his thoughts, there were probably very few that were given to how he might avoid the mayor's prescriptions.

Crump's secretaries state that he gave careful scrutiny to all the city's bills, and never signed a voucher until he had satisfied himself that the account was correct and the price paid was the best that could be gotten. To reduce waste to a minimum he inaugurated a city purchasing department. Under the old system every department had purchased what it wanted from whomever it pleased, and no one knew what supplies were costing until the bills came in. Now everything from lead pencils to automobiles was obtained by the purchasing agent through competitive bidding, with purchases over five hundred dollars requiring the authorization of the city commission. Each requisition had to have the approval of the commissioner from whose department it came, and so scrupulously were supplies administered that even postage stamps were brought under a strict accounting, and city employees had to purchase their own for their private mail.

New sources of revenue were uncovered. The collection of delinquent taxes from previous years was pressed. City money was put out to banks on a basis of competitive bidding with the result that the city was paid on daily balance and charged less for overdrafts. Twelve thousand dollars was saved with this arrangement in the first year of commission government. For the first time in history, the city collected the full amount of turnpike funds due from the county court, a sum of $22,500. Rentals of city-owned light poles by the light company amounting to $7,474.60, which previous administrations had been unable to get, were added to the treasury. Period-

31   *Commercial Appeal,* February 23, 1910.

ically, old bottles, scrap, and accumulations of feed sacks were gathered up and sold, and the money was turned into the public till rather than into the pockets of enterprising employees.

A basic reform was initiated in tax-assessing procedures. From 1900 to 1910 the yearly rate of increase in the assessment values of real estate was nowhere near the rate of increase in the actual value of property. One of the great weaknesses in financial administration before Crump came into office was the unwillingness or inability of the city to make equitable assessments of private and corporate property. For example, Crump found on becoming mayor that the Louisville and Nashville Railroad had been paying taxes on 1.73 miles of road within the city. Sending out the assessor's field force to make a check, it was found that there were actually 3.9 miles of trackage. An adjustment was secured from the company and back taxes collected. The result of this kind of attention to real values caused a rise in the assessment base from about $60,000,-000 when he took office to approximately $100,000,000 in 1915. It was this, plus efficient financial administration, that enabled the administration to lower the tax rate from $1.75 per hundred dollars of assessed valuation in 1909, to $1.58 in 1912. At a time of increasing expenditures to improve city services, the tax rate was reduced to the lowest point in the history of the city. In the years of Crump control that followed, the single thing that most forcibly demonstrated efficient administration was a continuing low tax rate, plus expansion of city services into areas important to general welfare.

Commission government, Crump's impeccable standards in financial administration, and his social awareness were characteristic aspects of a reform impulse in American society of that era that historians call the Progressive movement. In standard American history two other mayors, Samuel "Golden Rule" Jones of Toledo and Tom Johnson of Cleveland, are traditionally cited as exemplifying the best in the way of urban reform leaders. Crump stands with them, for not only was he honest and possessed of a social consciousness, but he embodied the most typical progressive traits in his profound conviction that the basic sickness in public administration was the alliance of government with corporate interests. It was a conviction that never left him, for even after he became something of a master of capital himself, he never ceased his fulminations

against the "interests," and there were few evils in government at
any level that he was unwilling to attribute to their diabolical machi-
nations.

The view that the common welfare was being subverted by the
corporate interests was practically a doctrine of faith for reformers
of the era. That Crump subscribed to it so passionately was likely due
to its having been so thoroughly a part of the climate of opinion that
he absorbed as a youth in Mississippi. Farmers and small town merchants could find no better object upon which to vent their frustration
at economic decline than the railroads. The prevalent mood was illustrated in a full page declaration in the Holly Springs *Reporter* in
1878 summoning the merchants and citizens of Marshall County
to a meeting at the courthouse to protest the tyranny exercised by
the railroad company over them. It was condemned for charging
"exorbitant prices . . . for carrying freights to and from this market;
its unjust discrimination against markets in which we are deeply
interested; its refusal to pay more than half-value for stock killed
by its trains; its oppressive and short-sighted course as practiced
towards the producing classes of this section, and its total want of
disposition to encourage the industries of the country through which
it passes and thus aid in building it up and enriching its population." [32]
One of the signers was "Crump & Co.," a business belonging to
Crump's uncle, James.

In Crump's catalogue of wicked corporations the railroads held
a special place. He conceded that they had "always maintained a
policy of 'Give and Take' but . . . they construe such a policy to mean
that they should take everything and give nothing." [33] In old age
when he had clearly won all his battles with the corporations, he railed
at them still: they had been "notorious tax dodgers for more than a
hundred years," and they had "never done anything in a civic way for
Memphis beyond a measly contribution of $50 a year to the Memphis
Chamber of Commerce." [34] He fought the railroads from start to
finish, and the battle commenced almost as soon as he had settled in
the mayor's chair. One of the first actions of his administration was
to hold a series of conferences with officials of railway lines entering
the city, seeking their agreement to build subways at important traffic
intersections. Contracts were signed, and by 1911, three subways had

32 Holly Springs *Reporter*, August 1, 1878.
33 Secretaries' notes.   34 *Ibid.*

been constructed. But one line, the Nashville, Chattanooga and St. Louis, showed signs of indifference toward the performance of its contractual obligations, and Crump issued an ultimatum. If an underpass was not begun immediately, the city would tear up the company's tracks over Lamar Avenue. Crump's word was not tested: the underpass was built. By the end of his six years in office the railroads had built eleven underpasses.

Battle was also done with the telephone company. It was, his secretaries wrote, "comparable to the Biblical account of the historical engagement between David and Goliath." The fight began in the Tennessee legislature where the Shelby County delegation, following Crump's lead, got the enactment of a rate-fixing law. The law was appealed through the state and federal courts to the United States Supreme Court. While it was pending there, a compromise was reached with the Cumberland Telephone and Telegraph Company whereby Memphis telephone users were refunded more than $105,000 and the city of Memphis was reimbursed $7,000 for the cost of litigation.

Then there was what Crump called the "streetcar gang." Perhaps to blunt the attack it knew was coming, the Memphis Street Railway Company announced in January, 1913, that it planned to modernize its system. Swinging metal gates were to be removed and collapsible doors substituted. There would be a gradual abandonment of all small cars, and new large double-track cars would be added. In Crump's view, progress was not fast enough. In December, 1913, he announced publicly that citizens were not getting the service they were paying for. The trouble was that the company was paying "dividends to a lot of Wall Street operators on watered stock." [35] The new cars had not been introduced as promised; the company was still using trailers on the main lines, and transfers were not issued to passengers. In the face of these demands, General Luke E. Wright, chief counsel for the streetcar company, protested that Crump was demanding more than other cities were getting in the way of service and that to fulfill the city's requirements would cause the company to spend more money than it was taking in. Such difficulties evoked no sympathy from the mayor. He was quite sure that the company could spend considerably more on capital investment and not hurt itself. If the

35 *News Scimitar*, December 19, 1913.

company could not provide adequate service to its patrons, Memphis would build its own street railway system.

Having seen Crump's performance for four years, the company realized that the threat of public ownership was not an idle one. Improvements were made. New equipment was added and new connections for transfer points established, removing the necessity of passengers having to go downtown to transfer irrespective of their destination. Crump insisted on, and got, lines into the new suburban areas. At his urging, a line was built to Riverside Park so that more people would have access to its natural beauty, concerts, and picnicking areas.

Yet for many years Crump lived with the conviction that there were scores with the Memphis Street Railway that remained to be settled. In 1895 the railroad had secured a fifty-year franchise from the city that was highly favorable to its interests. The secretaries note that on "many occasions, when Crump was informed that the street railway company was balking on the city's demands for increased and more efficient service to keep pace with the rapid growth of Memphis, he has expressed to his friends . . . the fervent hope that his life might be spared until 1945. We all knew what he meant. We also knew what to expect as the expiration date approached."

In Crump's view, the prince of darkness of the large corporations was the utility company, and, of the epic battles he waged in his years of running Memphis, the one with the light company was the one great struggle full of personal meaning for him.

By 1910 Memphis had two utility concerns, the Memphis Consolidated Gas and Electric Company and the Merchants Light and Power Company. The former furnished gas and electricity to the city's residential areas, while the latter supplied power to the central portion of the city and to large industrial concerns. From the first, Crump was not concerned so much with securing improved and cheaper service as he was with securing outright ownership. When he became mayor, the municipal government paid $225,000 annually for lights, and private consumers were paying ten cents per kilowatt-hour for current. "Crump insisted that Cleveland, Ohio, and other progressive cities, could get current at three cents per kilowatt hour, Memphis should get it for five cents . . . and that the city should manufacture its own electricity, for public and private consumption, at fifty per cent of what the private companies were getting for it, and, in addition, could furnish free light to charitable institutions throughout the city, just as free water was being supplied by the municipal water plant." [36]

The issue of public ownership of lighting facilities went back as far as 1887, when the state legislature had passed an act empowering Memphis to build or purchase its own light plant. In 1908 the legislature passed another act, this time providing for the issue of one million dollars in bonds to construct a plant. The sale of the bonds was so hedged with restrictions, however, that no action was taken by the municipal government.

With Crump in office, official declarations favoring municipal ownership became more frequent. The power companies were accused of meddling in local politics, of not cooperating with the city government, and of charging exorbitant rates in order to line the pockets of New York capitalists. In the growing argument over public ownership, the *Commercial Appeal* consistently opposed the idea, occasionally adverting to the danger of "socialism" but more frequently offering the opinion that Memphis could not stand a further increase of bonded indebtedness. The *New Scimitar* was a fierce advocate of public ownership and of Crump policies generally. It accused the *Commercial Appeal* of being a "mouthpiece" for the Consolidated Gas and Electric Company, and of attempting to "stem the tide of public sentiment in favor of a municipal lighting plant." [37]

Every time the state legislature met, it declared, "the *Commercial Appeal's* editorial writer is worked overtime in carrying out the orders of the corporations which control it. From a great and prosperous municipality, as the city is proclaimed in the same columns during the off season, Memphis suddenly becomes a debt-ridden wreck . . . if perchance there is a likelihood that bonds will be voted to displace one of the greedy corporate tentacles that guide the writer's hand."

And so the argument went, becoming more strident as the issue became more palpable. In the first three years of those that Crump served as mayor, it remained simply an argument, but after 1912 the subject of public ownership was overshadowed by a political power

36 Secretaries' notes.   37 *News Scimitar,* February 3, 1913.

struggle that had fateful consequences for Mayor Crump. As this issue developed and battles were fought on other fronts, there were even some lighter and joyful moments in the mayor's life.

The exciting clamor of Crump's public life contrasted sharply with the uninterrupted serenity of his domestic state. Throughout his life the two were kept almost totally disassociated. He never interjected his family into public affairs, even by allusion, and when he left his desk for home, it was to a cherished personal area of his existence upon which he refused to let public affairs encroach. The Crumps' third son was born November 5, 1910. He was named John after Crump's brother, and in later years it would be said of him that he had the most promise of emulating his father's political success. While John slept in his crib, Edward, Jr., and Bobby played cops and robbers in the livery stable.

Shortly after becoming mayor, Crump bought an automobile, a six-cylinder, sixty-horsepower Premier. The local agents of the Premier company stated that it was probably the biggest machine in the city. "It was but natural," the company announced in an advertisement, "that a man of Mr. E. H. Crump's sagacity and farsightedness should use rare judgment in the selection of an automobile for his personal use." [38]

In August Crump had his Premier shipped to Chicago where he, J. A. Riechman (president of the Memphis Associated Charities), Z. N. Estes (the county attorney general), and two Memphis businessmen began a journey to the races at Saratoga Springs. The trip was uneventful except for a minor accident at Meriden, Connecticut, where the Premier hit a cow. The Meriden newspaper got Crump's version of the affair and printed it as a bit of exciting local news. It was a fact, Crump said, "that all the way from Chicago through the intervening states, the White Mountains, and Massachusetts, we had not a single mishap except one puncture until we got within fifteen miles of Hartford. . . . There a cow got in our way. She slipped and fell and when she got up she stood still in spite of our shouts and the blasts of our horn." At the impact "we went up in the air . . . and when we landed on earth again, I looked back expecting to see a wreck of what was once a big Durham milk giver. Nothing of the kind. The cow had got up and was giving herself a shake." [39] Later

38 Scrapbook news clipping.   39 *Ibid.*

Crump wrote the mayor of Meriden, asking him to find the cow's owner so that he might make restitution. He was doing this, he said, despite the fact that "the cow was entirely at fault, attempting to turn and go back across the road just as the car passed."

Occasionally the Premier was used to transport the family to Holly Springs for the Sunday visit to Mollie Crump. The trip was an adventure, the car making its way precariously and sometimes laboriously over the rutted clay roads. Robert Crump, who was six at the time, recalls the excitement of those journeys, the lurching of the car, and the canvas bucket they used to dip water from a branch for the overheated engine.

In the summer of 1914 the family vacationed at Beach Haven, New Jersey, and one day Crump took his three boys crabbing. They crabbed from a small trestle-like walkway across a lagoon, where the water was shallow and the bottom was unfathomable mud. While Edward and Robert maneuvered their lines around the pilings, John, then three, found his sport in activities requiring less concentration. "John was in high spirits that morning," said Crump when recounting the episode in later years. "He stuck a fishhook in Edward's leg and thought it was funny. He was playing around on the narrow little bridge, and I told him if he wasn't careful, he would fall in. It wasn't a minute later when the little fellow toppled over backwards and went headfirst into the water and mud. I immediately leaped in after him, and pulled his head out of that mucky bottom." [40] Holding John with one arm, Crump grabbed a timber brace with the other, while Robert and Edward screamed for help. Shortly, they were rescued by two fishermen.

There are a few intimate glimpses into the Crump family life during this era—mostly episodes that had etched themselves into the minds of Edward and Robert. Both emphasize the great devotion of their parents. But "Father was a strict disciplinarian," E. H. Crump, Jr., remarked. "Whatever he prescribed he thought there should be strict adherence to it." He was firm, but "he was not the kind to flare up in a fit of temper." Bessie Crump read a great deal to the children and "Father would tell us stories. The main ones were Civil War stories. They were about ten per cent true—the rest was invention." Occasionally Crump took the boys hunting and fishing and saw to

40 *Press Scimitar,* May 10, 1939. Secretaries' notes.

it that they never missed the circus when it came to town. On the day it arrived they were all up at dawn and would watch the cars unload. He never lost his fascination for the highly developed precision of circus organization.

When the time came for the boys to go to school they were sent to the old Memphis University School, a private institution to which well-to-do families in town traditionally sent their sons. It had been conceived in the spirit of the Old South legend that required private schooling as one of the marks of gentility, and it was sustained in the twentieth century by a business class who sought to perpetuate the legend. Crump was not a snob, but he was perhaps thinking of giving his sons a mark of preferment that he himself had missed.

While his family was the calm focal point of his life during these years—and always would be—the tempestuousness in his public life continued, for Crump was always on the move. In the spring of 1913 the Crump administration met a crisis in the affairs of the city that did not originate in politics. On April 4 the Mississippi, rising to unprecedented heights from spring thawing, broke the levee in south Memphis and flooded a residential section in the southwestern part of the city. The situation became so acute that fifteen hundred persons were forced from their homes, and refugees came into Memphis from other flooded areas. The crisis had been anticipated, for by May 1 the Tri-State Fairgrounds at the eastern edge of the city had been transformed into a camp. Refugees were housed in tents laid out in rows with military precision, they were well fed from the camp comissary and were inoculated against typhoid fever. Aside from the excellent organization and efficiency of the camp, the most significant thing about it was that Negro refugees, who were in the majority, were given exactly the same consideration and attention as whites.

Many of the refugees in "Camp Crump" were from the county, and it was in such situations as this that Crump found efficiency impaired by the imponderable character of the county government. The Shelby County Court was made up of fifty-two members whose duties were both administrative and judicial. As an administrative body the Court met monthly, and, divided as it was into self-serving factions, its sessions were marked largely by the trading of favors calculated primarily to benefit court members rather than the county. In their judicial role the members served as justices of the peace, an office that could be made quite lucrative through its fee collecting prerogative. Some of the magistrates, to avail themselves of a more fruitful business, established offices in Memphis to mete out justice to Negroes arraigned for vagrancy and similar minor offenses. The *Commercial Appeal,* whose approach to the issue of race was rigidly traditional, nevertheless vigorously denounced the practices of these "migratory" magistrates, as they were called. "The greatest form of oppression among a defenseless people in this community is the business of dragging the ignorant into magistrates' courts, fining them for trifling infractions of the law, or for no infraction of the law." It was a common practice, the paper continued, "for a lot of negroes . . . to be surrounded and herded by . . . constables and run into a magistrates' court." [41]

Such obvious forms of injustice incensed Crump, but legally the city had no recourse against such practices. In the spring of 1911 he attempted to remedy the situation in the state legislature, where the Shelby delegation introduced legislation to abolish the administrative faculties of the county court and to substitute for it a three-man elected commission. Further, the number of magistrates was to be reduced from fifty-two to twenty-two, and they were to be prohibited from holding their courts outside their own civil districts. It was a "terrific fight" and Crump's victory "stands out as one of his greatest . . . in the Tennessee legislature." [42]

In subsequent years Crump effected further changes in the county government. In 1917 the number of magistrates was reduced to seventeen, and in 1935, to seven. Finally in 1941 the legislature abolished all magistrates' courts and established in their stead a court of general sessions, presided over by a salaried elected judge.

From the beginning, Crump received valuable assistance in securing measures to reform the county government from E. W. Hale. The association with Will Hale was one of the most enduring of his career, spanning the years from 1911 until Crump's death. As Frank Rice marshaled Crump's forces and fought his battles in the state legislature, Hale supervised the affairs of county administration. Hale was not a colorful man, but he possessed integrity and dedicated himself to his work.

41 *Commercial Appeal,* December 1, 1910.
42 Secretaries' notes. See also *Acts of the State of Tennessee, Fifty-Seventh General Assembly* (Nashville, 1911), 1188.

The aura of reform and the vigor with which Crump's personality invested commission government confirmed in many the judgment that the first two years of this form of municipal administration had been a success. In his 1909 campaign Crump had promised Memphis a business government, and if "business" government meant efficient government, Memphis had progressed a long way in two years. Generally it was a better place in which to live. It looked better, and it provided more and better services for its citizens. Inequities in the apportionment of taxes, when these inequities had favored certain large corporate interests, had been moderated, and more tax dollars were being used to better the lives of those oppressed by poverty.

Facing reelection in the fall of 1911, Crump worked from his first day in the mayor's office to consolidate his position. Memphis was getting reform government, and he made certain the public was informed of the fact. Assisting him in this matter was Tom Phillips, who, with Marvin Pope, began to publish a monthly report called "Commission Government." This newsletter, without reference to politics, described the accomplishments of commission government in an objective reportorial manner. It was circulated among the Memphis electorate and some of the newspapers of the country. In August 1911, shortly before election time, Phillips and Pope got out *One Year and Eight Months Under Commission Government,* a summary of administration reform and progressive measures, attractively printed on glossy paper and bound with a hard cover. The expense of the publication was borne by liquor license funds.

The "Commission Government" publications were aimed at the intelligent reform-minded segment of the electorate. But Crump was never one to go over the heads of the masses. Through the years he would say that his political success came from his giving the people of Memphis good government. This was true, but a class of professional and business people were perceptive enough to see the truth, without having the fact dramatized for them. With the immigrant class, Crump's appeal most certainly lay in his ability to champion their welfare not only actually but symbolically. He never deigned to be "objective" about his detractors and those who sought to frustrate his aims. They were evil-doers, enemies of the good, and he could always come forth with some rural homily or a quotation from Shakespeare or the Bible to illustrate in vivid fashion the execrable quality of their character. Occasionally an individual who had been seared by one of his rhetorical blasts would attempt to reply in kind, but it was always an ill-matched contest. Crump was a serious student of the art. His notepads are full of phrases that he had heard or culled from his reading that were later put to use in a political advertisement. It was a form of dragon-slaying that delighted the public and established him as an authentic hero.

His role as a public benefactor concerned with the plight of the unfortunate began during his first term as mayor when owners of the famous old riverboat *Kate Adams* offered him use of the boat for one day during the summer for any purpose he chose. The consequence was the inauguration of the annual boat ride for orphans, cripples, and the aged—persons whose lives were otherwise largely confined to the quarters of Shelby County institutions. He carefully planned the events with great solicitude for their comfort, seeing to it that every one of the voyagers had something to make his day a memorable one.

During his first term as mayor there occurred an event that in later years was occasionally referred to by journalists, although with some distortion. From time to time it would be stated that Crump had hired W. C. Handy to write the "Memphis Blues" as a campaign song when he made his first race for the mayor's office. *Time* magazine, for example, declared that Handy was hired to boost a Memphis politician named Edward Hull Crump, who was running for mayor. Handy wrote a song played on Memphis street corners with these lyrics:

> Mr. Crump don't'low no easy-riders here,
> Mr. Crump won't'low no easy-riders here.
> I don't care what Mr. Crump don't'low,
> I'm gonna bar'l-house anyhow,
> Mr. Crump can go and catch hisself some air.[43]

Crump did inspire the "Memphis Blues," as Handy declared later in a letter to Crump,[44] but he did not pay Handy to write the song that later became famous. "The truth is," Crump related in later years, "Handy came into my office in 1910, about a year after I was elected. He had the words of the song written out on a big piece of brown wrapping paper. He asked me to read them and asked my

43 *Time* XXVII (May 25, 1936), 56.
44 W. C. Handy to Crump, July 28, 1924. Crump Papers.

permission to name the song 'Mr. Crump Blues.' I told him it would be all right." [45]

As the fall election of 1911 approached, signs of partisan politics became more obvious. The *Commercial Appeal,* having treated the rise of Crump in the manner of a detached observer, grew critical of his politics. In August during the registration of voters for the November election, the paper noted critically that Memphis was having its heaviest registration since 1879. Unfortunately, it added, this seemingly laudable accomplishment was effected by Negroes being systematically registered in every ward under the supervision of the police department.[46] It further observed that the Sunday closing law was no longer being enforced and that it was beginning "to see political shrewdness of throwing the Sunday lid away. All the dive keepers are now enthusiastic and registering bums, black and white, that make business for their beer pumps."

When questioned about reports that city employees were registering Negro voters, Crump stated that he had no direct knowledge of it, and then he went on the offensive. If some of the city employees appeared zealous, it was because "constant unwarranted villification of the city administration no doubt prompted many friendly to us to become very active in registration." [47] The source of this critical attitude toward him was the Consolidated Gas and Electric Company which had used "every means in their power to defeat any one who has the temerity to oppose their plans."

But the *Commercial Appeal* pressed on, its editor, Charles Patrick Joseph Mooney, dipping his pen in ink of deepening shades of purple. On September 20 it declared that the issue was "up to the People": Crump had "made his commission a one-man organization" and had "grasped not only the political machinery of the city, but that of the county." So horrible had conditions become that "within gunshot of Court Square or the police station are dives that would not be tolerated in the tenderloin of a mining town."

The next day a "mass meeting" of citizens styling themselves the "Old Hickory Club" met in what was depicted as the dark hour of crisis to nominate a man to oppose Crump. The spear-carrying

45 *Press Scimitar,* April 11, 1938.
46 *Commercial Appeal,* August 22, 1911.
47 *Ibid.,* August 26, 1911.

Ithuriel for the Old Hickory group was none other than the battle-scarred veteran of former frays, Joe Williams.

It was not a very exciting campaign. On September 25 the Crump forces staged their "annual" municipal parade. Fourteen hundred city employees marched through the streets carrying banners proclaiming commission government and at their head, riding in his Premier, was Crump with Tom Phillips and members of the city commission. Then a week before the election, the supporters of Williams ran a full-page advertisement in the *Commercial Appeal* in which they accused Crump of being "very vindictive in character and dictatorial in manner." [48]

The election on November 8 produced a landslide for Crump. His majority over Williams was more than seven thousand, the latter suffering his worst defeat in his political career. Another candidate in the same election, running as congressman in the tenth Tennessee district, won by even a greater disparity of votes over his opponent. The *News Scimitar* noted that in "an election almost totally devoid of interest locally, Kenneth D. McKellar . . . was elected . . . over W. A. Weatherall, Socialist candidate." [49]

Crump's strong victory indicated an acquisition of new sources of strength that he had not had in 1909. When he denied a direct knowledge of what his supporters were doing in the way of registering Negro voters, he was truthful, for much was done at the grass roots level that he did not inspire. That was Frank Rice's work. But Crump favored Negroes voting. He had seen enough of Memphis politics to know full well that the Negro vote was an important element in winning elections and that successful candidates traditionally had Negro support. Joe Williams had won in 1898 because of it and had kept himself in office by it. Negroes had largely given their vote to him in the 1909 mayoralty, and it was only because of the growth of the suburban areas that Crump eked out a victory. The *Commercial Appeal's* agony over "wholesale" Negro registration in the 1911 election was feigned, since it never thought much of the matter when it was supporting Williams. Its sensitivity to Crump came from something more vital than Negroes voting, and it was becoming increasingly apparent that what was vital was Crump's disposition to push the issue of public ownership of utilities. This would become more apparent as Crump moved into his second administration.

48 *Ibid.,* October 29, 1911.   49 *News Scimitar,* November 9, 1911.

Crump did not cynically court the Negro vote. Negroes were beginning to realize that they were getting more vital benefits from his administration than they had gotten from former regimes. Under Williams they had gotten a few patronage jobs in the sheriff's department, but with Crump there was a more basic consideration of their needs. Negro medical inspectors had been placed in Negro schools; infants of indigent parents had been provided with milk; a movement had been inaugurated to purchase a park; and most important, Crump had moved to break up the inhuman business of preying on Negroes that was practiced by some of the county magistrates and their agents.

In 1911 Harry H. Pace, business manager of a Memphis Negro publication called the *Moon,* and partner of W. C. Handy, organized and became president of the Colored Citizens Association of Memphis, Tennessee. As election time approached, Pace interviewed both Williams and Crump to secure pledges of concessions for Memphis Negroes. In reporting back to the organization, Pace recommended that Negroes vote for Crump. "For," said he, "the other candidate promises everything and I fear he will do nothing; but this redheaded fellow frankly declines to promise some of the things we want, but convinced me that he will fulfill the promises that he did make." [50]

The *Commercial Appeal's* charge that there was a pre-election relaxation of the Sunday closing law for saloons was true. Some of the downtown wards were highly populous, and the saloon and divekeepers in those areas could hold the balance in a close election through their control of the registration books. It was part of the system to which Crump for a time made concessions.

Crump's election in 1911 assured him occupancy of the mayor's office until January, 1916, since previous to the election the legislature had amended the city charter to extend the mayor's term from two to four years. But after two years of his second term, it was reported that Crump was "toying with the idea of running for sheriff." [51] His friends were trying to convince him "that he owed it to himself to run for some office with generous fees attached before leaving a political career which he began nine years ago." When asked about

50   Merah Steven Stuart, *An Economic Detour: A History of Insurance in the Lives of American Negroes* (New York, 1940), 75–81.
51   *Commercial Appeal,* March 22, 1914.

this Crump said, "I have intended to serve out my term as mayor, and then retire from politics to re-enter business."

But he was thinking seriously of running for sheriff because the fees of approximately thirty thousand dollars annually that went with the office were becoming increasingly attractive as he found his personal funds dwindling. It was either business or the sheriff's office, and he chose the latter, probably because it kept him in politics. On July 11 he announced that he would run because he wanted "to break up some of the crooked work going on with the full knowledge of [Z. Newton] Estes," the Shelby County attorney general, and to "meet the assaults upon me personally . . . by the bloodthirsty outs." [52]

The next day Estes, who had been an usher in Crump's wedding, announced his candidacy for the lucrative office of county trustee, adding further that before the campaign was over he would prove that Crump had plotted to assassinate a detective.[53] The charge was fictitious, but such charges were in character with Memphis politics, and Estes probably thought it was dramatic enough to get his campaign off to a good start. Crump's only retort was that Estes was a "common crook." Several days later the *Commercial Appeal* stepped in and asked primly that Estes and Crump call a truce to "gutter talk." [54]

Crump's little flurry with Estes was largely pointless so far as his girding for the battle for sheriff was concerned. On July 28 he announced that he would not run because of the legal difficulties of holding two offices and that John A. Riechman would run in his place. Riechman, as president of the Memphis Associated Charities, had done a notable job of providing relief for the flood victims of 1913 by setting up the refugee camp at the Tri-State Fairgrounds. In his private interests he was president of the Riechman-Crosby Company, one of the largest mill supply houses in the South.

Meanwhile, Crump's onetime friend, Galen Tate, had announced that he would try for sheriff, thus making the race between Tate and Riechman. A legal technicality which kept Riechman's name off the ballot would ordinarily have ended the matter—but not for Crump. He decided to organize a write-in vote for Riechman.

Accomplishing this objective would have been difficult with a highly illiterate population writing in a candidate named "cat," but the task

52 *Ibid.*, July 11, 1914.   54 *Ibid.*, July 14, 1914.
53 *Ibid.*, July 12, 1914.

appeared insurmountable with a German name like Riechman, especially with the Crump force counting on Negro support. But Crump had a plan. Beginning in August Crump backers moved in large numbers into Beale Street with blackboards and slates to teach Negroes how to write "Riechman." Beale was plastered with banners, and trucks slowly toured the Negro area carrying large signs that spelled out Riechman's name. On the streets everywhere Negroes, delighting at the power of literacy, practiced their letters. "Put the 'i' before the 'e,' " they were instructed. The public stood aghast, and the *Commercial Appeal* became shrill in anger. Crump was "conducting schools on Beale Street . . . seeking to teach a gin-drinking nigger enough to make a mark and write a name." [55]

On August 6 Riechman was the victor by a large majority. Disgusted, the *Commercial Appeal* said the election was "a thorough exhibition of the power and evils of machine politics in Memphis." [56] Evil or not, it was legal. Riechman was an able and high-minded man, and his strength came not only from Negroes, but from the white suburban sections as well. Where the *Commercial Appeal* was concerned, the fearful thing was Crump's strength.

Crump was eventually stopped—not by the rise of political opposition in Memphis, but by the confluence of two issues that eventually enabled his foes to oust him from the mayor's office. The first issue was that of prohibition. On January 20, 1909, the legislature passed over the veto of Governor Patterson a statewide prohibition act. The law was supposed to go into effect July 1, but that day passed with scarcely a ripple in the liquor dispensing business.

The dry forces had made a long and spirited crusade in Memphis. In the minds of many, Memphis was the supreme challenge, a festering sink of iniquity, where gambling, murder, and whoredom were all begotten by alcohol. In 1898 a temperance lecturer from the Woman's Christian Temperance Union spoke at the Central Baptist Church. It was not heartening work, for at her appearance at Central Baptist she declared that "it was the smallest audience she had ever addressed in her twenty years of temperance work." [57] In 1902 the Tennessee Anti-Saloon League sent a team of lecturers, headed by the Reverend John Royal Harris, to press on with the work. "We have entered

55   *Ibid.*, August 5, 1914.
56   *Ibid.*, August 7, 1914.
57   *Ibid.*, April 19, 1900.

Memphis at last," the Reverend Harris proclaimed. "Memphis has more saloons than any other place in Tennessee." [58]

Still the temperance crusades in Memphis remained largely confined to the Protestant clergy and the more dedicated members of their congregations. The *Commerical Appeal* opposed prohibition from the start. In 1902 when the Anti-Saloon League was succeeding in getting an increased number of state legislators from the rural districts to support prohibition, the paper sarcastically observed that the paradoxical aspect of the business was that "men who never drew a sober breath during the session so long as they can buy or 'bum' a drink make the most impassioned appeals for restrictive legislation." [59] The *News Scimitar* declared that the "vast majority of the people of Memphis . . . are arrayed against prohibition." Such a law "could not be enforced." It would merely "transform the open saloon into a blind tiger." [60]

As the prospects for the passage of the law became more certain, a delegation of businessmen from Memphis went to Nashville to oppose enactment of the bill, but a "wild mob of state-widers" shouted and booed them into silence.[61] The *Commercial Appeal* filled its editorial page with bitter comment. "The condition before the people of Memphis is this: It is proposed to confiscate several million dollars' worth of property here, to render at least 10,000 people without any means of livelihood, and to force the city to cripple its business in order that the blind tiger may flourish and the bootleggers become sovereign." It blamed "preachers in Nashville" for what was happening and said that whenever "a minister of the gospel decides to get into politics he ought to be required to get out of the pulpit." [62] Several days later it blasted one of the leading clerical prohibitionists in Memphis, the Reverend William E. Thompson, for being a "political preacher." [63] One editorial was entitled: "Opposition to Prohibition Must Be Positive in Memphis."

Crump believed that the prohibition law could not be satisfactorily enforced; he was aware that a majority of the local business community opposed such a law; and he was convinced that prohibition

58   *Ibid.,* April 12, 1902.
59   *Ibid.,* November 8, 1902.
60   *News Scimitar,* January 6, 1908.
61   *Commercial Appeal,* January 12, 1909.
62   *Ibid.,* January 19, 1909.
63   *Ibid.,* January 13, 1909.

would create more evils than it would correct. Shortly after he became mayor, some representatives of the Law Enforcement League, a group of local church people of which the Reverend William E. Thompson was the central figure, called on Crump to get his stand on the prohibition issue. He did not equivocate. "I desire to say at the outset," he declared, "that I do not believe in compulsory prohibition for large cities. Prohibition might do well enough in rural communities, but it works poorly in large municipalities where local sentiment is opposed to it." He went on to point out that there were laws prohibiting the sale of cigarettes, Sunday baseball, and usury, and that they were not being enforced. "Usury is practiced by our best citizens every day," yet nothing was said about that.[64] Finally he did not believe in putting cities under the control of rural communities, and he saw no merit in the prohibitionist's argument that cities would also have to be dry to prevent the leakage of liquor into county areas, since most Tennessee counties could just as easily get their liquor from adjoining states.

The Law Enforcement League was not appeased, and several days later it demanded to know what Crump was going to do about the Sunday closing of theaters. Tom Phillips read to the league representatives a statement in which Crump took the offensive. He felt that the agitation from the league was politically inspired. "Since the hour we were sworn in, we have worked hard to put the commission form of government into practical effect" only to be confronted by "a great many useless and harassing suits" intended to "break us down" and "to throw every obstacle possible in our way." Some of the members of the league were doubtless "conscientious and sincere men," but some who were playing the role of public moralists, like Joe Williams and Reverend Thompson, did not have "a sincere bone in their bodies." As for closing the theaters on Sunday, "we must respectfully decline, for the present at least." It was a harmless amusement, and for a large army of working people, tired after a day of hard labor, it was too taxing at night for them to dress up to attend a theatrical performance. "Why should we deny them that pleasure, when it does not interfere in the least with those who do not care to go." If the commission were to ban Sunday

64 *Ibid.,* February 11, 1910.

theater, then it would also have to ban Sunday baseball, streetcars, band concerts, and the zoo. They were luxuries, too.[65]

The issue of law enforcement in Memphis, especially prohibition, was prominent in state politics, and it was also a divisive factor in the Democratic party. One faction, the Independents, had supported prohibitionist Republican Ben Hooper in the gubernatorial race of 1910 and had been the decisive factor in his victory. As the election of 1912 approached, some Democrats began to urge that action be taken to unify the party, among whom was Crump.

In his autobiography Ben Hooper states that on one basic issue he and Crump stood together. Both were anxious to regularize the state's financial administration and end the back tax collection racket. On this issue, Hooper wrote, Crump proposed a "deal." Crump would support financial reform if Hooper would cease his attempts to secure prohibition enforcement measures for Memphis. Hooper states that he rejected the proposition, and Crump accordingly aligned himself with the regular Democrats who were opposed to financial reform. "And thus," concluded Hooper, "was exemplified the certainty with which the boss of a city political machine will sacrifice the taxpayers . . . to save the system of commercialized vice and law nullification which feeds the coffers of his organization." [66]

Crump had not forsaken the path of righteousness to perpetuate whoredom in Memphis. He was interested in political self-preservation. On March 16 he sent out telegrams to prominent members of all Democratic factions stating: "Would you join in a movement for a Democratic mass meeting at an early date in Nashville with a view to bringing about harmony in Tennessee." [67] The convention that eventually resulted from his call produced enough unity to enable Democrats to agree on the candidacy of Benton McMillen for governor.

In the campaign McMillen studiously avoided the issue of prohibition enforcement in Memphis, but Hooper made it his major talking point. "When I am elected governor . . . I will with the help of an honest legislature and a good God, clean out every saloon

65 Scrapbook news clipping.
66 Everett Robert Boyce (ed.), *The Unwanted Boy: The Autobiography of Governor Ben W. Hooper* (Knoxville, 1963), 141–42.
67 Crump Papers.

and every low-down dive in Memphis." [68] The rural voter was in-trigued. The idea that he might with his ballot strike a blow at the very heart of sin in Memphis was a beguiling one. At any rate, enough blows were struck to elect Hooper governor.

A year later, Hooper, in a Memphis speech, indicated that the legislation respecting Memphis might be forthcoming. "Ten thousand," the *Commercial Appeal* declared, "heard Hooper denounce Crump for not enforcing the law." [69] The governor then stated that he was attempting to have bills put through the legislature designed to compel local authorities to enforce the statewide law.

What Hooper had in mind was revealed on October 16, 1913, just one week after his Memphis speech. On that day the legislature enacted two force bills. One prohibited the shipment of liquor from one county to another in the state and regulated the shipment of liquor into the state. The other, styled the "nuisance act," was specifically aimed at Memphis. It provided that any place that sold intoxicating liquor or any house of prostitution or gambling house might be declared a "nuisance" and closed by injunction. Designating a place as a "nuisance" could be done by the attorney general, or by one of the judicial officials of a city or county, or by any ten free-holders, and the injunction might be applied for from the state chancery, circuit, or criminal courts.[70]

The nuisance act did not effectively accomplish its purpose. During the remainder of 1913 its application was delayed by the customary court testing procedure. Finally, when it was obvious that the courts would sustain the act, 576 Memphis saloons surrendered their licenses on March 1, 1914. For many, if not most, this was a meaningless gesture, for almost immediately the "side door" trade began to flourish. "Few . . . bars are closed," commented the *Commercial Appeal*.

Thus, through 1914, the issue of prohibition in Memphis remained unresolved. In the fall of that year the state elected another governor. This time, with William Jennings Bryan helping out, Democrat Tom Rye took office. But this provided no especial comfort for Crump, since the Democrats were learning to sail before the wind.

68 *Commercial Appeal,* October 8, 1912.
69 *Ibid.,* October 10, 1913.
70 *Public Acts of the State of Tennessee, Fifty-Eighth General Assembly* (Nashville, 1913), 665–66.

Already, former Governor Patterson, who had unsuccessfully tried to stop the statewide bill with his veto in 1909, had announced his conversion to the crusade. In November, 1913, he attended a large Anti-Saloon League meeting at Columbus, Ohio, and there dramatically confessed his own past errors where drink was concerned.[71]

Crump faced a reelection contest in the fall of 1915, but on January 27 the legislature amended the city's charter advancing the date of the quadrennial Memphis municipal election from November to April. The change was sponsored by the Crump forces in the legislature so that city officials could go before the people on a platform to purchase a municipal light plant. If this action received the approval of the electorate, then the private power interests could be advised well in advance that the city intended to exercise its option to become effective on January 1, 1916, of taking over the power company.

On January 28 the legislature passed what became for Crump the epochal "ouster" law. This time the prohibitionists directed legislative action at public officials rather than at saloons. The law provided that any person holding public office in Tennessee "who shall neglect to perform any duty enjoined upon such officer by any of the laws of the State of Tennessee . . . shall forfeit his office and shall be ousted from such office. . . ."[72] Governor Rye signed the act the following day.

The storm was gathering for Crump, but in Memphis his position was stronger that it ever had been. On March 29 he and his fellow commissioners announced their candidacies for reelection, and a victory for the entire ticket was assured when the qualifying date passed with opposition only from the Socialist ticket. The Crump slate was easily elected on April 8, and in the same election it was voted ten to one "to acquire or build a municipal light plant." The following day the *Commercial Appeal* commented that "Memphis went through the deadest election in 25 years yesterday."

Meanwhile the ouster law was going through its court testing, and it was not until October that its legality was established and it could be applied to the situation in Memphis. On October 16 the *Commercial Appeal* joyfully reported that "The State of Tennessee

71 *Commercial Appeal*, November 13, 1913.
72 *Public Acts of the State of Tennessee, Fifty-Ninth General Assembly* (Jackson, 1915), 22.

through its attorney general . . . has come into the Chancery Court of Shelby County, and demands that E. H. Crump, mayor . . . be ousted from office." Also named in the proceedings were four other city officials. The *Commercial Appeal,* so recently and for so long the bitter opponent of anything and anybody that had given comfort to the prohibition movement, had completely reversed its position.

The ouster suit opened in the Shelby County Chancery Court on October 20. Crump and his co-defendants, having entered a formal plea of "not guilty," attacked the constitutionality of the act and demanded a trial by jury. But the presiding judge denied the request, and Crump knew that his position had become hopeless.

Several days after the ouster proceedings began, a delegation of Memphis businessmen went to Nashville prepared to promise Governor Rye that Crump would make an honest attempt to enforce the prohibition law if proceedings against him were dropped. But Rye would have none of the business and told the group that he had no authority to halt a judicial proceeding.

In commenting on this action, the *Commercial Appeal,* in view of its previous animadversions on the prohibition law, took an unctuous moralistic position. The committee should have called on Crump a year previous, instead of the governor, and the difficulty would have been avoided. "The great trouble in this town . . . is that when it suits us we take the administration of the law into our own hands. . . . This liquor law was violated so long . . . that violation was accepted as a matter of course." [73]

The case against Crump and the other defendants was called for a hearing on November 3. Crump, conceding that the state could prove its allegations of fact, waived trial in order to get the case before the supreme court as rapidly as possible.[74]

The committee that had called on Governor Rye had scarcely returned to Memphis when the chancery court announced that Crump could no longer hold office. An immediate appeal to the state supreme court followed, and as its decision was awaited a new aspect of Crump's ouster was brought to light. Since he had already been elected to a new term beginning January 1, 1916, could he be ousted from an office that he had not begun? There was no ready answer,

73 *Commercial Appeal,* October 30, 1915.
74 Secretaries' notes.

but when January 1 came and Crump was about to be sworn in, the supreme court issued a stay order. On February 12 the court found that Crump was guilty of the charges brought against him and that he had been properly ousted. While he might take office for his new term, the evidence used against him in the original suit could be used in a second ouster petition.

For a time Crump made no public statement of his intentions, but since the law required that he take office and file his mayor's bond within ten days after the legal beginning of his term, he was obliged to do so by midnight, February 22, or forfeit the office. On that date, a legal holiday, the city commissioners were mysteriously summoned to the residence of one of their members. There they found Crump and Vice-Mayor Utley. Crump took the oath of office, was handed a check for $678.31 in back salary, and immediately resigned as mayor. Vice-Mayor Utley took the oath as mayor, drew $439.65, and resigned. The commissioners then elected a fellow member as mayor, Thomas C. Ashcroft,—a choice made by Crump.

The day following Crump's resignation the *Commercial Appeal* sung hosannas that the tyrant had been overthrown and hastened to bludgeon the prostrate form. "Revelations as to the inner workings of the Crump machine, apalling to those who think that the government of the City of Memphis should be free from politics, have been made." There were "charges" as to the manipulation of registration certificates by the police. "Much evidence has been accumulated." Crump, by a "mere order" could sway "as many as 10,000 votes . . . one way or the other." It was a fact "that a free exercise of the ballot in the City of Memphis did not exist."

Such assertions appear calculated to have given Crump the *coup de grâce*. The charge of wholesale manipulation of votes was one that was made routinely throughout his career. In this instance there was no subsequent revelation of the "evidence" of manipulation to which the *Commercial Appeal* alluded. The paper's anguish over the thought that Memphis was not "free from politics" was farcical, since Memphis was always in politics up to its ears, and the *Commercial Appeal* with it.

Why, then, did the *Commercial Appeal,* long the bitter opponent of prohibition, change its position so completely? The paper's answer was that Crump had put himself so blatantly above the law and had maintained himself in a position of unassailable strength through such an extensive system of vote manipulation that the state had to take action.

But Crump insisted differently. His ouster had come from "intrigue on the part of the powerful utility interests, aided and abetted by a 'bought and paid for' Legislature and a strong build-up by the *Commercial Appeal* and other corporation controlled newspapers over the state." [75]

In 1949 a Memphis attorney named Lovick Miles stated that no utility company operating in Memphis had anything whatever to do with suggesting or approving the ouster suit.[76] Although Miles in his later years developed a paranoidal dislike of Crump, his testimony appears true because of the absence of any formal evidence to the contrary.

Yet one would not expect a large corporation to involve itself directly in a public issue. Its operations would be indirect and informal. Crump has given his own testimony, precise in detail, respecting the role of the utilities in his ouster:

1915 rolled around. I was elected on a platform to build or buy an electric light plant. A bond issue had been voted. The Merchants Power Co.'s franchise expiring on Jan. 1, 1916, simultaneously when I would take office for another term.

In the spring of that year, Gen Luke E. Wright, senior in the firm representing these utilities, called on me in the Mayor's office, or rather in the office adjoining the library on the second floor, which I used as a work office. My recollection is at the same time the Electric Light Committee, composed of five members, were present—James E. Stark, C. T. Kelly and I. D. Block deceased; Otto Metzger and Sam F. McDonald, living. Gen. Wright wanted to know if I was actually going thru with the purchase of the Merchants Power Co. when their franchise expired on the first of the year. I politely but emphatically told him that would be done—that I had been elected on that platform.

Gen. Wright was a large stockholder in the Commercial Appeal, which was controlled by an interlocking directorate. After his visit to my office and my reply on the light question, the Commercial Appeal came out the next morning and said Memphis was no place to raise a family and proceeded to cartoon me.

When the ouster suit was up, a very fine man, Mr. Jim Brinkley, came to my home, said he had authority to say from the president and general manager, chief attorney of the Electric Light and Gas Co., if I would drop the light question everything would be 'hunky dory,' the ouster suit would be withdrawn, no bother, no expense, no trouble, everything would

75 *Ibid.*   76 *Press Scimitar,* September 1, 1949.

be lovely and the goose would hang high. I thanked him and told him, "Never, I would go to my grave before I would desert the people who elected me on a platform to give them cheaper lights."

Mr. Brinkley reminded me that the ouster filed by the State Atty. Gen. Thompson was merely a tool for the crowd here and he was especially interested because he likewise represented a utility in Tennessee.

Mr. Brinkley further said, "Of course, you know there is no thought of law violation or reform on the part of these utilities—merely a matter of money. They don't want the city to take over the Merchants Power Co.—go in the lighting business." They didn't want anything municipally owned. [77]

The ouster suit remained an open wound with Crump throughout his life. The year before he died he wrote a further and more vehement account of the circumstances around it. *"I wouldn't turn traitor to the people,"* he wrote, underlining what he wrote. "Thirty seven years ago because I wouldn't turn traitor to the people, the vultures, the mighty power trust, sought to oust me from office. . . . They hoped to give me the death sentence—bury me beyond redemption—ganged up on me." Luke E. Wright had previously "assiduously wooed and flattered me, saying that I should be Governor, Senator, etc." But "I didn't fall for his taffy. I merely wanted the city to go into the electric light business for the benefit of all the people of Memphis and Shelby County."

He related how the utility interests in 1915 had hired the nationally known auditors Haskins and Sells to audit the city's books, certain that something sensational would be dredged up. But their final audit "made the revelation the city's books were out of balance 3¢ in my favor. They couldn't find one penny of graft or any irregularities on purchases or contracts; in fact on anything." They even had the Pinkerton Detective Agency "under the direction of the old master, William Pinkerton himself, dogging my tracks day and night. . . . A pistol shot was fired on two different occasions from my side porch when entering my home at midnight, trying to intimidate me. Yes, they resorted to everything."

He concluded with bitter comment on the two men he associated with memories of his ouster. He thought of Lovick Miles, who so recently had publicly taunted him by reviewing the ouster. He wondered what the "aging" Miles, "the snow white paragon of purity, existing on borrowed time, who is full of hate against me," would say

77 Crump memorandum prepared for Harry Woodbury.

if told that when Luke Wright was attorney general of Shelby County, handling cases on a fee basis, women from the red light district were hauled up and fined at intervals. "I dare say," commented Crump, "he would have said what happened back there long years ago was an old custom. . . . Most certainly I am not shouting, gloating over this. Merely showing the happenings of bygone days." [78]

That the ouster was fresh in his mind after thirty years indicated that its wound was deep. Others could have left it buried in the past, but not Crump. In 1916 the utilities may have thought they had heard the last of public ownership, but they were mistaken. The ouster laid bare all the implacable, savage thrust of his will. He would not be beaten. In time there would be a reckoning.

78   Memorandum. Crump Papers.

☒ ☐

Chapter V

BUILDING THE ORGANIZATION

THE OUSTER did not send Crump into a spirit-crushed retirement. He was more than ever determined to pursue politics to a final victory over the forces that opposed him. In the spring of 1916 he espoused the cause of United States District Attorney Hubert F. Fisher for the Democratic nomination for Congress from the tenth district. Fisher was nominated by a large majority. In May, 1916, Crump led a hotly contested fight before the state Democratic committee and was successful in having his own Democratic delegation from Shelby County seated in the state convention.

In Memphis he was still strong. Tom Ashcroft, who had been made a commissioner and then mayor through his backing, would presumably execute the affairs of his office while giving careful heed to whatever suggestions Crump might make. "Mr. Mayor," said Ashcroft, "I am eternally grateful for the honor you have brought to me and the confidence you have reposed in me, and so long as I occupy the mayor's office I shall always consider that you are the real mayor of Memphis." [1] Ashcroft seemed anxious to show that he was grateful. "I am quite desirous of having your photograph in my office. Won't

---

1 Secretaries' notes. "I quote his exact words," wrote Marvin Pope when giving Ashcroft's statement.

117

you personally favor me with one?" he wrote Crump in March.
Later he wrote a letter of thanks:

I don't want to let another day go by without expressing to you my
sincere thanks and appreciation for the splendid picture you sent me. I
certainly did not intend that you should be put to the expense of framing
it and am sorry you did so though, I am frank to say, I could not have
selected a more appropriate and attractive frame.

You have probably noticed that your picture occupies a very prominent
place on the wall of my office. Let me assure you that it will be a fixture
there so long as I occupy the office. [2]

He would have the picture as a kind of pledge that he would regard
Crump as the "real" mayor of Memphis.

Crump kept a close eye on administrative performance. He was
soon writing to the commissioner of accounts and revenues about
the budget for 1916, "which I have discussed with you and Mayor
Ashcroft two or three times. . . . Please let me suggest again that you
should have no trouble whatever in getting through the year very
nicely on the same tax rate of $1.58, with practically the same assess-
ment as last year." It would be necessary, of course, to keep down
expenditures while not impairing efficiency. The current deficit in the
treasury could have been avoided if all the taxes had been paid on
the first of the year. "Please let me suggest that you inaugurate some
system to collect all outstanding unpaid taxes. . . . I want you to feel
at liberty to call on me at any time," Crump concluded.[3]

After several months Ashcroft found that Crump's continuing
interest in administrative matters was creating tension in his life,
and he sought an escape. Increasingly, he lent himself to the purposes
of Crump's opponents. In July the same group that had brought about
Crump's ouster directed its attention to two Crump stalwarts in key
administrative positions. An ouster suit, filed in the name of the
state, was brought against W. T. McLain, the vice-mayor and fire
and police commissioner. It was charged that he was so controlled by
Crump that he permitted saloons to remain open whose operators
were friendly to the Crump machine. The bill of complaint said that
Crump had built a powerful political machine by permitting violations
of the law, "so that, through the influence of various saloons and
their allied lawless elements, large numbers of registration certificates

2 Thomas Ashcroft to Crump, March 27, 1916. Crump Papers.
3 Crump to Ennis M. Douglass, date obliterated. Crump Papers.

were collected and turned over to the Crump machine to corrupt elections." [4] Specifically McLain was charged with telling police officers not to molest a dive run by Jim Kinnane, "a notorious keeper of Negro dives and Crump ward boss, controlling a large number of votes of the most vicious element of the city."

In the hearing of testimony, Mayor Ashcroft testified for the state. He said that he and two other members of the commission had agreed that McLain was inefficient, that he could not handle the police department, and that a majority had agreed to transfer McLain to some other position, "not because of any prejudice against him, but because of his unfitness for the office." [5]

At the same time that McLain was undergoing an ouster suit, another was in progress against Shelby County Sheriff J. A. Riechman. Guston Fitzhugh, a utility attorney who was rapidly emerging as one of Crump's most dogged opponents, filed the suit. The principal charge was that "during his term of office as sheriff, he not only failed and neglected to enforce the laws against the sale of intoxicating liquors, but that through an agreement or understanding with the officials of the City of Memphis, he permitted saloons to be run in open violation of the law." [6]

Naturally Ashcroft's testimony against McLain irritated Crump, who shortly showed his displeasure in a striking manner. Stalking into Ashcroft's office in the county courthouse, he removed his picture from the wall. "Mr. Crump was immensely peeved with Mayor Ashcroft," the *Commercial Appeal* declared.[7] "Most of the boys thought that the end of Ashcroft had come when Crump went into the mayor's office . . . and took his photograph form the wall." [8] The episode was very distressing to Ashcroft, who gave a statement to the press, disclaiming any responsibility for the ouster suit against McLain. The mayor was very formal:

I have read a statement attributed to Commissioner McLain in an afternoon paper, in which the commissioner states that the mayor engineered the ouster suit filed against him.

I have to say that the mayor had nothing whatsoever to do with the

4 *Commercial Appeal,* July 16, 1916.
5 *Ibid.,* August 8, 1916.
6 *Ibid.,* August 9, 1916.
7 *Ibid.,* August 12, 1916.
8 *Ibid.,* August 13, 1916.

ouster suit; that he regrets that it was filed; that he offered the commissioner a place in the legal department of the city in perfect good faith . . . and that the mayor will have no further controversy regarding the unjust statement published. [9]

Crump had a simple explanation for the business. Ashcroft had "capitulated to the corporations and as a result the municipal lighting plant issue became . . . dead." [10] A year later an ouster suit was filed against Ashcroft. He resigned before his case came to trial. He hoped for better things. The story was that having "played ball with the Power boys," he would get an ambassadorship to Italy—but he never did.[11]

After his ouster, Crump was faced with the necessity of making a living. Marvin Pope stated that he personally knew Crump to be "deeply 'in the red' due to the terrific drain upon his personal finances and credit occasioned by the necessity for fighting political lawsuits throughout his incumbency as Mayor." [12] It happened that in the August following the ouster a county election was to be held, and among the available offices was that of county trustee. Actually the office was that of county treasurer and tax collector, and the fees attached to it provided an income of from twenty to thirty thousand dollars annually. Crump determined to run for it.

The "Crump slate," made up of Crump and Mike Tate, who was running for sheriff was announced in mid-July. Shortly thereafter the incumbent trustee, Harry Litty, proclaimed that Crump was running on a platform of "I need the fees," and that he, Litty, favored abolition of the fee system.[13] In an open letter, Litty asked Crump to join him in a debate on the issues of the election.

Crump replied candidly. "As you know, the office of County Trustee is merely a ministerial office. The County Trustee collects the state and county taxes and is custodian of the state and county funds. Therefore there are no 'issues' to be debated between us. . . . Why not be honest with ourselves and with the public as regards the whys and wherefores of our respective candidacies? We are both seeking the office for the emoluments attached thereto." Then Crump took the offensive: "I suggest . . . that you continue, as you have in

9   *Ibid.,* August 12, 1916.   10   Secretaries' notes.
11   Hugh Russell Fraser, "The Memphis Machine," *Real America* (April, 1935), 36–37.
12   Secretaries' notes.   13   *Commercial Appeal,* July 19, 1916.

the past, to make your daily reports to the Commercial Appeal, to the Memphis Street Railway Company, and to the Memphis Consolidated Gas & Electric Company and the attorneys of these corporations." Where the fee system was concerned, "I have a record . . . with which the public is entirely familiar and if you are not I suggest that you ask the governor of the state to acquaint you with it. He will tell you that I was a consistent advocate of the abolition of the fee system." [14]

Crump was aware that the legend of his political invincibility could have been shaken by his ouster, and strong efforts were therefore made to attract audiences for Crump rallies. In the fourth and fifth wards, where the saloon clientele was registered in impressive numbers, free beer heightened enthusiasm for the cause. Once when an anti-Crump banner on a wagon passed in front of Johnny Margerum's saloon, Johnny personally emerged to tear the banner to shreds. "Margerum is Crump's friend and loudest shouter," the *Commercial Appeal* declared. "He is also Mike Haggerty's stepson," it added darkly, realizing that everyone in Memphis knew that Haggerty was the kingpin of the gambling interests.[15]

The manager for the "good government—clean elections" candidates that opposed the Crump slate was the old warhorse, J. J. Williams. Williams was hopeful of victory. What popularity Crump had was because of his "giving away beer as if it was water," he said. It "must have cost a pretty penny." [16]

Crump won comfortably. The *Commercial Appeal* was bitter, declaring that the victory had come from Negro votes "and the dive keepers, chief among whom was Mike Haggerty and the old Monarch saloon bunch." [17] It pointed out that in the first precinct of the fifth ward, where Haggerty held sway, Crump got 291 votes to Litty's 41.

Crump's friends were jubilant. His cousin Dabney Crump wired him from Chicago: "Hurrah. The people have spoken. Had a jubilee at I.C. station with passengers." [18] A prominent Memphian sent congratulations and added a thought: "Why not lay off the local stuff and build with a broader pattern? The past has evidenced the

14 Crump to Harry Litty, July 26, 1916. Crump Papers.
15 *Commercial Appeal*, August 1, 1916.
16 *Ibid.*, July 30, 1916.
17 *Ibid.*, August 4, 1916.
18 Dabney Crump to Crump, August 4, 1916. Telegram. Crump Papers.

fact that you have personality. You have sons coming on to whom a heritage of Governor would rest better than County Trustee." [19] Thomas F. Gailor, the Episcopal bishop, vacationing in New York at the Park Avenue Hotel, sent his "hearty congratulations." [20]

Crump answered the telegrams and letters and made a point. To one correspondent he wrote: "All things considered, we feel that we have won a great victory. You see we have been bombarded day in and day out here for the past year or more by the Commercial Appeal. . . . It stooped to the foulest methods ever known to try and discredit me." [21]

Crump was more tired than jubilant. To a correspondent he stated that "the hard fight we had made the campaign very expensive and, while we won a great victory, instead of being able to enjoy it, we've had nothing but trouble since the election." Part of the trouble was Mayor Ashcroft who "had practically turned on me before the election. He, Love and Ennis, city commissioners, had formed a combination and he permitted old man Love to practically run the government." Furthermore, Ashcroft had fired Marvin Pope, whom he had inherited as secretary from Crump. Pope, unshakably loyal to Crump, had been "treated like a dirty dog," for Ashcroft "didn't have the common decency to tell him in person but waited until he had left for a little trip down the river." Crump concluded by saying he would like to take a vacation. "I know I need a rest and my wife needs a trip." [22]

He did need a rest, for he worked tirelessly during campaigns, and it is not unlikely that he was suffering from one of his "run down" spells, a periodically recurring complaint during his life. Nevertheless, he was able to prescribe for a friend. Three months after the election he wrote a prescription for Judge P. Harry Kelly, a political supporter, who was ailing at a Biloxi, Mississippi, spa. The letter was headed "Office of Edward H. Crump, Vetinery Surgeon—Foot and Mouth Disease A Specialty." "Let me prescribe for you," he began. "Get a pair of light dumb-bells and exercise with them night and morning. Walk no less than five miles each day, eat sparingly, especially at night. Every two or three nights take two or three tablespoons-

19   Nash Buckingham to Crump, August 4, 1916. Crump Papers.
20   Thomas F. Gailor to Crump, August 6, 1916. Telegram. Crump Papers.
21   Crump to William Crump, August 15, 1916. Crump Papers.
22   Crump to J. M. Brinkley, August 12, 1916. Crump Papers.

ful of 'Nujol.' " If Kelly would follow this advice it would do him "a world of good" and "there'll be no charge for it." [23]

Kelly responded two days later: "Dear Doctor, I think I'll try your dumb bells, but you can have the Nujol."

Crump entered the trustee's office on January 1, 1917. Shortly he was sending out letters to some of the prominent businessmen of Memphis stating his opposition to the fee system. The letters were in response to the articles in the *Commercial Appeal* impugning Crump's sincerity in opposing the fee system while holding a lucrative fee-bearing office. Crump wanted to assure the business community as to how he stood on the matter. He received reassuring replies. "I have not had time," one letter began, "to read the letter which you addressed to Messrs. H. H. Barker and Walter C. Chandler, but you are always on the right side of public questions, and I am ready to endorse you. . . . I believe in your integrity, and I believe you have the good of your constituents at heart, and that is all I want to know to endorse you and stand by you, first, last, and all the time." [24]

The support of the business community was possibly decisive in overcoming an obstacle that soon rose to halt his continued tenure in the trustee's office. On April 4, a bill commonly referred to as the "Retroactive Ouster Bill" passed in the house of the Tennessee legislature. It provided that any person who had been ousted from public office would be disqualified from holding office for a period of ten years from the date of the ouster. The inspiration for this action, Crump thought, was "the same old corporation crowd, bolstered by the support of Mayor Ashcroft." [25]

Crump fought back. Before the bill reached the state senate, a barrage of telegrams went out from Memphis businessmen to the Shelby delegation protesting the act. Then Crump went to Nashville to direct the fight to kill the bill. This time it was defeated. Crump described the action in a letter to Congressman Hubert Fisher in Washington:

Everything moved off fine at Nashville. I don't know just what you did but know that you did everything you could and I want to assure you of my appreciation. . . .

After old Ashcroft saw we had him beaten he then tried for an alibi.

23 Crump to P. Harry Kelly, November 1, 1916. Crump Papers.
24 Irby Bennett to Crump, January 29, 1917. Crump Papers.
25 Secretaries' notes.

He got Sam Bates to say, on the floor of the Senate, that he had been authorized by Mayor Ashcroft to say that he [Ashcroft] was taking no hand in the bill. Fauntleroy told Pope today that Ashcroft was the biggest liar he ever heard of, for he was very much interested in the bill and had done all he could to pass it in the Senate, just as he did in the House. . . .

Charley Metcalf told me he wrote you about a certain party grooming Sam Bates for Congress. I heard yesterday that Hunter Wilson had said that Judge Puryear had practically broken with Ashcroft because both of them wanted to run for Congress. Ordinarily I would not write you this kind of stuff, as to who might oppose you, but I know that you are not thoroughly satisfied unless you are figuring every day on some new candidate in the field against you. [26]

Crump won easy reelections to the trustee's office for three successive terms: in 1918, 1920, and 1922. There was nothing demanding about the job, but there were unpleasant occasions when he was asked to forgive delinquent fees for taxes that were paid late. In one instance he received a request from the county attorney asking that the late penalty on a client's taxes be waived because the payment check had been written out before the penalty period began and because the client had intended to send it on time. "In other words," the attorney wrote, "I think the intention of the party should be taken into consideration; and, while this should not be considered as a hard and fast rule, nevertheless, under the circumstances, I believe and give to you my opinion, as the attorney for Shelby County, that the acceptance of the check under the circumstances would not be contrary to your oath of office, or in violation of any law with respect to your collection of the taxes." [27]

Crump could see no reason to make an exception on the basis of the attorney's "opinion." "I gave the widest publicity possible to the period in which the taxes could be legally paid, without penalty, for at least three months prior to the date of delinquency," he wrote. "I advertised it in the newspapers probably more frequently than did any of my predecessors. . . . I wrote letters to all the real estate men who pay taxes for many individuals and to many other large taxpayers, calling their attention to the approach of the date of delinquency and during the last few days prior to that date I kept my

26 Crump to Hubert Fisher, April 11, 1917. Crump Papers.
27 R. Lee Bartels to Crump, March 1, 1917. Crump Papers.

office open evenings to afford every opportunity and convenience to those who had procrastinated."

"Now," asked Crump, "am I to understand that merely because [your client] states it was his intention to pay in time penalties were to be waived in his case, whereas the many taxpayers who have called since taxes became delinquent, offering various excuses, have been required to pay the penalties as prescribed by law?" Crump wanted to know "just where I am to draw the line in the matter of penalties," since he did not know that "a mere oral declaration of previous intention was entitled to consideration in the application of the law." Under the circumstances, he said, he would be compelled to return the check. "My commissions . . . would amount to $10.46 which amount I most cheerfully remit and am enclosing my personal check to cover." [28] The county attorney saw the point.

He wrote to Crump that he was advising his client to pay the penalty. As for Crump's check, he was returning that too, because he knew that his client "would not care to accept it." [29]

To a personal friend Crump wrote that he regretted to note that his taxes had come in late. "It would be my pleasure to waive the penalties that have accrued were it within my power . . . but I am entirely without discretion in the matter. . . . I have been compelled to apply the penalties on all alike and I assure you that it has been a most distasteful duty in your case as well as a great many of my good personal friends." [30]

Then the United States entered the World War I, convulsing Memphis with drama and hysteria.[31] Crump stuck to business, but lost an employee. Marvin Pope, who had been serving as a deputy in the trustee's office, went to Washington to take a government job. "Dear Boss," he wrote shortly after his arrival, "I think I am going to like it up here fine. Of course the work is still new to me but I have no misgiving as to being able to handle it as they tell me there never was a man appointed to a government job that he couldn't hold." [32]

28 Crump to Bartels, March 3, 1917. Crump Papers.
29 Bartels to Crump, March 5, 1917. Crump Papers.
30 Crump to Alex Y. Scott, April 2, 1917. Crump Papers.
31 James Curry, "Memphis in the First World War" (paper read before the West Tennessee Historical Society, May 5, 1951), 4.
32 Marvin Pope to Crump, December 1, 1917. Crump Papers.

At Christmas Pope wrote again to thank Crump for a Christmas gift. "I have frequently been asked in the past how I accounted for your popularity among those who knew you best and my answer has always been that it was because of your intense loyalty to your friends, and particularly because your attitude . . . never changed by reason of the fact that his days of usefulness to you had passed."

Pope was patriotically enthusiastic about the work of his office. "Everybody connected with this department seems to be thoroughly imbued with the 'help win the war' spirit and it is truly inspiring to see the 'Dollar a year' fellows go about their work." But he missed Memphis, and every Saturday afternoon he went over to Senator McKellar's office to read all the Memphis newspapers in sight and "am looking forward to doing that this afternoon." [33]

With the end of the war the country entered an era of enthusiasm for the "Great Crusade." The idealism of Woodrow Wilson reappeared in national life in grossly distorted forms—fanaticism and prejudice often being cloaked under the mantle of the flag. Those who dissented were labeled un-American or worse—Bolshevist. The Ku Klux Klan arose to exploit race and religion for their emotive value, contributing to demagoguery and political corruption.

After the armistice, Memphis lingered in the war mood. On Sunday, April 6, the soldiers came home, "bronzed and battle-hardened. . . . Home from the hells of Argonne and St. Mihiel—home to Memphis, mother of generations of Southern fighting men." [34] The following Saturday an air battle was staged over the city in the interest of the victory loan bond drive. Twelve planes—four Curtises, two German Fokkers, four Spads, and two British SE'5's—dived, rolled, and looped, pursuing one another to the intense excitement of onlookers below. In the *Commercial Appeal,* a war story ran serially, called "With the Help of God and a Few Marines."

Early in May a rumor began to circulate that there was to be a revolt of the Negroes on Saturday, May 24. Another rumor had it that certain groups of white people were organizing to go after the Negroes on the same day. The day came and passed without incident, but the *Commercial Appeal* commented that "if a drunken white man or a drunken negro had fired a shot Saturday in a crowded quarter there is no telling what would have resulted. There were

33 Pope to Crump, December 29, 1917. Crump Papers.
34 *Commercial Appeal,* April 7, 1917.

probably more people armed in violation of law and ready to break the law . . . Saturday . . . than for many years before." [35]

During the war there had been a tightening up of law enforcement. Mayor Ashcroft and Will Hayes, Crump's deposed chief of police reinstated by Ashcroft, made gestures at curtailing gambling, the sale of narcotics, and illegal liquor. Even houses of prostitution had been closed. With peace there was a pronounced relapse to the old ways. By April, 1919, according to the *Commercial Appeal,* fifteen thousand cases of whiskey were coming into Memphis every month. Despite the national prohibition law, it could be bought as easily as in the days when there were licensed saloons.[36] Gambling was widespread with "punch boards, crap games, poker sittings and even slot machines" operating with no interference from the police.[37] The red light district operated with "old stands . . . still in business because they pay 'protection' money to the police." [38]

The notorious Memphis homicide rate, which had been 43.7 per hundred thousand population in 1918, rose to 55.9 in 1919, continuing to hold the record as the highest among American cities. When it was observed that the lowest rate was in Milwaukee, Wisconsin, (2.5) the Memphis *News Scimitar* commented on the comparison with rare candor. "Milwaukee is a Socialist community. It is the home of Victor Berger, several times elected to congress and as often refused a seat in the councils of the mighty. It is in a state that was strongly suspected of harboring disloyalty during the war. It has a large element of foreigners—undesirables we call them down here." The paper thought the time had come to stop ignoring "this undesirable record. . . . Ignoring it doesn't seem to remedy the situation." [39]

The increase of tension and lawlessness in Memphis in the postwar months reflected a heightened mood of irritability in which the attention of citizens seemed to be directed inward on the city rather than outward to the world problems that had followed in the wake of peace. Abroad at least, International Bolshevism had become a very real menace. The well-known *Commercial Appeal* cartoonist J. P. Alley, who would syndicate his "Hambone's Meditations" in the twenties and thirties, depicted the Statue of Liberty together with a bearded, desperate "European anarchist" holding a lighted bomb

35 *Ibid.,* May 27, 1919.
36 *Ibid.,* May 19, 1919.
37 *Ibid.,* December 13, 1919.
38 *News Scimitar,* September 16, 1921.
39 *Ibid.,* December 11, 1920.

in one hand and a dagger in the other. The caption was "Come Unto Me, Ye Oppressed." [40]

There was however, a lighter side to the times. In October, 1920, Loew's State Theater opened on Main Street. To celebrate the occasion, a carload of Hollywood movie queens came to Memphis, and heading the entourage was Delores Costello. The excitement was palpable.

Crump's main concern in this era was his continued difficulties with incumbent mayors. After Ashcroft's departure, Harry Litty had served out his term, to be succeeded by Frank Monteverde in the fall election of 1917. Crump was assured that Monteverde would accept some of the established principles of Crump policy, the most important of which was the maintenance of the low tax rate. But Monteverde was not tractable on this point, and the kind of administration he thought the city should have caused the tax rate to rise from the $1.58 of Crump's last five years in office to $2.20 in 1919.

Crump's displeasure with Monteverde was reflected by the two Crump men on the commission and the other two who usually stood with Monteverde: there were frequent eruptions of antagonism and perpetual jockeying for positions of strength. Sometimes the attempts of one faction to discredit the other caused bitter verbal assaults and occasional forays into the field of character assassination.

Desperation forced the political opposition to the ultimate recourse: legislating the incumbents out of office. This stratagem had nearly worked for Joe Williams in 1905, and Crump himself had been legislated out of the mayor's office in 1915. Although Crump had opposed the use of such tactics in the past—when they applied to him—he supported a move to legislate Monteverde out of office by the adoption of a council–manager form of administration. In the summer of 1918 the reform element in the business community organized a "Committee of One Hundred," to promote the idea. By the following March the movement had become pretty much Crump's. The adoption of such a plan would supposedly deprive Monteverde of his office and leave Crump, who was still politically powerful and held the confidence of reform-minded businessmen, in a strong position to name the city manager and to formulate policies.

40   *Commercial Appeal,* June 6, 1919.

On March 24 he went to Nashville to lead the lobbying for the charter changes in person, as he had done ten years before when commission government was before the legislature. The city manager bill was approved by the Committee of House and Senate on Municipal Affairs and brought before the House for consideration on March 27. There to speak against it were the leading Memphis opponents of Crump—Judge David Fentress and Captain Gus Fitzhugh. It was Fitzhugh's oratory that brought the House to defeat the bill. "If you can face the Tennessee boys who broke the Hindenburg line, and tell them that you voted for a city manager bill without giving their people a chance to vote on the measure, then do it." He ranged widely over the phobias of the day and linked them with the city manager plan. "He bitterly assailed government by class," and he "spoke of the dread Bolsheviks as the natural outgrowth of such government. . . . He claimed the city manager bill contained the defects common to Bolshevik measures." Captain Fitzhugh was "wildly applauded." [41]

The defeat of the bill did not spell relief for Monteverde, for a city election loomed ahead in the fall of 1919. He had no stomach for the contest, and in July he announced that he would not run again but would support old Joe Williams. In August another candidate announced, a young businessman named Rowlett Paine, who was running with the support of a political group known as the "Citizen's League." The league was made up of some of the leading business and professional people of Memphis together with an element new to politics—women. The platform emphasized the necessity for strict law enforcement, honest elections, and improvement in the school system, which perhaps of all the aspects of Memphis government was the most neglected.

Crump, as usual, said nothing of his plans until two weeks before the election. In late September a Crump ticket, headed by Colonel William J. Bacon, was understood to be in the making, but difficulty was encountered in forming the slate, and on October 1 Bacon announced that he was withdrawing from the race.

The struggle was between Paine and Williams, and Williams, believing that Crump's strength was waning significantly, represented the contest as one between Crump and himself. It was Crump, he charged, who was the moving spirit behind the Citizen's League. The

41 *Ibid.*, March 27, 1919.

proof of his contention, he said, was Paine's support of the city manager bill, even to the point of going to Nashville to lobby for it. Colonel Harry R. Anderson, Williams' campaign manager, stated the Williams position in a session of campaign oratory: "The Citizen's League insists that it will have nothing to do with politics. My friends, that is the God's truth, because Mr. Crump and Roxie Rice will attend to all the politics for them." [42] Williams tried hard to make it appear that Paine was really Crump's candidate, but Paine was not.

On November 6 Paine won by a majority of 2,700 and took his whole ticket of city commissioners into office with him. It was the final race for Williams, still trying for a comeback in an era that had passed him by. He had been effective in the old days when winning an election was a matter of making oneself acceptable to certain corporate interests and to those who ran the dives and bordellos. But in 1919 there was a new interest group to contend with in elections—the ladies—and young, handsome Rowlett Paine, a devoted family man who occasionally presented his small daughter to the audiences he addressed, had the women with him.

Paine was mayor of Memphis from 1920 to 1928, a period in which Crump had no determinative voice in the affairs of city government. In Memphis, as elsewhere, it was a socially unsettled period, where problems of labor, race relations, and the rise of the Ku Klux Klan were reflected in knotty political issues. One of the most irritating of Paine's problems was Crump, who sometimes set himself against an administration policy with rigid inflexibility. But through it all, Paine provided Memphis with honest progressive government.

For Crump it was a period of consolidation. In politics this meant getting proven friends into key positions and bringing to the front a new generation of faithful bright young men who could wear the Crump yoke lightly—men who knew better than to harbor independent political aspirations. In his private life it was also a time of consolidation. Since his boys were growing up—Edward, Jr., was now sixteen,—Crump, thinking to provide for their future, joined Stanley Trezevant, a retiring United States marshal, in a business venture in 1920. The company of Crump and Trezevant, an insurance and brokerage firm, became the largest of its type in the mid-

42 *Ibid.,* October 19, 1919.

South, but in its first years it was manageable enough to permit Crump
to continue his work as county trustee.

The year 1920 found him facing a crisis in the condition of his
health, almost a lifelong concern with him. In later years, Phillips
observed that "E. H. Crump was never in perfect health during his
long life. With an iron will he fought off all physical discomforts, and
with a convincing smile invariably assured others that he was 'feeling
fine.' He had a genuine contempt for those who were always feeling
sorry for themselves." [43] The junior Crump remarked that "it was a
matter of pride with him never to admit to anyone that he felt badly."
Crump always succeeded in conveying to the public the image of himself as a man of rugged constitution and inexhaustible energy who
would probably live a century. His erect posture, his quick step, and
a complexion that seemed to glow with health reinforced the image.
Sometimes he would humorously attribute his "good health" to old-
fashioned, commonsense habits. "I owe my excellent health to the
fact that I wear long underwear the entire year," he told Blair Hunt,
a Memphis Negro leader. On another occasion he informed a Memphis newsman that he had had "only one real cold in thirty years.
. . . This I attribute largely to listening to the geese fly. When I hear
them flying south I run east to my home. Then I hustle into my long
pantaloons. Then when the dogwood blossoms . . . in the Spring
my undies are salted away in camphor until the next time the geese
fly." [44] This legend of glowing health was accepted by all except his
family and a few intimates.

Precisely what ailed him at particular times throughout his life is
not clear, but in old age he jotted on a notepad some of the ailments
with which he had been afflicted. "Sugar in urine, Low blood pressure, Iron deficiency in blood, Sub Nor[mal] Temperature for years,
malaria, typhoid fever, urinal infections, carbunkles," and the customary list of childhood diseases. Some of these conditions were
likely the consequence of malaria, and malaria probably had something to do with the periods of exhaustion that plagued him.

The problem of health became acute in the summer of 1920 when
he suffered increasingly from digestive disturbances and abdominal
pain. Late in August he went to Dr. C. W. Post's clinic in Battle

43 Thomas Phillips, "Edward Hull Crump, An Appreciation" (typewritten),
    3.
44 *Commercial Appeal*, November 19, 1940.

Creek, Michigan. Going to Battle Creek instead of entrusting himself to the care of Memphis doctors and hospitals can be explained partly by the tendency of Southerners of his generation to go afield to spas and resorts when seeking health. It was also a matter of pride: he did not want to display his physical vulnerability, and this would have been the inevitable result if he had been hospitalized for any length of time in Memphis. But the deciding factor was Battle Creek itself, with its rigorous dietary regimen and naturopathic approach to medicine.

Writing to his wife, Crump described his reaction to the clinic:

> I came here with misgivings—but its the place for me. Here one learns the fundamentals of Physiological or Biological living. No place today knows more about this subject. There are many important things we pay scant attention to until there is a rude awakening. Sugar in my blood is up—but my kidneys do not eliminate waste in my blood. Of course that's bad. However I never expected to reach the Biblical age of three score years, and while I haven't that confident attitude, yet I may go the time. Right here just think of the tragic mischance that sent Helen Keller into the world with such handicaps. All in all I am sure I'm going to feel much improved *in time,* but I must limit the load. That isn't just exactly consolation for the present, but hope for the future. . . . No one can *Work, Work, work,*—outrage nature without suffering the penalty. With dearest love for all my children and lots for Betty. [45]

Examinations revealed a diseased gallbladder, and it was decided to remove it. Phillips, left to keep watch over the trustee's office, writes how on the day of the operation he received a telegram from Mrs. Crump informing him of the serious nature of the operation and asking his prayers for recovery. "How earnestly the Trustee's staff responded," wrote Phillips, "even profane old Governor Bates!" [46]

In mid-October Crump returned to Memphis, much improved, and a profound respect for the Battle Creek clinic would carry him back for annual checkups and rest for the remainder of his life.

As Crump convalesced, Paine began his mayoralty auspiciously. A vigorous public health program was outlined, and a public health expert was employed to head the city health department. There was the customary brave talk of a campaign "to clean up the city of crooks, bawdy houses and bootleggers," the initial step being to hire

45　Crump to Mrs. E. H. Crump, undated. Crump Papers.
46　Phillips, "Edward Hull Crump," 3.

an ex-army sergeant to put the police under military discipline.[47]
Paine recognized the part women had played in his election by appointing a socially prominent matron, "somewhere near the age of
thirty six," Mrs. T. F. (Camille) Kelley, as judge of the juvenile
court.[48] Judge Kelley brought to the court ability and an effusive
maternalism that over the years gained her some national reputation.
In time she became an adornment of the Crump organization, and
a frequent object of the courtly gallantry that always characterized
Crump's relationship with women.

A significant accomplishment was a salary raise for teachers, whose
low pay made the Memphis school system a subject of adverse
comment by educators.[49] Among the exclamations of approval from
the populace, there was one critical voice—Crump's. He observed
that the raise had "carried no provision for Negro teachers and no
suggestion of improved school buildings for their use." They, too,
said Crump, "are entitled to better pay on account of the greatly
increased cost of living which has not been confined to a single
race." [50]

The teachers had scarcely received their raise when another segment of the civil service presented a petition for like treatment. On
April 20 the city commission received an "ultimatum" from Local
39 of the City Fire Fighters Union demanding something better than
a wage scale which paid its beginning "privates" one hundred dollars
a month. City officials and public leaders were full of sympathy but
pointed to legal barriers that prevented immediate action. Counsel-
ing patience, they assured the firemen that steps would be taken to
secure a wage increase. By the end of June nothing had been done,
and on July 14 after more fruitless exchanges, 260 firemen turned
in their resignations. To their surprise, Paine accepted them with
no conciliatory gesture, even after some backtracking and offers to
reconsider by the firemen. Perhaps emulating Massachusetts Governor Calvin Coolidge in the Boston police strike of the preceding

47 *Commercial Appeal,* January 3, 1920.
48 *News Scimitar,* January 14, 1920.
49 *Commercial Appeal,* January 18, 1920. This issue contains a report of
the survey of the Memphis school system by the United States Bureau of
Education; see also the *Commercial Appeal,* January 27, 1920, for the
comment on the survey by Albert S. Williams, state superintendent of
education.
50 Virginia Phillips, "Rowlett Paine's First Term as Mayor of Memphis,
1920–1924" (M.A. thesis, Memphis State University, 1958), 36.

year, Paine refused to negotiate. The firemen had resigned; the matter was closed.

Gradually new men were hired, but bitterness lingered, and on September 1 petitions were circulated for the recall of Paine and the commissioners. Eventually the recall effort failed because of the invalidation of a large number of signatures by the city clerk.

Crump had been home from Battle Creek only a few days when newsmen heard his opinion of the petition movement to recall Paine and of other matters of immediate political interest. He said that he would not go into the merits or demerits of the recall petition, but he was a strong supporter of the recall law, which he had helped to get through the state legislature of 1909. "The purpose of the recall," he said, "was for the people who had employed officials by their votes, to have the right to dismiss them by their same votes if the services of the officials are not satisfactory. . . . I am not only in favor of the recall law, but also of those giving the initiative and referendum, which allow the people to express themselves at all times." [51]

Of the approaching national election, Crump said that while he was at Battle Creek he had heard "Gov. Cox speak, and he made a strong, progressive argument for the national Democratic ticket, which plainly caught the crowd. However, as might have been expected, the Republican papers distorted the real facts and did not give him a square deal." He concluded by endorsing his slate of Democratic nominees to the state legislature, among whom were Lois Bejach, Frank Gailor, and Walter Chandler, names to be closely identified with the Crump organization in the decades ahead. Crump praised them as progressives—they had "voted for every woman suffrage measure, and for every labor measure that came before the legislature while they were members of it. . . . All four of these soldier candidates are wideawake young lawyers of splendid ability." [52]

They did indeed constitute a capable group. Bejach, the son of a Memphis department store owner, had gotten a law degree from Yale, returning to pre-war Memphis full of progressive fervor and enthusiasm for Crump's reform crusade. Frank Gailor, a Rhodes scholar, was the son of a widely known Episcopal bishop; and Walter Chandler was to represent over the years the member of the

51 *Commercial Appeal,* October 27, 1920.
52 Scrapbook news clipping.

Crump organization who best exemplified high-minded statesmanship.

The victory of these and the other Democratic nominees to the legislature in the November election was a foregone conclusion and was not considered particularly advantageous to either Crump or Paine. Yet almost at the same time as the election, dissension between Crump and Paine was developing that would have ramifications in the state legislature.

On November 4, 1920, the term of Abe Goodman on the Memphis park commission expired. Goodman, who had worked closely with Crump during the years of the latter's mayoralty, was strongly backed by Crump for reappointment. He had been a good commissioner, seeing that the taxpayers got a full return on money invested in parks, and it was he who had continued to represent Crump's view that there ought to be an extension of parks in Negro neighborhoods. But Paine passed over Goodman and appointed his own man.

With this action the mayor lost whatever support he might have gotten from Crump's friends in the legislature. Lois Bejach openly pronounced opposition to most of the Paine-sponsored measures in the legislature. But one measure especially dear to Crump and his supporters was eventually blocked by a Paine man in the state senate. In the fall of 1920 and the spring of 1921 there was a revival of talk for a publicly owned gas and light company for Memphis—talk given impetus by rumors of exorbitant profits made by the gas and light firm. "There is not one person in ten," declared the *News Scimitar,* "who believes that he consumes the amount of gas charged to him by the company. Apparently there is no redress for the situation, unless the city of Memphis shall own and operate its own plant." [53]

Both senators Chandler and Bejach were themselves in favor of a bond issue to buy gas and electric properties for Memphis, and in the latter part of the 1921 session Bejach got up a bill for a bond issue for a light plant which passed the legislature. According to Bejach, Governor Alf Taylor signed the bill, but he was later persuaded by Paine's influence to scratch through his name. [54]

In reality, Paine's actions were not the kind that brought out the

53   *News Scimitar,* December 21, 1920.
54   Interview with Lois Bejach, September 5, 1957.

deadly implacability that marked Crump's assaults on true foes. Paine was above venality, and his objectives were like Crump's—efficiency and better public services, especially in the field of health. But Paine was independent, and Crump could not abide half a loaf. Step by step he strengthened his position. In September, 1920, McKellar recommended John D. Martin, Crump's second cousin, as federal judge of the court of the western district of Tennessee. Martin, a graduate of the University of Virginia law school, had been practicing law in Memphis since 1905 and was president of the Southern League Baseball Association. In August, 1922, Joe Boyle took over the important position of poll tax collector for Shelby County. When news of the opening had first reached Crump at his vacation spot in North Carolina, he promptly wired Boyle: "The place of poll tax collector will have to be filled and I want you to know I am for you strong enough to come home at once if I can do you any good. You have been our loyal friend and fully qualified in every way for the position." Wishing his sentiments to be publicly known, Crump sent a copy of the wire to the *News Scimitar*.[55]

Of all the men associated with Crump over the years, Boyle exemplified the faithful servant—unassuming, hard working, scrupulously honest, and utterly loyal. His gifts as a politician were limited. Had it not been for Crump's appreciation of certain qualities of his character, he probably would never have gotten beyond his grocery store on Jackson Avenue—from whence Crump took him to serve as courthouse custodian. "Joe Boyle couldn't give a coherent statement to the press," one Memphis newsman commented.[56] But Crump gave this estimate of him: he "did not fear to call sin by its right name—could not be bought or sold. He stood for the truth and spoke it, worked and lived it, sincere and honest, filled every position with credit to himself and the entire citizenry of this community."[57]

The elections of 1922 demonstrated that Crump's strength was more imposing than ever. All of the candidates endorsed by the organization, from McKellar in the Senate down to the county commissioners, won by wide margins. Crump, who was a contestant in the election, swamped his opponent for the trustee's job. It was a

55 *News Scimitar*, August 15, 1922.
56 Interview with Harry Woodbury, October 29, 1957.
57 *Commercial Appeal*, December 26, 1951.

depressing spectacle for the *Commercial Appeal*. "The machine won in Shelby County. It was never better organized nor better disciplined. . . . The people of Memphis and Shelby County do not care for political independence. They do not mind a political boss." [58]

But Crump, who usually had an accurate sense of how far his political strength would carry him, chose not to make a direct contest with Paine in the 1923 mayoralty. Possibly his normal perceptions were upset by an imponderable element in the election—the Ku Klux Klan. It was a foregone conclusion that the Klan would have a slate of candidates for city offices, and in early September an anti-Klan candidate, Thomas Stratton, was the first to announce for the mayor's office. The most important issue in the election, he declared, was the Klan, and he stood positively and clearly opposed to it. "Paine," he said, had "played hands from beginning to end with the klan." [59] The issue was Paine's secretary, Cliff Davis, whose reputed association with the Klan had not been denounced by Paine. At the end of September Paine and the incumbent commission announced for reelection, and two days later the embarrassment the mayor suffered by his connection with Davis was relieved. When Davis returned to his secretary's job from a one-month's vacation, Paine discharged him on the grounds that he was planning to run for city judge.

Two days later Klan members, at a full dress night rally in a grove near Memphis, were instructed by the exalted Cyclops as to the candidates they would support in the coming election. Cliff Davis was named as the Klan choice for city judge.

What was Crump's position? On October 5 the *News Scimitar* announced that there would be a Crump ticket in the field and that the Crump choice for mayor would be Charles W. Thompson, the president of the National City Bank. But the next day Thompson said that he would not run because of his wife's strong objection, and Crump gallantly concurred, stating he would give way to the higher good of domestic felicity. Domestic concerns notwithstanding, it was evident that a Crump ticket against Paine would open the way for a Klan victory, and Crump never took a stake in an election contest except in the expectation of winning it.

The race was between Paine and the Klan, and as election day

58 *Ibid.*, August 5, 1922.
59 *News Scimitar*, September 8, 1923.

approached, speculation increased as to Crump's position. On November 1, one week before the election, he declared that he was neutral. "I have had nothing whatever to do with the . . . tickets and I have not been waiting to jump either way. I am quite sure, as the situation now stands, that I will not make a fight one way or the other. . . ." [60] He even suggested that he might leave politics, since he was feeling the effects of the many years he had given to it and he "could not continue it."

But he changed his mind. The day before the election Frank Rice, Joe Boyle, and several other organization stalwarts walked into Paine's campaign headquarters, took off their coats, and went to work. The word was sent down the line: the organization would support Paine. This eleventh-hour stand was decisive, for Paine's victory over the Klan candidate was short of five thousand votes. Davis was the only Klan candidate to win and he won by just two thousand votes. [61]

Why had Crump intervened? Only because it was clear that a Klan victory was imminent, and whatever differences Crump had had with Paine, they were slight when compared to the disruption of civic order and tranquility that might come with the Klan in office. All his opinions on race and religion in politics were in diametrical opposition to those of the Klan. Late in his life Crump noted some things he wanted emphasized by whatever future biographer he might have, and one of them was his opposition to the Klan. Characteristically, he did not hesitate to include the note of bold fearlessness in the description of his position. "Crump fought the Klan from start to finish," he wrote. "Many threatened his business, but he stood his ground and went on through—never wavered." [62]

Crump was to see more of the Klan issue. In June, 1924, he went to the Democratic convention in New York and witnessed the struggle between the Klan and anti-Klan elements in writing the platform

60 *Commercial Appeal,* November 1, 1923.
61 Interview with Lois Bejach, September 5, 1957. Bejach states that the mayoralty of 1923 was the only election he knows of in the recent history of Memphis politics that was stolen. He says that as names were called off the ballots for the talley-keepers to record, a name different from the one on the ballot would be called. Had it been strictly an honest election the Klan candidates would have won.
62 Memorandum. Crump Papers.

and choosing the candidate. In a letter to a friend, Mrs. Milus Nisbet of Washington, D. C., he gave his impressions of the conventions and some of his thoughts on those who contended for the nomination. "I can still hear the sing-song, 'Alabama, 24 votes for Underwood' [he wrote] and the good looking, tall red-headed angular girl calling out in the most dramatic way, 'Nevada, six votes for William Gibbs McAdoo'; and the young South Dakotan yelling that state's vote for McAdoo." He regretted that "Al Smith, a big man, always mag- nanimous and truly a sincere friend of the human race," had been disqualified because of the religious issue. That McAdoo was not nominated was "probably a blessing in disguise. . . . His oil and steel clientele would have put him on the defensive, without going into the merits or demerits of his connection." He thought McAdoo should be nominated in 1928 because he had proven himself an able administrator under the "great president, Woodrow Wilson" and because he had "strong progressive ideas." The "big interests," Crump declared, "will continue to pursue him," adding, "I know some little of their unscrupulousness, particularly that of the utilities and there is no limit to their intrigues." Crump thought that the nominee, John Davis, was "a man of fine character and sterling worth," although he was doubtful about his "Morgan connections." [63]

In contrast to Crump's generally favorable view of the Democratic presidential contenders of this era was his estimate of President Coolidge. His "appreciation" was in the form of a mock letter to Coolidge, sent in care of Senator McKellar. "My Dear Mr. Cal," he began:

I have been violently opposed to you, and I have said some mighty mean things about you, which I suppose have been told you repeatedly. I disapprove of: Your veto of the Bonus bill; giving aid and comfort of the oil grafters; charging the Legion $250 for making a stale speech in Connecticut; permitting your secretary of the treasury, and a malefactor of great wealth . . . to sell his liquor to chain drug stores throughout the United States in order that it might be bootlegged. . . .

I also disapprove of your posing as a farmer in the Sunday illustrated magazine and wearing that artificial smile; your play to the Big Interests in their unscrupulousness; your permitting Senator McKellar . . . to ac- company your wife to a party, which certainly requires more nerve than I thought you had. . . .[64]

63 Crump to Mrs. Milus Nisbet, July 22, 1924. Crump Papers.
64 Crump to Kenneth D. McKellar, October 22, 1925. McKellar Papers.

The tie that bound Crump and McKellar was political, but in the twenties their correspondence indicates a personal association based on a number of mutual interests. One, apparently, was a bit of sensational reading involving the revelations of Harding's purported mistress. "Dear Ed," McKellar wrote to Crump, "I am . . . sending you a copy of 'The President's Daughter.' I had never read it until last night. It is a horrible affair and I am sending it to your office so that you can read it up there if you have time and not at home." [65]

Both were interested in sports, especially horse racing, allusions to which appear frequently in their correspondence. "The Kentucky Derby will be run on May 19," Crump wrote to McKellar, "and we are expecting you to join us. You might write Governor Sampson to be there with his long hair to pull our horses first around the track." [66]

Crump was an ardent football fan, and there were few major games in the mid-South that he did not attend. October 18, 1924, was the occasion of one of football's epic performances. He recalled the event, sitting in his office some twenty years later. "It was a redletter day," he said, "which I shall always remember." On that day Red Grange, "one of the greatest backs of all time, 'arrived' as a star of the first magnitude, and I was among those present. The game was between the University of Illinois and the University of Michigan, played at Urbana in the new university stadium which was dedicated on that memorable occasion." He had been in St. Louis, attending to the business of his office there, and had decided to go to Bloomington the night before the game and then to take an early train to Urbana the next morning. "But I missed the night's sleep." A "lot of young people had come in from Missouri, Iowa, and throughout the Middle West, and bedlam reigned. They talked over the past football games, sang songs and danced all night long." He remembered the stars of the Illinois line. "I recall . . . Capt. Frank Rokusek, end; C. E. Kassell, end; and C. A. Brown tackle. Wallie McIlwaine did most of the blocking for Red, although many of his runs were attributable to the fine blocking of Earl Britton." [67] And then he went on to name the stars of Michigan's team.

The era that produced its golden moments found Crump also enjoying some of the deeper satisfactions that attend a man's life. His

65 McKellar to Crump, December 22, 1927. McKellar Papers.
66 Crump to McKellar, May 13, 1928. McKellar Papers.
67 *Commercial Appeal,* October 18, 1944.

business prospected phenomenally. By 1925 subsidiary offices had been opened in St. Louis, Pittsburgh, and Little Rock, and mortgage correspondents were established in a number of other Southern towns. In October, 1929, he bought the Coca-Cola franchise in a central New York merchandising area. It was an opportunity he thought offered "a big chance to make a lot of money." [68]

The family was expanding too, for in April, 1925, Edward, Jr., married Louise Fly of Memphis. Young Edward had his father as his best man, the latter thoughtfully bringing a bottle of ammonia to the ceremony for those who might be emotionally overcome.

Politically, he was more solidly entrenched than ever before. In August, 1927, the organization announced a full ticket of contenders for the city government, the composition of which was described as "a testimony to the political genius of Ed H. Crump." [69] For mayor, Crump offered the scion of a distinctive and wealthy family, Watkins Overton, great grandson of John Overton, one of the founders of Memphis, and grandson of Napoleon Hill, one of the grand seigneurs of the cotton factorage business in the eighties.

Young Watkins, or "Wat" as his friends called him, was born in Memphis on June 5, 1894. He studied law at Harvard and then joined the ambulance corps in World War I. After the war, he entered the University of Chicago law school, graduating with an LL.D. degree in 1921. Back in Memphis he practiced law and showed a taste for politics. In 1925 he went to the state legislature and became friendly to Paine, but Crump, impressed with his education and lineage, wooed him into the organization. Overton's blue-ribbon family background and education made him Crump's mayoralty choice.

Running with Overton as the candidate for fire and police commissioner was Judge Cliff Davis, the Klan candidate of 1923. But Davis was not a Klansman at heart; he was a politician, and Crump, recognizing his large personal following, had brought him into the organization. Davis announced on August 20, and he immediately made it clear why he was joining the forces opposing Paine, his former employer. Paine had beseeched him "night and day" to run on his ticket, Davis declared, but "Mayor Paine unfairly turned me out of his office . . . when he knew I did not have a penny, just after

68   Crump to McKellar, October 24, 1929. McKellar Papers.
69   Scrapbook news clipping.

my wife's illness. I have no faith in him." [70] Others on the organization ticket were a labor leader and a YMCA secretary.

Even before Paine announced, the organization was hard at work. The veteran theme was played up. At the opening rally the keynote speech was made by veteran Abe Waldauer, a rising organization man, who emphasized that "this is the first time that an ex-service man has ever been placed on a ticket for the position as mayor of Memphis." Another speaker lauded the Spanish-American War Veterans, saying that they really had not received their just recognition. Overton declared that he would speak in the army language to which he was accustomed and asked his hearers to support "my squad." He closed by saying that if he were successful at the polls, he would still be "Buck Private Watkins Overton, mayor of Memphis." [71]

Four days later Paine announced. "Keep bossism from power," he cried. He was critical of Crump for having the support of Negroes, declaring that so long as he was in office "there will be no negro policemen, no negro firemen, nor removal of the restrictions now governing the admission of negroes to the white parks of the city." [72] Later he was critical of Crump over the "low tax" issue which Overton had raised and emphasized. He charged that Crump, "the political boss" who "was ousted from the office of mayor," had had a low tax rate by allowing city bonds to become due, then refinancing them with other bond issues "which have matured in succeeding administrations." His administration had paid most of them, Paine said—something that Crump's administration should have done except that "he was too busy with his demagoguery about lower taxes." [73]

The next day Crump bought newspaper space and answered Paine. "All right, Mr. Mayor, come and tell how I was ousted 12 years ago. All I ask is that you tell the truth. . . . Don't dodge and tell lame untruths about how I was ousted, similar to the manner in which you so unfairly dealt with the negro people after begging them for their votes in 1923, nor like you sidestepped and disclaimed any knowledge of your secret salary raise to $12,000." [74] As for the tax issue, Crump pointed out that refinancing bond issues was a practice common to Paine's administration too.

---

70 *Press Scimitar,* August 20, 1927.
71 *Ibid.,* August 24, 1927.
72 *Ibid.,* September 8, 1927.
73 *Ibid.,* October 7, 1927.
74 *Ibid.,* October 8, 1927.

The new recruit to the organization, Cliff Davis, did not dwell much on the issues, but he was hugely entertaining and drew large crowds. He would give "a short snappy talk" and then send the crowd into uproarious laughter by his impersonation of Paine.[75] After that there would be loud demands that he tell his "ham" story, and he would oblige with a lugubrious tale, richly embellished with Negro humor and dialect.

A week before the election, the Paine forces fell heir to a sensation which they hoped could be turned to good political account. Galen Tate, Crump's friend of yesteryear, accused Crump of jury fixing. In space purchased in the *Press Scimitar* the testimony of a deputy who had served under Tate when the latter had been sheriff, was given in bold type.

> When Mr. Crump came in the office he stated to Galen Tate:
> "We've got to arrange to take care of those fellows over in Criminal Court tomorrow."
> And Mr. Tate said: "Exactly what do you mean," in a loud voice.
> Mr. Crump replied: "We've got to get men on that jury who won't convict."
> At that instant I heard Galen Tate push his chair back from the desk and at the same time knock one of his hands on the desk as he got up and apply an epithet to Mr. Crump and ordered him from the Sheriff's office and told him never again to appear there as long as he, Galen Tate, was Sheriff of Shelby County, Tennessee. [76]

No doubt the electorate was amused by this "revelation," a melodramatic concoction that might have garnered a few votes in the 1890's but not in the era after the First World War. Overton won by nearly 13,000 votes. "As expected," Davis led the ticket for fire and police commissioner.[77] A month later, Overton announced that Walter Chandler would be the new city attorney.

After the inauguration, Crump stated his high confidence in the new mayor. "Overton will be standing when others are gone," he noted in his memorandum book. On January 30 there was a final evening-up of the score: Galen Tate was stopped by sheriff's deputies and searched for a gun. "I know who's to blame," said Galen darkly.[78]

75 *Ibid.*, November 2, 1927.
76 *Ibid.*, November 3, 1927.
77 *Ibid.*, November 11, 1927.
78 *Ibid.*, January 31, 1928.

⊠ ☐

Chapter VI

STATE POLITICS

AFTER the city elections of 1928 Crump thought of leaving politics. He now controlled all the major city and county offices, and he felt he could direct the administration along broad policy lines and leave the piloting to Overton. "I have reached a point where I must call a halt," he wrote to McKellar. "I do not intend ever to go through the gruelling demands of such a campaign as the last one, and I am going to leave the active management of future struggles in the hands of others." [1] But he was soon caught up in another political struggle— the national election of 1928.

As in 1924, he was chosen in 1928 to be delegate-at-large to the Democratic convention meeting in Houston. He went supporting Cordell Hull, Tennessee's favorite son; but as the tide moved toward Al Smith he went along enthusiastically. When the New Yorker's name was introduced and the issue of religion brought up, he wrested the Tennessee banner away from a North Carolina delegate and joined the demonstration for Smith. Later he explained: "When Sen. Robinson referred to Thomas Jefferson's beliefs on religious freedom, the Tennessee banner was held by the North Carolina delegation." Not to join the parade, he felt, was a reflection on

1 Crump to McKellar, December 9, 1927. McKellar Papers.

Tennessee. "Then it was we took the banner and went into the parade, following the banner of religious freedom." [2]

After the convention he spent a month in Saratoga at the races and in New York City, returning to Memphis in mid-September. He was full of enthusiasm for Smith and the Democratic platform. "The Republican newspapers and the big monied interests who fattened on the Harding and Coolidge regimes realize they have a big fight on their hands," he said.[3]

But it was obvious that everyone in Memphis did not share his enthusiasm. As early as February Protestant clergymen were protesting the possibility of Smith's nomination. "A Catholic, if elected president of the United States, would be subject to the pope's authority," one said. Another said that Smith's religion "has for centuries tried to dominate politics, set up kings and prevent or abolish free and public educational institutions." [4] Though some of the clergy protested, Mayor Overton sent Smith an official invitation to visit Memphis.

As the election approached, the political prognosticators thought that the religious issue would carry Tennessee for Hoover. Walter Davenport, writing in *Collier's,* stated that if Hoover won in Tennessee, he could thank "the Rev. Horace Mellard DuBose, D.D., bishop of the Methodist Episcopal Church, South, for Tennessee. . . . To his following, amongst which the Ku Klux Klan found so many eager recruits, Governor Smith means The Saloon, Tammany Hall and The Church of Rome. And they wouldn't vote for any one of them, much less the three." [5]

The *Collier's* article did not reflect the situation in Shelby County. The Democratic executive board, meeting with Mayor Overton, declared it was solidly for Smith and deplored the interjection of the religious issue into the campaign. There was "no place in the state of Andrew Jackson for such tactics," the board declared. "We have no doubt of the result in this county and we confidently expect to contribute materially to the success of the entire ticket throughout the state." [6]

2 *Press Scimitar,* July 2, 1928.   3 *Ibid.,* September 20, 1928.
4 *News Scimitar,* February 10, 1928.
5 Walter Davenport, "Tennessee for Hoover—Missouri for Smith," LXXXII, *Collier's* (September 29, 1928), 42–44.
6 *Press Scimitar,* September 24, 1928.

Religion and the liquor issue were not Smith's only disabilities. Gossip had it that he was too common, and his wife was too plain and lacking in culture to grace the White House. It was this, as much as the religious question, that irked Crump. On October 29 he bought a double-page statement in both the *Commercial Appeal* and the *Press Scimitar*. "Alfred E. Smith, the Plain Man—the Snobs Can't Beat Him!" was the leading statement in large black type. Then Crump looked at the issues:

Snob women, the three ninety-eight variety and would-be "Four Hundred," in a meeting in New York, said they could tell how a man or woman was going to vote by their [*sic*] clothes, looks, accent, and airs (they no doubt mean artificial airs). I had not supposed it was possible to tell Hoover men and women from Smith men and women by that formula. It is being whispered by these snobs, and what malicious injustice, that Mrs. Smith, having come up in a plain, humble way, without a college education, would not grace the White House. This is an old trick of the snobs who fear defeat. The same cry was raised against Andrew Jackson, a great Democrat and Tennessean, yet despite the slander and opposition of the snobs, he and his beloved wife, Rachel, were swept into the White House by an enormous plurality.

I can not believe the time has arrived in this great, free and Democratic country, when a man or woman can be barred, when they are deserving, simply because he or she hasn't a college education, nor artificial airs and have risen from obscurity.

Then he outlined why he supported Smith—Smith's progressivism, his "unrelenting and courageous stand for the preservation of water power against the power trust," his "far-reaching and beneficial farm relief measures," his humanitarianism. "Governor Smith . . . has done more than any other living man to better the conditions of those of his people who are poor, needy, aged, afflicted, diseased and distressed. . . . He is a friend of the common people and a lover of mankind."

Finally, he took up the matter of Smith's religion. "Let's Face plain Facts":

The man or woman who votes against Alfred E. Smith merely because he is a Catholic betrays his American citizenship and violates the letter and spirit of the constitution of his country.

Before responding to false propaganda, let's be fair and just enough to judge the Catholics by first-hand knowledge of their work in our own community.

In 1841, some twenty years before the Civil War, the Catholics founded

Saint Peter's Orphanage. During the entire history of the institution, 80 per cent of its children who now average 300 per year, have come and are now coming from Protestant parents.

St. Joseph's hospital, the first hospital in Memphis worthy of the name, was founded by the Catholics in 1888. Ninety-two per cent of the charity patients of this hospital, who numbered 1548, an average of 129 patients per month, in 1927, were Protestants.

At the outbreak of the Civil War in 1860, the population of Memphis was 22,623, including men, women and children, white and black. Of that number, about 2,000 gallant Catholic men shouldered their muskets for the cause of the Confederacy. The Catholics of Memphis and Shelby County made a proportionately gallant and patriotic response in the Spanish-American and World Wars.

In the yellow fever epidemics in 1873–78–79, in the City of Memphis, 25 Catholic priests and 19 nuns laid down their lives mercifully nursing the victims of these horrible plagues, Protestants and Catholics alike. This series of epidemics well-nigh depopulated the City as every inhabitant of this community knows.

In the face of these services, merciful, heroic, and charitable to the whole people of Memphis and Shelby County, how can any man or woman, capable of reasoning, damn the Catholic people by giving ear or tongue to malicious political propaganda against them? "Thou shalt not bear false witness against thy neighbor."

As a Protestant and as an anti-snob, I earnestly hope the people of Shelby County will reflect and deliberate fairly before casting their votes against Governor Smith merely because he is a plain man and a Catholic.

Yet it was probably not the advertisement, but the Crump political organization, with its support from the Negroes, the city and county employees, and the loyal "small" people that gave Smith his meager 6,367 majority in Shelby County. Indeed, Shelby was the only Democratic stronghold in Tennessee that carried for Smith. The Nashville–Davidson County organization, where the financial giant, Luke Lea, had an important voice, contributed the majority of its votes to Hoover's 35,100 margin over Smith throughout the state. Crump, at least, had made his point. He had been loyal to Smith and had not been labeled, as had some others, as "talking for Smith and praying for Hoover." [7]

Six months after the election those who had perhaps felt cheated by the lack of sensational exploitation of the menace of Rome inherent in Smith's candidacy found a mild catharsis through hysteria when the Reverend J. Frank Norris came to Memphis. Addressing

7 Scrapbook news clipping.

upwards of five thousand persons in Peabody Park, he was at his dramatic best. His first action after being introduced by the Great Titan of the Ku Klux Klan was to take from his hip pocket with a great flourish a pint bottle of whiskey and place it on the speaker's stand. "I have been asked to bring proof of liquor being sold in Memphis. There it is!" he cried. Then his manner suddenly changed. He stood immobile, silent, looking at his tensely expectant audience. After a long, dramatic pause he said in slow measured tones: "I came here tonight to speak on 'The Menace of Romanism.'"

Then he laid bare the whole frightful business and placed it at Crump's feet: "I want to say right now . . . that Memphis has the lowest down political boss inside or outside of hell! He ought to be in the state penitentiary right now. . . . Memphis would have gone for Hoover . . . if your low-down politicians had not stolen it for Smith!"

Norris's assistant pastor told of the terrible things he had witnessed in his short stay in Memphis. "I saw chips, money and cards on the table right across from the Gayoso Hotel. . . . On Pontotoc Av. I was openly solicited by a prostitute." [8]

Since there were many in Memphis who were of one mind with the Reverend Norris, Smith's victory in Shelby County showed that the Crump organization had become a potent political force. Every important political office was headed by men who were bound to him, not only by ties of political obligation, but frequently by strong personal loyalty. The presidential contest was a brief skirmish, but the struggle that shortly developed between Crump and the powers that ran the state gave the organization a real test of strength.

In the background of the contest were forces that characterized the twenties—the rising wave of speculation that reached its peak in the last years of the decade and then broke on shallow sand. In Tennessee the wave was Caldwell and Company and Luke Lea, and before it broke it had engulfed the state administration.

The Caldwell family began business operations in Nashville in 1870, when James E. Caldwell began an insurance business and later added utilities and banking to his interests. In 1910 one of Caldwell's younger sons, Rogers, who had been attending Vanderbilt University, moved into his father's insurance business where he found a growing

8 *Press Scimitar,* May 11, 1929.

opportunity for profit by dealing in municipal bonds. As the insurance and security business expanded, Rogers Caldwell established closer connections with the major banking interests of Nashville, which provided the company with sources of funds and outlets for some of its securities. In all of these maneuvers, the historian of the Caldwell Company has concluded that its lines of advance were not always solidly marked out and it was "not adequately protecting the interests of its clients nor its own reputation as a sound investment analyst." [9]

Associated with Caldwell in two banking ventures in the early twenties was Colonel Luke Lea, a newspaperman and politician. Lea had been a protege of Edward W. Carmack, editor of the Nashville *Tennessean*. When Carmack was killed on the streets of Nashville in 1908, Lea attempted to use the prestige of his late leader and the *Tennessean* to further his own political interests, and in 1910 he was elected to the United States Senate. But he was defeated by Kenneth McKellar in 1916, and shortly after the United States entered the war, he organized the 114th Field Artillery and eventually became its colonel. At the end of the war he thought up and actually undertook a hare-brained scheme to kidnap the Kaiser and present him to Wilson at the peace conference. He was probably acting from the instincts of the politician, thinking that such a coup would greatly magnify his political prestige at home. The plan miscarried (the Kaiser refused to cooperate), and Lea barely escaped serious consequences with the army. Soon afterwards, he returned to Nashville to edit the *Tennessean* and to expand a banking and real estate business with Rogers Caldwell.

In 1927, with the backing of Caldwell, Lea bought the Memphis *Commercial Appeal* from a group of some twenty local owners. To finance the operation, Lea and Caldwell formed the Southern Publishers, Incorporated, a holding company, of which Lea was president at a salary of fifty thousand dollars per year. It is interesting to see how the purchase was financed:

The purchase money was raised by two bond issues which were secured by the entire preferred and common stock issue of Memphis *Commercial Appeal*, Incorporated. This collateral was placed in trust with the Minnesota and Ontario Power Company, and the entire issue of bonds sold to the *Commercial Appeal* and Lea's *Tennessean*. As this company was in

9 John Berry McFerrin, *Caldwell and Company* (Chapel Hill, 1939), 17.

turn controlled by the Minnesota and Ontario Power Company, the newspapers through the sale of these bonds became financially tied up with the power interests.

The sale of both issues yielded a total of $3,750,000 which was almost $500,000 more than needed to complete the purchase. The cash balance was not turned over to the publishing company, but, instead, Lea and Caldwell interests retained the cash and paid the publishing company in bonds of Lea's real estate companies and Caldwell issues. Lea was made president of Memphis *Commercial Appeal,* Incorporated, and was publisher of the paper and although he retained his office in Nashville and was not particularly active in the management of the company, except in dictating its policies on political matters, he was paid a salary of $24,000 a year, in addition to the $50,000 he received as president of Southern Publishers. [10]

Thus, the complicated structure of the Caldwell Company was brought to interact with state politics in two ways: first, by dealing in municipal bonds; and second, by the company's tie-up with Luke Lea, politician and publisher.

Yet there was still another more direct connection between the Lea–Caldwell interests and the operation of the state government. In 1926 the Caldwell Company incorporated the Kentucky Rock Asphalt Company of Delaware to acquire the property of the Kentucky Rock Asphalt Company of Kentucky, which quarried and marketed rock asphalt under the trade name of "Kyrock." It was primarily Luke Lea, with Kyrock as the binding factor, who established the connection between the Caldwell Company and the state administration.

In 1922 the Lea–Caldwell interests successfully supported Austin Peay for governor. Peay was an able administrator and was reelected in 1924 and 1926. While he was governor, there was no indication of improper conduct in state administration. He died in office, October, 1927, and was succeeded by the speaker of the senate, Henry Horton.

Already, an attempt had been made to place the state in a position of contributing more solidly to the profits of the Caldwell interests. In September, 1927, Lea approached C. Neil Bass, state highway commissioner, with the suggestion that he specify the use of Kyrock without competitive bidding in the building of certain state roads.[11] Bass refused, but with Horton in office more pressure was brought

10   *Ibid.,* 89.   11   *Ibid.,* 103.

upon him to use Kyrock. In a conversation with Bass's father-in-law, "Horton suggested that he convey to Bass the idea that he was not using the Highway Department to the best political interests of the Governor and that his policies be directed more to that end." [12] In January, 1928, the Nashville representative of Kyrock informed Bass that his company expected Kyrock to be specified without competition for a contemplated west Tennessee highway.

Bass's refusal to cooperate brought Horton on February 13, 1928, to ask for Bass's resignation, which he received. Horton then appointed Colonel Harry S. Berry, a lifelong friend of Luke Lea, as state highway commissioner. "Thereafter Kyrock was specified for a number of roads, assuring a good market for a Caldwell product." [13]

Horton as governor faced the electorate for the first time in 1928. His opponents in the August state Democratic primary were Lewis Pope, a first-time candidate, and Hill McAlister. Horton had, of course, the ardent backing of the Lea–Caldwell complex, but there was a growing question of how much good it would do him, since the towering growth of the Lea–Caldwell financial empire had been given much press attention throughout the state, and many were probably saying what the *Press Scimitar* said in an editorial on April 10: "The chief objection to Horton is that there is supposed to be a string running from his office to the office of Col. Luke, and that all that the colonel has to do is to pull the string."

As was his custom, Crump made no early announcement of his choice. In May he wrote McKellar that he expected to vote for a candidate for governor, but "with all my might, . . . I am for Kenneth McKellar first." [14] It was not until July 20 that Crump declared his choice. He, Overton, Rice, and other organization stalwarts took a two-hour drive to Covington to hear McAlister speak and to give him "a real old-fashioned welcome" to west Tennessee.

The meeting produced some novel excitement. In Memphis, Clarence Saunders, fortune builder, czar of the great "Piggly-Wiggly" grocery chain and strong ally of the Lea–Caldwell forces, sent two airplanes to Covington after McAlister's speech to drop circulars attacking Crump.

Crump responded with a large advertisement in the *Press Scimitar*.

12 *Ibid.*, 103–04.
13 *Ibid.*, 104.
14 Crump to McKellar, May 21, 1928. McKellar Papers.

"Who is This Fresh Upstart?" asked the headline. "Is this the same Clarence Saunders of stock-peddling fame? Many widows and orphans in their sorrow and distress answer, 'Yes.' " Saunders was peeved, said Crump, because "I would not enter into an agreement, or have any kind of an understanding with this upstart, in whom I have no confidence whatever, and who has already been found guilty in federal court of 'Fraud, embezzlement, misappropriation and defalcation.' " The "upstart" had been emboldened to attack him, Crump continued, because he was supported by the "chain newspaper owners, seekers, and procurers of non-competitive road contracts, promoters and political hijackers"—namely, the "three Rock-Asphalteers, Lea, Caldwell and Horton." [15]

Crump then declared that the Lea–Caldwell group had "repeatedly made overtures to me to become associated with them in business, as well as politics. I declined, and am now pictured as a vile, wretched character." He, Crump, was not the issue in the campaign. The real issue was "whether Hill McAlister or Henry Horton is the better man for governor. . . . However," he continued, directing his remarks again to Saunders, "I say to this fresh upstart, if you only propose to deal with me personally, come on with all your dirt and filth, for I am going to the mat with you. This is not the first time that some little squirt has sought to make me the issue."

The day after Crump's blast, the *Commercial Appeal* introduced an old issue with a new twist to the tumult of the conflict—the Negro vote. The paper ran a large picture of a white man instructing Negroes how to vote. "This Must Not Happen Again in Memphis," the caption piously proclaimed. From Crump and members of the organization came the counter charge that the picture was faked. The *Press Scimitar* declared it was a fake. But the *Commercial Appeal* persisted, and shortly was urging the chairman of the Shelby County primary board to exclude Negroes from voting on the grounds that "the Democratic party is the white man's party in the south." [16] For Memphis, this was a novel doctrine.

In the election on August 2 Horton won by a scant 2,548 votes. In Shelby County the organization's control had never been more tautly exercised. Horton got 3,723 votes to McAlister's 24,019.

15　*Press Scimitar,* July 27, 1928.
16　*Commercial Appeal,* July 29, 1928.

From the first, the Horton administration got opposition from Shelby County. Luke Lea's choice for speaker of the senate was blocked, and the administration's choice for secretary of state had to be shelved. When Horton proposed a sales tax, Crump strongly opposed it. The big fight was on the Horton redistricting bill, which would give the Republicans three more senators and ten more representatives, while depriving Shelby of a senator and two representatives. It was simply a matter of "Fairness to all," said the *Commercial Appeal,* inasmuch as Davidson and Shelby counties had "banded together to stifle the interests of rural Tennessee." [17] Crump had a different version. "The Republican redistricting bill is only a windshield for the water power grab. Under Gov. Horton's proposed water power bill they hope to get control of 100 million dollars worth of water power in the Cove Creek district in East Tennessee. . . . The ones who get Cove Creek hold the key to the Muscle Shoals and other power sites on the Tennessee River, as the Cove Creek dam will increase or diminish the power at Muscle Shoals." [18]

Crump was certain he smelled a rat in the redistricting bill, and the rat was the "Luke Lea–Rogers Caldwell combination and its bullying papers," that never had another thought than "water power, road building material and road bonds." He declared again that back in July "they wanted us to go with them, not only politically but also in a business way, but we respectfully declined. Had we gone with them the Lea–Caldwell papers would have pictured us as statesmen of the type of John C. Calhoun and patriots like Benjamin Franklin, just as they have been 'soft-soaping' others." Lea's papers "prate about the election frauds in Shelby. Its closest approach to fraud, and for which it will ever apologize, was when Shelby cast the deciding vote that elected Luke Lea to the United States Senate" back in 1910.[19]

As the bill was being prepared for its testing in the legislature, Crump cancelled reservations he had made for a California trip so that he could go to Nashville to fight it. Even Senator McKellar went to Nashville. He went at Crump's bidding, the *Commercial Appeal* declared. Very likely he did.

The redistricting bill was defeated, and after this the cannonading

17 *Ibid.,* February 10, 1929.
18 *Press Scimitar,* February 8, 1929.
19 *Ibid.,* February 14, 1929.

between Memphis and Nashville quieted. All was peaceful as the twenties entered its declining months—peaceful in Memphis politics, but in the world of finance the cloudless skies of the golden era grew suddenly black, and by October the bubble had burst. The sound of woe filled the land.

In Tennessee the Lea–Caldwell empire became a shell, but still the structure stood. On February 10, 1930, the *Press Scimitar* carried an account that clearly indicated the empire was cracking and that frantic efforts were being made to prop it up. The news was that the state treasurer, John Nolan, had the state's general fund on deposit in the Lea–Caldwell banks in amounts up to five times in excess of the legal limit. It was further stated that the highway commissioner was juggling funds between banks.

Yet, almost strangely, there was no cry of alarm from Shelby County—no sensation. On June 10 there was a sensation of a different order. News came that "Edward H. Crump, Memphis political boss, had announced for Congress from the Memphis district." Poor old Hubert Fisher, the incumbent, "appeared puzzled and disappointed," and although he had already made known his candidacy, the Memphis attorney whom he had asked to file his papers decided against entering Fisher when Crump appeared in the contest. Fisher had been friendly to Crump for more than a decade, but as Tom Phillips explained it, Fisher had grown hard of hearing and was letting things pass in his work that should have had attention. Crump had "the courage to be either a friend or an enemy," said Phillips.

A story in the *Press Scimitar* gave a more sophisticated analysis of Crump's action. Crump had decided two years earlier that Fisher would not do, but he had hoped that some rising public servant, close to the organization, could be substituted for him. When it became apparent that none would do, Crump placed himself before the electorate.

After his announcement Crump went to Battle Creek for a rest and then to the East on business. Yet the summer of surprise had not ended, and the biggest was still in the offing. Returning home in time for the Fourth of July, Crump announced that "Horton will be the next governor of Tennessee." [20] Both he and Overton expressed appreciation for Horton's help in getting good roads into Memphis

20 *Ibid.*, June 10, 1930.

and enlarging the state mental hospital at Bolivar, some sixty miles from Memphis. Then Crump said he would vote for Horton "with the greatest pleasure" and expressed the hope that "every taxpayer and citizen in this community will show his or her appreciation for the assistance he has rendered by rolling up a tremendous majority for him, in the August primary." [21]

Then surprise again: Luke Lea's *Commercial Appeal,* which for nearly two years had been thundering the awful wickedness of the Shelby organization, endorsed Crump's candidacy with oily obsequiousness. "The nomination of Edward H. Crump as the Democratic candidate for Congress . . . without opposition, is but another evidence of the esteem in which Mr. Crump is held by the people of Shelby County." Since he had become mayor in 1910, the article continued, "Mr. Crump has had a continuous series of elective triumphs. He has been engaged in all in more than 40 campaigns before the people of Shelby county and has never lost a single fight." Then putting itself heart to heart with Crump, the *Commercial Appeal* declared that "it believes with Mr. Crump" in the "wider sphere" of service that his election to Congress would bring. [22]

When L. E. Gwinn, Horton's opponent in the primary, heard of Crump's action, his comment was: "I trust that those who now think so highly of Gov. Horton's record and so little of my candidacy will at least be sportsmen enough to join in such measures as may be necessary to insure to [me] all the votes . . . [I] actually receive." [23]

In the election Horton won in the state by 123,642 votes to Gwinn's 88,416. Shelby County made the difference, giving Horton 27,634 and Gwinn, 2,267. Crump had made a governor, but most remarkable was that some twenty thousand voters who had been against Horton in 1928 changed their minds at Crump's suggestion and voted for Horton in 1930.

It was, in fact, so remarkable that Senator Gerald P. Nye, chairman of a Senate investigating committee, came to Memphis to hold hearings on the tactics of the Shelby group which was charged with "herding carloads of negroes from one Democratic primary polling place to another, expulsion of designated watchers, and wholesale distribution of tax receipts." When the hearings closed, Senator Nye

21 *Ibid.,* July 5, 1930.
22 *Commercial Appeal,* July 11, 1930.
23 *Press Scimitar,* July 7, 1930.

said: "There is [*sic*] no substantial grounds for the serious charges brought against the party here." His problem, as he explained it, was that "tho a number of witnesses, in affidavits prepared after the election, said they saw irregularities in the conduct of the election, they testified . . . they saw no irregularities. . . . That is what makes it so hard for the committee to reach the bottom of any situation." [24]

Crump's candidacy for Congress produced little public debate. Only Bishop DuBose of the Methodist Episcopal Church, South, wanted the issues clarified. In response to the bishop's query as to how he stood on prohibition, Crump said that he would make no iron-clad pledge, but that prohibition had bred a disrespect for law, which in his judgment was "the greatest curse of American life today." [25] The Nashville *Tennessean* stated that Crump's reply to Du Bose had required "courage," but obviously not much was at stake in Shelby County. In November Crump got 23,756 votes to 1,500 divided between his two opponents.

The 1930 election in Tennessee was interesting from several points of view. It was not only that thousands of voters in Shelby County had reversed themselves on Horton, but that Crump had reversed himself also. It was not in character for Crump to level his artillery at an opponent and charge him with corrupt collusion with the "interests" and then alter his position, especially when there was good evidence that the charge was true.

The *Press Scimitar* (formerly the *News Scimitar*) called it a "trade with Nashville," but what did Crump get out of the trade? The answer is not clear. As a candidate Crump in no way depended upon Horton–Lea–Caldwell support for his election. That he was clearing the way for a future senatorial contest was thought to be the explanation by some, but Crump denied it. "I have no ambition ever to interfere with the good work Sen. McKellar has been doing for Tennessee," he stated shortly after announcing for Congress.[26] If there was any agreement at all, it probably involved the Shelby delegation's hope to have Scott Fitzhugh elected as speaker of the state senate, a position equivalent to lieutenant governor. Fitzhugh was one of the more sparkling members of the Shelby legislative group; he had wanted

24   *Ibid.*, October 21, 1930.
25   *Commercial Appeal*, September 14, 1957.
26   *Press Scimitar*, June 11, 1930.

Hubert Fisher's place in Congress, but with Crump taking that position, an acceptable alternative would be the speakership.

Crump stated his reason for supporting Horton. "We fought the Caldwell–Lea–Horton crowd for many years in Memphis," he explained to a Chattanooga *Times* reporter, "but last year we supported them because the governor came down there and promised to do a lot of things which were good for Memphis and which he did." [27]

It was quickly apparent that Crump had supported a broken reed. On November 6, two days after Horton's election, the Lea–Caldwell Bank of Tennessee closed. Since 1927, on the authority of the state legislature and with the Shelby delegation concurring, the Bank of Tennessee had been receiving state deposits: $40,000 in 1927; $50,000 in 1928; and on June 30, 1929, following the sale of $21,000,000 of bonds, the state's balance jumped to $2,269,000. In July and August, 1930, between the primary and general elections, the state treasurer deposited over a million more to keep the bank open until Horton had passed the election barrier. At the time of the collapse the state's total deposit balance with the Bank of Tennessee was $3,418,400.[28] To this amount was added the loss of $2,500,000 with the collapse of the Lee–Caldwell Holston Union National Bank of Knoxville. In Memphis the *Commercial Appeal* went into the hands of receivers.

The crash of the Lea–Caldwell empire found the Shelby delegation on the defensive. Why had it voted for the bills that had let down the bars for the Lea–Caldwell raid on state funds? Delegation members answered that they thought they were safeguarding the money, and if state officials had demanded the "good bond" provided for in the bills for which they voted, the state would not have been left holding the bag.[29]

Crump gave new marching orders. "At the state capitol there must be an absolutely thorough and sweeping investigation of state affairs," he announced. "The guilt or innocence of anyone should be determined by the facts. . . . This must be done without regard to how it will affect the political future or ambitions of any individual, big or little." [30]

27 Chattanooga *Times*, January 8, 1931.
28 McFerrin, *Caldwell and Company*, 113–14.
29 *Press Scimitar*, January 1, 1931.
30 *Ibid.*, January 2, 1931.

After his Sunday dinner on January 4 he left for Nashville to take a hand in the organization of the new administration. By Tuesday evening he and Frank Rice had marshaled the strength to elect Scott Fitzhugh over the administration candidate. "Mr. Crump came to Nashville on Sunday night as the boss of Shelby County. In two days' work he was elected to the 'boss' of Tennessee politics," said the Chattanooga *Times.*

On Tuesday evening a reporter found Crump in the lobby of his hotel, talking briefly with one and then another person, frequently ending his conversation with "loud chuckles." The reporter asked Crump if he had changed his mind about pushing for an investigation of the state's financial mess. Crump was positive. "No sir," he said, "we haven't gone back on a thing we said yet. We mean every word in that statement and haven't anything to take back." As it frequently happened in Crump's encounters with newsmen, the interview was turned into an instruction session with Crump's sermon-like pronouncements on positive living. "You know, I have rules for my work. These rules are: First, observe, remember, compare; second, read, listen and ask; third, plan your work and work your plan." Pointing his finger at the reporter, he declared that there were many people who could plan their work but could not work their plans. He hastened to another thought. "Another thing you should do is to trust people. You know, I trust people. I can get more out of them by trusting them than I can by distrusting them." Then a final thought: "I have found that very few people can stand prosperity. This is true in business, in politics and in social life." [31]

The next day the reporter got something more solidly political. Crump explained why he had made such a strong fight for Fitzhugh's election as speaker. "With all these bank failures in Tennessee, Arkansas, and Mississippi and this financial situation, I saw how things were heading and that we would not be able to support the governor's man . . . although he is a good man. I told him we could not support him when I came up here. I looked over the field and then decided to put in Fitzhugh, a fine and able lawyer, an honest man." [32]

But "fine and able" Fitzhugh was shortly in the soup. Without consulting Mayor Overton or the Shelby delegation, he personally

31   Chattanooga *Times,* January 7, 1931.
32   *Ibid.,* January 8, 1931.

had drawn up a bill authorizing Sunday movies in Memphis, then had "secretly" rushed the bill through the legislature and had gone to the governor's office to urge him to sign it. A Memphis theater owner appeared to have been closely involved in the matter, but had "withheld" some of the facts that explained why Fitzhugh had acted for him.

Crump was exasperated. He was not opposed to Sunday movies. He had always favored "innocent amusement on Sunday." But he thought the Shelby legislators should have consulted Mayor Overton before introducing such important legislation. "I think it is an act of discourtesy to the mayor and city administration for any member . . . of the Shelby delegation to have introduced a bill affecting the city of Memphis. . . . Some of the members of the Shelby delegation undoubtedly are permitting a little success to carry them off their feet." That, he said, was "a dangerous sign for anyone in political business or social life." [33]

Two days later the Shelby "boys" at Nashville declared that the measure would be withdrawn. Fitzhugh appeared confused. He had thought "that some of the other 'boys' had talked with the mayor about it. . . ." [34]

Several weeks later a troubled Fitzhugh, accompanied by the house speaker "Pete" Haynes, journeyed to Memphis to speak with "Mr. Crump." "I am just getting away from Nashville with Mr. Fitzhugh," Haynes explained. "There seems to be a little misunderstanding." [35] Haynes sat in Crump's office most of one morning, explaining, while Fitzhugh awaited a call to join the session, hoping that the cord of trust and esteem that had once bound him to Crump could be tied again. The call never came. As Fitzhugh left for Nashville, his mournful comment was: "My life is and always has been an open book." [36]

For the moment, Fitzhugh was left alone to contemplate his error. Crump had a more pressing concern at hand. On March 4 the principal Tennessee newspaper gave banner headlines to his statement denouncing Horton and calling for his impeachment. The forces were in line, the weapons primed, and Crump was out ahead, full speed, delivering thunderous volleys. The Chattanooga *Times* gave its front page over to the statement:

33 *Press Scimitar,* January 24, 1931.   35 *Ibid.,* February 19, 1931.
34 *Ibid.,* January 26, 1931.   36 *Ibid.,* February 20, 1931.

The governor of our state, Henry H. Horton, sat in his office, supine and docile, an easy prey for designing selfish interests, gougers in the taxpayer's money, and has permitted possible mismanagement of commonwealth affairs. The result of this colorless and utterly inefficient nonexecutive's feeble attempt to run the state makes it clear that he was possessed solely with the illuminating and brilliant idea of being governor in name only. . . .

A very great principle is involved. Are the people to have officials who will guard their interests, or to look after those of private individuals? All of these officials, from the evidence adduced, are undoubtedly guilty in the estimation of the people of Tennessee of being tools and figureheads for Luke Lea and Rogers Caldwell, the quick clean-up men.

Then Crump asked for articles of impeachment against Horton, to be drawn up "the very first day the Legislature resumes its session." Moreover, the state treasurer and comptroller should not be reelected when the session reassembled. He had no desire to "dictate state politics," but sufficient evidence had been gathered to show that the time for action had arrived. "Every individual who has stuck his wicked claws into the state's affairs for personal gain, whether he be Luke Lea, Rogers Caldwell or anyone else, should be dealt with most severely, just as the poor ragged individual is handled in the criminal courts every day and given a free ride on the log chain."

Early in May he made his annual pilgrimage to Battle Creek. Returning leisurely to Memphis he watched the seventh running of the Kentucky Derby and then visited the birthplaces of Abraham Lincoln and Jefferson Davis, "two of his favorite historical figures." [37]

On Saturday, May 23, the Shelby organization and its leader left Memphis for Nashville to begin the assault on Horton when the legislature began its work on Monday. " 'Boss' Crump has 100 rooms reserved in a local hotel," the *Press Scimitar* reported. "All roads were leading to Capitol Hill," and by Monday, "Nashville is expected to be a teeming center of politics, and the battleground for what may prove to be the greatest 'shakeup' in the state's history." [38]

Before he left, Crump gave an estimate of Horton: "If one of the learned mathematical professors were to condescend to throw away that much time in discussing temporary Gov. Horton, he would no doubt brand him the square root of zero. . . . Some circus clown

37 *Ibid.*, May 20, 1931.   38 *Ibid.*, May 23, 1931.

should get this: Horton says, 'It is marvelous how few irregularities have been found.' He no doubt is proud of the fact that no one has stolen the penitentiary or the capitol building." [39] To Horton's charge that he wanted to boss the state he said, "Would I, if I could, try to 'boss' Tennessee's horribly mismanaged affairs, with millions of dollars stolen and practically every branch of the government enmeshed in the octopus of corruption and unscrupulousness? I say most emphatically 'No!' I would not any more than I would buy and be troubled with a gully-washed farm, a mangy, egg-sucking dog or a distempered, wind-broken horse." It was Horton's responsibility. "Gov. Horton, the question with the people is not 'who furnished the stone or who owned the quarry, but who chiseled the statue.' You are the governor, you are the responsible head, and you must take the consequence." [40]

There is a story repeated in Memphis by an older generation of political savants, that when Crump arose to breakfast on Sunday morning in the Nashville hotel, he had Scott Fitzhugh as his guest. In substance, Fitzhugh was summarily told in terse, colorful, and coarse language, that he was to resign as senate speaker upon the resumption of legislative business. Crump was terse and colorful, but he was never coarse, and that element of the story is apocryphal. In any case, Fitzhugh was informed that he must resign, and in the background, to enforce Crump's order, was the unfortunate business of several months previous, when Fitzhugh through some special inducement from a theater owner had attempted to sneak through the Sunday movie bill.

Accordingly, when the legislature reassembled, Fitzhugh announced to the senators that he was resigning as their speaker. "I feel," he said, "that I have fulfilled my duty to the fullest of my capacity. The smoke screen thrown out over the state that I was anxious to get into the governor's chair or that my political friends were anxious for me to get there to capture control of the state government must be put to rest." [41]

The same day lengthy articles of impeachment were laid before the house. Horton was charged with failure to perform his sworn

39 Nashville *Tennessean,* May 23, 1931.
40 Chattanooga *Times,* May 24, 1931.
41 *Press Scimitar,* May 29, 1931.

duty by willfully neglecting to fix and obtain surety bonds from subordinates handling state money; he was charged with having given active cooperation to the Lea–Caldwell interests "for the pecuniary aid, assistance and advantage of their numerous private, separate and joint schemes, ventures and enterprises"; he was charged with wrong-doing in dismissing the highway commissioner who had refused to specify rock asphalt for paving as demanded by Lea and Caldwell; and he was charged with the misuse of his pardoning power.[42]

The house voted on June 4, and Crump lost his battle forty-one to fifty-eight. It was only a temporary setback, Crump said. And indeed a week later the power of Horton over the state government was broken when, as Crump had urged, the Democratic caucus refused to renominate Horton's state treasurer and comptroller. Hill McAlister, supported by Crump, and a longtime enemy of the Horton–Lea–Caldwell faction, was nominated state treasurer, and thenceforth no more money would go into banks friendly to the administration.

The great battle on Capitol Hill had come to an end. Horton had not been ousted, but he was broken, and somehow where Crump moved, there was always the satisfying sequel of retributive justice. Already, Luke Lea and Rogers Caldwell had been named in a federal indictment for conspiracy to violate the national banking laws. In Davidson County a grand jury at Nashville indicted Caldwell for fraudulent breach of trust in connection with the taking down of securities pledged to protect the deposits of Hardemann County. In August a federal court in Asheville, North Carolina, sentenced Luke Lea to serve from six to ten years in the penitentiary.

Later, when everyone was back in Memphis, Crump gave a picnic at Horseshoe Lake in Arkansas for the members of the organization who had worked in the impeachment battle. They ate, fished, and napped beneath the trees, and later, had a baseball game. It was some game. "You know Joe Hicks?" Crump asked. "Why he knocked a ball into the lake. It looked like a home run, but three or four fellows tackled him football style between second and third and held him until Bunyan Carter had fished the ball out of the water and tagged him. . . . And you ought to have seen Frank Gailor. He knocked a beauty right over second base and Roane Waring, who was umpiring, called it a foul. . . . We had a great time." [43]

42 *Ibid.*, May 29, June 1, 1931.   43 *Ibid.*, September 29, 1931.

☒ ☐

Chapter VII

CONGRESS

IN THE summer of 1930 the Great Depression settled down for its long siege, and kids all over the country were trying for tree-sitting records. In Memphis one fell from his perch, prompting police commissioner Cliff Davis to warn parents of the dangers of the pastime. That June the city's firemen held a ball, and Crump was asked to lead the dance. He wrote Senator McKellar to urge him to attend. "I am to lead the great march and expect to pull off a real tricky high-stepping illusive march and want you to take part. . . ." [1] He was as good as his word. He began the ball with an old-fashioned quadrille and the Highland fling. "They're the best kind of dances, anyway," he said.[2]

Late summer brought an oppressive heat to Memphis, causing perspiration to come with the slightest exertion. Even after sunset, waves of hot air rolled off the sidewalks and pavement, settling motionless around people sitting on their porches. After work Crump sat in his side yard with his shirt unbuttoned and read newspapers until the light failed. To Mrs. Crump, vacationing at Daytona Beach, he telegraphed that he would "just as soon say Noah Webster could

1 Crump to McKellar, February 6, 1930. McKellar Papers.
2 *Commercial Appeal,* June 30, 1930.

not spell cat or that Newton was a Bushman and could not count above five as to say it is not hot here." [3]

Unemployment increased, and shortly the city was pushing work on public improvements to provide jobs. Apple-selling appeared on the streets in November, the city staking the vendors to their first box and making repayment a matter of honor. In homes where there was no money for fuel, city trucks took men to wood lots.

That winter a Memphis theatrical manager got the idea of having a cotton carnival in the spring. It would add a note of gaity to the sober times and would stimulate business. Crump worked with the idea, which was to become an annual event: for a season Memphis society solemnly adopted the manners of royalty, and lesser folk witnessed the ceremonial pomp and toured the carnival that was set up on the levee.

The worst was still to come. One day long lines queued up in the lobby of the north Memphis branch of the Union Planters Bank, just beneath Crump's office. He went downstairs and told the bank officials to get all the currency they had and stack it where the people could see it. Then he walked along the line trying to reassure those waiting to get their money. The bank was strong and weathered the crisis.

One Saturday afternoon in the closing days of the dreary year of 1932, Crump snapped a rubber band around the last pile of papers on his desk, pushed his hat back over his bushy locks, and philosophized about the Depression to a group gathered in his office. "Yes sir," he declared, "the rainy days are here. The people must go back and live over again the hard days of the past. They must have patience and endurance, but in the end they will come thru, just as they did when I was a boy." A brilliant sun leveled across the Arkansas shore and flooded through the window behind him, lighting the faces of his listeners, one of whom was Edward, Jr. "You take Christmas," he continued. "When I was a boy we got a measly apple, a sour orange, a stick of candy and maybe one toy. All the fall before we saved pig bladders for Christmas out of the hogs we killed. Christmas Eve we'd blow them up and on Christmas morning we'd pop 'em."

Edward, Jr., laughed. "You know we've heard this story before, and one Christmas that's what we gave him for Christmas, a dried

3   Crump to Bessie Crump, August 17, 1930. Crump Papers.

up apple, an orange, and a stick of candy, and Robert found some bladders somewhere."

Returning to the currently bleak economic scene, Crump concluded:

"We're overbuilt and oversold." [4]

The continuation of hard times brought unrest. In June, 1932, four hundred unemployed veterans moved into Memphis. Police chief Will Lee suggested that they "be marched to a large building at the Fairgrounds and be locked up there until they make up their minds. Then open the doors, load them on . . . the railroads that brought them here . . . and ship them back to their homes." [5]

There was no trouble, and eventually they left. Crump was sympathetic with the veterans. "They have been well behaved, harmless, and if one would mingle with them he would find many a Distinguished Service Medal or Croix de Guerre pinned on a tattered coat." [6] He could be as sentimental as the next one about veterans.

In the summer of 1933 police officials thought they had a Communist conspiracy on their hands. Commissioner Davis was reported as saying that many Communist leaders had come to the city and were organizing Negroes. "Their followers ran into the thousands," he said.[7]

Then Boris Israel appeared on the scene, and his very name struck fear into the hearts of those who supported the established order. He had come to Memphis to protest pay cuts on the Reconstruction Finance Corporation projects. When he planned a speech, he was told he would have to have a permit. Chief Lee informed the city attorney that he was not going to give any "communist-son-of-a-bitch" the right to speak and left the matter in the hands of the city attorney. Finally, Israel was given the permit, but as a precaution Lee was authorized to deputize additional men to preserve order.[8]

Israel soon left Memphis, but Lee remained suspicious and alert. He was very preoccupied with what he called the dictatorship of the "pro-lat-erate," a word he pronounced by accenting the second syllable.[9] He announced his intention of arresting "six to eight Com-

---

4 *Press Scimitar*, December 31, 1932.
5 *Ibid.*, June 6, 1932.
6 *Ibid.*, June 23, 1932.
7 *Ibid.*, June 14, 1933.
8 Interview with Abe D. Waldauer, September 17, 1957.
9 *Ibid.*

munist agitators" and turning them over to immigration officials for deportation. "We intend to stamp out the seed of Communism in Memphis," he sternly declared.[10]

The *Press Scimitar* was indignant. "Chief Will Lee has a penchant for annoying and arresting men suspected of being Communists. He has no more right to arrest a man suspected of being a Communist than he has to arrest a man suspected of being a Methodist." [11]

The Depression caused many businesses to founder, but Crump's weathered the storm. Crump had seen the Depression coming and had prepared. In 1927 the Metropolitan Life Insurance Company offered Crump and Trezevant mortgage correspondent agencies in Boston, Cincinnati, and Toledo, in addition to those operating in St. Louis, Pittsburgh, and Little Rock. "We looked over those cities," Crump explained, "but finally decided we didn't want to take them on in view of the Coolidge artificial prosperity when call money was 20% . . . [and] stocks were selling for $1,250 that were worth $350. Therefore we declined to expand—take on those cities and requested that we be permitted to sell everything but Memphis, which we did." When the Depression hit, the company was braced. "We had . . . sold mortgage bonds over the counter to the public," Crump continued, but they were all paid with interest—"one of the few concerns in America that can make this boast. We are proud of that record." [12]

In any circumstance, Crump would go to extraordinary lengths to protect the integrity of his company's name. John Martin, Jr., a company attorney and Crump's cousin, tells a story that illustrates his scrupulous business ethics. In 1938 a Chicago casualty company for which the Crump company was an agent went into receivership. The company had been given an "A" rating by the insurance rating manual and by the Illinois and Tennessee insurance rating commissions, and therefore was presumed to be strong. When the telegram arrived telling of the company's difficulties, Crump called in Martin and the local representative of the Chicago company, and both assured him that he had neither legal nor moral responsibility to 610 local policyholders. Even so, the Crump company bought new policies, costing about thirty thousand dollars. As Martin pointed out,

10   *Press Scimitar*, December 15, 1933.
11   *Ibid.*, February 2, 1934.
12   *Commercial Appeal*, October 16, 1947.

this was good business, for it gave the company a reputation for protecting its clients.

Yet this was not the end of the matter. Just when the Chicago company failed, one local business concern, a policy holder, had a truck involved in an accident that killed four WPA workers and injured others. Unprotected, the business was in the way of losing a considerable amount of money. But the Crump company itself paid the claims, finally amounting to $45,626.39. This, said Martin, was unprecedented in the history of the insurance business, in that an agent, rather than the insuring company, paid the claim. Crump saw to it that his action was appreciated. "John," he said to Martin, "they ought to be grateful for what we did. I think you ought to go down there and claim their insurance business for the next ten years." [13] Martin got the contract.

Over the years there was a continuing hope among Crump's detractors that some evidence could be found that would prove a link between Crump company financial success and city politics. Except that the name "Crump" brought business, there was no link. Crump absolutely avoided involving his company in any aspect of city or county financial administration. It was not until after his death that the company began to hold a portion of the city's insurance.

In business as in politics Crump liked to put himself in the way of aiding young people. He made it a practice to offer jobs to those whom he regarded as worthy graduates of Memphis high schools. One, Clara Muller, joined the company in 1924, becoming over the years an integral part of the company organization. She worked hard, and Crump recognized her efforts by taking a helpful paternalistic interest in her affairs. This was characteristic of him, she explained, bearing out his belief that if employees were happy, they would work better. Yet his paternalism could go beyond the objective of an efficient office force, and Miss Muller cited the case of a girl who had worked for two years and then was forced to retire because of tuberculosis: she was kept on the payroll "for many years." [14]

Crump enforced an old-fashioned propriety in the relationship between male and female employees. He did not abide over-familiarity, insisting that men address the ladies as "Miss" or "Mrs."

13 Interview with John Martin, Jr., November 6, 1957.
14 Interview with Clara Muller, August 6, 1957.

rather than by their first names. Once, overhearing a male employee refer to a retreating female figure with phrases that were indelicately descriptive, he severely reprimanded the man.

In December, 1936, Crump bought out the interest of associate founder Stanley Trezevant, and the firm was reorganized as the "E. H. Crump Company." Since 1930, E. H. Crump, Jr., had practically managed the business, and with the reorganization, he, Robert, and John were placed in top executive positions.

Crump was fifty-six years old in 1930. With his success in politics and business there was a widening of the family circle, bringing an added measure of the family felicity he cherished above everything else. He and Mrs. Crump were now grandparents, with two small daughters in Edward, Jr.'s, household. On May 21, 1932, another daughter-in-law was brought within the family fold with Robert's marriage to Sara Louise Taylor.

John, in 1930, was at the University of Virginia. One month he sent his father an accounting of his monthly expenses that came to $241. Crump was exasperated. "John, you don't realize that 95 per cent of the world's population are supporting large families and putting money aside on what you spend each month." [15]

When the semester ended, John left school. In the summer he went to Colorado hoping to clear up sinus trouble. He wrote breezy letters home, listing his expenses, discussing the Memphis political situation, and telling of a meeting with a "beautiful girl." He wondered if his father had heard the Coca-Cola program that was broadcast every Wednesday evening from New York. Had he heard Grantland Rice and Graham McNamee? If he would tune in the following Wednesday, he would hear Iris Speaker. "This 'hour of refreshment' might serve to stimulate you. . . ." Then, as an afterthought, he added that "the other evening while driving home from dinner, I ran into a Buick sedan from behind. . . . The officer stated that the fault was mine. I acknowledged it." [16]

Crump wrote his sons old-fashioned sermonizing letters from Congress. "Bear in mind," he counseled John, "that you crawled before you walked; the great football players played on the scrub before the varsity. . . . You must prepare for the eventuality. Eagerness and ambition are praiseworthy, but without preparation faulty and

15   Crump to John Crump, April 15, 1930. Crump Papers.
16   John Crump to Crump, undated. Crump Papers.

defective." He was concerned about John's reading. "There are a lot of good books in the Cossitt Library, which are interesting and informing, dealing with the City of Memphis, State of Tennessee, the United States and all the various countries of the world." He suggested that John read "The 'Epic of America,' . . . also Claude Bowers' 'Tragic Era' . . . the 'Life of Sam Houston . . . Andrew Jackson' . . . 'Life of Andrew Johnson' . . . most interesting." In a side note he added: "First, read the Declaration of Independence and the Constitution of the United States. It is worth anyone's time. Joy riding, hot dog eating, ragtime dancing, John Barleycorn, late hours—all have their attractiveness, but avail little in afterlife the worthlessness of that time and money spent and wasted. . . ." [17]

In one instance, he addressed his thoughts to Robert in a memorandum. "It is a fine thing to be an important person in the world, but this always takes conscientious preparation. None of us just spring to fame or distinction overnight. There is no royal road to anything worthwhile. It is a rough road." He counseled Robert to practice self-discipline. "It was self discipline that enabled W. E. Henley to write that inspiring poem 'Invictus'. . . . So long as we live we shall remain our best friend and our worst enemy. No one else can master us without our own consent." [18]

Crump's sons had their shortcomings, but one they emphatically did not have was a lack of affection and respect for their parents. They all appeared to realize that they were in advantageous circumstances compared to most people, and that their welfare had been the foremost concern in their parents' life. The family relationship was marked by effusive displays of affection. Customarily the boys saluted their father with a kiss on the cheek, and they were even more demonstrative toward their mother. Robert Crump spoke of her as "the dearest and sweetest mother a boy could ever have," [19] and once John in a letter to her told her that he was "thanking God that I am so fortunate as to have you—just you as my mother. . . . Xmas is not long off, and when I step off of the old 'Special,' prepare yourself to be kissed and hugged as you have never been before." [20]

Crump took his seat in the Seventy-second Congress on March 4,

17 Crump to John Crump, March 31, 1933. Crump Papers.
18 Memorandum. Crump Papers.
19 Interview with Robert Crump, January 3, 1958.
20 John Crump to Bessie Crump, undated. Crump Papers.

1931. When he walked into his office in the old House Office Building, it was filled with flowers from well-wishers back home. The next day he got down to business and had the flowers sent to Washington hospitals. Joining him again in his office was Marvin Pope, his secretary of the years past when he had been mayor. He had rescued Pope from a languishing Washington haberdashery business.

Among the beloved aphorisms that Crump had recorded among his random jottings were a number that dealt with the perils of vanity that came from worldly success. He studiously avoided the airs and affectations characteristic of some who were newly blessed with wealth and success, and when he went to Congress, he attempted to keep a balanced view of his position. He "had come to Washington with no illusions as to the importance of his position," Marvin Pope noted. "He did not feel that the fate of the nation rested upon his shoulders." [21] When Clara Muller wrote that she was keeping a scrapbook of his accomplishments that was growing daily, he replied that he did not think he would need a very big scrapbook because "I am only a very little frog in a big pond." [22]

Shortly after he arrived in Washington, a journalist attempted to get the viewpoint of the new congressman on some of the issues. Crump was always positive, and when the subject under discussion was not on familiar ground, he would be positive about something else. "It has become very clear to me," he said, "that a newcomer must observe, remember, compare, read, confer, listen and ask questions. As a business man I have always sought to plan my work and then work out my plans. I see that will be a little difficult here." [23]

He played a minor role in Congress. Unwilling to speak publicly, he was part of no historic moment of debate on a vital national issue. The seeming lack of discipline in Congress, its confusion, and the ponderous way in which it moved to accomplish its objectives appalled him. "I shall appear before the very next session of the Tennessee Legislature and offer an . . . apology for some of the things I have said of that . . . body in the past," he remarked to Pope.[24] His job, as he saw it, was to scrutinize closely the bills that

21 Secretaries' notes.
22 Clara Muller to Crump, December 11, 1931; Crump to Clara Muller, December 14, 1931. Crump Papers.
23 William G. Shepherd, "O Say, Can You Hear?" *Collier's* LXXXIX (May 7, 1932), 13.
24 Secretaries' notes.

came before the House and vote on them as the welfare of his constituency indicated. Otherwise, he did what a hardworking congressman must do: he attended to patronage matters, secured passports for constituents, mailed out government bulletins, answered from one hundred to three hundred letters daily, and greeted Memphians when they came to Washington.

At his request he was placed on the House Military Affairs Committee. He chose this post because he felt that he might be in a position to aid legislation dealing with the water power development of the Tennessee River area. He was obviously thinking of the possible development of hydroelectric power. Later he requested and obtained a transfer to the Rivers and Harbors Committee, again in the hope of furthering the cause of federal power projects.

His record in Congress was progressive all the way. When he announced for the office, he declared that he was "unalterably opposed to the high tariff being foisted on the people by the Republican party at the behest of the big and tremendous money interests. . . . I pledge a vote and helping hand at all times for those sadly neglected citizens who would bear the burden of the high tariff measures." [25] He was anxious to get the government to take charge of the eradication of malaria in the Mississippi Valley. He wanted a large government hospital in Memphis to treat venereal diseases. "Health is the first requisite for a contented people," he declared.

His first term in Congress occurred during those trying days of 1931–32, when Hoover and the Democratic Congress stood at odds while the Depression lengthened. In June, 1932, Crump explained his position on some current issues. He was strong for the soldier's bonus bill. "We need more money in circulation if prosperity is to return." He had voted for the bonus bill and added that he regretted that "all of my constituents are not in accord on the bonus question, but I simply cannot concur in the theory that my constituency is limited to those who can enjoy the privileges of a Tennessee Club, a country club . . . or an outing club." [26] These were words that every politician likes to intone, but Crump meant them. He had voted for the Reconstruction Finance Corporation Act, "designed to care for 'big business,' . . . for the home loan banking bill, for the measure to enlarge the discount facilities of the federal reserve system, and, in fact, for everything . . . which I thought held any

25 *Press Scimitar,* June 10, 1930.   26 *Ibid.,* June 23, 1932.

hope of helping the American people in these dark days." He had voted for Hoover's plan for a moratorium on foreign debts because conditions throughout the world amply justified "the rich American government in postponing the payment of all inter-governmental debts for one year." [27]

He had a solution for the impasse between the Democrats and Hoover. "The Democrats might say to President Hoover, 'You lower your high tariff, and we'll vote for your moratorium.' And further, 'Correct the cotton and wheat evils of the Farm Board and we will look your way.' " [28]

He made a striking figure in Congress. His red hair had turned gray, and he affected a cane, yet he continued to give the appearance of great energy. With his shoulders thrust back and his quick step he had an almost severe military bearing. His actions and speech were quick and direct, and his transparent skin with its pinkish tint suggested robust health. "Bland, perfectly self-possessed, he ambles as quietly about the Capitol as a tiger stalks its prey on a Persian rug," wrote an observer. "The gentleman from Tennessee is no longer called 'redsnapper,' only his wife dares to recall the word." He was a compound of "polish and suavity and custom made clothes. . . . Smooth words and gentle hints." [29]

He wrote newsy letters home telling of some of the events in his life as a congressman. To daughter-in-law Louise he gave an accounting of his social life and his thinking on some of the issues on which he would soon vote: "After three weeks tussel [*sic*] on the tax bill, our school let out Friday evening and a crowd of us 'took off' for Saturday, going over in Maryland and playing a little at the Bowie races." The party included "Speaker Garner, Richard Cleveland, son of the former president, Charles Crisp of Georgia, Fred Vinson of Kentucky, Lindsey Warren of North Carolina, Marvin Junes of Texas, and E. H. Crump of Tennessee." Spring was coming and "Washington's attractiveness, which appeals to everyone, is just beginning to impress me. Of course, with everything we have declining, it is hard to really enthuse as one should over anything for any length of time." The Philippine independence question would be coming up and he would vote for it. After that, the Kunz-Granata election contest, affecting Al Capone's district in Chicago. "Kunz is

27 Scrapbook news clipping.   29 *Ibid.*
28 *Ibid.*

a very sorry, no account Democrat and Granata is one of Capone's men. I suppose I'll vote for Kunz as the less of two evils." [30]

He was not long in making up his mind whom he would support for the presidency in 1932. He was for Roosevelt. "Gov. Roosevelt . . . has made a good governor. . . . In fact he has filled every position he has ever occupied with honor, credit, dignity, and ability. Any man who has the nerve to conquer the disease with which Gov. Roosevelt was afflicted most certainly has the stamina to wrest this country from the Republican depression." [31]

When the Republicans wrote their platform in June, he declared that it was as "weak as evaporated dishwater." On the liquor question he emphatically wanted to repeal the Eighteenth Amendment. The Republican liquor clause contained "everything from near beer to canned heat," and "Hoover on this proposition has been blowing hot and cold just as he has on economy appropriations, and balancing the budget." He was asked whom he would support if Roosevelt could not get the nomination. Crump showed yet again that he was positive: "I never make a second choice. . . . I am for Franklin D. Roosevelt." [32]

The *Press Scimitar,* under its new editor, Edward Meeman, took a position contrary to Crump's. "Franklin Roosevelt in our opinion would prove another Hoover—lacking the necessary vision and courage of great leadership. The country knows this. There is no enthusiasm for Roosevelt." [33] As the Democratic convention got underway, the paper saw Roosevelt "slipping fast." His duplicity had "sickened enough of . . . [his] own following to cost him the nomination—and, if not that, his election. . . . There are too many millions of American voters with a feeling for sportsmanship to trust that kind of a leader." [34] The *Press Scimitar*'s portrait of Roosevelt as a calloused trickster derived from Roosevelt's attempt to break the two-thirds nominating rule.

Crump entered just as enthusiastically into the state gubernatorial election. He announced he would support Hill McAlister, the recipient of his support in previous contests. As usual, he thundered his opinions in a large political advertisement. Rather than concentrating on McAlister's virtues, he downgraded Malcolm Patterson,

30 Crump to Mrs. E. H. Crump, Jr., April 3, 1932. Crump Papers.
31 *Press Scimitar,* September 25, 1931.   33 *Ibid.,* June 27, 1932.
32 *Ibid.,* June 18, 1933.   34 *Ibid.,* June 25, 1932.

an old hand in Tennessee politics who was running against McAlister. He used the kind of language that got through to the simpler folk and made them slap their thighs with delight. Judge Patterson "was the same local and long distance liar that he has been for years. His unfair and unjustified remarks about me at the auditorium last Saturday night to a small crowd emphasizes one thing above all else—that a leopard cannot change his spots nor can a hog remove the swallowfork brand from its ear. Drunk or sober, he is the same Patterson today as of old." [35]

The *Press Scimitar,* reflecting the point of view of its new editor, gave a high-minded endorsement to its own candidate. It was for Lewis Pope, because he was "the people's candidate." The paper admired "Patterson's courage . . . in leaving the secure quiet of the bench for the turmoil of a campaign. We are with him in the splendid fight he is making against corrupt elections in Shelby County." As for McAlister he did not have "aggressive courage" nor "freedom from political entanglements." [36]

Neither was the paper satisfied with Watkins Overton's candidacy for mayor. Overton was a "good" man, but he had a queer sense of loyalty to Edward H. Crump "that made him disloyal to himself. . . . Does not Watkins Overton realize that he has it in his power to get a new deal for the People of Memphis?" asked the paper. "Does he not realize that he could wipe out the shame of Shelby?" [37] Overton apparently did not realize all of this.

In the midst of electioneering another voice was raised against Crump and the organization. On July 19 Senator William Edgar Borah, the venerable Idaho Republican, made public two letters from Memphis informants stating that government relief flour was "being used by the political machine of Memphis . . . and . . . that no unemployed can secure this flour unless he is pledged to vote for Crump's . . . candidates." [38]

Overton immediately denied the charge, stating that neither the county nor the city had anything to do with the distribution of flour. In a telegram to Borah, Crump said it was "inconceivable" that "a supposedly reputable member of the United States Senate, with a background of 25 years of service, would permit himself to be used as a tool of irresponsible political scavengers by giving publicity,

35 *Ibid.,* June 7, 1932.   37 *Ibid.,* July 8, 1932.
36 *Ibid.,* July 6, 1932.   38 Memphis *Evening Appeal,* July 19, 1932.

without the slightest investigation," to "false" and "utterly absurd
charges." The "lying misinformation sent you was inspired by the
Patterson interests." [39]

McKellar was puzzled. "I think Borah acted very peculiarly about
the matter," he wrote Crump. "I was here and he could have called
me and found out about it, but he never said a word to me and the
first I saw of it was his statement to the newspapers." [40]

Borah had been used, but perhaps he was unaccustomed to the
spirited competitiveness of Tennessee politics. The scheme to which
he had given the prestige of his name was obviously calculated to
shake the Negro voter's confidence in Crump.

As the election approached, the *Press Scimitar* increased its
attacks on the organization, shortly claiming that "phantom voters"
were being registered.[41] Crump answered these charges in full-page
advertisements. The *Commercial Appeal* was controlled absolutely
by the railroad interests, and the *Press Scimitar* was a "Hoover Depression Republican paper." [42] To the charge of election irregularities
he proclaimed in large type that "Thieves Don't Work for Something
They Intend to Steal." [43] The newspapers, he declared, knew full
well "that every ward in Memphis and every district in Shelby County
had been thoroughly and systematically organized for weeks in behalf of Mr. McAlister's candidacy. . . . These newspapers know
that the McAlister Campaign Committee and I, personally, have
spent large sums of money for paid advertisements (the only newspaper publicity available to McAlister), and for banners, cards,
stickers, bands, hurdy-gurdys, picture show slides . . . in order to
keep Mr. McAlister's name and the things for which he stands
before the people."

Organization and intense campaigning accomplished its purpose.
On August 4 Shelby County gave McAlister 31,439 votes; Patterson,
6,661; and Pope, 2,318. In the state count McAlister won over Pope
by less than 8,000. Had the Shelby vote not been included, Pope
would have won by 20,000. Finally, the election revealed that the
electorate was scarcely influenced by the editorial opinions of the
Press Scimitar.

39 Crump to W. E. Borah, July 19, 1932. Telegram. Crump Papers.
40 McKellar to Crump, July 30, 1932. McKellar Papers.
41 *Press Scimitar,* July 21, 1932.
42 *Commercial Appeal,* July 10, 1932.
43 *Press Scimitar,* August 3, 1932.

The *Press Scimitar* did not graciously concede defeat. "Pope Must Not Lose by a Negro Majority," it said. "To allow Shelby each two years to return arbitrarily a 30,000 vote for its candidate, nullifying the vote of white Democrats in a score or more of the smaller counties in Tennessee, is a disgrace that will not be tolerated by the state at large." [44]

The challenge to McAllister's victory would have to be made on something more than just the fact of Negro votes, which were as legal as any. Shortly after the election Pope filed a contest before the state Democratic committee, seeking to have himself named the true Democratic candidate on the grounds that his supporters in Shelby had been intimidated. At the hearing before the committee the Shelby organization successfully disproved the intimidation charge. Organization attorneys Charles Bryan and Abe Waldauer secured affidavits from Pope supporters from every polling place in the county attesting that they had in no way been intimidated. McAlister remained the official Democratic nominee. [45]

But Pope was not finished; he decided to run as an independent in the general election. His campaign was strong, and Crump was worried. A week before the election Crump wrote McAlister a strong letter, pointedly criticizing him on two counts. First, he felt that McAlister had been apologetic about the support he received from Shelby County. "There is a lot of feeling among our strong supporters that you regret our assistance, and have given wordy evidence of that fact on every occasion," Crump wrote. "Your Paris speech, in answer to the Press Scimitar here, was a complete and deliberate apology for your acquaintance with us." Even in Memphis, McAlister had said the wrong thing. In this speech "your allusion to me apparently confused and embarrassed you so that you forgot my name and referred to me as 'Edwin' Crump." Irrespective of what McAlister or anyone thought, said Crump, "we all feel that we have worked, lived and thought in this life just as fairly, just as honorably, and just as well as you or any of your advisors have. For many years we have stood a lot of unnecessary abuse for you and there is no reason for our giving thought, time, labor and money to the cause of one who is playing the role of 'Dr. Jekyl and Mr. Hyde' with us."

The second point for criticism was that McAlister was not cam-

44   *Ibid.*, August 5, 1932.
45   Interview with Abe D. Waldauer, April 10, 1962.

paigning hard enough. "Even Roosevelt, candidate for the great and dignified office of President is making a more spirited fight, in dealing with Hoover, than you are making in running for governor." Crump concluded by saying he realized he was writing a strong letter, but "I would be an awful hypocrite, and I am not one, if I didn't tell you that we feel that your candidacy is anaemic, devoid of fighting spirit, wholly colorless, and is getting you nowhere." [46]

In the election on November 8, McAlister won easily. This time he had over 60,000 votes to spare. A month later Crump wrote McAlister another letter, but it was never sent. Perhaps he felt that the governor had heard enough from him. The letter does contain a statement of what he expected from McAlister in the way of patronage and performance, and principles were formalized that served as guidelines for the organization's subsequent dealings with state administrations.

"My dear Governor-elect," Crump began. "The opposition all over the state to your candidacy for governor said that my support would embarrass you in the operation of the state's affairs. The inference was that . . . I would try to use you and would endeavor to dictate the policies of your entire administration, with no good purpose in view. In order that they may not be disappointed, I now come forward with my suggestions. . . ."

Then he listed what he wanted McAlister to do: First, insist that before the legislature elected its speakers, it should require that they "pledge themselves absolutely to a strict economy plan." The way to do this was to put all available patronage jobs on a slip of paper, then let every legislator draw lots to see who got the jobs. For the other state jobs, he laid down the following proposition: "While Shelby County . . . pays about one-fifth of the taxes of the state . . . we will ask for only one-ninth of the state's patronage. *This is certainly more than fair,*" said Crump, underlining his words for emphasis. "After you have cut out all useless boards and jobs, combined a great many, reduced salaries in excess of work, labor and responsibility involved; in fact, after you have cut the operation of the state's affairs within reach of the taxpayer's money, then count us in Shelby as one-ninth."

Finally, Crump wrote, "There has been much talk and evidence of a 'rake-off' someone has been getting on contracts and purchases. . . .

46 Crump to Hill McAlister, September 27, 1932. Crump Papers.

This, of course, should never happen again and anyone projecting himself to that extent ought to go to the penitentiary without delay, for the taxpayers only are entitled to the best contracts, prices, quality, weights, etc." McAlister should take Memphis as his model, where "the taxpayers . . . and not grafters . . . get the benefit of any shrewd business methods to obtain the best at all times." The grafters had played for big stakes in dealing with the taxpayers' money. "Only determination, eternal watchfulness and a strong hand will break the practice up." [47]

Crump's concluding advice to McAlister was inspired by a recollection of another governor he had helped elect—Henry Horton. He later called his support of Horton "a bad day's work," and it was an experience he did not want to duplicate. He might be stung once, but not twice; and McAlister, who was governor because of Crump, would always have that fact impressed upon his mind by the numerous questions, probings, and detailed advice he would get from Crump. For a man who valued freedom of action it was a high price to pay for an election victory, and certainly there must have been times when he would have liked being governor just by himself, knowing that Crump was not looking over his shoulder. But that was not to be, for Crump was determined that his man in Nashville be far above even the merest hint of corruption and inefficiency.

While he thus stood ready "to assist" the new governor "in any way possible," [48] his immediate responsibility was his job as congressman. There were hopeful expectations of what Roosevelt and the Seventy-third Congress would do to combat the Depression, and as the inauguration approached, the attention of the country was directed to Washington.

Recognizing the historic character of the event, Crump invited all of his immediate family, a niece, and Rebecca Trezevant, the daughter of his former associate, to witness the event. Louise Crump thanked him for the invitation. It would be "a memorable event with a Democratic President going in," she wrote.[49]

With the organization of the House of the new Congress, Crump became actively involved in the politics of electing a speaker—appar-

47   Crump to McAlister, December 5, 1932. Crump Papers.
48   *Ibid.*
49   Mrs. E. H. Crump, Jr., to Crump, undated. Crump Papers.

Crump as a child . . .   as a young man . . .

and in later years.

Crump's mother,
Mollie Nelms Crump.

Crump's wife Betty,
as a young woman.

The Crump home at 1962 Peabody in Memphis.

Crump's boyhood home in Holly Springs, Mississippi.

Mayor Crump (seated behind the door bearing his initials) poses in 1911 municipal parade.

The public Crump—hat on head, hand held high—sits among youngsters at a 1942 circus.

Crump Day at the Fair, 1935. Left to right are Mrs. Robert Crump, Crump and his wife Betty, Robert Crump, Mrs. E. H. Crump, Jr., Mrs. John Crump, John Crump, and E. H. Crump, Jr.

Crump at the Democratic National Convention in Chicago, 1940. Standing in front of him are, left to right, Will Gerber, Senator Kenneth McKellar, Tennessee Governor Prentice Cooper, and Will Hale. To Crump's left are Walter Chandler, then mayor of Memphis, and John Vesey.

Crump plays the shell game in this cartoon which
appeared in the Nashville *Tennessean* April 25, 1936.

Statue of Edward Hull Crump looks out over the city of Memphis.

ently the only time he put his talents to use in Congressional politics. House majority leader Henry T. Rainey of Illinois was a candidate, as was Joseph Byrnes of Tennessee, John Rankin of Mississippi, and William Bankhead of Alabama. It was Crump's work to engineer a compromise which resulted in the election of Rainey as speaker and Byrnes as majority leader, with each having nominated the other for the post to which he was elected. Bankhead, left out completely, protested "somewhat vehemently," but his chance was not far off. When Speaker Rainey died, Byrnes assumed the office, and during his tenure he too died, opening the way for Bankhead.[50]

Crump's role in the Seventy-third Congress was almost exclusively one of supporting the New Deal. Without exception, he voted for every administration measure that came before the House. In two instances his vote brought repercussions at home. When he cast his vote in favor of the "Beer Bill," his action was so contrary to that of many of his regional associates that "some of his colleagues nudged him . . . thinking that he had made a mistake." [51] It was no mistake; indeed he probably cast that vote with more personal satisfaction than any other, remembering back to the days of 1916, when the prohibition issue had been used to oust him from the mayor's office.

In voting for the Agricultural Adjustment Act, he went against the interests of the powerful Front Street cotton firms. Writing in his column in the *Press Scimitar,* Ralph Millett declared that he was "proud of the way Rep. E. H. came thru because I knew of the pressure the Front Street boys were bringing on him. . . . He resisted the cotton men just as he had resisted the opponents of the economy bill and those against the beer bill." [52]

After a year of Roosevelt, Crump was certain the New Deal had come to stay. "I don't believe those 'good old days,' when anything could be sold, money could be had for any purpose and there was no limit to credit, will ever return," he said. He gave the credit to Roosevelt. "The President has made wonderful headway. He not only has creative ability but executive ability. . . . He is in touch with the people, not a few certain classes, but all the people." [53]

Crump's admiration for Roosevelt is easy to understand. He liked

50 Secretaries' notes.   52 *Press Scimitar,* March 24, 1933.
51 *Ibid.*   53 *Ibid.,* December 30, 1933.

the President's energy, flair, and forcefulness; he was especially impressed with the way in which Roosevelt had risen above his physical handicap. They were men alike in several respects. Both were of the aristocracy of their particular regions, yet both came to be thought of as the benefactor of the "little" man. Possibly the most significant characteristic they held in common is revealed in an observation that Samuel I. Rosenman made of Roosevelt: "He was most generous and forgiving about human weaknesses; but he was implacable and vindictive toward those who deliberately were unfair to him, especially in political matters." [54]

After the excitement of the early days of the New Deal had passed, life in Washington became increasingly burdensome to Crump. His family was much on his mind. On Mother's Day, 1933, he scattered telegrams broadcast. To Mrs. Crump, having a physical checkup at Battle Creek, he wired: "This is not only a message to a dear mother but to a loyal and devoted pal who will monopolize my thoughts on Mother's Day." To his own "dear mother" he sent "love and affection," and to his mother-in-law his "dearest love." [55]

Early in May he went to Louisville to witness the Kentucky Derby. It was an outing in which pleasure was mixed with business. Meeting there with Crump were Tennessee senators McKellar and Bachman, and organization stalwarts Will Hale, Frank Rice, Tyler McLain, and Mayor Overton. It was a unity meeting, marking the end of a breach between Crump and McKellar that dated back to the previous January, when McKellar had successfully supported his brother Clint's bid for the Memphis postmastership. At the time Crump stated that "someone other than a brother of a United States senator" should have the job. McKellar, on the other hand, insisted that the fact that he was a senator should not deprive his brother of a promotion merited through fifteen years of service as an assistant postmaster.[56]

It was politics that bound Crump and McKellar in an alliance that each found useful. Beyond that, they had one thing in common—their mutual love of horse racing. If there was any rancor left in the feeling of each for the other, it was soon dissipated in the bright Ken-

54   Samuel I. Rosenman, *Working With Roosevelt* (New York, 1952), 84
55   Crump to Bessie Crump, May 13, 1933; Crump to Mollie Nelms Crump, May 13, 1933; Crump to Mrs. Robert McLean, May 13, 1933. Crump Papers.
56   *Press Scimitar*, January 17, 1933.

tucky sun and the pageantry of the race. Part of the color was Crump himself, with his navy blue sport coat, white flannel trousers, and two-tone shoes, looking like a Kentucky colonel with his mane of white hair curling from beneath a broad-brimmed Panama.

Back in Washington he wired Mrs. Crump about a trip to Europe they had been thinking about for some time. "Am all pepped up over the thought and think by all means we should go." [57]

They left in mid-June, 1933, the local press carrying a picture of them before their departure standing on the deck of the White Star liner *Majestic*. Crump was togged out in his usual elegant two-tone combinations, except the floppy Panama with its deep Southern accent had been discarded for the continental styling of a Homburg.

Leisurely touring Europe, he sent home postcards, addressed and signed in a sprawling scrawl that left no space for a message. He gambled a little at Monte Carlo, was critical of the strutting and posturing of the Italian Facists, and was most impressed with the frugality of European farmers, who "could live comfortably on what American farmers waste." [58]

They returned in late September on the *Europa*. While Mrs. Crump went on to the World's Fair at Chicago, Crump lingered three days in Washington to attend to the more pressing business before he joined her.

In October he was back in Memphis, catching up on his business affairs, and then in November he returned to Washington. The stress of work during those weeks was beginning to tell on him, and he, who never admitted to any weakness to anyone outside his family, wrote a plaintive letter to his mother. It had been "hard going" with "stacks of work confronting me each morning." Further, he had not felt "at all well." He was "terribly run down" which was the "natural consequence of constant, never ceasing work."

He had happier news for his mother. That summer, while he and Mrs. Crump were in Europe, John had stayed with a neighboring family and had fallen in love with the daughter, Jane Boyce. "Betty writes me that Jane's worthiness is more impressive all the time," Crump told his mother. He had written Jane that day, "in response to a very dear letter she wrote me, and I told her she deserved the highest happiness. . . . We'll do our part," he added confidently.

57 Crump to Bessie Crump, May 22, 1933. Crump Papers.
58 *Press Scimitar*, September 30, 1933.

Writing Jane, Crump told her all about her new relatives-to-be, including "Cousin William, with his three foot whiskers," who would "relish" one of Jane's "charming kisses." That provoked an amusing picture, and Crump was reminded of one of his nieces whose face, after kissing Cousin William, would be "all puckered up . . . as if she had swallowed a quart of quinine." [59]

He returned to Memphis in the first days of December. The fourth was a bright warm day, and the press of work had eased enough to permit a promenade, an event that was becoming part of the body of legend that surrounded him. With his cane flashing and several of the courthouse faithful in attendance, he strode down Second Street by the old Lily Bakery, around Court Square, and then back toward his office. Frequently he stopped, removing his hat and making a courtly bow to a woman, or shaking hands with a representative of the humbler segment of the citizenry—all of whom were addressed by their names. Back at Second and Adams he stopped to look up at some Civil Works Administration workers who were cleaning the police building. Turning to courthouse custodian Joe Boyle standing at his side, he brought up the matter of some leaks in the police station roof. "Joe," he said, "why don't you look up Cliff Davis and suggest we have those leaks stopped since the men are working up there anyway?" [60] Boyle agreed that that was a good idea and turned to seek out the police commissioner.

John's marriage took place on Christmas eve. It marked the end of a phase of Crump family life, since all of the sons now had their own households. Yet Crump did not completely surrender them to their own concerns, but charmed his daughters-in-law into a participation in a close-knit family activity with the big house on Peabody as its center. It was about this time that he initiated the custom, about which all Memphis knew, of the family in all of its parts assembling for the midday meal. The event signified domestic felicity of a high type. Crump would have it that way. It was traditional, and in his life there had to be order according to the way in which he viewed things.

He announced his decision to leave Congress in March, 1934. He did not like his work. Washington and Congress were not efficiently organized systems circling in his orbit. He wanted to re-

59 Crump to Mollie Nelms Crump, date obliterated. Crump Papers.
60 *Press Scimitar*, December 5, 1933.

turn to Memphis and especially to his family. "I knew there was a labor more fitting and fertile awaiting me at home with my boys," he later wrote in his notes. Publicly, he expressed the same thought. "With a business in Memphis, an office in Washington, a thousand miles apart . . . I must choose between the two. This being the situation, I prefer my business, with my boys at home." [61]

The relief he felt at knowing that his Washington days were drawing to a close was communicated in a telegram he sent his mother on her ninety-first birthday: "Another birthday for my dear mother and how happy we are that her health is very good and that with her strong alert mind she is still thinking of the future and not of the past." How he wished he could be with them all, but he knew his "dear Betty" would serve well in his place. "Keep her with you several days for she needs the rest and change. Hold in reserve some of the chocolate cake cheese wine and crackers for I say with joy I will be there before long." [62]

Since his time in Washington was growing short, he arranged to have Tom Phillips and Clara Muller visit the capital. Would Phillips care to come, Crump wrote, "if I could arrange it around April 1st, where your railroad fare would be taken care of and not a heavy expense here." Think it over, Crump suggested.[63] Phillips wired immediately: "Don't need to think it over. Rarin to go . . . and looking forward eagerly to pleasures in store." [64]

He was in Washington two weeks, living at the Popes' apartment and taking tours that Crump arranged for him. Among the "pleasures" he experienced was one completely unexpected. One day as he and Crump walked down a street, a chauffeur-driven car was curbed alongside them and a hearty greeting called out to Crump. It was the President. Crump took Phillips over to the car and introduced him to Roosevelt.

Then Clara Muller came. "Make your arrangements to leave Memphis on Sunday night, the 15th," Crump wrote. "You will have Saturday and Sunday to help Edward. . . . Reserve your berth, and

---

61 *Commercial Appeal,* March 4, 1932.
62 Crump to Mollie Nelms Crump, March 24, 1935. Telegram. Crump Papers.
63 Crump to Thomas Phillips, March 1, 1934. Crump Papers.
64 Phillips to Crump, March 4, 1934. Crump Papers.

get a 15-day round trip ticket. . . . We have mapped out an itinerary for Tom Phillips, and will have the same thing for you." [65]

Finally, he had all of his daughters-in-law to the capital. Mrs. Crump, acting as chaperone, wired their acceptance of his invitation. "We feel we shouldn't and Jane hates to leave her little husband but we haven't the moral courage to refuse. . . ." [66]

When the second session of Congress ended on June 18, all of the tours had been completed. Now Pope had to clear the office. On June 14 Crump had received a letter from McAlister, the new Tennessee governor. Addressing Crump as "Dear Ed," McAlister urged him to represent Tennessee at ceremonies arranged by Harry F. Byrd at the grave of James Madison on the anniversary of his death. Crump wired a short reply: "I will not be here." [67]

65 Crump to Clara Muller, April 4, 1934. Crump Papers.
66 Bessie Crump to Crump, May 7, 1934. Crump Papers.
67 Crump to McAlister, June 16, 1934. Crump Papers.

▮▮

☒ ☐

Chapter VIII

THE ORGANIZATION

WHEN Crump came home from Congress, he employed a new chauffeur. Since neither he nor Mrs. Crump drove, the new man found chauffeuring practically his sole work. His name was Clint Cleaves, and the first thing Crump told him was that he wanted his car kept clean. "He didn't have to tell me more than once, because that is the way I like them," Cleaves reminisced. "He wanted the garage kept clean, too, and about twice a year he would go around and inspect it thoroughly to see that everything was in its place." Neither Crump nor Mrs. Crump were fussy, Cleaves said. "If you made a mistake, Mr. Crump would correct you in a quiet way. He knew how to talk to a man." [1]

The family had a 1928 nine-passenger Buick touring car and a new 1933 Lincoln sedan. The Lincoln was used around town, whereas the Buick was for evening tours in the country. On many evenings during the hot summer months the Crumps took rides. Sometimes they put down the Buick's jump seat and took Mr. and Mrs. Mason Jones with them. The trips ranged widely, a typical one taking them to Oakville, Germantown, and then northward along the eastern edge of the Shelby County penal farm to Cordova. This

1 Interview with Clint Cleaves, August 7, 1957.

part of the ride was through territory that over a hundred years before had been the site of a young Scotchwoman's dream of eventually bringing an end to slavery. It was Frances Wright's Neshoba colony, where slaves would be educated and instructed in crafts that would enable them to work out the price of their freedom.

Crump knew the history of the area, and he related it to Jones as they drove along. It was a relaxing moment, driving through the cotton fields and Wolf River bottoms, with the warm night air fanning their faces. As they entered the village of Cordova on an oak-lined road, the dusk deepened into night. From behind wisteria and crepe myrtle glimmered an occasional light from an old home. At the end of the town they passed the heavy gloom of an antiquated warehouse that stood by the railroad track. The aged quiet of Cordova reminded Crump of Hudsonville and the scenes of his youth, and he and Jones fell to reminiscing about bygone days.

He returned from Congress to five years of close association with his sons and their families. He directed his sons in their growing familiarity with the business and concerned himself with their personal welfare, sometimes in matters they probably wished that he would overlook. Noticing a disposition toward faulty posture, he made them promise to exercise while repeating to themselves words of encouragement: "Get on the floor, face down and raise up my hands and toes; also to stand up and touch the floor with my hands." By following this regimen they would learn that "exercise of this character will develop my chest, broaden my shoulders, and eventually force me to stand perfectly erect with my head up." [2]

The grandchildren were employed to enforce the agreement at a salary of ten cents a day. Since there were no children in John's household, Jane was the enforcing agent. In deference to her maturity she was to receive 16 2/3 cents, but would "have to keep a daily record of performance."

He tried to shield his sons from publicity. Once when the *Commercial Appeal* printed some names in connection with a personalty tax and included Edward, Jr.'s, he wrote the president of the publishing company to protest publication of the assessment "which was emphasized . . . over and above everyone else . . . who might have

2 Crump Papers.

been assessed too low. . . ." It was "unjustifiably severe on a young man," and he did not think it "right or just." [3]

The *Commercial Appeal* did not ordinarily deal in sensationalism for its own sake. It probably included Edward, Jr.'s, name along with others because journalistic ethics precluded its exemption simply out of deference to Crump.

The paper was fair with Crump. It had only recently urged the Memphis board of education to name its new football stadium after him. Crump had frequently declined proposals to name public property after him, the paper said, but in view of his interest in football, he should have this "deserving tribute." [4] The paper's recommendation was taken, and it was at Crump Stadium that a later generation of Memphians came to recognize the Shelby leader through his appearance at football games.

He went to most of the college games in the area, and frequently it was a family affair. "I will be up for your parade and have three friends for the football game," he wired Governor McAlister. "Hope you can obtain four tickets for me." [5] McAlister would send an aide for the tickets, but sometimes he had trouble convincing athletic officials that it would be a favor to him if they would rescind their complimentary status. It was not easy to return Crump's check to him.

He especially enjoyed a trip to Oxford to see the University of Mississippi play, and frequently on one of these occasions he would take a party with him. On December 28, 1935, when Mississippi played Mississippi State, he took his sons, daughters-in-law, police commissioner Davis (sportingly attired in knickers), attorney-general Chandler, and his cousin, Judge John Martin. Passing through Holly Springs, Crump and his group would have lunch with his mother before going on the short distance to Oxford.

His stopovers in Holly Springs came to be a ceremonial occasion for the townspeople. The party would stop at the bus terminal restaurant on the town square, and Crump, cane in hand, would walk along the store fronts greeting everyone by name as he was saluted from all sides by "How are you, Cousin Edward?"

3 Crump to Enoch Brown, December 6, 1935. Crump Papers.
4 *Commercial Appeal,* February 25, 1934.
5 Crump to McAlister, November 15, 1934. Telegram. Crump Papers.

In the fall of 1935 Mrs. Crump and a companion toured Europe while Crump and his sons relaxed at football games. He kept her informed on the state of things at home with frequent cables. "Wish you and Miss Fredericka a wonderful trip, lots of enjoyment also lots of sleep and rest. All fine here." [6] He cabled Mrs. Crump in Paris on her birthday: "You now top Heinz by one. Wish you much happiness with dearest love." He signed it "Rudy." [7]

In the thirties he brought his political organization to the peak of its effectiveness. It ran with well-oiled efficiency, so smoothly balanced that the energizing force behind it could almost stand aside and watch it work from its own momentum. If dissonance developed, the trouble was quickly corrected. A telephone call, a word, a hint from Crump restored the balance.

When the organization assembled for formal deliberation it performed with the precision of a well-coached football team. In May, 1938, there was a meeting of the Shelby County Democratic Executive Committee. Crump was not present. He had gone over the final arrangements with the key members of the "team" in the trustee's office of the county courthouse a half hour before the meeting. Afterwards, he had come from the office to walk through the corridors, stopping every few feet to shake a hand and extend a greeting.

The three hundred visitors that jammed into the courtroom to witness the proceedings appeared pleased with the certainty of the action. After all, many had just shaken Crump's hand, and there were few people who, after shaking his hand, did not have the feeling that here was a man truly interested in them and to whose keeping their welfare could be safely entrusted.

The press gave the following account of the occasion:

President Roosevelt was praised by every speaker. Time and again the name of E. H. Crump was mentioned and on each occasion applause broke out. . . .

The audience enjoyed it. They knew that everything was going off according to the program. It was no secret. Several speakers referred to the outline they held in their hands. Laughter broke out when Percy McDonald appointed a committee of 50, hesitating only long enough to turn the proper page. . . . [8]

The efficiency of the organization, so pleasing and assuring to those

6 Crump to Bessie Crump, August 24, 1935. Telegram. Crump Papers.
7 Crump to Bessie Crump, September 13, 1935. Cablegram. Crump Papers.
8 *Press Scimitar,* May 13, 1936.

Memphians assembled to observe it, was not universally approved. Crump was becoming the subject of an increasing amount of journalistic preoccupation, and much of it was critical.

There were several reasons for his rise to a figure of national interest. He was, first, an intriguing subject for writers. His personality, always positive and colorful, became more flamboyant with age. His appearance took on new exotic tones. Few who wrote of him failed to include a seasoning of their viewpoint with a physical description, caricatured to whatever image they wanted to establish. One, written in this era by Fred Hixson of the Chattanooga *Times,* was vivid and accurate:

Crump is rather tall. . . . His hair is brilliantly white, thick and bushy at the sides and back, and thinning at the middle. His eyebrows, as heavy as mustachios, are shaded in brown from cream to cocoa, and the deep blue of his eyes is made almost indescernable by the covering of eyeglasses and by its setting in a face of deep, bright pink complexion. Often, as he talks, he raises his brows high in wide-eyed critical inspection of the topic under discussion; or, in reflection, purses his lips far outward. These mannerisms give him the appearance of a venerable pixie who is under no misapprehension as to the way the world wags and who will correct its shortcomings with no dilly-dallying on the way.

His . . . appearance was set off by toggery leaning to the dandified; a light gray suit with small checks, a blue shirt with white semi-stiff collar, and a red tie. [9]

It was frequently the liberal press that found Crump a subject of interest. It was not just that he was "the last of the old-fashioned bosses." It was that in outlook and philosophy there was fundamental difference between him and the liberal spirit of the times. Whether it was the consequence of his Old South heritage, or just his nature, he was an absolutist. There was right and wrong, truth and error, and one man's point of view was not always as good as another's. He was an absolutist in everything he did from the way he kept order in his dresser drawer to the way he organized the Memphis political machine. He did not ride in the stream of things, pushing for goals that were plausible in the existing situation. He set an objective and then reshaped the progression of affairs—over years if necessary—to support his objective.

Especially to the liberal press of the thirties and forties, he represented an unhealthy if not dangerous factor in American politics.

9 Chattanooga *Sunday Times Magazine,* October 24, 1937.

His principles were too rigid, too rooted in absolutist convictions reflective of a feudal mentality. His place in affairs was not expressive of a working cooperative democracy of people; he represented a feudal *noblesse oblige* operating in a twentieth-century city. Liberalism meant change, discarding outworn values for new—a continuing flux of men and ideas moving toward an autonomy and creativity for every person.

At its roots it was a philosophical difference that marked the separation between Crump and his honest critics. He was the formalist, rooted solidly in his Old South manners and values, while his critics moved in the stream of a pragmatic pluralism–liberalism.

By the thirties the most characteristic feature of the Crump phenomenon was its longevity and the totality of its hold on Memphis. Here, in the heart of America, was a political boss at a time when political totalitarianism in any form was becoming increasingly suspect by thoughtful citizens. Dictators abroad were providing the world with sickening evidence of their aberrant behavior. There were little "Fuehrers" in America, too, capitalizing on a lingering depression to put forth their programs of class and race hatred.

As for Crump, a new generation knew little of the "Redsnapper" of the Progressive era; he was looked at anew, and a new image began to form. The trouble was that the character of the times disposed some who were concerned with Crump to read into his character sinister overtones that did not exist. Some were apparently sincere; some were obviously trading in sensation, incapable of resisting the flourish of a large generalization, no matter how illogically derived.

He was a "boss," a particular kind of Southern boss, full of affectations, poses, and hypocrisy. His physical appearance suggested something uncommon: the white curling hair that was permitted to grow overly long; the ruddy delicate complexion; and the kind of secretive distance he kept between himself and the public by retreating beneath the heavy shade of his broad-brimmed Panama and his horn-rimmed glasses. With this facade of elegance he combined an old-fashioned courtliness: he bowed low and addressed the ladies of Memphis as "Miss Mary" or "Miss Sue" in the manner of the Old South.

From his physical appearance the image was expanded to include all the sins from which demagoguery profited. He was a megalomaniac, and there was an automatic assumption that he was venal. He beguiled the simple-minded with side-shows, picnics, boatrides, and hypocritical charity. Minority groups were used, but kept down. This was especially true of Memphis Negroes, who were universally "voted," but who got nothing but their chains for supporting the machine. Elections were grossly fraudulent—voting Negroes were imported from Arkansas; dead men whose names were taken from tombstones filled election rolls; and the inmates of asylums, hospitals, and the penal institutions all contributed to the Crump majorities. When opposition did develop, it was silenced through coercion, economic pressure, and, if necessary, by an occasional street beating to serve as an object lesson.

In time the stereotype became so fixed that it was scarcely possible to disassemble it, to reduce it to its basic ingredients for independent reconstruction. For there was always enough evidence to give the appearance of faithfulness to any aspect of the image. The problem was whether those parts really added up to a total picture that was assumed "proven."

The outlines of the image were begun by the Memphis *Press Scimitar* when Edward J. Meeman took over as editor in November, 1931. It was a star-crossed event for Crump. Until the end of his days, the gadfly in his life was edtior Meeman of the *Press Scimitar*.

Meeman began his newspaper career with the Evansville *Press* in his hometown of Evansville, Indiana. Working his way up to managing editor, he left Evansville in 1921 to help found the Knoxville *News* which he merged into the *News Sentinel* in 1926 as a member of the Scripps-Howard chain. In Knoxville Meeman showed himself in a characteristic pose—that of the crusading editor whose cause was smashing city machines and promoting the city manager form of government through the organization of "citizens movements."

From the first, the *Press Scimitar* bore Meeman's mark. He was the hard-driving editor who could deal in headlines and sensation; he was a man of ideals who believed in freedom, and government of and by the people. He was an ardent devotee of "Nature," and lamented that by building highways and clearing land man was laying "foul sores and . . . giant scars" on the beneficent face of nature. But in the end, nature would have its way, for a "befouled nest drops to earth and by the beneficent process of Nature, soon becomes clean . . . again." [10]

10 *Press Scimitar*, September 12, 1938.

Meeman did not explain how "Nature" could have its way and also maintain for man the benefits of a technical culture: his idealism would sometimes leap over problems that in the realm of practical affairs would require a solution.

The new editor had not been long in Memphis before he launched the *Press Scimitar* upon the major crusade of his journalistic career— that of bringing down the Crump organization. On June 21, 1932, the paper editorially attacked "Shelby's hydra-headed organization" and declared that "Mr. John Memphis" was being robbed by bureaucracy and extensive duplication of administration facilities. In November, a year after he had arrived in Memphis, Meeman addressed a group of women who were lunching at a downtown department store. The aim of the Crump machine, he said, was not "to make democracy work, but to work democracy." Streets had been straightened and bad spots removed. "We should be proud of all these, but—'For what is a man profited if he shall gain the whole world and lose his own soul?' " [11]

He admitted that Crump had done good things for Memphis. He recognized his "undoubted concern for efficient government, his usually quick appreciation of the needs of the people, his vision for the future of the city." But Crump was the head of a potent political machine, and on this point the editor made it plain where he stood: "May his machine be cast into the junk heap. . . ." [12]

Meeman would substitute for Crump's organization one of a different character. "Let us have . . . an organization of citizens and taxpayers which would be the basis of our political system and underlie everything else." The politicians would not organize the people; rather "a community committee" would draft unselfish public-spirited citizens for city and county councils. "Let the office seek the man. . . ." [13] A "Young Memphis Voter" wrote a letter to the *Press Scimitar:* "I . . . would like to start now doing my job of citizenship but I don't know just how to start." Meeman immediately provided a plan of action. "Start by associating yourself with other young men who have the same idea. . . . Let your organization be non-partisan and non-factional," nor should it be anti-administration, for it was "obvious that the majority of the people of this community like the public services they receive from the city . . . and take pride

11 *Ibid.,* November 5, 1932.   13 *Ibid.,* August 15, 1939.
12 *Ibid.,* June 9, 1939.

in them." But "when the servant says: 'This is the best food in the country, ask no questions, but eat it, or I'll ram it down your throat,' the master begins to wonder if he is as fortunate as he thought." [14]

In the years that followed, the *Press Scimitar* stood poised to pounce upon any indiscretion that Crump and the organization might commit. In its zeal to expose, it sometimes grasped at trifles. Murky and sinister doings lurked behind the facts. If an occasional fact happened to be wrong, a crisp acknowledgment would sometimes be made, although combined with added strictures on the organization.

Another newspaper that had much to do with creating the popular image of Crump that liberals held in the forties was the Nashville *Tennessean*. In 1937 the *Tennessean* was bought by a Texan named Silliman Evans who had recently been a fourth assistant to Postmaster James Farley. Evans was an open-handed gregarious person who liked politics and good whiskey. He was also a New Deal liberal, and like fellow editor Meeman, he was a man with a mission. For a newspaper, which according to one of its writers held positions that "in the great main [were] liberal and progressive," there was work to be done in Tennessee in a world increasingly menaced by totalitarianism.[15] The "work" was, of course, Crump, who in addition to possessing the dragon-like qualities against which a newspaper might crusade, had the well-known disposition to roar back after an attack, and this would be good for circulation.

In 1944 a writer for the *Tennessean,* Jennings Perry, reviewed the *Tennessean*'s holy crusade against Crump in a book called *Democracy Begins at Home.* In the book was a capsulized representation of the *Tennessean*'s image-making: Crump was drawn to conform to all the stereotypes that went with the totalitarian mentality. He was an "arrogant, vain, vindictive, self-righteous old man" who could "render political decisions binding upon the state and bearing upon the nation. . . ." [16] He could do this because Memphis had given itself to Crump "body and soul—and if its soul shriveled in the process, Memphis did not notice or care. . . ." Absurdly, "this despot—this semiliterate old fellow with the steamed-apricot face and amazing, hairy-eye-brows, was benevolent. For instance, he was tender toward

14 *Ibid.,* June 14, 1939.
15 Jennings Perry, *Democracy Begins at Home, The Tennessee Fight on the Poll Tax* (New York, 1944), 58–59.
16 *Ibid.,* 24.

birds, wrote letters to the paper about them and he had laws passed against cats." [17] Finally, Crump was identified with the poor white Southerner: when he had left home in 1892, he "rode his Mississippi mule to Holly Springs to take the train for Memphis." [18]

The theme of Crump as a breed of backwoods demagogue was too irresistible to forego. The St. Louis *Post-Dispatch* had Crump looking "like a faun from the more remote woods that has strayed by mischance into the marts of trade." When he strolled "into the lobby of the Hotel Peabody (and Mississippians thereabout—of whom Crump is one—are said to believe that when they die and go to heaven it will be just like the Peabody lobby), there is no bigger sight in Memphis." [19]

Periodicals presented the image to a national audience. One of the 1939 editions of the *Saturday Evening Post* contained an article that discussed his qualities as a "fuehrer." [20] *Time* contributed its distinctive characterization. When Crump drove along the streets of Memphis in a new Chrysler during the cotton carnival, sidewalk spectators "gawked as if they had spied the Mad Mullah of Tud, nose ring and all, cracking pecans on the Hope Diamond." Memphis had "amazingly clean streets, dozens of parks and playgrounds, fine schools, libraries, one of the finest zoos in the U.S., a fairgrounds, and E. H. Crump Stadium, good hospitals, good health. . . ." Yet there was something rotten at the core. "Memphis 'niggers' (40% of the population) were quiet: and whites, some of whom had Negro mistresses, could say contentedly: 'No trouble here; no hifalutin' ideas.'" Crump had given Memphis citizens almost everything "but the right to vote for a candidate of their own choosing—a luxury he firmly believes that few but the maladjusted miss anyhow." [21]

In his own copy of *Time,* Crump underlined statements that he regarded as untrue and defamatory. The one about whites having Negro mistresses was heavily underlined. He put brackets around the part about the people of Memphis not being able to vote their choice.[22] When the *Commercial Appeal* asked him for a reaction to

17   *Ibid.,* 33.   18   *Ibid.,* 36.
19   Rufus Terral, "An Intimate Study of Dixie Demagogues," St. Louis *Post-Dispatch,* June 9, 1946.
20   Jonathan Daniels, "He Suits Memphis," *Saturday Evening Post,* CCXI (June 10, 1939), 22–23.
21   *Time,* XLVII (May 27, 1946), 22.
22   Crump Papers.

the article, he replied mildly. "It seems that the Northern writers are imbued with the idea of belittling the South." They liked to picture Southerners "as a lot of ignoramuses and with nothing progressive." He thought the tide was against the North. Industry was moving South. "I'll live to see the day when there will be more cattle, hogs, poultry, soybeans, alfalfa and wheat and less cotton and more manufacturing," he predicted. "Saturday night payrolls build cities and weekly and monthly market crops and livestock sales will build up the country." [23]

Usually he was not so mild. He was very sensitive to press opinion, and when he felt he had been unjustly dealt with, he would send an editor a harshly worded letter of protest. His reaction to criticism was strongly personal, and he developed in time an implacable detestation of Meeman and Evans, the two editors whom he regarded as devoid of honor and principle. "Oh! how you do hate me," he wrote Meeman; "you live on a diet of hate and your hate is mirrored in the columns of your paper. . . . Your paper has written many lies about me—your hate for me is growing." [24]

His protests did little to change the evaluation that liberal America was making of him. All that was wrong with Memphis—the narrow-minded complacency of some of its citizens, with their suspicion of any new idea and their insensitivity to injustice—all was attributed to Crump.

He was never able to understand the temper of his critics. "Boss? Who said boss?" he asked a Washington newspaper reporter. "I am no boss. I am no dictator. I am just an unassuming good citizen, working with and for the people." [25] He never mentioned it publicly, but he was probably irritated by some of the characterizations of himself as an uninformed rural bumpkin. After he finished his work at night, he read, and he awakened early in the morning to read. He read history, and always the newspapers—the Memphis papers, the Nashville and Chattanooga papers, the Chicago *Tribune* and the New York *Times*. The *Times* was his favorite paper, and in it he followed with much admiration the career of Turner Catledge, who had once been a reporter for the *Commercial Appeal*. He read *Harper's,* and the *Atlantic Monthly*. In the last ten years of his life he took the

23 *Commercial Appeal,* May 24, 1946.
24 Crump to Edward J. Meeman, November 10, 1946. Crump Papers.
25 Washington *Times Herald,* April 22, 1946.

leading Negro newspapers and *Ebony* so as to keep abreast of Negro thinking. He was, in fact, so concerned with "improving himself" with his reading that he refused to read fiction, although he read *David Harum* several times. He was "familiar with anything you mentioned," exclaimed Mason Jones. "And memory—My God! he remembered everything." [26]

When Meeman attacked him because he had a political organization, he could see no sense in it at all. "What of it?" asked *The Tattler,* a Crump paper that was published briefly in Memphis in the late twenties. "Every successful enterprise has its boss, and every organization that functions successfully has its machine." [27] Organization was at the core of Crump's soul. He had known Memphis in the days when it was more chaos than order, and he knew what a great task of planning and organization it had been to bring even a semblance of order to the city.

Neither could he understand the attitude of the press that would have only those elections that were closely contested as exemplifying democracy at its vital best. He felt something closely personal between himself and the electorate. "Some people have wondered how we have been successful in politics in Memphis and Shelby County for all these many years," he once said. "I'll tell them in a few words. It is simple. We have been fair with the honest poor and the honest rich and they know it." [28]

Walter Chandler, one of the most perceptive of the organization stalwarts, attributed Crump's success to a "great capacity for learning what people wanted." He had "native ability and indefatiguability," Chandler said. Further, he was absolutely honest, even avoiding "the appearance of evil." [29]

But to say that his phenomenal success was the result of giving the people good streets, beautiful parks, and a low tax rate omitted the person of Crump. The "people" were made of many interest groups, and it was one of his gifts as a politician to make each group recognize that because of him its vital interest was served. As a

26 Interview with Mason Jones, July 11, 1957.
27 *The Tattler* (Memphis), June 15, 1929. *The Tattler* was organized as an administration newspaper to counteract the anti-Crump position of Luke Lea's *Commercial Appeal*. John D. Martin was one of the organizers, and Crump was a stockholder.
28 Nashville *Tennessean,* May 24, 1936.
29 Interview with Walter Chandler, July 10, 1957.

consequence, political factionalism rising from struggling group interests was minimized.

Further, he kept himself above an identification with any particular group. He shunned special attachments, even in his private life. He "never did permit anyone to get too intimate with him," related Clara Muller. "He was simple in his tastes and associates. People who had money did not impress him at all. When he sat in his side yard at night and talked with people he did not like 'chit-chat.' He liked intelligent, informing conversation." [30] A Memphis labor leader made the same point. "Crump had no real confidants. Various people were accepted as friends, but there was always a line." [31]

He identified himself with no particular group, yet most groups thought of him as their special friend—Baptists, Jews, Catholics, Irish, Italians, and Negroes—all felt that there was a special understanding between Crump and themselves that united their interests on a plane higher than political expediency. Within the circle of his friends there was usually a representative of one of these groups, serving as a channel of communication with them. For years he maintained an association with a Baptist minister, the Reverend D. A. Ellis. Ellis, like most of the men whom Crump admired, was a simple sincere man with little interest in politics. Through Ellis, Crump sometimes helped the Baptists, and in time they came to regard him with much favor, although some thought he was too partial to Negroes, and most thought he was wrong on the liquor issue.

Ellis recalled one instance particularly in which Crump had interceded for the Baptists. A small congregation had just bought some land on which to erect a church, but after the sale it was discovered that twenty years of back taxes were owed on it, and the pastor could not see where the money was coming from. The Reverend Ellis took the pastor to Crump's office, where the sad story was recited. The pastor had hardly concluded before Crump picked up the telephone and called the mayor's office. "Is the city of Memphis so hard up that it has to assess this struggling and worthy church for a bill that should have been paid by the previous owner?" he asked.[32] Of course, the city was not.

The Reverend Ellis was proud of his friendship with Crump, and

30 Interview with Clara Muller, January 10, 1958.
31 Interview with John R. Gorman, September 22, 1957.
32 Interview with the Reverend D. A. Ellis, August 7, 1957.

sometimes he would take a delegation of Baptist ministers to Crump's office to meet him. Crump was always very hospitable and very interested in what they had to say. It was the minister's feeling that Crump privately leaned toward the Baptist point of view.

Yet Catholics felt that Crump looked with interest and favor on their faith. He had made a strong attack on religious bigotry in the 1928 Presidential election, and he donated to Catholic charitable institutions in Memphis. He admired the dedicated and sacrificial character of the lives of some of the priests and nuns he knew, and he revered Catholic religious practices. Writing to the Sisters of the Good Shepherd who maintained a home in Memphis for delinquent girls, he thanked them for a Sacred Heart badge. He had worn a similar one "continuously since you presented it to me some four or five years ago; in fact, it has about worn out from constant wear, hence the new one is doubly appreciated." [33] He took the badge to the grave with him. One of the city's better known priests, with whom Crump maintained a friendly association, stated that he had blessed Crump "on many occasions." [34]

His favorable disposition toward the Catholic church earned him some private criticism, but he got much more for his openly pro-Jewish point of view. He admired the Jews; their history attracted him because of their fierce struggle to survive in the face of harsh inequities. He had a kind of intellectual's curiosity about their faith and their role in the plan of Providence. Sometimes late at night a Jewish member of the organization would be awakened by a phone call from Crump, wanting to know something about their belief.

When Hitler's campaign against the Jews began to crescendo, Crump denounced it. "If we value good citizenry—and we should—the Jew need not ask to be defended as a Jew. But, when the Jew is persecuted, driven from his home, denied a living, and his property confiscated, there is no longer any safety for freedom or tolerance among the members of any race. In our days there should be no Jews, and no Gentiles, but freedom and equal rights for all. . . ." [35]

Crump's opposition to anti-Semitism, even in its seemingly innocuous forms, was not shared by all members of the organization. Some, among lesser ones, thought there had been too much of one

33 Crump to the Sisters of the Good Shepherd, May 24, 1917.
34 Interview with the Monsignor M. F. Kearney, January 10, 1958.
35 Scrapbook news clipping.

Will Gerber in the affairs of the organization, and they could not understand why Crump insisted on placing Gerber in a high position on the council seat. In the forties "Willie" Gerber became the principal object of abuse from all the anti-Crump sentiment in the state. He was "Gerber the Jew," who finely sifted the dirt to winnow out the slightest detail that could be used against Crump's enemies. He fought for the organization in the factional struggles of state politics with a fierceness that only Crump could equal. All thought Gerber was shrewd; some thought him boorish. One observer of the Memphis political scene commented that Gerber could "act polished and high-classed or could use vile street language." [36]

Gerber's parents, Russian Jews, arrived in Memphis in 1906 when young Will was six years old. He went to the old vocational school on Poplar Avenue, and for eight years he delivered the *Commercial Appeal* in the morning and sold afternoon papers on the streets in the evening. After service in the Army during World War I, he married and soon began to study law in the evenings. He passed the state bar examination in 1923 and entered the law firm of McLain and Bejach, a partnership of two high-ranking organization men.

Gerber was recommended to Crump as a young man who had "come up in the world," a type that Crump liked. He held public office for the first time in 1925, when he was appointed an assistant attorney general under Tyler McLain. He became the assistant city attorney under Walter Chandler in 1934, and the following year, when Chandler went to Congress, he became city attorney. In 1940 Governor Prentice Cooper appointed him Shelby County attorney general.

As a prosecutor, Gerber had a "bullying, boring way of prosecuting a case. He would roar and then whisper—crescendo and diminuendo." [37] Controversial as he was, he always had the unflagging support of Crump. Years later the dying Watkins Overton publicly paid tribute to him. In all the years of his public service, "no one ever dared to question the integrity of Will Gerber. There was no back door to the attorney general's office, and many resented him because as attorney general he steadfastly fought the forces of

36 Interview with Clark Porteous, August 13, 1957.
37 *Ibid.*

crime and evil without fear or favor." [38] His impeccability as a prosecutor was underwritten by Crump. Gerber himself testified, "Mr. Crump at no time ever asked me to do anything one way or another on any controversy in the courts." [39]

Politically, Gerber served a useful purpose. He "brought the Main Street Jews with their financial support into the fold," said one Memphian who was well versed in the Memphis political situation.[40]

The core of the organization's voting strength, it was frequently said, was the city's several thousand employees and their friends and relatives.[41] Local rumor had it that Crump kept a file on all of them and knew how each voted. This charge, like some others, was one of the fictions that was embroidered around him. Actually, there was no cause to have a poll watcher peer over the shoulder of a voting employee or to mark a ballot so its user could be later identified. As in most groups where organizational rapport was emphasized, those who were critical of the organization were found out and soon felt the censure of their superiors. In one publicized incident, Percy McDonald, successful corporation lawyer and county school superintendent, removed a school principal for anti-organization activity—or so the newspapers charged. McDonald himself would say no more than that he removed the principal because he thought "the situation required it." [42]

Through the years the *Press Scimitar* was critical of the sometimes intense political activity of city workers, and it did not hesitate to make broad accusations of coercion from the top. With coercion, it pointed out, there was fear and toadyism. Loyalty to Crump was affected for the sake of preferment.

In an organization based on the principle of one-man leadership there could not help but be included among its numbers many who would find it convenient to take a short cut to security by anticipating Crump's wishes on every point. Such men were timeservers, and the role of sycophant came easily to them. Yet the principal office holders associated with the organization were men of intelligence and ability—Overton, Chandler, Bejach, Joyner—and they

38   *Commercial Appeal,* August 17, 1958.
39   Interview with Will Gerber, July 30, 1957.
40   Interview with John R. Gorman, September 22, 1957.
41   Gerald Capers, "Memphis, Satrapy of a Benevolent Despot," in *Our Fair City,* ed. Robert S. Allen (New York, 1947), 224.
42   Interview with Percy McDonald, July 30, 1957.

were not the type to work well on a tight rein. Within broad lines they were free agents—up to the point of ultimate authority. There were times when some of these men must have felt an inner rebellion at the loss of final free choice, but they managed for the most part to submerge resentment, since they knew it would be pointless to kick at the pricks.

Yet in talking with organization men of all levels five years after Crump's death, not one showed any bitterness toward Crump. Their recollection of him was touched with respect and real affection. There were positive reasons why this was true. He was able to elicit loyalty to an unusual degree because all knew that short of a betrayal of trust he was absolutely loyal to them. Most of the men who worked with Crump over the years eventually obtained positions of modest affluence in the community. Crump saw to it that some of the high-paying patronage jobs came their way. Sometimes there was a more personal basis for the deep loyalty to Crump that his associates had. One person, a minor figure in the organization, had the problem of chronic alcoholism. Time and again he fell from grace, and each time Crump helped him to his feet and encouraged him to try again to defeat the problem. Eventually he did.

For most city workers Crump came to represent a kind of father, an image that was reinforced by stories of his having interceded in the affairs of this or that city employee to resolve some personal problem. This, combined with the efficiency of the city government, produced loyalty and an *esprit de corps* that made city workers politically active.

From the time he first entered politics, Crump had the support of the local business community. Businessmen believed in their own way of life as an ideal for political management—no-nonsense efficiency. Crump, preeminently successful in business, was their man. He had brought Memphis an efficient administration of city services, low insurance rates, and the development of a climate of opportunity for growth. In time it came to be almost the first rule of sound business procedure to support the organization. It was even more: it was a mark of status signifying that a businessman's values were in order. Liberal journalists, however, noted how solidly Memphis businessmen stood behind Crump and criticized them for being insensitive to basic human values and interested only in having "the trains run on time."

By the thirties large industry had come to represent a significant portion of the economic activity of Memphis, with Ford and Firestone operating large plants in the city. In view of Crump's attacks on the "mighty corporate interests" it might be supposed that industrial management would have reservations about supporting the local political organization. Yet large industry in Memphis supported Crump with almost total dedication. No other interest group in the electorate put out more effort to get votes for the organization. The employees at Firestone and Ford had considerable pressure put on them to vote, and some industries used a check-off system to insure the registration of their employees. Frequently company transportation was furnished to take employees to the polls.

Why was industry so enthusiastic for Crump? Because he stood for what industry wanted: cheap power, cheap transportation rates, and a settled political climate in which to operate. There was also Crump's opposition to the CIO. Lucy Randolph Mason in her "personal story of the CIO in the South" states that "Mr. Crump . . . made an agreement with the AF of L that if it would lay off organizing any large plants—he wanted to attract large industries to Memphis and desired to assure them that they would not be bothered by union efforts to organize their employees—he would protect the AF of L in its promotion of craft unions." [43] This assertion is obviously true. Crump had cordial and close relations with local labor unions, and he fought the CIO from the time it entered Memphis in the thirties until he saw, as he did after the Second World War, that it was a permanent fixture in the Memphis labor scene.

Memphis labor, white and black, was made up overwhelmingly of people who were close to the manners and traditions of the rural South. Except for a few CIO organizers, members of labor saw nothing contradictory in the fact that they, as well as management, supported Crump. In the rural South there had been no great chasm between the aristocracy and yeomanry. Lines of communication were open between them, and they shared a common point of view on the issues of the society in which they lived. In the conduct of important affairs the yeomanry accepted without question planter leadership, never doubting that their interests would be better served by this class than if they themselves were in charge of affairs.

43 Lucy Randolph Mason, *To Win These Rights, A Personal Story of the CIO in the South* (New York, 1952), 106–07.

Crump carried this tradition into the city and kept it alive as long as the Memphis population continued to be swelled with rural immigrants. They looked upon him as their patron and protector. He possessed an easy affability that enabled him to speak their language—perhaps to discourse upon their ailments and to suggest valued remedies his mother had used when he was a boy. He knew their names and in many instances an amazing amount of their personal history. As they repeated among themselves the numerous stories that circulated about Crump's timely intervention in the affairs of one of their number to set aright some fearful problem, they developed an unshakable faith in "Mr. Crump," and to fail to vote his ticket on election day was a betrayal of a trust.

In his role as patron Crump would sometimes have a "possum" hunt, barbecue, or some other festive event, and very often he would invite representatives of the humbler segments of society to attend. There were also his boatrides for the shut-ins, theater parties for orphans, and later the benefit football game for the blind, all of which contributed to the image of Crump as a great benefactor.

One of the largest Crump parties took place in September, 1935, when the whole populace was invited to a "Crump Day at the Fair." Children were given free rides on all the midway devices; there was dancing, old-fashioned community singing, boxing, wrestling, and track contests to entertain the older folks. When the fairground gates were opened at 3:30 on September 23, Crump was there in front of the band on the midway, wearing a brown plaid coat, brown and white striped pants, white shoes, and a bronze dahlia the size of a saucer. As the people entered, he bowed and smiled while organization personnel passed out paper hats with the label: "Mr. Crump's Party." Then, with Mrs. Crump and his three sons and their wives marching with him, he twirled his cane and led the band up and down the midway. It was estimated that over fifty thousand people attended the event.

The *Press Scimitar* viewed the affair with suspicion. It smacked too much of the Roman carnival, of a Nazi sports rally. Several months later the paper ran a story which said that Memphis firemen had each been assessed from $7.50 to $15.50, depending on their rank, to pay for the outing. In a letter to Meeman, personally delivered by an aide, Crump declared that the statement was a "deliberate lie," and that "not one penny of the firemen's money was used." He explained the source of the money. "Merchants over the city contributed prizes and the actual expense for the concessions was less than Fifteen Hundred Dollars, which was made up by the city and County organizations. All entertainers gave their services free except the bands."

"I realize," Crump continued, "you preferred to involve me if possible for you do not like a bone in my body and came here from Knoxville with the very great desire to try and smear me, but you have failed. . . . Your paper is trying hard to involve me. Your statement yesterday was a deliberate lie and if you have the honesty of a common pick-pocket or the manhood of the lowest coward you will print this letter." [44]

The *Press Scimitar* printed the letter and rejoined forthwith: "The news story to which Mr. Crump objects was handled in the regular routine" by a reporter "who has the name and address of the fireman in uniform who gave . . . the information." The editor added a thought: "When civil service is restored to the fire department it is hoped firemen can complain of conditions without saying: 'If you use my name I lose my job.'" Several days later the city firemen signed a statement denying "emphatically" that "we were ever requested to or made any contribution to the Crump Festival at the Fairgrounds. . . ." [45]

The spectacle that more than anything else caused the outside liberal to view Memphis politics with concern was that of Negroes voting the Crump ticket on election day. Negroes did not vote in Memphis; the charge was that Crump "voted" them. Thousands of them, with sheeplike credulity, were herded to the polls, handed marked ballots and then rewarded with policies that underwrote all of the vicious principles of a rigid racist doctrine. [46] To see Negroes voting was enough to underline the truth of this view. At the close of the day's work, lines of them stood outside polling places, to a man waiting to cast their vote for Crump's candidates.

Why did they do it? Crump was a racist, for he held to the point of view in which he had been reared—that the Negro was a being set apart. But the Negro of the South has at times been grateful for a little, and even though Crump held the traditional view, it was

44 *Press Scimitar,* February 7, 1936.
45 *Ibid.,* February 10, 1946.
46 Charles W. Van Devander, *The Big Bosses* (New York, 1944), 172.

certainly more advanced than that of a great majority of the city's inhabitants. Over his whole career he worked to improve the basic condition of Negro life in Memphis. In the latter years of his life one finds pages of memoranda of things he wanted done for the Negro community. Housing, health, and education were his main areas of concern. In a memorandum, made sometime in the late forties, there are these notes: "New School south of Parkway . . . Negro Sanitary officers . . . Park and Swimming Pool in rear of Lauderdale St. School . . . Negro Doctors and Negro nurses . . . Another Slum Clearance." [47]

He opposed the practice, so common to the whites, of addressing the Negro in demeaning and opprobrious terms. He never used the word "nigger," and he did not permit his sons to use it. "Father never let us use any term that would be offensive to the dignity of a person," said E. H. Crump, Jr.[48]

Neither did he sanction police brutality where Negroes were involved. It was a common enough crime—almost inevitable with the prevailing racist doctrine and the high value that sadistic men attached to the use of force against Negroes. There was enough of it in Memphis, and in aggravated cases Crump would go over the head of the police and commissioner to denounce it. In 1938 a policeman killed a Negro boy on the supposition that he was a prowler, and Chief Will Lee, after a perfunctory investigation, whitewashed the policeman. Crump dumbfounded Lee and the department by publicly denouncing the act. He had, he said, made a personal investigation of the matter and had come to the conclusion that the officer was to blame. "This boy was not a late prowler, because the affair occurred around 10 o'clock. He was not a pickpocket; he was not a burgler and he was certainly not a desperate criminal. The police had not been called. He was up on the tracks in plain view of everyone, and there is no doubt in the world he could have been easily arrested without being killed or injured. . . . This isn't the first time that I have called the officials' attention to matters of this kind." [49]

Possibly there was some truth in the contention of the opposition that Crump's statement had been made for political reasons,[50] but

47 Memorandum. Crump Papers.
48 Interview with E. H. Crump, Jr., April 10, 1962.
49 *Press Scimitar*, August 16, 1948.
50 *Ibid.*, August 11, 1938.

the political effect was probably incidental to his primary concern with the inhumanity of the act. He had spoken out against police brutality before.

As with other groups, Crump established contact with the Negro population by taking into his counsel one of its respected members, Blair T. Hunt, principal of Memphis' largest Negro high school. Hunt was an intelligent and kindly man, whose conservative leadership was accepted by Negroes. He had a high opinion of Crump. "He was a great benefactor to the Negro race," Hunt said. "I may be prejudiced—I am—I ought to be." He thought that Crump had become increasingly misunderstood in the latter years of his life. Crump had lived the best of his life in that era "when a man knew what was what," Hunt concluded.[51]

By the end of Crump's life it was apparent what the years of his political leadership had accomplished for Negroes. Especially in health and housing, advances had been made that represented a significant step forward.

Crump saw to it that some of those whom he considered the most worthy Negroes of Memphis were memorialized. "Fuller Park" was named for the Reverend T. O. Fuller, a Negro humanitarian who worked with underprivileged Negro boys. "Foote Homes," a housing development, was named for a Negro attorney, Will Foote. "I knew him when he was a young boy riding the Beale and Main line," reminisced Crump. "I lived on Polk Street and he lived in the neighborhood west of Walnut. He was afterwards a mail carrier, then he became a lawyer—always a good boy and a good man." [52]

On the bluff overlooking the Mississippi there is a tall marble shaft commemorating the valorous action of Tom Lee, a Memphis Negro who used his rowboat to rescue thirty-one people from the river when a steamer capsized in 1925. Crump suggested the monument and organized a committee to raise funds for it. After the disaster, he occasionally ran into Lee: "always admired him—unassuming and very polite." [53]

The Negroes to whom Crump extended civic recognition were conspicuous also because they moved wholly within the bounds of Southern racial traditionalism—"Uncle Toms," some might call them.

51   Interview with Blair T. Hunt, August 27, 1957.
52   *Commercial Appeal*, April 3, 1952.
53   *Ibid.*

Crump recognized them out of some feudal sense of *noblesse oblige,* much as a planter might have memorialized a beloved slave. Until World War II there was an almost universal response by Memphis Negroes to his benevolence, but after the war, with equalitarian ideas abroad in the world, an increasing number came to prefer equal rights to *noblesse oblige.*

In the decade of the thirties and through World War II the great majority of the city's inhabitants, white and black, felt no restiveness under Crump's leadership. A columnist for the Atlanta *Journal,* after visiting Memphis in the fall of 1945, reported that he doubted "if there has ever been a city boss who is held in such genuine affection by all classes of a city's population. The citizens are apparently absolutely contented with . . . [Crump's] benevolent despotism." [54]

The "benevolent despotism" that the journalists liked to roll off their pens was, in substance, organization. Crump often declared that there was nothing mysterious about his political success. He attributed 95 per cent of it to organization. He expressed this belief in a letter to Governor McAlister, which he wrote on the eve of the 1934 election campaign. It was marked "Personal," and addressed to "My dear Hill":

We are in for another tough fight, therefore please put every man upon whom you have a call in Tennessee on the "MUST" list; that is, *they must help you actively.*

Please get off somewhere with two or three who are able to assist you and figure on your ORGANIZATION in every county.

Senator McKellar's and Senator Bachman's appointees in every county and their relatives of course, ought to be merged (and quickly) with such ORGANIZATION as you might have.

Working and thinking separately simply means no ORGANIZATION.

A good ORGANIZATION should know how every man and woman in the country stands. Please get that to them, for it is so very necessary.

Senator Bachman hasn't the slightest conception of ORGANIZATION.

Chattanooga has never gotton out a vote because there is no compact hard hitting ORGANIZATION.

If you drive hard, others will hit the same stride. If you hesitate in forcing an ORGANIZATION those down the line will also hesitate.

If your friends—those working for the State and those working for the Government, friendly to Senators McKellar and Bachman,—would paste something like the following on their windshields, and live up to it, it would be most helpful:

54 Atlanta *Journal,* January 6, 1946.

Don't sit down in the meadow and wait for the cow to back up and be milked—GO AFTER THE COW.

Any ORGANIZATION can be handicapped by one single man who places himself out of harmony with it.

No one is any bigger than the terms they use in thinking. Let's holler it loud and long to all of our friends throughout the State—

"We want ORGANIZATION!"

We want an army of vote marchers, men and women, to be in thorough training for the Parade Day, August 2nd. [55]

There was, to be sure, ORGANIZATION in Shelby County. "Crump was the general, Watkins Overton, Tyler McLain and E. W. Hale were the corps commanders, and Frank Rice was the field marshall," said Lois Bejach.[56] It was like a general staff meeting when the group assembled to plan an attack. "Take this down, Mrs. Humphreys," Crump would say, getting the discussion started. Then somebody would say something—and somebody else—until the idea came forth that he wanted. His eyes would flash and his eyebrows go up and down. "Now, that's a good thought. Take it Mrs. Humphreys." To witness Crump working with lieutenants "was an experience," an observer said. "He was dynamic." [57]

It was he who decided what ideas were valuable. Whatever his view of himself as one "who worked with the people," he was boss in everything from directing overall procedure down to the manner in which he conducted his conversation. In a controversy, oral or written, he was not sidetracked from attack by a lengthy consideration of his opponent's argument. He used his energy in pressing his own position. When he had said what he thought was necessary to cover the subject, he changed it. "The way to get along with Mr. Crump was never to bring up a subject after he had closed it," commented one of his friends.[58]

No one around him could grasp the details of a conception so quickly as Crump. Most of the men in the organization readily admitted this. Will Gerber stated that Crump seldom had to summon anyone to his office for instructions. "They sought his advice," said Gerber. They knew further that to intrude an extraneous or con-tradictory plan of their own onto one of his would result in absolute

55 Crump to McAlister, June 11, 1934. Crump Papers.
56 Interview with Lois Bejach, September 5, 1957.
57 Interview with Harry Woodbury, October 29, 1957.
58 Interview with O. H. Miller, December 9, 1957.

unyielding opposition. Prudent men knew better than to challenge him.

The recognition of Crump's ability for organization produced organizational efficiency. So did discipline. Discipline came from knowing what was what. It came from the "line" Crump drew. He was "Mr. Crump" to all—"Ed" to none. It came from knowing the rules. "Crump never deceived or lied to anyone," wrote Marvin Pope.[59] The rules were clear and anyone acquainted with Memphis politics knew what they were: loyalty, absolute honesty, and a satisfactory performance of one's duties. The Nashville *Banner* summed it up: "He will stick to a political friend to the bitter end," or "until that friend violates the Crump high code of ethics. When and if that infraction takes place, the infractor is ruthlessly dropped into the discard." [60]

By the thirties there were few discards. The rules were known. Muckraking journalism found little to feed on. There was no need for anything to be brought to light from the outside. If some infraction of the rules did occur, the first the public knew of it was when someone was dropped from the organization.

There were repressive aspects in this kind of discipline. Some thought it almost uncanny how Crump could know in such detail the private and even secret history of so many people. Once when he and a companion were taking an automobile trip to New Orleans, he passed the time by relating a complete history of all the prominent families of Memphis. When they reached their destination, the companion remarked, "Mr. Crump, you scare me. If you know all of this about these people, you might start dredging up my background." [61]

"Don't worry, don't worry," said Crump. "I know it already." The companion, a prominent Memphis industrialist, said that he had once given Crump a job applicant's file to have copied.

A veteran Memphis newsman, Malcolm Adams, related another story that illustrates how closely Crump kept in touch with what was going on. The event had occurred in the early thirties when Adams had worked on the *Labor Review,* a paper that served the Memphis American Federation of Labor unions. "Mr. Crump always managed

59 Secretaries' notes.
60 Nashville *Banner,* May 22, 1936.
61 Interview with O. H. Miller. December 8, 1957.

to keep the AFL men politically happy," Adams said, but on this occasion one of the leaders "kicked the traces which kept him 'inside' Mr. Crump's organization." He began to campaign against Crump's choice for governor. He dropped by Adams' office one day to get some help on a speech he was going to make. "I did what I could," Adams said. "As far as I know, no one saw my union friend enter or leave. His talk went over big. The daily newspapers gave much space to his attack on the 'red-snapper.' " A few days later Adams got a call from Crump. "Malcolm," he said, "I'm surprised about those red-snapper remarks. . . . Don't you know I'm snowy white-haired?" asked Crump with a laugh.[62]

Finally, there was Crump's "red book," where names of those who had been assigned a final excommunication were placed: Galen Tate; later, his brother Mike; Frank Fentress, the judge who had ruled in favor of his ouster; and Lovick Miles, the lawyer who in later years conducted his eccentric crusade against Crump and publicly reopened the old ouster wound. There was no softness in him toward the excommunicated. Walter Chandler stated that he would sometimes say to Crump, "Wouldn't it be better to forget this incident?" and Crump would reply, "I despise him; I despise him." He was "absolutely implacable," Chandler said.[63]

It was discipline that kept the organization taut from the Shelby delegation to the state legislature in Nashville down to the captains of remote county precincts. Writing in the Chattanooga *Times*, Fred Hixson stated that he had closely observed the state legislature for over a decade "and no delegation from any section . . . is better qualified . . . than the men the Crump organization sends to Nashville. All are highclass men." Hixson described the working procedure of the delegation. "Nearly everyday the assembly is in session the delegation holds a conference to discuss legislation. All bills introduced are fully digested at these conferences and if there are members who don't understand them there is always someone present who can give a full explanation." If there was a division of sentiment among the members, the matter was worked out in a delegation conference. Therefore, "Shelby County acts in unison on practically all matters." [64]

Ordinarily, the broad lines of organization policies were so well

---

62 *Commercial Appeal*, November 17, 1954.
63 Interview with Walter Chandler, July 10, 1957.
64 Chattanooga *Times*, June 27, 1934.

known by Shelby legislators that there was little referral of issues to Crump. When an important matter arose which called for a policy definition or the mapping of strategy, Frank Rice was the coordinator. Occasionally, however, the delegation would run afoul of some established principle, and when it did, it would hear about it. In February, 1937, it fell flat on its face when it introduced a bill exempting the Memphis Street Railway Company from a state gross receipts tax that would have taken around $70,000 a year from the state.

"What do you think about the bill affecting the Memphis Street Railway Company's taxes, Mr. Crump?" asked a reporter when he found Crump standing on the corner of Second and Adams. "Do you want a statement?" asked Crump. "Say that I was astounded to read in the papers that Shelby County had introduced the bill. I most certainly disapprove of the Shelby delegation sponsoring a bill for the street car company—Wall Street crowd. Roane Waring [president of the company] is a nice gentleman and a good citizen, but the street car company is owned by the electric company, a tremendous Wall Street outfit—cold-blooded institution." [65] It was a "new thought and a new day for the Shelby delegation to introduce a bill for the electric light and street car company." [66] The Shelby group was stunned to silence by Crump's attack. Later a member indicated that an "understanding" had been reached and that the measure would not be heard of again.[67]

In his later life Crump wrote a memorandum for a future biographer that covered the subject of organization. It was compressed into two brief paragraphs:

In every campaign Crump's work was to get up the various committees, including finance, publicity, ward organizations, platform, speaking, newspaper advertising, etc.

The organization in each ward looked after its own vote; that is, tried to get everyone to register, and then get them to pay poll taxes. A list was made out by the ward organization of those who could not pay their own poll taxes and this list was furnished to general headquarters, where such poll taxes were paid. [68]

The memorandum reveals nothing extraordinary, but Crump stated

65 *Press Scimitar,* March 3, 1937.
66 *Commercial Appeal,* March 3, 1937.
67 *Ibid.*
68 Memorandum. Crump Papers.

many times that there was nothing extraordinary to reveal. It was all a matter of close organization, especially at the ward level. Each ward chairman possessed a list of names of all persons eligible to vote. Workers made house-to-house calls urging residents to register, pay their poll taxes, and vote. "We teach people how to vote and we urge them to vote," Crump told a Chattanooga newspaperman. "Most people don't know anything at all about how to vote. You'd be surprised how little they do know. They don't know the candidates they want to vote for, and they don't know where to mark the ballot." [69]

This awareness of lack of voter perception and interest was reflected in the realism with which the organization dealt with the electorate. It was almost as if the voter were taken by the hand and led to the polls, where a little attention and flattery from organization workers induced him to vote the organization ticket. The disposition of so many voters to be led galled those of the Memphis electorate who would have their elections cast in a more noble framework in which democratic man supposedly fashioned his destiny through the unfettered use of his own pure reason.

Organization pressure to get poll taxes paid was at times considerable. One Memphian recalled a time in the thirties when he had applied for a job on the police force. Ward leaders promised their support if he would first sell a certain number of poll taxes. In time he sold them and got his job. When this incident was recounted to an organization veteran, he acknowledged the practice, explaining that the payment of poll tax was required by state law and that Memphis political leaders were doing no more than helping citizens to conform to the law. [70]

Some poll taxes, as Crump stated, were paid at headquarters. Paying the poll tax of a well-disposed voter was an ancient practice in Memphis. Long before Crump, the gambling and vice interests took care of their clients, and thus armed with their ballots they could fend off any reform-bent political aspirant. Inasmuch as a red light district was tolerated in Memphis through the thirties, there was a lingering suspicion among many that the old practice still obtained to the benefit of the organization. In 1938 the St. Louis *Post-Dispatch* sent

69   Chattanooga *Sunday Times Magazine,* October 24, 1937.
70   Interview with Abe D. Waldauer, April 10, 1962.

an investigator to Memphis to find out about organization financing. The investigator reported that Crump "flatly denied" that commercialized vice financed any part of the organization. There was no "system of collection," although Crump said that he could not vouch for the honesty of individual policemen. Bootlegging admittedly existed because "prohibition's a joke like it always was."

Crump told the investigator that political funds were gathered by a finance committee which "received contributions from business houses and individuals." City employees who made "adequate salaries" were "encouraged" to contribute to campaign funds. He described the practice as a "voluntary assessment system" that was "common to most political organizations." [71]

What Crump said, others close to him verified. Tom Phillips, always painstakingly exact, declared that there was no shakedown of the vice interests. The money came from business groups.[72] When Crump ordered the final dissolution of the Memphis red light district the bitterest complaint the ladies could make was that they had just purchased their poll tax receipts and had "voted faithfully for Shelby County political candidates." All denied ever having paid graft.[73]

Crump covered the subject of his personal role in organizational finance with several short sentences which he wrote for his biographer. "Never handled a dollar in any campaign in my life. . . . Never signed a pardon or accepted a pass of any kind or character whatsoever. . . . Never accepted a present from anyone that had any monetary value. Always encouraged that in others. . . . Nothing in Memphis for any official to graft on in the way of vices. . . . After all, every public official should watch his step—be careful how he lives, for he may be the only Bible that some one will read." [74]

The drive for organizational efficiency made for a tautness that Crump's opponents called ruthlessness. Crump's desire to achieve a high level of unanimity among the people of Memphis on election day tended to make his lieutenants deal severely with those holders of public jobs who were not in harmony with the grand design. A person who did not go with the grain of things was either fired or harrassed

---

71 Spencer R. McCulloch, St. Louis *Post-Dispatch* Magazine Section, July 4, 1938.
72 Interview with Thomas Phillips, April 11, 1962.
73 *Press Scimitar*, April 27, 1940.
74 Memorandum. Crump Papers.

out of the picture. In the early days it had been Judge Jacob Galloway, the ousted chairman of the park commission; Galen and Mike Tate; police chief Will Hayes; and Tom Ashcroft, the mayor. In time there was left a train of grievously wounded sensibilities, representing a company of outcasts, and always in the background of Memphis politics was the chorus of their wailing.

In the thirties and forties the charges against Crump of political blackguardism reached a sympathetic ear in some of the Tennessee newspapers, and the years just prior to World War II produced the classic examples of Crump's supposed wickedness: the CIO beatings, the Charlie Brown affair, and the expulsion from Memphis of a Negro druggist.

In 1937 the Crump-constructed equilibrium in the labor movement was threatened by an invasion from the CIO. For over a decade Crump had worked to bring organized labor within the organization, and he had been successful. A labor representative customarily sat with the Shelby delegation in the state legislature, and the organization sometimes sided with the workers against management in a labor dispute. Once, during a strike of operators against the Memphis Street Railway Company, Crump had the police cooperating with the strikers against the use of strikebreakers. When the American Federation of Labor began to organize the Plough pharmaceutical company, police actually aided strikers by sometimes arresting strikebreakers for breaching the peace.[75]

The CIO, however, represented a radical doctrine that Crump would have none of, and when word came out that Norman Smith, an organizer for the United Automobile Workers, was in Memphis to organize Ford and Fisher Body, there was a reaction from Mayor Overton. Memphis did not want "Imported CIO agitators" and "Communists" whose tools were "violence, threats, sitdown strikes, destruction." The CIO and its "unAmerican" policies would be opposed "from start to finish," said Overton. "Let them go elsewhere, if anyone wants them. We don't and won't tolerate them." [76]

Police commissioner Davis added the emphasis of his office: "I am 100 per cent behind Mayor Overton in his attack on the CIO. We will

---

75   Interview with John R. Gorman, September 22, 1957. Crump had been critical of the "sweatshop" conditions at Plough. Later, improvements were made and Crump and Abe Plough became friends.
76   *Press Scimitar,* September 20, 1937.

not tolerate these foreign agitators in Memphis. We have started today and will free Memphis of these unwanted people. . . . We know Norman Smith and his whereabouts and will take care of that situation very soon." [77]

The Overton–Davis statement was announced in the press on September 20, and two days later word came out that Norman Smith had been severely beaten. The United Automobile Workers headquarters in Detroit protested that the beating had been incited "by statements of the mayor and chief of police," and the American Civil Liberties Union sent a telegram of protest to Davis.

After the affair, both Davis and Overton seemed to back off. Davis declared that the city government was opposed to violence, and a week later Overton announced that, if requested, "the Police Department will furnish police escort to Smith or others who fear attacks while performing legitimate duties. All persons violating any of our laws or ordinances will, when apprehended, be vigorously prosecuted." [78]

Today Congressman Clifford Davis recalls the time of the CIO trouble, when he was the Memphis police commissioner, and states his belief that the Smith beating was the outcome of an interlabor dispute,[79] which probably was what it was. But the fact of the truculent Overton–Davis statement and the beating that closely followed aroused in the minds of many the suspicion that there was a cause-and-effect relationship between the two, and that somewhere along the chain of command some city official knew a lot more than was let out for the public. According to Walter Chandler, Crump would never have suggested an attack of this kind, although he might express the opinion that the person who was beaten had placed himself in the way of inviting an attack.[80] It seems likely, too, that when Overton and Davis retreated to the higher ground of law after the Smith beating, their more moderate position could have been suggested by Crump.

Crump disliked the CIO, but when he recognized an unalterable fact of life he tried to live with it. For a few years during World War II, Crump and the CIO found themselves political allies in their mutual support of Roosevelt; and in 1942, Walter Chandler, then

77 *Ibid.*   78 *Ibid.*, September 22, 1937.
79 Congressman Clifford Davis to the author, July 16, 1962.
80 Interview with Walter Chandler, July 10, 1957.

mayor of Memphis, welcomed the Tennessee CIO state convention to Memphis. "I am very happy to have you come to Memphis," he said, "not only to see our city, but to give us an opportunity to show our city to you. You are genuinely welcome. . . ." [81]

In 1946 Crump and the CIO split again, this time over McKellar's candidacy for the Senate. He accused the CIO of being "very solicitous" about Senator McKellar, "just about like buzzards flying around over a herd of cattle inquiring about their health." [82] Like McKellar, Crump was getting old, too, and he was standing with his old friends. But Crump was merely expressing a personal feeling. There was no official opposition to the CIO. It was in Memphis to stay.

One of the charges against Crump was that he mercilessly broke his enemies and hounded them out of Memphis. If anyone asked for the citation of an instance, he was invariably told of the Charlie Brown affair. Brown was a lawyer, highly intelligent, with a streak of nonconformity in his makeup. Sometimes the posturings and pretensions of fearful little men trying to curry favor with those who determined how far they would rise in the world of affairs evoked in him a mordant humor, which he expressed in satirical commentaries on the local situation that were mimeographed and served out to a small audience.[83] He was regarded as having great potential, and it was probably through his senior associate, Percy McDonald, that he was recommended to Crump and subsequently made a member of the Shelby delegation to the state legislature.

Then came the fateful day of Crump's outing at Moon Lake, Mississippi, which he held for a large number of his political associates. All was going well—games in progress and spirits high—when Crump observed Brown lazing beneath a tree. This was not good; all members of the organization should loyally have fun at Crump's picnic, and so Crump ordered Brown to a nearby game where a catcher's position was open. And Brown, who thought the whole business was juvenile, rose to his feet and muttered loud enough for Crump to hear: "When the boss says you gotta go, you gotta go."

This was *lese majeste,* and Brown paid for it. He was broken in the organization and forced to leave Memphis, eventually taking up

81 *Press Scimitar,* July 6, 1946.   82 *Ibid.*
83 Percy McDonald showed some of these to the author.

a law practice in Nashville. There an increasing despondency ruined his health and hastened his death.

This was the story that was passed among Memphians who were critical of Crump. It followed him all of his life. At the time of his death the Knoxville *News-Sentinel* even included it in the obituary. Crump "couldn't take criticism," the paper said. "One of the few who dared challenge his authority, a lawyer and for years a member of the Legislature, had to leave Memphis and set up practice in Nashville." [84]

The story originated in the *Press Scimitar* and was presumably reported on the basis of *something* that occurred at Moon Lake. What did occur and the consequences of it are a matter of dispute. In the sketchy memoranda Crump set up for a biographer the Brown issue is discussed. He said it was a "conspicuous example of journalistic juggling of facts, designed for the consumption of an uninformed public." The story had originated with a "Memphis Press-Scimitar reporter who was not there" and concerned "an alleged incident which did not occur." Then Crump gave his version of what did occur:

[The story's] publication followed immediately after an outing in Mississippi at which I, among a large number of my Memphis and Shelby County friends, enjoyed a day of pleasure and relaxation. According to the yarn written by this reporter, without the semblance of a fact to support it, a young Memphis attorney, affiliated with our Shelby County organization, was invited to join in the organization of a soft ball game, declined, where upon I was quoted as saying "You gotta play ball—if you don't you are out!" No bigger falsehood was ever put out, because no such incident occurred, yet it was given widespread circulation over the state in an effort to portray me as a political tyrant. [85]

At a later date, apparently toward the end of his life, he wrote another statement about the charges in which he termed them "Another one of the Press-Scimitar's cooked up lies that Crump said at a picnic at Moon Lake—'You gotta play baseball.' . . . Crump didn't use those words. He was free and easy with any crowd, good humor, never talked business or politics. Joined in the spirit of it. Always cheerful." [86]

84 Knoxville *News-Sentinel,* October 18, 1954.
85 Memorandum. Crump Papers.
86 *Ibid.*

Percy McDonald says that Crump had nothing to do with Brown's going to Nashville. Brown went because Nashville offered a more fruitful field for the practice of his legal specialty, which was interstate commerce. Then, to add credence to his point, McDonald cited instances of a number of large transportation companies that had moved to Nashville in the thirties.[87]

The most likely explanation of the business is that Crump suggested to Brown that he play ball, and Brown retorted with a quip that was out of harmony with the pleasantness of the occasion. In the transmission of the incident to the reporter, words could have been put into the mouths of both Brown and Crump. What Crump objected to was the implication in the story that he had acted the part of a tyrant.

Then there was the case of a Negro druggist who was harassed by police to the point that he had to leave Memphis. The action began early on a Saturday morning when police were stationed outside the drugstore and began to seach everyone who entered. Blair Hunt, Crump's Negro friend, quickly heard of what was going on and went himself to the drugstore. When he got there, he found several policemen stationed outside, one of whom recognized him. "Professor, what are you doing down here?" the policeman asked. Hunt said he wanted to see the druggist and was permitted to enter without being searched.

Then he went home and called Crump, but Crump was at a football game. The next morning Hunt was visited by a spokesman from Crump. Crump wanted to be called at a certain time. When Hunt called, Crump said, "I know what you want." And Hunt said, "We're going to lose a lot of Negro votes because of this." To which Crump responded, "We might lose every Negro vote, but I'm going to clean up Memphis." The drugstore, Crump explained, was a front for dope peddling, and the owner had to be run out.

Hunt said he had no firsthand proof of Crump's charge, but he was "convinced" that Crump was correct. He had heard that some of the clerks who worked at the store had dope connections and, further, it seemed to him that the owner was far too rich to have gotten all of his money through legitimate business operations. The druggist "was a bad influence on the Negroes in the community," Hunt concluded.[88]

87   Interview with Percy McDonald, July 30, 1957.
88   Interview with Blair T. Hunt, August 27, 1957.

Crump's detractors exaggerated and perhaps fabricated to try to show a black viciousness in his character. To the extent that such stories implied a mean and treacherous nature they were largely incorrect, but otherwise Crump was a fighter, and there were occasions when he could indulge in a harsh, direct, and personal form of verbal assault. But he did not fabricate base untruths in order to discredit an opponent, and when he called into question a person's character, it was, figuratively, a face-to-face confrontation, based on solid evidence. Judge John Martin stated that he had had an "intimate knowledge" of Crump that extended over many years, "as a friend and relative, and as his attorney," and that he had "never known him to hit below the belt." [89] A Memphis labor leader who knew something of the in-fighting of the organization said that he would be "very loath to believe that Crump would take an unfair advantage of an opponent." [90]

The "all-out" character of Crump's political fights came naturally to him, although in Memphis, politics traditionally left off gentlemanly rules. Before Crump there had been a long list of figures who had been duped and doped into a compromising situation with some notorious local playgirl and then were rudely interrupted in their Elysian venture by a reporter or cameraman who happened on the scene. Crump's moral scrupulousness was basic to his nature, but he also knew how the game was played, and he wanted no chinks in his armor. Crump left off this traditional aspect of waging political war, but he was a past master at working up an old-fashioned majestic personalized wrath against an opponent. If the voters missed the delight of witnessing a public figure brought low by being caught in a festering sink of iniquity, Crump gave them heroes and devils as in the old days.

That some of Crump's public displays of wrath were aimed at voter entertainment is indicated by an interview he gave to the St. Louis *Post-Dispatch*. He "alluded to the fact that in the South politics is highly personalized; family connections are large, personalities rather than issues figure in campaigns; there is no such thing as an impersonal attack." [91] Crump's opposition in the thirties and forties, while

89   Interview with Judge John Martin, September 16, 1957.
90   Interview with John R. Gorman, September 22, 1957.
91   Spencer R. McCulloch, St. Louis *Post-Dispatch* Magazine Section, July 4, 1938.

numerically insignificant, was vocal. There were the outcasts and the slighted and those who had been stung by his verbal assaults. There was editor Meeman and some independent souls like Gilmer Richardson, a Memphis realtor who shared something of Meeman's point of view. When asked what Crump had done to him to arouse his opposition Richardson said, "Nothing—nothing at all." He thought Crump was a good man who had accomplished many good things for Memphis, but he was utterly opposed to the kind of one-man rule that encouraged sycophancy and discouraged the really free exercise of opinion and initiative.[92] Further, as he once declared in the midst of a political campaign, he disliked the fact that the "entire vote of the people of this great city and county can be given to any candidate, regardless of qualifications, simply on the whim of one man. It is undemocratic and unAmerican." [93]

Richardson had made the most basic criticism of the Crump phenomenon. It was easy for sensation-mongering writers to come to Memphis for a two-day stand and then write up their piece on how Crump was frustrating democracy in the city. The people of Memphis could have voted Crump into insignificance any time they chose. The matter for concern, as Richardson said, was that twenty to thirty thousand voters would unquestioningly do Crump's bidding in the use of their votes, even to the point of completely reversing in one election their vote in a previous election. It did not bespeak a viable electorate, conscious of its own integrity, that would vote over twenty thousand against Henry Horton for governor in 1928 and then vote for him by the same amount two years later just because Crump said so.

Bossism in Memphis was a problem that involved the electorate, but it would be pointless to blame the people of Memphis for having a boss. They were not sophisticated enough politically to supplant Crump with another sort of effective leadership. The business community, interested in the dollar-and-cents aspect of politics, was pleased to have Crump take over a political role that it might have played. As for the leadership of intellectuals, there was little. The Southern mentality was so beset with traditional sectional dogmatisms that those in academic circles were given little attention.

92 Interview with Gilmer Richardson, September 23, 1957.
93 *Press Scimitar*, August 1, 1938.

When people are incapable of making political choices along lines of enlightened self-interest, the avenues of demagoguery and corruption are opened, and frequently political bossism develops to feed upon and perpetuate these evils. Between the end of the Civil War and the 1920's bosses were a familiar part of the American city scene. Crump, it was frequently said, was the last of the old-fashioned city bosses. How typical of this group was Crump?

One study of twenty city bosses, published in 1930, attempted to produce a profile of a typical boss based on a great mass of empirical evidence. Beginning with the "Honorable" William Tweed of New York in the 1860's and ranging to the big city bosses of the twenties like "Czar" Martin Lomansney of Boston and Cincinnati's George B. Cox, the conclusion was that a typical city boss did not exist. About the only thing that a majority of the bosses appeared to have in common was that "most of them had wives and children to whom they were reasonably devoted"; that they "made more or less use of relatives in politics"; and that they lived "to a respectable old age." [94]

These revelations were not especially startling, but the study did show some traits of bosses that occurred with sufficient regularity to offer points of comparison with Crump. Of the twenty, only eight remained free from prison, trial, or indictment. Two of the twenty served prison terms, while six others came to trial for alleged offences varying from perjury to murder.[95]

Further, bosses tended to die rich. Ten of the twenty died leaving fortunes in excess of a million dollars. In almost every instance of large fortune-making the bosses combined politics with their own personal economic ventures. Not one of them appeared motivated to achieve ascendancy in politics solely to effect social reform. In many instances they seem to have drifted into politics, and circumstances over which they exercised no vital control raised them to the status of boss.

Crump differed from his predecessors in the character of his political morality. The organization was scrupulously honest; there were no rackets in Memphis and no privileged groups. He died a wealthy man, as Memphis people accounted wealth, but there was always a clear line drawn between business and politics.

94 Harold Zink, *City Bosses in the United States* (Durham, 1930), 33.
95 Interview with Walter Chandler, July 10, 1957.

There was more than just his honesty to differentiate him from most of his predecessors. For thirty years he labored long and hard to improve the whole society of Memphis. He did this without financial compensation. Neither did he seek rewards in the way of social preferment, for he studiously avoided involvement in the affairs of Memphis "society." Finally, under his control Memphis was spared the kind of demagoguery that comes when political figures invoke the issues of race and religion to perpetuate themselves in power.

What motivated him to give himself so completely to the work of improving Memphis? Deep down he was a romantic. He seems always to have held to the fancy that he was yet the poor country boy who had come to Memphis to conquer it and make it good for all its inhabitants. It was *noblesse oblige.* He was a romantic, but unlike most men, he possessed a unique combination of abilities and an implacable determination to actualize his romantic fancy. Memphis, the legendary town of sin, was the test of his mettle, and even in old age he continued to enjoy responding to its challenge.

Many of the criticisms made of Crump during his years of political ascendancy landed on thin air because his methods were always within legal and traditional limits. The most serious criticism to be made of him was that the pride-driven thrust of his will operated abrasively and sometimes unfairly on those who could not keep the pace or who represented a challenge to his policies. He made liberal concessions to human frailty and honest differences of opinion, but if their existence involved him personally in a way that reflected on his judgment, or if they frustrated the achievement of an important objective, he became an avenging angel. Sometimes men received more blows from him than were their due. Henry Horton was not the craven, timeserving soul that Crump made him out to be, nor at a later time was Governor Gordon Browning the completely depraved person that Crump depicted.

The issue, many insisted, was that of bossism, for Crump was boss absolutely. Authoritarianism does indeed restrict the freedom of others. But the extent of freedom is bound by the ordering factor of its intrinsic worth. Had there been no Crump there doubtless would have been more freedom for independent political action, but would the people of Memphis have been as free in those areas that represent the basis for any humanized society—order and material well being? Considering the character of Memphis as Crump found it, it is doubtful that they would have been.

⊠ ☐

Chapter IX

TVA

BY 1934 Crump had been in Memphis politics for three decades. Battles had been fought and won, but there remained one unresolved contest that acted as a goad throughout his years of political power-building. It began on November 4, 1915, when he had been ousted as mayor of Memphis—all because, as he so passionately insisted, he had made a determined move to bring public power to Memphis and to break the hold of a cutthroat Wall Street monopoly on the city. He had been ignominiously driven from office, and the directors of the old Merchants Power Company probably thought they had heard the last of him and of the public power issue. Perhaps some of them had, for his planning stretched into more years than were allotted to many of them. But one thing was certain: there would ultimately be a reckoning with the "Wall Street vultures," as he called them.

The era of the twenties was not, however, a time for reckoning. Crump built up his business and his political organization during a resurgence of the spirit of *laissez-faire* that permitted the utility corporations to spread across America in complicated webbings of intercorporate control. The holding company had superseded the large, local corporation. In Memphis the pyramiding process began in 1921 when the Electric Bond and Share Company, a member of the General Electric group of holding companies, organized the

224

National Power and Light Company to acquire certain investments, among which were securities of the Memphis Gas and Electric Company. The Memphis Gas and Electric Company was itself a merger of two groups—the Memphis Consolidated Gas and Electric Company and the Merchants Power Company. In November, 1922, the Memphis Gas and Electric Company turned its assets over to a new corporation, the Memphis Power and Light Company, and it was to this agency that the people of Memphis paid their light bills for the next fifteen years.[1]

But even as the holding companies waxed, the idea of public power did not die. In the Senate the old progressive George W. Norris maintained an insistent clamor that the government develop the World War I Muscle Shoals project; with this as a guide it would be possible to find out how much Americans were paying as a bounty to corporate structure in their monthly light bills. Crump remained alert to capitalize on any opportunity that might develop which would enable Memphis to get public power. In 1925 the Shelby delegation in the state legislature got through a bill that would give Memphis the right to build and own a transmission line between Memphis and Muscle Shoals in the event that the government should ever begin to generate power there.

One of the lures that the office of congressman held out to Crump in 1930 was the hope that in Washington he might do something to forward plans for public power development in the Tennessee Valley. But whatever he might have done under normal conditions was completely superseded by one of the great projects for social and economic development that was part of the New Deal. In 1933 Congress passed H. R. 4859, the bill creating the Tennessee Valley Authority. At the national level, Crump's objective was attained.

The Memphis city government reacted quickly to the prospect of federal power. On April 11 Mayor Overton announced the appointment of a commission to make a study of the possibility of transmitting Tennessee Valley public power to Memphis. In October,

---

1 On the development of the Memphis Power and Light Company see Ralph G. Hon, "The Memphis Power and Light Deal," *Southern Economic Journal*, VI (January, 1940), 347. On the development of holding companies and particularly the Electric Bond and Share Company, see *Utility Corporations, Summary Report of the Federal Trade Commission to the Senate of the United States*, Seventieth Congress, first session, Senate Document 92, Part 72-A (Washington, 1945), 36–38.

David Lilienthal, the director of TVA, visited the city and informed the city commission that if a sufficient local market existed, the government itself would build transmission lines.[2]

These developments presaged trouble for the Memphis Power and Light Company—and its owner the National Power and Light Company—and its owner the Electric Bond and Share Company. Early in December Memphis applied to TVA for engineering aid in making a power survey to see if federally constructed lines could be built to Memphis. On the heels of the city's application the Memphis Power and Light Company came forward with a proposed "Voluntary rate reduction," being willing, it said, to "sacrifice for the public good of Memphis." [3] That the company could afford a "sacrifice" was strongly suggested by the fact that in the depression year of 1933 it paid the Electric Bond and Share Company $1,333,612.54 as a "service fee." [4]

Concluding his days as congressman, Crump put pressure on Governor McAlister to spread the good news of TVA. "I hope very much, Hill, that you will lose no time in advocating the stringing of TVA wires into every city, town, village and hamlet in the state for there is no question in my mind, but that the people of Tennessee want just that." [5] McAlister, as usual, could not agree more with his mentor. "Dear Ed," he began. "I feel exactly as you do about the TVA. The last Legislature authorized me to appoint a committee to work with TVA, and I suppose I had better do it right now." He wondered if "Watkins" would agree to serve.[6]

Privately, Crump continued to have misgivings about McAlister. At times the governor seemed to lack decisiveness in the execution of state affairs. Only recently he had written Crump because he was worried about a letter he had received from the Secretary of the Interior, Harold Ickes, which he enclosed to Crump. Ickes was unhappy because Tennessee was not pressing on with Public Works road-building projects. Allotted money had not been used. "I regard this as an unsatisfactory showing," Ickes had written. If something were not done, he would "advocate that power be reserved to rescind

2   Hon, "The Memphis Power and Light Deal," 350.
3   *Press Scimitar,* December 7, 1933.
4   *Ibid.,* March 8, 1934.
5   Crump to McAlister, March 23, 1934. Crump Papers.
6   McAlister to Crump, March 27, 1934. Crump Papers.

allocations to those states which are negligent in putting . . . money to work." [7] McAlister wanted Crump to intercede to prevent such action. "I don't think he should be given the right to withdraw money from the state in the event he don't [*sic*] think we spend it as promptly as we should." [8]

Worse yet, McAlister in announcing his candidacy in the 1934 gubernatorial election had declared himself for prohibition in Tennessee. Nevertheless, Crump shortly announced that he would support the governor for another term "even though his prohibition views are not in accord with mine." [9] McAlister had done some good things: he had balanced the budget, and he had refinanced a lot of bad financing which he had inherited. Most important, he was "absolutely honest." At the bottom it was simply that no one else was available. Crump would have nothing to do with McAlister's opponent Lewis Pope, with the odor of his Lea–Caldwell–Horton association about him.

With the other candidates the organization supported, there was no question. Chandler was running for Crump's position in the House, and McKellar and Nathan Bachman were Crump's choices for the Senate.

During the campaign Crump offered McAlister helpful suggestions. Should he not consider advocating game and fish legislation that would appeal to outdoorsmen? What about the gas tax—he had read that the oil people were protesting it. "Please write me fully . . ." concluded Crump in his letter to McAlister.[10] On one subject he directed McAlister specifically, investing his thoughts with the urgency of a telegram:

SUGGEST YOU REPLY TO PRESS SCIMITAR QUESTIONNAIRE AS FOLLOWS QUOTE REGARDING YOUR QUESTIONNAIRE I AM THOROUGHLY CONVINCED THAT IT IS NOT YOUR PURPOSE TO PLAY THE GAME FAIR WITH ME PERIOD IF I WERE TO ANSWER EVERY QUESTION ONE HUNDRED PER CENT YES YOU WOULD PICK ON ME JUST AS YOU HAVE FOR A LONG TIME UNQUOTE. [11]

Late in July an investigator from a U.S. Senate committee came to Memphis to inquire into the political methods of the Shelby group.

7   Harold Ickes to McAlister, March 15, 1934. Crump Papers.
8   McAlister to Crump, March 21, 1934. Crump Papers.
9   *Commercial Appeal,* May 21, 1934.
10   Crump to McAlister, July 13, 1934. Crump Papers.
11   Crump to McAlister, July 21, 1934. Telegram. Crump Papers.

The prober, R. L. Ballentine, talked at length with Frank Rice and Joe Boyle and then visited Crump. "We had a very pleasant talk," commented Crump. "I told him that our crowd is trying to elect McAlister and Bachman, and that McKellar and Chandler are already in with practically no opposition. . . . I asked . . . [him] to stay over and go around on election day and further asked him to make a careful survey of what little the opposition is doing here." [12]

In the August primary election all of Crump's candidates won. McAlister was especially grateful for Crump's support and immediately after the election he wrote him a letter.

> I am leaving town for a few days but before I go I want, once more, to tell you the deep gratitude I have in my heart for all you have done for me this hot strenuous summer. I have heard it said several times that we have defeated them "without Shelby." So we did. But the knowledge that Shelby was always there gave me courage and an assurance of victory that never left me from beginning to end. It likewise caused cold chills to run down the backs of their viscious [*sic*] slanderers. They never forgot that Shelby was always right there. . . .
>
> I want you to know the affectionate esteem in which I shall always hold you. [13]

With the primary over, Crump turned his attention to the general election of November 6, with its local referendum on the issue of TVA power for Memphis. There was little question but that a majority of the Memphis populace wanted TVA power, but for Crump an overwhelming endorsement of the bond issue to purchase local distribution facilities would represent a final vindication of his policy on the power issue when he was mayor. Interestingly, his position on TVA was duplicated by the *Press Scimitar*. Meeman gave almost daily editorial support to what had become his crusade too, and assigned one of the paper's most capable reporters, Null Adams, to interpret developments.

As the day for the election approached, the organization staged an all-out effort to get out the voters. Banners urging a vote for TVA gave a carnival appearance to the downtown area: bands rallied people to mass meetings, and houses were systematically canvassed.

12 *Commercial Appeal*, July 27, 1934. The index for the *Congressional Record* of 1934–35 does not show either a committee or subjects that pertain to an investigation of election practices in Memphis.
13 McAlister to Crump, August 6, 1934. Crump Papers.

"Even fake fights in the streets to attract crowds for TVA speakers were a daily occurrence." [14]

Amidst the height of the shouting for TVA, Crump had to enter a hospital. Edward, Jr., wired Senator McKellar: "Doctors have advised father to have an immediate operation but to assist you . . . and TVA he hopes to delay until November sixth." [15] But the crisis in his health passed, and on November 5, the day before the election, he published a heroic size statement in the *Commercial Appeal* in which he discussed his part in the history behind the issue of the next day's election: "Twenty years ago, after a long, hard and expensive fight, and with the assistance of my friend, Frank Rice, I finally got a bill through the Tennessee Legislature calling for a referendum. The people voted 'Yes,' giving the city the authority to buy or build an electric light plant. . . ." To deter him from this course he had been spied upon, and "every form of blackmail had been attempted. I owed some money at that time—that was published. My personal checks were stolen." He would not yield because the "people were entitled to cheaper lights and I wanted them to have them." So he had been ousted "on the wholly unrelated subject of prohibition."

Crump came to the current issue: "Some are hollering 'The TVA will be a calamity,' but it won't. In a great majority of such cases it is but the echo of propaganda put out by the money barons who control the Memphis Power and Light Company from their love nests in Wall Street. It's the same old financial quackery—the old two-medicine man prescription—that the city is overbonded and will probably break and crumble to pieces—just anything to save the monopoly."

Wall Street, he declared, had always opposed every progressive move. "They were against the Federal Reserve banking system which Woodrow Wilson gave the country. They also fought the guarantee of bank deposits and passage of the Securities Act, both gifts of Franklin D. Roosevelt." In view of this record, "the people of Memphis should open their eyes to the tremendous opportunity they

---

14 Hugh Russell Fraser, "Memphis Votes for Cheaper Power," *The Nation*, CXXIX (November 28, 1934), 615–16.

15 E. H. Crump, Jr., to McKellar, October 25, 1934. Telegram. McKellar Papers. Crump may have had a hernia, and it is possible that his hospitalization was related to this condition.

now have by voting 'Yes' for TVA. If you didn't groan the dentist would never know he had hit the nerve. The power monopoly has hit our nerve, so let's groan loud on Tuesday and write it 'Yes.' " [16]

The next day Memphis voted "Yes" by eighteen to one—32,735 for TVA and 1,868 against. In true revolutionary fashion the city named a street for the occasion. A downtown alleyway was rechristened "November Sixth Street."

One year later a contract was signed between TVA and the city of Memphis, clearing the way for the construction of transmission lines. The ceremony took place at noon on November 22 in the Shelby County courtroom. In an atmosphere perfumed by flowers, Mayor Overton and Major Thomas H. Allen, chairman of the board of light and water commissioners, wrote their names on bulky contracts as Congressman Chandler and Senator McKellar looked on. Congressman Chandler made a statement: "So today we express in no uncertain terms our sincerest thanks to our great leader, Hon. E. H. Crump," he said. Then Dr. E. A. Morgan of TVA made a speech. When he finished and as the meeting was about to break up, Grover McCormick, Shelby County public defender, stepped up and added a final word. "Just a minute, gentlemen, I think this occasion should not be allowed to pass without some tribute to the great service rendered by that rugged old United States senator who . . . fought . . . to make the signing of this contract possible. I refer to . . . Senator George Norris." [17]

Twelve days after the November-sixth election Crump went to Nashville at the invitation of McAlister to welcome President Roosevelt, who was passing through the city. Roosevelt was the principal attraction, but Crump was not far behind him. Riding in his big touring car, he arrived at the reception point just before Roosevelt, exciting "the interest of thousands" and starting a crush of politicians around his car. He was a striking figure with a large brown crouch hat and high-fashion brown ensemble, shaking hands heartily and addressing pleasantries in a booming voice to all around him.

"It is not hard to understand why his great Memphis machine runs ahead, oiled and gathering speed," wrote Joe Hatcher in his column in the *Tennessean*. Hatcher noticed something else he thought was significant: As soon as Crump had gotten his car placed in the parade

16   *Commercial Appeal,* November 5, 1934.
17   *Press Scimitar,* November 23, 1935.

line, he seized Congressman Gordon Browning by the arm and led him down the parade picket line before thousands to show him the Crump car and to invite him to ride with him over the thirty-mile parade route. "Gordon's star has been in the ascendancy for the 1936 governorship for some time now. It has been rumored that the Crump boys would like to extend the hand of fellowship to West Tennessee . . . for the next governor," wrote Hatcher.[18]

The following six months demonstrated one thing for certain: McAlister could have no further claim to Crump's support. In January, 1936, when the legislature convened, McAlister tried to push through a state sales tax. At first its passage seemed inevitable, but gradually forces were organized to oppose it. By the end of July its defeat was final. In Memphis the *Press Scimitar* explained how it had happened:

[In January] everybody thought a sales tax was inevitable. . . . Governor McAlister "controlled" the Legislature and Governor McAlister was committed to a sales tax. . . . Nearly all thought we were sure to have it.

But the editor of the Press-Scimitar does not believe that anything which is wrong is inevitable. He said the sales tax was wrong and should not be passed. He said it again and again.

Soon this met response. Individuals and organizations joined in. Other newspapers took up the fight. . . .

The Press-Scimitar does not claim to have defeated the sales tax. We claim only that we "gave the light" by which "the people found their own way" to throw off this threatened burden.

The paper graciously acknowledged Crump's assistance. He had thrown "his great strength into the fight . . . even though it meant a break with the governor. That decided it. The sales tax was doomed." Meeman admitted that "we have had our sharp differences with Mr. Crump, and no doubt will have them again, but that will not prevent our giving him due credit." [19]

In the spring of 1936 there began the biennial spring guessing game as to whom Crump would support for governor. On the front page of its Sunday edition for May 24, the *Tennessean* carried a cartoon of Crump pointing to a Shelby County ballot box and asking office contenders, "What am I offered?" Crump was irritated. "Your cartoon of me 'To the Highest Bidder' is unfair, is not right, is unjust,

18 Joe Hatcher, "Politics," Nashville *Tennessean*, November 19, 1934.
19 *Press Scimitar*, July 31, 1935.

is destitute of the truth," he wrote the paper. "I am not a slight-of-hand [*sic*] magician nor an optimistic palmist. I have merely worked to the extent of my humble ability, trying to do something helpful for Memphis, Shelby County and the State of Tennessee, and I know I have done it honestly without fear or favor." Crump said he knew he had supported some bad men for office, but he had also supported some good ones. "Our vote for Senator Kenneth McKellar has been a real pleasure. . . . However I differ with him at times. . . ." Crump differed with McKellar "when he praises Governor McAlister's administration." McAlister had been ungrateful. "He made one speech in our county, contributed not one penny, nor did he spend five minutes soliciting votes." Finally, there was McAlister's attempt to put through a sales tax, which was a "monstrosity." [20]

It appeared that he would differ with McKellar again. The two announced candidates were Burgin Dossett, president of one of the state teacher's colleges, and Gordon Browning, congressman, and opponent of Nathan Bachman in the 1934 senatorial election. McKellar supported Dossett because, said the Chattanooga *Daily News,* he "fears that Browning may run for the Senate four years hence." [21] In announcing an endorsement of a candidate, the usual procedure was for McKellar to allow Crump to select his candidate first. Crump, however, was slow to arrive at a decision, and it was well into July before he made a statement. He had been looking over both Browning's and Dossett's record, he said. He was going to vote for a man who would keep down taxes, cut out useless jobs, and "throw unworthy Ernest Haston, secretary of state, out of office." It had also been reported to him that the state boys' industrial school had been using a whipping post, and he was concerned about that. "This thing of beating children up . . . with a cat of nine tails and keeping it up is an outrage." But he was "not surprised at anything under McAlister's administration—our sorriest governor," who had "tried in a sneaking way to put the sales tax on us—kept it hidden in his stony heart—before election." [22]

Crump had not mentioned Browning by name, but it was obvious he supported him, since Dossett had as his campaign manager the "unworthy Ernest Haston." This did not mean a break with McKellar,

20 Nashville *Tennessean,* May 25, 1936.
21 Chattanooga *Daily News,* July 18, 1936.
22 *Press Scimitar,* July 18, 1936.

Crump said, just an honest difference of opinion. In the *Tennessean,* Joe Hatcher doubted that McKellar would make a real fight for Dossett. "Browning was destined to go to Shelby with a substantial majority even had Crump declared for Dossett." Everyone agreed that Dossett's case was "hopeless." [23]

It was not much of a race. Crump made no heroic charges against the Dossett position, only chided him for making "wild, impractical, impossible statements" about Shelby County. It reminded him "of a levee camp cook scrapping around for anything he can find to make hash." [24] The election on August 6 showed that Hatcher's prediction had been correct. Browning got 225,815 votes to Dossett's 96,704. Of Browning's votes, 60,218 of them came from Shelby County; of Dossett's, only 861. With or without Crump, Browning could have been governor, but he was properly appreciative of the help he had gotten and remarked that there were sixty thousand reasons why he liked Shelby County. Privately, no doubt, he felt quite strong and independent.

After the election, Crump mentioned some of the things that had influenced him to support Browning. "Gordon Browning, a poor boy, born on a farm, has had to shift for himself, worked his way through Valparaiso college, which was the poor man's college of the Middle West at that time." Also, he predicted, Browning would "consign the unworthy . . . Haston to the scrap heap." [25]

The November general election would be even more crucial than the primary. Roosevelt was up for reelection, and Crump was very interested in getting Leon Jourolmon, a strong public power advocate from Knoxville, elected as one of the state's public utility commissioners. For the moment though, he rested from politics and caught up on his correspondence with Mrs. Crump, who was vacationing at Daytona Beach, Florida.

What was there to write about from Memphis in August execpt the weather? "Why condemn the nudist?" he asked his wife. "We are experiencing the hottest yet." There was sad news: "Johnnie Linder's splendid little boy five years old died this morning—appendicitis, peritonitis and double pneumonia. Johnnie hasn't a dollar

23 Nashville *Tennessean,* July 21, 1936.
24 *Press Scimitar,* July 24, 1936.
25 Nashville *Tennessean,* August 21, 1936.

on earth but we will help him." [26] He concluded with "lots of love
to you all, and a big kiss for dear Betty."

Three days later he wrote a longer letter. He wished that they
could be traveling in Europe, and they would be, were it not for
the presidential election. Then he moved into one of his humorous
fantasies, recalling the old Sells Brothers Circus that featured the
"Wild Man of Borneo." He thought the latter had many descendants
scattered throughout Tennessee and in Memphis. "I could perhaps
name them easier than Adam named the animals. Adam must have
been a very smart man to have thought of such suitable names for
some of the animals—only it was not hard to name the hog or the
jack-ass." Someone living to the rear of them had some new dogs
and "how they do love to fight, which they stage between 2:00 and
3:00. From what I understand they will not last more than two or
three more rounds. The revelation that they have killed one another
will be receptive news." [27]

He wrote again the next day, adding more drollery to the subject
of politics, the weather, and some Memphians. "There is a truce
between the President and Landon and other leaders in Omaha on
the drought situation. There is a truce between the occupants of
the apartments and boarding houses—all assembled on the lawn
looking for a breath of fresh air. That's one time when people are
more or less on equal terms. . . . In time of overflow the snake,
rabbit, deer and wolf make a truce while they are on some knoll
waiting for the water to recede." [28]

But politics was soon pressing upon him again. Jourolmon had
been attacked by the president of the Tennessee Manufacturers Association as "too red" to fill the office of state utilities commissioner.
Crump answered: "Jourolmon is red—yes, red, white and blue—a
good American." He was "absolutely honest and fearless, and the
big interests and utilities can't dominate him." [29]

On the national election, he noted that "every kind of big business
is cussing Roosevelt . . . notwithstanding the fact that their business
has greatly improved." It was a matter of Wall Street wanting "to

26 Crump to Bessie Crump, August 18, 1936. Crump Papers.
27 Crump to Bessie Crump, August 21, 1936. Crump Papers.
28 Crump to Bessie Crump, August 22, 1936. Crump Papers.
29 *Press Scimitar,* October 27, 1936.

torpedo its own ship to get rid of Roosevelt and make sure they won't have further exposure of their crooked transactions." It was "hard to cure a dog of chasing sheep once he has tasted blood," he concluded.[30]

In September Roosevelt took a sightseeing tour through the Smokies enroute to Charlotte, North Carolina, to deliver an address to a seven-state Democratic rally. On September 9, the party, occupying twenty cars, had a picnic lunch on Clingman's Dome—fried chicken, sandwiches, beer, coffee, and cold drinks. As they ate, Roosevelt chatted and laughed with senators and governors. Above the sound of the wind and mingled conversation could be heard Crump's high voice, kidding senators McKellar and Bachman about the big hats they wore. Then Roosevelt entered the conversation. "Well, Ed, what about that dog house down in Memphis?" He spoke of a $15,000 WPA-built steam-heated city kennel that had provoked critical comment. "Oh, the dog house is fine," said Crump. "It will mean a lot of votes for you down there." [31]

He stayed with the caravan until it reached Asheville. There he wired Mrs. Crump. "Wonderful trip. Picnic Dinner with President in Smoky Mountains Yesterday. Enthusiastic crowd all along line. . . ." [32]

In October he went to Battle Creek to replenish his store of energy before the final election push. While he was away, the Mortgage Bankers Association held its national convention in Memphis, and a number of its officials used the occasion to make speeches criticizing Roosevelt and the Democratic administration. Reading the speeches at Battle Creek, Crump decided the association had gone too far. Wiring Edward, Jr., he announced, "Crump . . . resigns from the Mortgage Bankers Association."

The neighboring Crittenden County *Times* commended Crump for what he had done and added its own incisive criticism of the Mortgage Bankers. Every other "decent" mortgage banker in the country should have done the same thing. It would be a fitting reproach for those who, "as broke bankers in 1933, rushed pell-mell to Washington, fawning, whining, pleading for assistance, and now,

30 *Ibid.,* December 19, 1935.
31 Nashville *Banner,* September 10, 1936.
32 Crump to Bessie Crump, September 10, 1936. Telegram. Crump Papers.

as vicariously rejuvenated big shots of finance seek to destroy the very man and the very rehabilitory system that yanked them from the brink of ruin a bare four years ago." [33]

Shortly after his wire to Edward, Jr., on the Mortgage Bankers, Crump wrote Mrs. Crump on the political situation at Battle Creek. All of its wealthy clients were discrediting Roosevelt, so much so that he was "beginning to wonder if the horse really had horse sense." As for himself, he had never admired Roosevelt more. "The President looks fine and not for a single moment has he cringed or weakened and never has he worn the armor of a fighting man so admirably." He was the champion of the people "against 'Princes of Privilege' and 'economic royalists.' . . . He meets colossal crowds with his usual smiling joviality while throngs greet him with lusty cheers. He is just now putting the Republicans on the defensive. That's what we want." Roosevelt, he said, was passing through a time "of unprecedented slander of the vilest sort, while fighting to maintain Democracy for America, and a living for the plain people." Crump thought at the moment Roosevelt's chances were fifty–fifty, but the situation was improving every day, and he was "entertaining high hopes of victory." [34]

He would be happy to return home, although he was "not a bit well." Back in Memphis, he went to bed with a cold, but not before assuring reporters that Roosevelt would win. The *Literary Digest* poll was "rigged. There was big money behind it." [35]

The election on November 3 eased the tension. Roosevelt had won and Jourolmon had won. No new impediment had been raised against TVA, and some had been removed. The election brought sweetness of another kind. Crump revealed that while at Battle Creek he had bet three hundred dollars to one hundred that Roosevelt would win.

On the last day of the year he announced some of the plans he had for the future. He wanted a consolidation of more city–county agencies; he wanted a further restriction of loan companies; and he wanted a hospital for crippled Negro children. "Negroes have to work for their living. Nobody goes out of their way to take care

33   Crittenden County *Times,* October 13, 1936.
34   Crump to Bessie Crump, undated. Crump Papers.
35   *Press Scimitar,* October 29, 1936.

of them. They have a hard time. It is pitiful to see them hobbling about, deformed—forced to keep on going day after day." [36]

There was one thing further—all important: TVA power would have to be brought to the Memphis public. It would be a while yet; dams were being built and great steel-tower transmission lines put up through the Valley area. Then would come negotiations with the National Power and Light Company to buy its local distribution facilities. In the meantime, he looked for energetic state leadership from Browning in getting federal power into Memphis.

One week following Browning's nomination in the August Democratic primary, Crump received a letter. "We have been requested to communicate with you," it began, "by Mr. Inlow of Detroit, Mich." Then followed this statement: "We are very much interested in the general distribution of Kentucky Natural Silica Sand Rock Asphalt thruout your state. We are desirous of making an appointment with you at your earliest convenience and would ask you to advise us by return mail the earliest opportunity that this conference can be consummated." [37]

Crump was curious and also concerned. Who was "Mr. Inlow," and why did someone representing the old "Kyrock" outfit of the Horton days want to talk to him? Especially, why had this letter come right on the heels of Browning's nomination—was there a connection? Finally he did not like the peremptory tone: "advise us by return mail the earliest opportunity that this conference can be consummated."

Crump wrote his reply out in longhand on the back of the Rennie letter and three days later had his secretary, Mrs. Humphreys, type it and send it to Rennie.

Yours of the 15th asking for a personal appointment is at hand. It would be useless for your man to see me about road paving. For 30 years I have insisted that all city and county contracts be awarded on merit and not pull or money considerations. I hold the same opinion about state contracts. Therefore you would not need me or anyone else if you have merit and I will be terribly disappointed in Gordon Browning's administration if he does not adhere to that policy. [38]

36 *Commercial Appeal*, December 31, 1936.
37 G. H. Rennie to Crump, August 15, 1936. Crump Papers.
38 Crump to Rennie, August 18, 1936. Crump Papers.

Then Crump had copies made of both letters, sending one to Browning and the other to Browning's campaign manager, A. R. Broadbent.

There was shortly another disquieting development. Will Gerber explained it: "In the fall of '36 we learned that certain people were to be appointed of questionable character"—specifically, Wallace Edwards, Governor Horton's private secretary, who was to be appointed as state commissioner of administration. Gerber was delegated to go to Nashville to protest this move. "He gave us the brush-off," said Gerber, "and appointed Edwards. . . . Later, when he sought Crump's advice, we knew he was phony." [39]

Browning was inaugurated in January, 1937. Gerber was put to checking on the governor, and Overton wrote to McKellar asking for Browning's history in Congress respecting the issue of TVA. The answer contained some mild surprises, and Overton forwarded the letter to Crump. "I have looked up Browning's record and find he did not vote for the TVA," wrote McKellar. Not only that, in the hearings on the TVA bill before the House Committee on Military Affairs, Browning had sought to add a crippling amendment to the bill. What he had proposed was this:

Now, the Government has the policy of constructing self-liquidating projects, and if a bid is offered by a private concern to lease this dam after completion for power purposes, providing for the amortization of the entire cost of the dam and taking care of the interest on that part of it chargeable to power, I believe it would be a fine proposition for the Government. . . .

Then Browning offered his "small" amendment to permit private concerns to lease TVA power on terms that "will return the bond interest on the investment *chargeable to power purposes. . . .*" [40]

McKellar explained the Browning amendment to Overton. It meant "that the government would build . . . dams along the river and lease them out to the power companies, not on a basis of what the dams cost . . . but after deducting that portion of the cost that might be applied to flood control and that portion of the cost that might be applied to navigation, and charging the power companies

---

39 Interview with Will Gerber, July 30, 1957.
40 *Muscle Shoals, Hearings Before The Committee on Military Affairs,* House of Representatives, Seventy-third Congress, first session, April 11 to April 15, 1933 (Washington, 1933), 56. The italics are mine.

a price based only on that part of the dam used for power, generally estimated at about one-third of the cost of the dams."

This, said McKellar, was "exactly what the Alabama Power Company had been doing at Muscle Shoals. They had been leasing . . . power generated there *at the switchboard* for less than one-fifth of one cent and selling it . . . as high . . . as twelve cents in some instances." McKellar also noted that Browning had been closely associated with one "W. G. Waldo, reputedly one of the leading power lobbyists here."

McKellar cleared himself of any irregular complicity with Crump against Browning. "I am simply giving you what, as my constituent, you are entitled to have. I do not wish this letter to be considered a criticism, except that, as you know, I have at all times been in favor of . . . disposing of the power generated . . . for the benefit of the people rather than . . . the power companies." [41]

Of Browning's amendment, Crump noted beside it in his own copy of the committee hearings: "Not in conflict with TVA! It would only gut it!" Browning had, of course, spoken in favor of TVA during the campaign, but what was his real position? Crump wondered.

Crump made memoranda of his suspicions and the evidence. "First of June Luke Lea was in Washington in conference daily with . . . Browning's brother. He spent a couple of hours for dinner at the Occidental Hotel with him. . . . We had hoped that he would see it unwise to associate with Luke Lea, or have employees associated with him. Pull away, but he hasn't done it. . . . We have talked to Browning about Luke Lea on three different occasions." [42]

On August 1 there came another disquieting sign from Nashville. A number of state officials gave Browning a new twelve-cylinder car, equipped with a radio and "dual air-compression horns." It was a big "surprise" to the governor, who was "arrested" in his office by the chief of the highway patrol and led to the capitol steps for the presentation. "It is our tribute of love and affection to you," said Secretary of State Broadbent.[43]

Crump made more memoranda on Browning, verbalizing his suspicions and jotting down striking phrases on notepads to store in

41 McKellar to Watkins Overton, June 3, 1937. Crump Papers.
42 Memoranda. Crump Papers.
43 *Commercial Appeal*, August 2, 1937.

his arsenal of verbiage for possible future use against the governor. What about "Browning's pardons?"

"Include his letter to Overton wanting to sell street signals . . . Willie Gerber knows several bad things. . . . Letter he wrote he would not run against Bachman, but he did.[44] . . . Browning refused to earmark a lot of taxpayers money in the appropriation bill. He has a lot of loose money to spend here and there. It is now earmarked. Luke Lea will tell him how it will be spent. . . . Browning has a designing crowd around him. There is no tower of Babel—they all speak the same language. . . . A case of Birds of a feather —water seeking its level."

He experimented with a piece of homespun imagery that was his trademark in political writing: "In the old circus days a man rode horse back ahead of the parade, hollering 'hold your horses.' 'Wild men, man-eating vampires, big elephants are coming.' Now I say to the tax-payers of Tennessee, 'Hold your pocket-books,—Browning's Luke Lea, old Henry Horton, and Lew Pope are coming.' " [45]

In August he went to Battle Creek, where he continued to check on Browning. The name of "G. Hall Roosevelt" of Detroit had been mentioned to him as one of the figures behind the "Kyrock" letter of the previous year. He telephoned a banker friend in Detroit to check on Roosevelt.

"I have checked," came the response. "He is a brother of Mrs. Franklin D. Roosevelt, and has been away from Detroit for quite some time." Roosevelt could have been connected with the Kentucky Rock Asphalt letter, but that was one of the things he did not know about. He was currently spending time in Washington, and "as far as my information goes, he is strictly a promoter of public utilities of various kinds." As for the mysterious "Mr. Inlow," there was only one listed in the city directory, and he was a broker. "Just what he is broker of, I do not know. I thought I knew every broker in Detroit through my banking and brokerage experience, but he is a new one." [46]

Crump knew little more than before, except that one thing was

44 This letter, written to Abe D. Waldauer, contains this sentence: "I will support Bachman and McAlister fully." Crump Papers.
45 Memoranda. Crump Papers.
46 H. C. Newland to Crump, August 9, 1937. Crump Papers.

clear: there had been some conniving behind the letter he had received a year ago.

In September he was back in Memphis, refreshed and planning a boat ride for the inmates of Shelby County's charitable institutions, crippled children, incurables, the aged, and poverty-stricken. Sitting in his office with Frank Rice, Crump told newsmen that he was not going to talk politics until the following spring. He had had enough for a while. Rice agreed.

He meant what he said, and he did not exclude the state liquor referendum set for September 23. When Methodist Bishop H. M. DuBose, president of the Tennessee Anti-Saloon League, visited Crump at his home to determine his sentiments on the referendum, Crump replied that "we will have no interest in the repeal referendum." [47]

The statement, "they are privileged to vote as they see fit," prompted editor Meeman to deliver a political instruction to the people of Memphis in the form of an editorial sermonette in satire. "What a red letter day," he rejoiced, "a day in which the political organization leaves the election entirely alone, and also leaves the voters alone, permitting them to vote as they see fit!" [48] What a pleasant time they would have—"no city hall and courthouse employees, firemen, policemen, school teachers and their sisters and their cousins and their uncles and their aunts, swarming the polls and bravely pretending . . . an enthusiasm they don't feel." Think of it, exclaimed the *Press Scimitar*, "you'll be able to go to the polls just like people do in other cities. . . ." [49]

The drys won the election, but as Crump pointed out, it meant nothing, since either way the referendum was not binding on the legislature, and the legislature, with its abundance of rural drys, could be depended upon to vote dry, referendum or no. Crump thought the vote was "remote and silly." He made a prediction, though: "We will pull the silliness out next time." [50]

47 Scrapbook news clipping.
48 *Press Scimitar,* September 22, 1937.
49 *Ibid.*
50 *Commercial Appeal,* September 24, 1937.

☒ ☐

Chapter x

THE BROWNING BATTLE

ON SEPTEMBER 29, 1937, Joe Hatcher wrote in his column in the Nashville *Tennessean* that Crump was on the verge of a break with Browning over the appointment of Lewis Pope as a "special investigator" to collect back taxes, and also because Browning had announced that he was "personally voting dry" on the liquor referendum.[1] Crump was irritated and wired Hatcher immediately: "You are trying to convey the impression Governor Browning and I have had a difference over the referendum. This is an untruth. . . . I have never discussed the referendum with the governor. I am not falling out with anyone in Tennessee over the whiskey question. But you are endeavoring to create that impression. I probably made a mistake in talking to you in a gentlemanly way."[2]

Hatcher sent his "regrets" and said he had not intended to mislead anyone.[3] Even so, his prediction of a break was close to the mark. Had it been made solely on the matter of Browning's appointment of Pope as a back tax collector, Hatcher would have been dead center.

1 Nashville *Tennessean,* September 29, 1937.
2 Crump to Joe Hatcher, September 29, 1937. Telegram. Crump Papers.
3 Hatcher to Crump, September 29, 1937. Crump Papers.

Browning initiated the break. It came suddenly, explosively. On October 1 he announced that the legislature would be called into special session to shear Crump's power. A county unit system of choosing certain elected officials was to be devised, which would nullify the great Shelby majorities.

When Crump heard of the plan, he was aghast. "I can't believe it, for only a crazy man would do it. . . . Huey Long in his desperation didn't dare try a thing that is now proposed for Tennessee. . . . I don't believe a Tennessee Legislature will attempt anything of this sort." [4]

On November 6 he answered Browning's attack with a bomb of his own. He revealed that the governor had come to his office on September 13 to propose a gigantic political trade: Browning would run for the United States Senate in 1938, taking the place of his own appointee, George Berry. Lewis Pope would run for governor with Crump's support. In 1940 Crump, with Browning's support, would run for the Senate against McKellar.

Crump wrote two detailed accounts of his meeting with Browning, one of which was for the press. The press statement was published in Tennessee's leading newspapers, and it was not long before its first paragraph was being quoted around the state. "My quickly declining to swallow Governor Browning's roguish eye Luke Lea and his Nero heart Lewis Pope angered him and his artificial smile and laugh faded. Now he must slaughter me if possible and disenfranchise Shelby County voters. Therefore, he is trying to put over the County Unit Voting vote cutting plan which he denied until finally cornered. The sneak is desperate. He wants to go to the United States Senate. His vaunting ambition was getting the best of him."

The circumstances of the meeting were related. "The sneak came to Memphis, September 13th, Mid South Fair Day. He called at my office at 9 A.M. His Senatorial aspirations had been worrying him. Should he try the next year or wait until 1940, the McKellar year. . . . 'Anyway,' he said, 'I have a proposition to make to you this morning. I want you to go to the United States Senate in 1940. I can send you!' "

To which Crump replied: " 'Governor Browning, when we sup-

4 *Press Scimitar,* October 2, 1937.

ported you in 1936 we told you then we did not want anything of a personal nature and would bother you less than any part of the State. . . . We have kept our word.' "

Crump then asked:

Would I trust him three years even if I had ambitions to go to the Senate? No, I wouldn't trust him three minutes. Of all the people I have known in Tennessee politics I believe he is the least trustworthy. The three year contract meant a complete "sell-out" on my part. I would have to join in and condone his secret personal Lewis Pope contract, put my feet under the same table with Luke Lea, support the sneak next August for the Senate, while he throws George Berry in the Holston River, support Nero heart Lewis Pope for Governor and the legislative program for 1939; say all the sneak's 1937 legislative Bills, many very questionable, were right; say his tax raising schemes high minded and noble; and that Gordon Browning is an honest, upright, sincere man and he didn't have a hypocritical bone in his body. [5]

In the other draft, details are added. The meeting had been arranged by Abe Waldauer, a friend of Browning and a rising figure in the Shelby organization. Crump also added this information: after Browning told him that he could send Crump to the Senate, Crump told Browning that "he had the substance in his hands and could have appointed me when he appointed Berry and I was surprised that he appointed Berry after he told us what he did about Berry's claim against the TVA. As the Governor went out I told him he had the substance but he didn't offer it and now he was offering me a mere shadow." [6]

Before the *Press Scimitar* published Crump's statement, it gave Browning a preview. His response appeared with the statement. There was not, said Browning, "a truthful statement in his whole harangue." Crump apparently imagined that "his flamboyant language and silly prattle will becloud the issue, and that he can drag me down to his level." The core of the matter was that "Mr. Crump's pride was hurt when I failed to appoint him to the United States Senate. Detecting that, I intimated . . . that there might not be a conflict with any aspiration of his for the next vacancy from West Tennessee. . . ." Browning denied that he had any plans for the

5   There are several typed copies of this statement in Crump's papers. The *Press Scimitar's* publication of the statement had Browning arriving at Crump's office at 11 A.M. It deleted the word "sneak."
6   Memorandum. Crump Papers.

Senate. "I will be elected to succeed myself as governor that year, and I hereby announce my candidacy. He will live under my administration, whether he likes it or not."

He concluded by putting his conflict with Crump on a plane of the "larger issues": "No, this is not a power fight, nor is it a contest between him and his old enemies. It is a fight between decent people and ruthless corruption, and I shall carry it to him until he is satisfied." He would not submit to "the dictation of a mere man. I take my orders from the people. . . ." [7]

There is was: Crump said he had been offered a gigantic trade; Browning said Crump's pride was hurt when he had failed to appoint the Memphis leader to the Senate in the spring of 1938 when a vacancy had occurred. Could Crump's statement to Browning on the morning of September 13 that "he had the substance in his hands and could have appointed me when he appointed Berry" lend weight to Browning's claim that Crump was hurt when he was not appointed? It would seem so, except for the following memorandum made by Crump:

Sunday evening April 25th [1937] about 8:00 after Mrs. Crump and myself had returned from a country ride with Miss Muller I went by the Baptist Hospital to see Frank Rice. He told me some of my friends had gotten Abe Waldauer to leave that afternoon, I think by plane, for Nashville, to see the Governor in my behalf for Senator.

I told Rice I didn't want it and was sorry they made that move. I called Mrs. Waldauer to get Abe's number in Nashville. She gave it to me at her parent's home. I called several times but was unable to locate Waldauer. He returned home the next morning, Monday. I got him immediately and had him call Browning and under no circumstances to consider my name and to forget it. [8]

Apparently, he really did not want to go to the Senate, but then why did he seemingly reproach Browning for not appointing him? Crump was simply pointing out that if Browning had wanted him in the Senate, he could have made the effort in 1937 rather than in 1940.

Whatever Browning said at the conference, or whatever he meant, the fact remains that he, the governor, went from Nashville to Memphis to see Crump in Crump's office, and in view of the basic differences that were developing between them, a proposition was the

7 *Press Scimitar,* November 6, 1937.
8 Memorandum. Crump Papers.

only thing he could have had on his mind. And the most plausible proposition he could make was that he would support Crump in a senatorial contest in 1940 in return for Crump's acceptance of Browning's policies.

Nevertheless, Browning's action seems almost incomprehensible. Crump had been burned once by the Horton–Caldwell–Lea coterie, and anyone who knew Crump even slightly should have known that it would be impossible to get him to agree to any kind of association with them again. Moreover, Browning's assumption that Crump would run against McKellar was self-delusion. Crump knew how jealously McKellar clung to his office, and he knew also that McKellar could be more effective in the Senate in achieving certain objectives for Memphis than he himself could be.

Browning had acted out of desperation. He had failed, but he was bold, and he was a gambler. He called a special session. On October 10 the legislature, responding to Browning's pressure and expressing a sectional jealousy over the strength of the giant on the bluff, passed the county-unit bill. The "county-unit basis shall mean," the bill read, "that the candidate who receives the highest number of popular votes in any given county shall be considered to have carried such county and shall be entitled to the full county unit vote of such county." The number of county-unit votes was to be determined by dividing by 100 the number of votes "which such county in the past general election cast for the party nominee for governor." The maximum county-unit vote of any county, "irrespective of total vote cast, shall be one-eighth of one per cent of the population of such county according to the latest . . . federal census." [9]

"Be it further enacted," the bill significantly added, "that nominations provided by this act for candidates elected by the electors for the entire state, to-wit, governor, U.S. senator and railroad and public utilities commissioner, shall be determined on the county-unit basis." The inclusion of the public utilities commission as one of the offices to be placed under the county-unit system no doubt struck Crump as ominous in that it could lead to changes in the state's TVA program.

With the county-unit bill, Browning called for and got another weapon against Crump: a registration purge bill that gave the state

9 *Press Scimitar,* October 11, 1937.

administrative power to check Shelby County's registration lists.

To all this Crump reacted momentarily with verbal pyrotechnics. "Oh . . . this mighty faker-pretender!" he exclaimed. "He realizes there is increasing distrustfulness of the sneak over the state. He is mad. Bites himself. He will spew in his own grease before it is over." [10]

Nor was it over where Browning was concerned. On November 12 the legislature was set to work again. The governor wanted even more power. A bill was passed increasing the membership of the state board of elections from three to six, an action that would in effect give the governor control over the state's election machinery. Another repealed the requirement of a jury trial for ouster suits, a provision that opened the door for mass firings. In addition to these legislative measures the governor appointed a "Crime Commission" to investigate political methods employed in the state.

Browning's massive assault on Crump placed one of his Memphis friends in an anomalous position. It was Abe Waldauer, an assistant city attorney until 1936, when, as he declared, he resigned rather than vote against Browning who was then running for the Senate against the Crump-supported Nathan Bachman. Waldauer's action did not represent a break with Crump: it was just his decision to adhere to principle where a personal friendship was involved.

It was a friendship with sentimental overtones, going back to the days of the First World War. Browning was the captain of Battery A, 114th Field Artillery, and young Waldauer served under him. "His campaign for Congress was planned in the dugouts of the Argonne Forest," Waldauer said. Captain Browning was popular with his men, for he "had sense enough to let the Battery run itself." [11] When the war was over and the boys were back home, Waldauer allied himself with Browning's political fortunes and saw him rise to the governorship.

With Browning as governor, it fell to Waldauer's lot to act as liaison between Nashville and Memphis. When Browning made his appointments, he named Waldauer as a member of the state election board. The board's principal function was that of appointing one member to each county election commission, and in the performance of this work Waldauer was most conscientious. The board held open

10 *Ibid.*, November 8, 1937.
11 Interview with Abe D. Waldauer, September 17, 1957.

hearings regarding appointments, and "every citizen who wished to do so was invited to appear before it to make such representation as would be helpful in securing capable and honest election officials in each county." [12]

When Browning requested an increase in the board's membership to six, it was, as Waldauer pointed out, an expression of "no confidence" in its personnel. So Waldauer decided to break the cord which over the years had bound them together. He announced his decision in a dramatic radio address on the evening of November 9. "I had always accounted myself the governor's friend," he declared. "Why would he repudiate me? If I have not measured up to the duties and responsibilities of the office, will he advise the people wherein I have failed?" If the governor's purpose was to purify elections, Waldauer had constructive suggestions. He would have a permanent registration in all counties and require each person to sign his name on the registration book. When the registrant voted, he would have to present a matching signature.

The break was an occasion full of pathos—the end of a "comradeship born in the fire of battle—a fire that welds men's souls. . . . As Kipling wrote of Tommy Atkins: 'Was there aught that I did not share—/Of vigil or pain or ease,/One joy or woe that I did not know,/Dear heart across the seas.' " [13]

The next day the *Press Scimitar* stated that "many could detect intense feeling in Mr. Waldauer's voice and delivery." It further reported that Browning, hunched over a radio in a Nashville hotel, "heard Waldauer's talk with a trace of tears in his eyes." [14]

Crump was also "reported" to have been glued to his radio during the address. It was the first knowledge he had of Waldauer's position, for he had "never mentioned" Browning to Waldauer.[15] If the governor had wept, Crump might have smiled, for Waldauer, progressive and astute, would be a welcome ally.

The next day the Shelby boss laid down his arms and relaxed. He took his granddaughters, Betty and Demetria, to a football game. But the battle continued. In December the state cancelled $306,500 of Crump-held insurance on the buildings of the West Tennessee Teachers College at Memphis. Crump wrote the refund check of

12 *Press Scimitar,* November 10, 1937.
13 *Ibid.*   14 *Ibid.*
15 Interview with Abe D. Waldauer, September 17, 1957.

$21.46 in unearned premiums, making it out to "Luke Lea, Lewis Pope/or State of Tenn." The check was returned and another sent, this time made out just to the state. On the last day of the year the *Commercial Appeal* whimsically reprinted a picture of Crump and Browning together that it had published shortly after the governor's nomination. Crump cut out the picture, drew bars across Browning's face, and filed it in his papers.

From the first, Crump had insisted that the power issue lay behind his difference with Browning. "This is a utility fight pure and simple. . . . Browning is merely fronting for them. They know him. . . . He wouldn't dare call an extra session if the utilities, with their Wall Street money, were not supporting him." [16] In January, 1938, Browning made a move that Crump thought suspicious. The governor proposed that the state of Tennessee "cooperate" with the federal government in setting up "privately financed non-profit corporations" which would operate in districts to be set up by a "Tennessee Rural Electrification Commission." [17]

The government was not cooperative. McKellar had gotten to Roosevelt first, explained the *Press Scimitar*.[18] So had Crump. In a letter to the President he said he wanted to "protest" Browning's scheme to alter the TVA distribution arrangement for Tennessee. "To begin with Governor Browning hasn't a sincere bone in his body. . . . And, too, Governor Browning is surrounded by a coterie of bad men. He has them sitting in his white ribbon." [19]

Meanwhile, the governor was firing Shelby County holders of state jobs. Only one, J. M. Smith, commissioner of education, was permitted to remain. On January 8 Browning named Marshall Priest state comptroller, one of the stalwarts of the Lea–Caldwell–Horton regime. In February he fired the state highway engineer "for the good of the service." [20] The engineer said he had been discharged for "resisting pressures" that would rob the state. Would Browning please explain? asked the Nashville *Banner* in an editorial.

The fight ended abruptly with Crump the victor. On February 12 the state supreme court declared unconstitutional the county-unit law.

16 *Press Scimitar,* October 7, 1937.
17 *Ibid.,* January 28, 1936.
18 *Ibid.*
19 *Commercial Appeal,* January 25, 1938.
20 Nashville *Banner,* February 7, 1938.

The Shelby majorities were safe. Judge Grafton Green wrote the majority opinion. Citing cases involving the U.S. Supreme Court's interpretation of the Fourteenth Amendment, he stated that the state could not confer the right to exercise the franchise upon one class of voters and deprive another, unless the discrimination could be logically justified. His final point was a thrust at those who saw the magnitude of the Shelby vote as something bad in itself: "In our form of government a large vote in a constitutional election cannot be regarded as an evil, and dealt with as such under the police power of the state. . . . Devaluation of full participation in primary elections cannot be justified as a commonplace exercise of police power. Such participation in itself does not menace the safety, health nor morals of the state. Discrimination against the citizens of a particular county cannot be sustained on the bare ground that they took a large part in a primary election." [21]

The following day the *Press Scimitar* handed down its decision. The people of Tennessee had won a victory, but "We trust that the victory will not make our Shelby politicians too cocky. . . . The people of other parts of Tennessee envy Shelby its good city and county government, but they detest and distrust our political methods." Since Crump gave both government and politics, he should "bring the politics up to the level of the government." [22]

The court's decision put Shelby into politics again, and just one week later a Shelby candidate announced for governor. Walter Chandler said that he was in the race and that he had the support of Crump and McKellar. Across the state, people who hoped for statesmanship and dignity in the statehouse were pleased. Five days later, however, state senator Prentice Cooper of Shelbyville, west Tennessee, announced. He declared that he had no political ties with any Tennessee faction.

Quickly, doubts arose over Chandler's candidacy. Crump, always hesitant to test his own candidate across the state, saw the possibility of a Chandler victory diminished by another west Tennessean in the race. Further, said the *Commercial Appeal*, McKellar's endorsement had been only "lukewarm." [23] The *Press Scimitar* thought that while Chandler was "an exceptionally able man," he had "never questioned

21 *Commercial Appeal*, February 13, 1938.
22 *Press Scimitar*, February 14, 1938.
23 *Commercial Appeal*, February 27, 1938.

the election methods of the Shelby County machine," and he therefore could not carry Crump across the state. Crump wondered. A canvass was made of the state's leading newspapers and the concensus was that a candidate from beyond Shelby County would have a better chance of defeating Browning. On March 2 Chandler announced that he was withdrawing from the race. Crump announced that he would support Cooper.

A week later, Cooper wrote to Crump, thanking him for his endorsement. Crump responded by drawing up a platform for Cooper, delivered by a third party. It was a litany of pledges to rectify Browning's grievous errors:

I propose to eliminate Browning's Hot Taxes.
I propose to tear up the $50,000.00 Contract he gave Lewis Pope.
I propose to fix it so Luke Lea will not have his long fingers around the State's affairs.
The Power Trust will not handle me against the interest of the people.
I will not issue Pardons for the sole purpose of permitting someone to make big money. . . .
I will not bribe Legislators to pass any kind of Bill.
I will not fire worthy people for political purposes. . . .
I propose to give TVA to all the homes, farms and factories and the Power Trust will not tell me how to do it.
I will give the people of Tennessee an honest administration. Goods will be bought on Merit and price. Contracts will be awarded the same way. [24]

Cooper apparently did not sign the pledge and return it, but he reported periodically on his campaign activities.

When April came, yellow jonquils bloomed everywhere, and personal cares faded before the advent of spring. Mrs. Crump was in Miami, so Crump, anxious to forget politics, took off with some of his office force to the Hot Springs races. He wrote Mr. Crump a relaxed account of the group's activities. The "sucker" had been Ernest Coleman, the careful, correct man who acted as Crump's aide. At first Coleman had declined to bet, "said he didn't know how, where or anything about it." The next day "the touts got him. They pulled their usual trick. One was owner—the other was a big shot—lot of tickets in his hand—betting commissioner." Coleman, "even with his usual timid-ness, never an extra dollar to spare, fell for it.

24 Crump to Prentice Cooper. March 7, 1938. Crump Papers.

He bet his whole wad. . . . I had no idea what had happened, but I said, 'Coleman, how about the Phillistines, the Touts,' and he said, 'to tell you the truth, I've been to Krauses.' " [25]

He had other light news. There was the man from Mississippi who "wants to be Mayor of Memphis—crazy. Called me several times. . . . Said I came from Mississippi and got to be Mayor, Why shouldn't he?" [26]

He was shortly writing her again—this time a more serious letter. In the April 9 issue of *Collier's* there had been an article, "Mista Crump Keeps Rollin' Along." He did not like it, called it "inexcusable" and "incorrect." The "biggest prevarication of all" was "that we have all the County's Insurance. Of course, you know that is a willful and malicious fabrication." Yet there were "some very good lines. They say we are not grafters, and of course we are not, give a good Government, stick with our friends and are winners. We are given that credit." [27]

Home in Memphis he took in a baseball game. "I am going with a large crowd, probably twenty five or thirty." He gave the home news: "John and Jane are in Nashville—Edward and Louise in New Orleans." Frank Rice was in the hospital, "really a very sick man. . . . Your yard, grass, shrubbery looks beautiful and in the next two or three days we will have the house from cellar to garret spotless." [28]

As Crump watched the azaleas bloom in his yard, Browning's program for the purification of Shelby politics went into the first act of its comic-opera sequence. On March 18 the governor's election board threw out the Shelby election commission that was friendly to Crump and replaced it with three Browning backers. One of the new commissioners was Crump's fierce foe of yesteryear, Galen Tate.

It was not until April 12 that the flurry of court activity had subsided sufficiently to enable the new commission to set about its work. Meeting at 9 A.M., the group chose Tate as their commander-in-chief, who forthwith announced: "We are going to Lytle McKee, the former chairman, for the keys, then go to the courthouse and take charge of the books." With a *Press Scimitar* reporter and cameraman along to bear faithful witness, the group "resolutely" led by Tate,

25 "Krauses" was a large Memphis dry cleaning establishment.
26 Crump to Bessie Crump, April 4, 1938. Crump Papers.
27 Crump to Bessie Crump, April 7, 1938. Crump Papers.
28 Crump to Bessie Crump, April 14, 1938. Crump Papers.

began its mission. "Down Third to Union, up Union to Front, they walked, and into the office of Sternberger and McKee Cotton Co., where Mr. McKee has his office." There, the following colloquy occurred:

"Mr. McKee in?" Mr. Tate asked as he walked in.
"No, he isn't," replied a clerk.
Mr. Tate walked around the office, spied Vance Hill, who is with the cotton firm.
"Hello Vance," said Mr. Tate.
"Why, hello, Galen," replied Mr. Hill.
"When will Mr. McKee be in?"
"I don't know," replied Mr. Hill. "He doesn't usually come down until pretty late, just about when he feels like it."
"You don't know when he will be here?" asked Mr. Tate.
"No, I don't know what to tell you."
"Well, I guess the best thing we can do is come back," said Mr. Tate, and the three left the room.

After brief deliberation, it was decided to visit Ross Mathews, secretary of the old commission. They walked down Front to Monroe, through Monroe to the alley behind Lowenstein's Department Store, emerging on Main in front of the Commerce Title Building, where Mathews had his office. In the lobby all huddled to scan the directory and found that Mathews and his associate, Lake Hays, had an office on the eleventh floor. "Maybe you all had better wait and let me sneak up on this fellow," said the leader, but "they all got into the elevator. . . ." Then again:

"Hello Lake," said Mr. Tate as he entered the office.
"Why, hello Galen" replied Mr. Hays, sitting in his office with a client and a stenographer. "Well, what's all this, the reporters following you around for a story?"
"Is Ross Mathews here?" asked Mr. Tate.
"No, he isn't in, Galen, and I don't know when he will be here," said Mr. Hays.
"Well, goodby Lake," said Mr. Tate.
"Goodby Galen," said Mr. Hays.

From the Commerce Title Building the group angled across Court Square and northward past the old Lily Bakery to the courthouse. There they sought out George Finlay, the custodian. He stood in front of his office as the new commission approached:

"I want to see Mr. Finlay," said Mr. Tate.

"This is he," replied Mr. Finlay.

"Mr. Finlay, this is Galen Tate," the chairman said, extending his hand, which Mr. Finlay took. "I am chairman of the Shelby County Election Commission. . . . Are you the custodian of the building?" Mr. Tate then asked.

"Yes sir."

"Have you the keys to the election room?"

"No sir," replied Mr. Finlay.

"Well," said Mr. Tate very formally, "here are three members of the Shelby County Election Commission who make demand and request of you for the keys to that room."

"About the only way I know to let you in that room . . . would be to get an acetylene torch."

"Then you haven't the keys?" Mr. Tate said.

"No sir."

"All right, thank you," said Mr. Tate, and the three left. [29]

At 11:15 A.M. a Nashville court enjoined chairman Tate and his associates from proceeding further with their plan to take over the election machinery. The issue was back in the courts.

In June the state supreme court put the final stamp of legality on Browning's election board. But before Tate and his group could take over the registration books, Abe Waldauer, as a member of the state election board, seized the books himself and began his own purge. Personally checking the addresses of registrants, he found, he declared, explanations of specific situations that Browning forces might claim as instances of fraudulent registration. How, for example, could a dozen people be registered when claiming the same address? Waldauer investigated and found the address covered one whole interior court of dwellings.[30] His findings, to be sure, strengthened the organization's claim to the purity of the ballot box.

Three weeks later, representatives of the state election board came into Memphis to assist Tate's local election board with a supplemental registration of voters for the approaching primary. There were, of course, misunderstandings between the state and local registration personnel. Crump supporters claimed that Browning registrars were closing the books, leaving many standing in line. When a supplemental registration at a residence was halted at the closing hour of 9 P.M., leaving "nearly 100" persons crowded around the house,

29 *Press Scimitar,* April 13, 1938.
30 Interview with Abe D. Waldauer, September 17, 1957.

Crump men set up a table on the sidewalk and held a "supplemental supplemental" registration. Knowledge of this brought Waldauer rushing to the scene in a police car, where the owner of the residence, clad in long underwear, received him at the door. He had closed the books, he said, at 9 P.M., on the "personal" orders of Galen Tate, who had telephoned him. "Put this down, too," he commanded a reporter: "They've tried to bribe us and threaten us, too. They came here yesterday, one of the big men in the organization and tried to buy us off." Who was the big organization man who tried to buy him off? He did not know, but he "could sure find . . . out." [31] Commissioner Waldauer decided that the "supplemental supplemental" registration was valid and ordered it sent to the courthouse.

On July 12 the "crime commission" moved into Memphis. A spokesman stated that "we intend to have a thorough investigation and go fully into all reported lax law enforcement conditions." Crump immediately dubbed it the "slime commission," and had Will Gerber do an investigation on some of the commission's personnel. Gerber shortly provided a memorandum on the subject. One member of the commission had "at least on three occasions" been investigated by the Veterans Bureau. "As a result of one of these investigations, certain money was paid back to a veteran," after the subject of the investigation had "on a certain day, a certain month and year, in a certain place in Ripley [Tennessee] gotten down on his knees and pleaded with an investigator for the Veterans Bureau out of Nashville, and in the presence of four witnesses, not to institute proceedings looking toward sending . . . [the subject] to Atlanta [federal penitentiary]. Another member had had disbarment proceedings filed against him in chancery court, but they were dropped after he had made restitution to the party he had attempted to defraud."

"A fine pair of jail birds to turn loose on the people of Shelby County," wrote Crump on the margin of the memorandum Gerber had given him.[32]

The crime commission's hearings produced more conflict. Overton and Gerber attended to observe the proceedings and to answer questions. In the midst of the hearing Overton arose, "quivering with anger—perspiration pouring down his face," to shout his resentment

31 *Commercial Appeal,* July 9, 1938.
32 Memorandum. Crump Papers.

of "star-chamber" testimony by "paid witnesses who could not be cross-examined. . . . Our elections are as clean, or cleaner in Memphis than in any other city in the state. . . . There were charges made about an election in Knoxville, but you have made no investigation of Knoxville." The Nashville attorney conducting the hearings tried to soothe the mayor, but he "rushed on without a pause."

Overton's verbal barrage was interrupted by a question shouted by Gerber: The mayor "would like to know whether there will be a cross-examination of these rats. . . . We would like to know what these witnesses are being paid. Why don't you answer now? Answer it now!"

Eventually the chairman got on with the questioning. Yes, Overton agreed, there was an organization in every ward of the city, and policemen and firemen took part in the work. Were they ordered to work in the wards? "We don't have to order them. They have never been ordered to do ward work."

Did the policemen on the beat haul voters to register and vote? "No Sir."

Was it true that "a certain vote is allotted to each ward and they have to bring it in?"

"Absolutely untrue."

Was it true that whiskey was distributed on the day before the election, "especially among the colored population with promises of more if they returned the next day? Do you approve of such practice?"

"If such a condition exists, of course I don't approve. Who said that—this fellow who got $500 for testifying?"

Was it true that "negroes are voted in large numbers in Democratic primaries in Shelby County?"

Yes, they voted; they had the right to vote; they vote for us "because we have been fair with them."

And on it went. The testimony did bring out that the Shannon Lumber Company paid the poll tax of its Negro employees, deducting it from their wages at the rate of twenty-five cents weekly. Negroes were taken to register and to vote in a company truck.[33] But this was hardly a revelation.

---

33 The crime commission hearing was covered by the *Commercial Appeal*, July 15, 1938.

Several days later the crime commission left Memphis, its attorney announcing that it had discovered "13,437 names not lawfully listed" on the registration lists.[34] No details were provided.

On July 4 in the midst of registration checks and the crime commission furor Tyler McLain, the attorney general for Shelby County, died. A huge colorful man and one of the original stalwarts of the Crump organization, he had been an exacting prosecutor, securing a high conviction rate. He was the first major figure to thin the ranks, but soon there would be more.

In mid-summer the governor's race began to gain momentum. On July 1 Crump revealed that the Shelby organization had contributed $25,000 to Browning's 1936 campaign fund, a revelation calculated to suggest the extent of Browning's perfidy in his attack on Crump. Even worse, added Crump, on the day before the election "Browning phoned that he wanted to see me. We made an engagement. He came to my office and said he wanted more money. I told him all the money had been reported and there was no more." [35]

Browning roared his indignation. "I never mentioned money to him in my life. . . . If Crump sent any such money as he says to my organization it was without knowledge on my part." He could not "personally" verify it, but he had been told that Crump "never turned in what he was supposed to. . . . He is a liar," Browning concluded.[36]

Among the numerous memoranda Crump made and placed in his "Browning" file was one on the subject of a contribution to Browning's campaign fund: "After Browning's primary and the November election was figured on I was asked by Washington to raise money for the Roosevelt election—[I] named W. G. Durr [as collecting agent]. He raised the money, we gave Broadbent, Manager for Browning $25,000.00. . . . After the election Browning came down, and said he wanted to see if he couldn't get more money. Frank Rice and I told him we just couldn't go any further—thought plenty had been given. Whether he got any from the utilities—some big mighty interests or not I don't know." [37]

Browning represented the real issue between him and Crump as that of prohibition. Speaking at Erin, Tennessee, he said that "Shelby sent a man to dangle their registration of 117,000 voters over my head. By innuendo he brought out that the boss expected me to

34 *Press Scimitar,* July 26, 1938.   36 *Ibid.*
35 *Press Scimitar,* July 1, 1938.   37 Memorandum. Crump Papers.

accept a wet platform. I frankly told him I was not interested." [38]

Crump denied it. Sending identical telegrams to all of the major Tennessee newspapers and fourteen lesser ones, he said he would give $1,000 to "any charitable institution in your City if a fair Committee of five will say after hearing proof that a reliable person representing us" had advised the governor that he "should run on a wet platform next time if he expected Shelby County's support." He would give another $1,000 if he failed to prove that he contributed $25,000 to Browning's '36 campaign.

Crump had more to say: "I said the State sent Charles Phillips in Memphis $500.00. Browning said that was a lie. Phillips received that amount before he testified before the Crime Commission. If I can't prove this I will give a third one thousand dollars to some charity." Browning's trouble was that he was "frantic." He "realizes he is licked. . . . He feels the ground shake and tremble under him. I realize he would like to see me dive three times and come up twice. However that does not justify him telling falsehoods about Memphis and me." [39]

Browning played full upon the theme of Memphis "corruption." He announced that he contemplated sending troops to the city to insure an honest election. On July 30 there was a report in Memphis that 1200 troops would arrive on election day. Immediately, organization attorneys sought a federal injunction to prevent the action. They did not have far to go, for sitting in the federal building on the bluff was U.S. District Judge John Martin. He quickly obliged. "I could not," he said, "be called upon to issue a more just writ, placing the judicial power of the United States by court order at the disposal of the citizens of this county to defend them from the unjustified, tyrannical, unconstitutional, despotic invasion by a swashbuckling governor. . . ." [40]

Fired by civic patriotism, Judge Martin's words soared above the even, judicious tones associated with the court. Commented the Nashville *Banner:* "And think of a judge on the bench indulging in the abuse of a person in court which the Memphis judge directed at the state's governor!" [41]

38 Nashville *Tennessean,* July 20, 1938.
39 Scrapbook news clipping.
40 *Press Scimitar,* August 2, 1938.
41 Nashville *Banner,* August 2, 1938.

Browning had one spokesman in Memphis—Gilmer Richardson. He defended Browning's plan to use troops. "I personally saw hundreds of names copied from the registration books to the poll sheets and later saw the ballots put into the box. . . . This was in the Second Precinct of the First Ward in the 1932 primary, and two of the men who were officials at that polling place at that time have been appointed to serve again this year." [42]

Three days before the election Browning announced that he would not send troops to Memphis "unless he changed his mind." That night he came to Memphis and addressed a rally of over 8000 persons at the Fairgrounds. "There is nobody, my friends," he said in connection with the troop issue, "that is afraid of the good clean boys of the 117th Infantry. . . . They have been talking about those boys as if they were outlaws, and I want to say to you that they come from the best families in Tennessee." No federal judge, said the governor, could deter him from the use of troops if he so chose, because "I am the chief executive of a sovereign state, and I know exactly what my rights are!"

He explained the reason for his break with Crump. The Shelby group knew that they could not beat him for governor, so "they got on the band wagon. After we had gone down the road a little ways there began to be some fussing. The organization said 'What's wrong?' I said there is nothing wrong. I said you got on the wagon and you can ride as long as you want to, but you can't drive. I've got the reins."

He explained at length how he had been invited to speak to a Methodist men's group by a local minister, but "the political Sanhedrin of Shelby County descended upon his church" and forced the minister to publish a statement repudiating the governor. "I don't know who it was the Sanhedrin talked to. . . . But I do know that a delegation of ministers who came to see me today, who are as fine as ever trod God's footstool, told me that he [the minister] never signed the statement. . . ." [43]

It was a clever performance. The *Press Scimitar* reported that the crowd was friendly, and not a "single hostile incident" occurred. That there had been none seemed almost inconceivable to the paper; there had to be harassment, so a boxed insert was placed in the

42 *Press Scimitar*, August 1, 1938.   43 *Ibid.*, August 2, 1938.

Browning story: "A switch engine on the Southern Railroad, just south of the Fairgrounds, did considerable whistle-blowing and letting off of steam as it shuffled cars about during the early part of the governor's speech. There was noise as the cars were banged about."

"Had it thundered, we would have been blamed!" exclaimed Crump.[44]

Browning's arrival in Memphis the night before the election was a bold political stroke, but it did not save the election for him. He lost to Cooper by nearly 70,000 votes. The governor-elect had not needed Shelby County. Indeed, the surprise of the election was Shelby itself, where Browning got nearly 9,000 votes. Possibly Browning had convinced some of the church people that the issue was truly prohibition and had awakened in their minds a suspicion that Crump, with the coterie of Jews and Catholics around him, was not really with them.

On the other hand, it seemed that Crump had gotten his message across the state. Horton and Luke Lea evoked unpleasant memories. What was Browning really trying to do about TVA? And his war on Crump seemed needlessly reckless.

Years later, Browning sat in his bare, old-fashioned office in Huntingdon, Tennessee, and recollected his great battle with Shelby. Time had not erased all of the bitterness. Crump's charges were imaginary, he said. The men he had appointed were capable and honest; that they had been caught in the backwash of the Lea–Horton debacle was not their fault. It would have been unworthy of him not to have appointed them, for they were experienced and had supported him. Crump was a puritan, whose high principle and rectitude were not signs of morality, but a mere shield for his ego. The break had been caused by his interference in appointments, his seizing on every piece of evidence, no matter how circumstantial and remote, and magnifying it to damaging proportions. If Crump had remained in Shelby County and left the administration of the state to him, all would have been well.[45]

There may have been substance to Browning's position, but Crump had learned to be wary of governors. Browning came at a time when the central issue of Crump's whole political career was just short of realization. TVA power had to come into Memphis. Browning, it seemed to him, was not firm on TVA.

44   *Ibid.*, August 3, 1938.
45   Interview with Gordon Browning, October 21, 1957.

But Browning was gone, and already workmen in Memphis were building the substations to receive TVA power. The remaining barrier was the presence of the National Power and Light Company in Memphis, for it seemed not yet convinced that the war had been lost, although battles had been going against it for several years. In the Ashwander case of 1936 the U.S. Supreme Court had decided that the sale of federal power was constitutional. A major reverse for private power had been the reelection of Roosevelt in 1936. In Tennessee the presence of Leon Jourolmon on the state utility commission made for a favorable view of public power from that agency. Continued court actions aimed at blocking Memphis from constructing its own power supply system failed.[46] By March there seemed to be no further hope. On the thirty-first Paul B. Sawyer, the president of National Power Company came to Memphis to negotiate.

Although the city was prepared to build its own distribution system, the sensible course was for it to purchase the already existing facilities of the Memphis Power and Light Company. The city would buy, Crump had said, but "of course, that means draining the water, junking the scrap and some real bookkeeping figures." [47] The problem was to arrive at "real bookkeeping" figures. There was also the question of the city purchasing the gas properties. It was a matter that Mayor Overton was "reluctant to consider," but since Sawyer and his associates refused to consider a sale of the electric properties alone, Overton agreed to negotiate informally for the purchase of both.[48]

Negotiations went on sporadically throughout the summer, but the positions of the company and city were so far apart that Sawyer left Memphis at the end of June. He returned in September, apparently in a more tractable mood. On the twenty-third he made an offer to sell the electric properties at a new low figure of $16,401,418.77. It was refused. The following day, J. A. Krug, chief power planning engineer for TVA, sitting with Mayor Overton and Major Thomas Allen, chairman of the city light and water board, submitted to the company an offer of $13,000,000, with TVA paying $1,750,000 of this amount for its share of the joint-use properties.

46 The full story of the TVA coming to Memphis can be found in Hon, "The Memphis Power and Light Deal."
47 *Commercial Appeal,* January 25, 1938.
48 Hon, "The Memphis Power and Light Deal," 358.

Two days later Crump was asked what he thought of the city's offer. "The power company ought to snap it up like hot cakes," he said.[49] He complimented Overton for his work on the matter, but added significantly that the city ought also to buy the gas properties. "Gas rates here are entirely too high."

On the twenty-seventh the company made two counterproposals, naming two figures at which it would either sell the electric properties alone or both the gas and the electric. Both were refused. Three days later the city and TVA made an offer of $13,500,000 for the electric properties. The company refused, but late that evening Sawyer indicated that he would accept the figure if the company's office building and some minor properties were excluded. Overton then joined the conference, and an agreement was reached.

The following day there were the customary statements from Overton and Sawyer expressing pleasure that the deal had been made. The *Commercial Appeal* ran a large picture of the smiling negotiators, and the *Press Scimitar* carried a full-page statement by fifteen business concerns expressing their gratitude to Mayor Overton and Major Allen for their work: "A grateful city acknowledges its debt to you for having accomplished the greatest progressive step in our long and proud history." [50] There remained one small matter—ratification of the agreement by the city commission.

Even before the commissioners got a copy of the Overton-negotiated contract, lightning flashed across the sky. On October 11 Crump publicly denounced a recently enacted grocery-closing ordinance that Overton had sponsored and which the commission had unanimously approved. He said it was unfair to the small grocer, and it was also "impractical . . . and unsound."

Immediately finance commissioner Joe Boyle added his criticism. He thought "the ordinance was impractical and silly and said so at the time." But Overton wanted "unanimous votes in the commission and I went along with him. I haven't felt good about it since. I used to be in the grocery business." [51]

Asked if this meant a "break," Crump referred reporters to Overton. Overton referred them back to Crump. Manifestly, it was, and it concerned more than the grocery ordinance which, a few days

49   *Ibid.*, 359
50   Quoted in Hon, "The Memphis Power and Light Deal," 361.
51   *Press Scimitar*, October 12, 1938.

later, all commissioners excepting Overton's man, Ralph Picard, dutifully repealed. Boyle was Crump's voice, and the issue was the secrecy that had surrounded negotiations leading to the September 30 agreement. "The first thing I knew of the power company purchase was when I read it in the newspapers. . . . I can't find out anything about the contract. But I am going to find out how that money was spent and what we got and I'm demanding that the entire deal be aired." [52] Had Overton negotiated the deal without consulting Crump? He had; in fact at the time the agreement was made, Crump was at a football game. It seemed a strange course for the mayor, for it was Crump who had laid out the grand strategy and who had fought the battles that made public power a reality. More than that, the agreement was the culmination of the most personally significant objective in Crump's public life. With the goal at hand, Overton had stepped in personally to direct negotiations!

Why had he done it? "Arrogance and peevishness," said Crump.[53] There were also indications that Overton, after the long years of following the main plans of city development laid out by Crump, wanted to move to the forefront of things. In the summer of 1938, Frank Rice, who was ill, asked to be relieved of ward organization work, and his job was detailed to Picard for the residential wards and Boyle for the downtown district. At the time of the break reports were circulating around the courthouse "that Mayor Overton and Commissioner Picard were building their own political lines, using the residential wards as a nucleus." [54] Perhaps in the power company negotiations Overton thought the time had arrived to dignify his office, and himself personally, by an autonomy that it did not altogether possess. The mayor's feelings were understandable, but to assert his independence on the issue of negotiations with the power company was a graceless move.

With commissioners Boyle, Cliff Davis, and O. P. Williams siding with Crump, it was immediately obvious that the Overton agreement rested on thin ice. Editor Meeman attempted to give it a firmer basis. "Our TVA Contract—Let No One Harm It!" proclaimed a *Press Scimitar* editorial.[55] Crump was not going to be stopped by the *Press*

---

52 *Commercial Appeal*, October 16, 1938.
53 *Press Scimitar*, December 16, 1939.
54 *Ibid.*, October 20, 1938.
55 *Ibid.*, October 17, 1938.

Scimitar. "I've been fighting the power trust for more than 30 years now. We had them licked once before under Mayor Ashcroft but there was a slipup. There will be no slipup this time. I'm determined about this business and, if the trust doesn't believe it, I'm ready to square with them any time." If the Overton agreement, still being worked out, "was not what it should be, Memphis will continue with its own TVA plant and go to the last ditch to own its gas plant. . . ." [56]

On November 23 the city commission got all the details of the deal of September 30 with an inventory "showing down to nuts and bolts just what the utility retains and what the city gets." [57] On November 30 the city made a new offer. It would give $17,385,000 for both the gas and electric properties.

Company officials declined. The new proposition was a "surprise" to them. In a letter to Major Allen the company stated its case. In the September 30 agreement "we made a great sacrifice in connection with the sale of our electric properties, this was by reason of the federally financed destructive competition to which we are being subjected." But the situation did "not obtain in connection with our gas properties, which are capable of independent operation and expansion on a remunerative basis irrespective of any electric competition." [58]

Yet the company had no rancor toward the people of Memphis. It was giving them a "Christmas present." As of December 1 it would reduce its electric rates to that of the TVA level.

Then Meeman entered the negotiations. He advised going ahead and buying on the basis of the September 30 contract. "We want no destructive competition in Memphis, no torn-up streets, no further investment of funds of taxpayers, either local or federal, in a duplicating system which will not be needed if that reasonable offer is accepted." There was no good reason "why the city should go into the gas business, and many reasons why it should not." [59]

Company officials knew what Crump knew—that they had to negotiate, and on December 14 they advised the city they would accept the original offer of $13,500,000 for the electric properties and negotiate for the gas. Crump was not impressed. No negotiations

56 *Commercial Appeal,* October 30, 1938.
57 *Press Scimitar,* November 24, 1938.
58 *Ibid.,* December 3, 1938.
59 *Ibid.,* December 5, 1938.

were necessary; the city had made its offer. Moreover, it had a new federal allotment of $2,700,000 available to complete its own distribution system. The city's position was invulnerable, and Crump could not only stand firm but indulge in some observations on the character of the "Power Trust." He was sure that Diogenes with his lamp would have passed it up. "Now with their matchless gall, they say they will talk some more about a trade. I am certain they will sell their old electric light plant at their price and throw in a slice of cheese and crackers, and a sack of goobers." He made reference to the *Press Scimitar* by saying that anybody who had favored Browning in 1938 should have nothing to say about the negotiations. "I say again if their Gordon Browning had been elected, there would have been an extra session long before now, and no thought of a trade on the part of the Power Trust or reduction in lights." [60]

But the *Press Scimitar* was out to call the play if it could. The day after the company offered to negotiate the sale of its gas properties, the paper carried a large front-page editorial: "Memphis Business Leaders Say: 'We Want No Wasteful, Duplicating Power Systems: The City Should Complete Its Agreement to Purchase.'" Over half of the front page featured pictures and statements from businessmen as to why the city should go ahead with the Overton agreement and not try to get the gas properties.[61]

The paper was at it again the next evening. "Citizens Speak," ran the editorial lead. "But when politics stepped in, and officials tore up this agreement, to indulge passion, prejudice and political advantage . . . interfering with local business and branding this city as one which has no respect for the rights of honestly invested capital—Then public opinion parted company with the officials. . . ." The people of Memphis would not stand for it, "littering . . . streets," interfering with business, and the projection of an "advertisement of Memphis as a city that does not deal fairly." [62]

Crump was not disturbed, but he did make an observation concerning one of the businessmen who had been lined up by the *Press Scimitar* to support its position. "One living high up on the hog," he sermonized, "forgets how those live who toil for a living and

60   *Commercial Appeal,* December 16, 1938.
61   *Press Scimitar,* December 16, 1938.
62   *Ibid.,* December 17, 1938.

disregards what a reduction in gas rates would do for them." [63]
Meeman printed Crump's statement and appended an editorial rejoinder. Crump lived "as high on the hog" as did the businessman in
question, and if it had not affected one, it need not necessarily affect
the other.

The *Press Scimitar's* campaign continued throughout December,
but it availed nothing. The power company knew it had to sell, and
on January 8 Paul Sawyer stated that the National Power and Light
Company was willing to sell "and the city is willing to buy, so we
should get together." [64] One week later a ten-hour negotiating session
was held in Crump's office, interrupting his customary Sunday visit
with his mother. The city raised its offer for both gas and electric
properties to $18,127,000, but Sawyer rejected it. In February
TVA's two negotiators, J. A. "Cap" Krug and Joseph Swidler,
arrived in Memphis to help out. They held a lengthy meeting with
Crump on the sixth. Afterwards, Crump exclaimed, "I can smell gas
and my fingers are tingling with electricity." [65]

The final agreement was reached shortly before midnight on
February 15. The company received $17,360,000 for its properties,
$15,250,000 of which was paid by the city and the remainder by
TVA. There was also a detailed addendum of properties excepted
from the sale. The key to removing the impasse faced by the city and
the company was furnished by TVA. The company-owned steam
generating plants were excepted from the sale, with TVA agreeing
to use the power generated for a period of from one to three years.
For this service TVA would pay operational expenses of the generating plant and $100,000 a year to the company. Thus Memphis was
relieved of a property that it did not need, and the company was
able to continue to use it at a profit.

The essential difference between the Overton and Crump deals
lay in the disposition of the generating plant and gas properties. With
Overton, the city was to acquire the generating plant and not the gas
properties, whereas Crump's agreement provided for the acquisition
of the gas properties and not the generating plant.[66]

63   *Ibid.,* December 20, 1938.
64   *Ibid.,* January 9, 1939.
65   *Ibid.,* February 7, 1939.
66   Hon, "The Memphis Power and Light Deal," 368. Concluding his article

As the negotiators concluded the final details, Overton and members of the commission sat in the mayor's office in the courthouse poised to ratify the agreement. There was no sign of strained relations; they sat smoking and quietly talking.

A block away Crump sat in his office, leaning back in his chair. Shortly after 3 A.M. word came that it was over. The commissioners, including Overton, had signed the agreement, and it then went to the office of the attorneys for the city in the Commerce Title Building. There, representatives of the company and TVA attached final signatures. Hearing the news, Crump got up, put on his hat and coat, and started down the narrow corridor to the elevator. "All's well that ends well," he told a sleepy reporter.[67]

---

on the power transaction, Hon asks several questions and then attempts to answer them. Who made the better deal, Overton or Crump, and was bringing TVA to Memphis in the public interest? The Overton deal was a good one, he says. Further, it could "be safely asserted that the gas rates charged by the Memphis Power and Light Company were not exorbitant." But Crump had made the better deal. It precluded any disturbing competition between publicly owned electricity and privately owned gas. Moreover, the city had no need of the generating plants included in the Overton deal. The question of whether or not bringing TVA to Memphis was in the public interest could not be answered for "years." The doubts of the author arose from the frequently made assertion that publicly managed power tended toward inefficiency and even corruption.

Hon's article was written one year after the power deal. Time has provided more positive answers to the question of the value of public power in Memphis. The assumption that public ownership means inefficiency has been proven untrue in the operation of the Memphis Light, Gas, and Water division of the city government. Through the years of its direction under Major Thomas Allen, standards of the highest efficiency and integrity were established. Not only has low-cost TVA power provided the city with inexpensive lighting, but it has been largely responsible for the city's remarkable industrial growth in the past twenty years.

67 *Commercial Appeal*, February 16, 1939.

⊠ ☐

Chapter XI

"MR. CRUMP"

THE WINTER of success had been shadow-crossed. Frank Rice did not live to see the realization of the most important objective of the Memphis progressive crusade. He had just turned seventy when death overtook him in a New York hospital. "My old friend, Frank Rice," Crump wrote on one of his memorandum pads.

The winter dragged through its dull grayness until March, when there seems to have been a consensus that relaxation was in order. On the third, two special trains left the Memphis Union Station bound for Hot Springs and the "E. H. Crump Day at the Races." About fifty members of the Tennessee legislature were aboard, a great proportion of the Shelby organization, and the remainder "just plain race folk"—like Crump and Lem Motlow of Lynchburg, Tennessee, the state's only whiskey distiller.[1] Naturally, all of the public servants had a good reason for going. They and the legislators wanted to see firsthand how the situation was managed in Arkansas. The state administration was represented by the late Senator Estes Kefauver, then the state finance commissioner, who wanted to look into the revenue-raising aspects of racing.

Crump enjoyed the excitement of some mild betting, yet recognized

1 Jack Daniels and Wild Turkey.

that anyone "who can beat the races or any gambling game can grow oyster in a cornfield or raise chickens on a mill pond." But it was "good to be a little foolish occasionally—lose your naturalness—and Hot Springs is the place to blow off, if you don't overdo it and make it too costly." [2]

By May the weather was mild enough for the Crumps to take their evening rides around Memphis, and Clint Cleaves frequently had the car in the backyard polishing it before they began their trip. He was working on it on the evening of May 2; the light was growing dim and he hurried to finish. Through the open back door he heard a telephone ring. A few minutes later Crump came out and stood by him, observing the work. "You are doing a good job, Clint," he said. He paused a moment, then, "Clint, Mr. John has been in an accident." He turned to go into the house, and Cleaves noticed that he had a strange look on his face. Inside, he went upstairs to where Mrs. Crump lay resting. Shaken to the depths, he did what he knew he must: he told his wife that John had been killed in an airplane accident. Then he went downstairs, called all the servants together, and told them. His composure left him and he wept.[3]

The accident occurred at Grenada, Mississippi. John, Ted Northington, and pilot George Stokes were in the *Commercial Appeal*'s new white Cessna monoplane, visiting towns and cities as goodwill emissaries for the Memphis cotton carnival, soon to open. Stokes was attempting to land on a pockmarked field. His approach was too cautious, too slow. At 150 feet the plane veered off and spun in.

"My son passed in the noontide of his day," Crump wrote to a friend in Grenada. "I have never before fully appreciated the pathos expressed in the lines of the Athenian orator who said 'when a young man dies it is as if the year had died in the Spring.' " [4]

John was buried in the family plot that Crump had acquired in the old Elmwood cemetery in Memphis. The next day Crump attended George Stokes's funeral at Covington, Tennessee.

After John's death the city became alive with rumors about Crump—that he had aged perceptibly, that he carried a Bible with him and was wont to cite passages from it, and that he had "gotten religion." The death of a son would indeed cause a father to age,

2 *Press Scimitar*, March 1, 1939.
3 Interview with Clint Cleaves, August 7, 1957.
4 Crump to Wick Ranson, May 16, 1939. Crump Papers.

and for a time Crump's appearance showed the effects of the loss. Cleaves added that Crump seemed to slow down, even to the point of having him reduce driving speed when they were on a trip.

Statements that he carried a Bible with him and quoted it to all who would listen are fanciful. He quoted the Bible as readily as any Southerner, but he also quoted Shakespeare or any other literary source when he thought it apt. Willie Thomas, Crump's gardener, said that Crump used to like to talk to him about the Bible. "He really knew the Bible," Thomas said. "He liked to talk about the old prophets. Sometimes he would ask me about some of them I wouldn't know much about and I would say, 'Mr. Crump, I don't believe I can follow you there.' " "Willie," he once asked, "what do you think is the most important thing in the Bible?" Willie thought, then said, "Love the Lord thy God with all thy heart and thy neighbor as thyself." Crump said he agreed with that.[5]

He possessed a copy of the Goodspeed edition of the New Testament, and judging from the frequent underlinings and notations that appear in it he did indeed read it. He read it as a person looking for guideposts to live a more meaningful life. "When you fast, do not put on a gloomy look, like the hypocrites, for they neglect their personal appearance to let people see that they are fasting." "Good," Crump wrote across these lines. He underlined the passage "Peter asked how many times he was to forgive his brother, and Jesus said not seven but seventy times seven," and wrote "Forgive" at the top of the page. There were other passages underlined. In one instance the message had a local political application. "And if a household is disunified, that household cannot last." Over this he wrote, "Park Board." [6]

Nominally Crump was an Episcopalian, but he never attended church. Why he did not is not clear. Corporate, formal worship seemed to touch no responsive part of his nature. He would rather work. Further, Sunday mornings were reserved for the visit to his mother, and he would rather not attend at all than to attend infrequently. But he did possess a religious belief. A Baptist minister, the Reverend D. A. Ellis, stated that he had a firsthand knowledge

5 Interview with Willie Thomas, August 8, 1957.
6 Crump Papers.

of Crump's religious convictions. "The trend of his life as I knew him was to be a better man every day," said Ellis. "He had an intense desire that every man be clean and honest." [7] Once Ellis went to Crump's office, as he said, for the sole purpose of talking to Crump about his soul. Crump positively assured him that he believed there was no hope outside of Christ. "He was a real believer," said Ellis.

His religious convictions did not, however, come from the loss of John. He was not the type to "get religion." He accepted the basic principles of Christian orthodoxy as true, and worried no more about it. He loved his sons with the deep affection of a man who found his only surcease from the cares of the world in his family. Yet John was gone, and lamentations and cloaking himself in an unnatural piety could alter nothing. The mystery of it all was beyond his knowing. It was not his gift to possess the intuitions of the mystic—principle and duty were the only meaningful forces in his life. He pursued them with the complete dedication of a man who knew that somewhere there was the fulfillment of truth, and it was only along this path that he could travel to reach it.

In August, 1939, he turned again to politics. It was the year for a mayoralty, and there was, of course, the question of Overton. Overton himself answered it shortly. He announced that he was having a check made of voter registrations at his own expense. A week later he stated that he would not run in November. Presumably his registration check revealed that Crump's majorities could not be easily challenged.

On August 28, just before leaving for Battle Creek, Crump advised Memphians to "be prepared to vote on November 9 for a man who will give Memphis the best business government we ever had." Who would be mayor? "Why do you ask me?" replied Crump archly.[8]

While he was in Battle Creek, there was much speculation over his choice. For a while it appeared that it would be police commissioner Davis. Crump had just recently spoken well of Davis. He was a "high-minded gentleman. He has the faculty of looking at things as they are—seeing them as they might be." [9] But a week later the *Commercial Appeal* cited "sources" that indicated the choice would be Congressman Chandler. "Friends of Captain Chandler say

7 Interview with the Reverend D. A. Ellis, August 7, 1957.
8 *Commercial Appeal,* August 29, 1938.
9 *Press Scimitar,* August 31, 1939.

he would welcome the opportunity to return to Memphis, especially as mayor." [10]

Chandler it was. E. H. Crump, Jr., was the emissary who informed Chandler that it was Crump's wish that he become mayor. Chandler "readily agreed," but with the appearance of reluctance, for he was making a good record in Congress.[11]

Crump returned to Memphis on September 22 and made the announcement. Chandler was his choice, but he, Crump, would run instead. He explained how it would work. "If the people of our great city elect me on Nov. 9, I will be most appreciative of their vote. I will take the oath of office on the morning of Jan. 1, and immediately resign, thereby opening the way for Mr. Chandler to be elected mayor by the City Commission." The reason behind this unusual course was that "Our lawyers . . . advise it will be necessary for Walter Chandler to resign as member of Congress before he can file his qualifying petition to run for mayor." In Washington the important issue of the repeal of the neutrality bill was before Congress. "For him to resign at this time," said Crump, "while a measure of great importance is right on the threshold of Congress . . . would be a serious loss." He did not feel, therefore, that "Mr. Chandler should be called upon to vacate his seat, and lose his vote for democracy." He realized that this method of choosing a mayor was unusual, "but in the election of a President of the United States, the people do not vote for the President. In other words, I am simply an elector for Walter Chandler." [12]

The *Press Scimitar* objected to the procedure. "And what do the people think of this method of choosing their city government? . . . From the expressions we have heard, they don't like the process that gives them no part in choosing their mayor." Chandler was "intelligent . . . hard working . . . [and] efficient," but he was also "quite subservient to the machine. If there are limits to that subservience we have not seen it." What Memphis needed was a council–manager system, the paper added.[13]

Memphians were not disturbed by the procedure. On September 30, thirty thousand of them went to the Fairgrounds to participate in

10 *Commercial Appeal*, September 6, 1939.
11 Interview with E. H. Crump, Jr., January 7, 1958.
12 *Commercial Appeal*, October 23, 1939.
13 *Press Scimitar*, October 23, 1939.

the E. H. Crump Day celebration, and on election day "elector" Crump was chosen mayor without opposition.

As Overton concluded his days as mayor, it occurred to him to add constructive suggestions for the better administration of the Memphis light, gas, and water division. The mayor touched a nerve that had been sensitized in his recent relationship with Crump, and Crump exploded: "Watkins Overton's mind is as warped and out of shape with his peevishness and insincerity as a bale of cotton with three hoops off. He is now declaring for certain things which he consistently opposed during his 12 long years as mayor of Memphis, and I have the facts and the proof. After the first of the year . . . I propose to show and I believe to the satisfaction of the people . . . his insincerity and the role he has as a perfect hypocrite." Overton had begun "to lose his naturalness, assuming arrogance and peevishness . . . [which] reached their heights, when he proposed to put over a power deal omitting the gas plant, without consulting . . . any of us who had been struggling and fighting for municipally-owned lighting . . . for 30 years—long before he returned from Wisconsin." [14]

Overton had made his suggestions in good faith, he thought. Crump's unexpected slashing assault was more than he could take— especially the phrase "before he returned from Wisconsin," with its smug inference that Overton was not really a simon-pure native. Crump, always so quick to loose his cutting verbiage at some hapless, fearful, and tongue-tied opponent, could now take some back. Three days later Overton gave a reply that was full of the bitterness of wounded feelings:

The poison pen writes on. The author's path to eternity is strewn with the wreckage of men who have dared to stand up for what they believe to be right. No one dared to challenge his omnipotence, lest they be blasted.

For 12 years I worked for Memphis, to give Memphis good government. Memphis had good government. So good that the great author boasted of it, and used it as his chief argument as he gradually extended his political and personal empire. Memphis' good government was used as a 'front' to cover all sins. . . .

For over a year the author and his poison pen tried to get me to engage in a mud-slinging contest, at which he has been a master for 30 years—long before I returned from Wisconsin and from serving my

14 *Ibid.,* December 16, 1939.

country in France, to make my permanent home in Memphis—the place of my birth and the home of my forebears. He did not succeed and this he also takes as a personal affront.

Everything he says about me—and I know what the poison pen will write—he has said before with different plagiarisms [*sic*] about every freeborn American who dared differ with him, or stand up for what is right and just.

I am aware that every means in his political and financial power, or available through those who bow before him, will be used in an attempt to ruin me, distort the truth, to destroy my record of good government. Can his poison pen deceive the people always?

I say now to the author and his poison pen:

I will never bow my knee to any tyrant. I will never raise my hand in the Nazi salute to any dictator. I still believe in Democracy. [15]

It was quite a document, florid, melodramatic, taut—almost hysterical. Overton was obviously distraught. Crump let it rest. Basically he respected and appreciated the dedicated leadership Overton had given the city government. In the time ahead he gave evidence that he regretted the break and wanted it forgotten. He never alluded to Overton's bitter words—perhaps the harshest that had ever been spoken of him. And if one thing could dispel the charge that Crump was eternally unforgiving toward those who crossed him, it would be that Overton was later invited to return to the fold.

"He came to the peak of his power in 1938–39 with a twin demonstration of his ability to make candidates successful and to drive the same men from office," said the *Commercial Appeal* in a retrospective look at Crump's career.[16] He had helped to make Browning governor, and then he had worked to defeat him. Overton was removed with hardly a ripple of disturbance in Memphis politics.

The climax came on January 1, 1940, at the Memphis Central Station at 12:15 A.M., when Crump was sworn in as mayor and then resigned moments later. He arrived at the station a few minutes after midnight, Will Gerber on one arm and Mrs. E. H. Crump, Jr., on the other. They stopped on the platform beside the baggage truck, and the city clerk stepped forward to administer the oath. "Have I got to be serious, or can I do it with a smile?" asked Crump, but then he removed his hat and became very serious. His eye caught

15 *Commercial Appeal*, December 19, 1939.
16 *Ibid.*, October 17, 1954.

mayor-designate Chandler standing in the group. "Walter, Walter Chandler, come over here," he cried. "I want my old friend with me here," he said, putting his arm around Chandler. Turning to the clerk again he said, "Well, what do you say, Eenie, Meenie . . ." —then became instantly serious.

After the oath he took a paper from his pocket, and speaking loudly said: "Now further, I wish to hand in my resignation, and the City Commission will elect a very distinguished, honorable and upright man, a man with real ability—Walter Chandler. . . ."

Ascending the steps of his car, he turned on the platform to wave goodby. He saw a newspaper reporter and paused to make an observation. " 'There's Ned Trapnell down there. . . . He's a fine boy but he usually disagrees with us. But that's all right. We're going to beat the newspapers. . . . Here is the Commercial Appeal with CIO writers,' he said, holding out his hand, and 'here's the Press Scimitar with CIO writers,' holding the other, 'and down here is John L. Lewis between them—Communist. . . .' "

Joe Boyle, standing with Crump on the platform, threw a snowball at a photographer and started a battle. Then Crump got a chrysanthemum from the "boys from the Nineteenth Ward" to wear at the game he would attend.

He called out to Edward and Robert: "You all better run along home. . . . we've all had a big time." The train began to move. "Goodnight to all of you," he called out as he entered the car.[17]

The next day the press published a statement from Crump that represented his only official act as mayor. It rescinded an invitation "extended by my predecessor, Watkins Overton," to the CIO American Newspaper Guild to have its 1940 meeting in Memphis. "I know the people of Memphis are against all CIO activities and you will not be welcome," the Guild was told.[18]

On January 2 the city commission elected Chandler mayor. Immediately after the swearing-in ceremony reporters asked him what he thought about Crump's revocation of the invitation to the Newspaper Guild. Said Chandler: "My judgment is that his position is sound." [19]

Chandler began his mayoralty in a year that saw burgeoning de-

17 *Press Scimitar,* January 1, 1940.
18 *Ibid.,* January 1, 1940.
19 *Ibid.,* January 3, 1940.

fense preparations in the Memphis area. At Millington, just north of the city, a gigantic powder manufacturing plant was erected, with scores of buildings stretching out across the pine flats. Near Milan, a hundred miles northeast of Memphis, a great shell-loading plant was under construction. Within weekend commuting distance of Memphis, two great army training centers were located—Camp Peay near Tullahoma, Tennessee, and Camp Shelby, near Hattiesburg, Mississippi.

The appearance of uniformed young men on the streets of Memphis brought the city to the final chapter of the cleaning-up process that Crump had initiated in 1912, when vice and gambling were rampant. During the mayoralty of Rowlett Paine, continued progress had been made against these evils until by Overton's administration they were fairly under control. Crump tolerated a curtailed and policed red light district and some gambling in the form of bookmaking probably because he felt that there was always a class whose sporting impulse would have its out, one way or another, and the best way was under police supervision. But with draftees crowding into Memphis on weekends, the system had to be eradicated. Joe Boyle, superseding Cliff Davis as police commissioner, gave the order for the final dismantling of what was undoubtedly the oldest continually existing institution in the history of Memphis. Having already declared a ban on the bookies, the city, on April 24, gave the houses of prostitution ten days to close.

Pipe-smoking Clark Porteous, ace reporter of the *Press Scimitar,* went among the dispossessed to get their story. It was rather sad. The order had come on a Wednesday, and the madams said that on the previous Monday they had been sold poll-tax receipts by political workers. They had been told to vacate by Captain Lee Boyle of the police department, who defended himself against his unchivalrous conduct by saying the fault was not his.

Not only had all of the girls paid their poll tax, but they had "voted faithfully" for Shelby County political candidates—even Boyle. "Where will you go?" asked Porteous. " 'We can't go to Mississippi,' a dark-haired girl in a baby-blue negligee said. 'We aren't wanted there. Chicago is closed up tight' " and New Orleans was overstaffed. There was nothing they could do. "It's just Joe Boyle," they agreed.[20]

20   *Ibid.,* April 27, 1940.

As an old institution crumbled and vanished, Crump launched Memphians on a new interest. On the day before the ultimatum was given to the madams, the Crump Audubon Society was organized. Mayor Chandler explained to a gathering of civic leaders how it had happened:

Our friend, E. H. Crump, as you all know, has been interested for many years in the protection of birds. . . . In a recent conversation Mr. Crump told me how he has looked around for bluebirds and how he never sees one any more. He said it was strange we don't see many of them any more and thought that something ought to be done. . . . Mr. Crump said that we still see redbirds, but unless something was done, soon they would be gone, too. So, some of us encouraged him to have this meeting and therefore a letter was sent by Mr. Crump to each one present here.

The mayor recalled that there had once been another Audubon Society in Memphis, and he read a passage from the notes of its founder: "Without the birds, man could not exist, because the insects would destroy all plant life. Birds constitute a mounted, swift-moving insect police force which travels from the Arctic region to the equator and the Antarctic Circle."

"This is what Mr. Crump has in mind," said Mayor Chandler.

Thereupon Mr. Crump was nominated as honorary chairman of the new group. Chandler called for other nominations, but there were none. He observed that probably before the work was completed the organization would be known as the "Crump Audubon Society."

"Why not do that right now?" asked juvenile court judge Camille Kelley. Did Mrs. Kelley care to make that in the form of a motion? asked Chandler. She would, and she did. It passed unanimously.[21]

Editor Meeman, well-known friend of nature, was delighted. "The Press-Scimitar will cooperate with the society in its endeavors," he announced, adding that the "Crump Audubon Society will do well to pay some attention to the domestic cats that have gone wild." [22]

It was one year and one week after John's death that Mollie Nelms Crump died. Crump was with her at the time. Three years more, and her life would have spanned a century. She was a woman of the Old South throughout her life, enduringly committed to the manners and values in which she had been raised. At the age of

21 *Ibid.,* April 25, 1940. 22 *Ibid.,* April 26, 1940.

ninety-three she opened her home for the Holly Springs centennial, and four hundred people passed through her door. She stood to receive them all. "I have always welcomed my friends standing," she said.[23]

The day after her death Crump ordered funeral notices placed in every home in Holly Springs. The service was held in the old Episcopal church in which she had been married, and was attended by the notables of Tennessee politics. Her body was placed beside her husband's. Though he had preceded her in death by over sixty years, she had never failed to respect his memory.

Time moved swiftly. Nineteen-forty was the year of a Presidential election and a gubernatorial one for Tennessee. In the state Crump backed Cooper again. For once, he had found a governor who suited him. Cooper's administration had been unspectacular, but solid. He gave the state a good financial administration, granted few pardons, and used the state highway patrol in drives against illegal liquor, gambling, and roadside dives. One half of the state's sixteen toll bridges had been freed, and the governor had vigorously prosecuted violators of the small loan act.[24] It was the kind of administering that Crump appreciated.

In June the Shelby leaders went to the state Democratic convention in Nashville. Sitting in his room in the Hermitage Hotel with the state's Democratic leaders as his auditors, Crump expounded strategy for the approaching Chicago Democratic convention. He thought Tennessee ought to have an uninstructed delegation, for if Roosevelt decided not to run, they could throw their strength to Cordell Hull. Would he be one of the four delegates at large, he was asked. "Well, I'm just like an old horse that used to haul express in my home town," Crump answered. "That horse had been working for a good many years and they'd often say they were going to turn him loose on the streets just to rest. But when the trains would pull in that old horse would run down to meet them." That was just the way he was about political conventions, he said. "I've been going for a good many years." [25]

He remained in his hotel room during the one-day state convention, but he was not forgotten. His career was praised in a keynote

23 *Commercial Appeal,* May 10, 1940.
24 Nashville *Tennessean,* January 14, 1940.
25 *Commercial Appeal,* June 20, 1940.

address by Senator Tom Stewart, provoking loud and prolonged applause from the nearly five hundred delegates from Shelby County. There was talk that the Tennessee delegation might give him its support for the vice-presidency if Hull refused.[26] Writing to Senator McKellar, Blair Hunt declared that "thousands of Memphis Negroes will be happy if you'll use your influence in having Mr. E. H. Crump's name presented for Vice President. Please do so." [27] McKellar felt the "same way," but the effort would be useless. "We tried our best to get him to let us endorse him, but he would not do it." [28]

Crump's most talked-about action at the Chicago convention came just after Senator Alben Barkley's tribute to Roosevelt. Hearing that James A. Farley was sulking over the prospects of a third term which would frustrate his own Presidential ambitions, Crump mounted the platform, sought out Farley, and "practically dragged" him to the front. Pointing to the surging mass shouting for Roosevelt, he ordered Farley to "look at that demonstration!" [29]

Crump would have been for Roosevelt no matter whom the Republicans had nominated, but the choice of Wendell Willkie with his utility background brought him back from Chicago full of fight.[30] He was contemptuous of those Democrats who were deserting Roosevelt—Senator James Reed of Missouri and: "Now comes Senator Burke of Nebraska," with his threat to call a meeting of dissident Democrats. They were "quitters," and their plan for a meeting was "just a lot of bunk." Cotton Ed Smith of South Carolina could join them if he wished, but South Carolina was a "cinch bet for Roosevelt." [31]

Then he directed his fire at the Republican party and Willkie. "The most corrupt influence that ever nominated a president was behind Warren Harding, the Republican president of moral sloth and Teapot Dome fame, and practically the same Wall Street influence is behind Wendell Willkie, president of a utility holding company, whose only thought in life has been to exact high electric rates from the people."

26 *Ibid.,* July 15, 1940.
27 Hunt to McKellar, July 17, 1940. McKellar Papers.
28 McKellar to Hunt, July 23, 1940. McKellar Papers.
29 *Commercial Appeal,* July 18, 1940.
30 *Ibid.,* July 17, 1940.
31 *Press Scimitar,* July 23, 1940.

Willkie himself did not help his cause where Crump was concerned. At the beginning of the campaign he remarked that he was gratified at the type of person that supported him—not a "Mayor Hague . . . nor a Mayor Kelly . . . nor a Crump . . . in the list." This remark, thought Thomas L. Stokes, a syndicated columnist who was carried in the *Press Scimitar,* by pointing up the "unholy alliance between New Deal idealists and corrupt city machines may become, before it is all over, one of the decisive influences in the presidential campaign." Crump, Stokes added gratuitously, looked "like something out of *Gone With the Wind,*" who, instead of being "one of the cleverest city bosses left in the United States," should have been sitting "on the front porch of a colonial mansion against a backdrop of wisteria, sipping mint juleps and saying 'by Gad, suh.' " [32]

Crump's being linked with other "corrupt" bosses was unfortunate, but he had another good reason for opposing Willkie. Both the Memphis newspapers supported the Republican nominee. At the moment Crump was more than usually annoyed at the *Press Scimitar.* It had opposed the appointment of Marion Boyd, a rising young lawyer, as Shelby County attorney general. "Mr. Crump," the paper stated, "has incurred resentment by passing over his old friend Judge Sam O. Bates and the many other mature and seasoned men who are qualified for this high responsibility to pick a comparatively young, inexperienced man who, tho he has his merits, most observers believe would scarcely have been in the running in any untrammeled meeting." [33]

Crump burned, and Meeman received a letter. The *Press Scimitar* found fault with "every man whom I have voted for, every man whom I have advocated for any office—select another." The editor was obviously incapable of seeing anything wrong with himself. He was "always meddling, always enormously busy doing something colossally unimportant to this community." He had come from Knoxville "for the sole purpose of trying to knife me in the back—to kick me out of Memphis if possible—but he has failed. He has never been able to get a comfortable seat in the front row." And now he was objecting to Boyd's appointment—"honest, capable Marion Boyd"—condemned "because he broke up the loan shark

32 *Ibid.,* August 9, 1940.   33 *Ibid.,* August 10, 1940.

racket—a racket extracting money from the poor and unfortunate."

"I say again," concluded Crump, "you are nothing more in this community than a venal and licentious scribbler [a phrase Crump enjoyed rolling off his pen] hiding behind the cowardly privilege of writing lying, mis-leading and colored stuff in your sheet." Meeman had "failed to publish my letter . . . of October 23, 1939." Now, said Crump, "I'll see if you publish this one." [34]

The letter was published and an editorial answer given. "What has occasioned this volley of abuse from Mr. Crump?" The progress of Memphis was "not a one-man drama. It is the cooperative effort of 360,000 citizens of Shelby County." The *Press Scimitar* had "always cheerfully, and even warmly, appreciated Mr. Crump's part in that progress. We have valued his leadership and supported him in all his endeavors which we believed to be good. . . ." But the paper had "just as warmly resisted his attempts to be a dictator, rather than a leader, and we have defended those whose honest disagreement with him he has rewarded with vile abuse."

Since Crump had "not refrained, with unbecoming modesty, from taking credit for the good things that have come to Memphis, we shall take advantage of the opportunity his attack affords us to point out that the Press-Scimitar, too, has had a part in bringing about that progress." The editor had also been a staunch supporter of TVA, even during his years in Knoxville. "Mr. Crump and the Press-Scimitar worked together to bring this boom to Memphis." And when Crump had recklessly gone ahead with plans to build a city-owned distribution system, the *Press Scimitar* had taken the lead in preventing this "calamity of duplication."

When the paper had urged Crump to come to terms with the power company, it "was the champion of the underdog, as this newspaper always is, whether that underdog is some poor negro beaten up at the workhouse or some wealthy man who, like Mr. Crump, lives 'high on the hog.'" [35]

The *Press Scimitar,* obviously, wanted to be loved, too.

The *Commercial Appeal* received its letter from Crump when it complained that the Crump Audubon Society was made up of politicians. "We know that you have frequently had spasms of editorial pain over some of our selections and I would be glad for you to say

34 Crump to Meeman, August 9, 1940. Crump Papers.
35 *Press Scimitar,* August 10. 1940.

who should be booted out of the Audubon Society in order to make it pure and perfect," wrote Crump.

He wanted to make another point with the *Commercial Appeal*—the Presidential election. His views, he knew, would not suit the paper or its "headquarters in New York." He was supporting Roosevelt because "he gave us Tennessee Valley Authority . . . while your candidate, Willkie, was fighting it." Further, the New Deal had provided Memphis with five large housing areas, "providing cheaper rents for the poor." The price of cotton had been raised from five to fifteen cents a pound "and remade this devastated country which was ruined under Republican administrations." Roosevelt was "the best friend Memphis . . . and the South ever had. No other President did half as much for us." If Willkie "should accidentally stumble into the Presidency, in a very short time every interest in this Southern area . . . would set up a groan of despair that would be heard from Dan to Beersheba." [36]

As for the governor's race, Crump had no worries. On August 2 Cooper won an easy renomination over his primary opponent. "Congratulations," wired Crump. "Thank you for all you have done for me," responded Cooper careful not to make the mistake of appearing ungrateful.[37]

Several weeks later Crump went to Battle Creek to diet and rest before the final push for the November election. The atmosphere there was not reassuring for Roosevelt's prospects. He wrote to McKellar, asking him to inform the President that "the Republicans are putting out a lot of scare stuff for the doctors to read. . . . They are contacting every doctor here. . . . *Doctors can spread a lot of propaganda*," warned Crump, underlining the phrase for emphasis. He thought that "something should be done," for he really did not consider the "election any two and one-half to one bet on Roosevelt by any means." [38]

After resting a month, he returned to Memphis to inaugurate the election drive. Mrs. Crump, vacationing at Mineral Wells, Texas, received an account: "We opened Headquarters today in the Hill Building. . . . Senator McKellar, Mayor Chandler, Congressman

36 *Commercial Appeal*, October 24, 1940.
37 Crump to Cooper, August 2, 1940. Cooper to Crump, August 2, 1940. Telegrams. Crump Papers.
38 Crump to McKellar, October 2, 1940. McKellar Papers.

Davis, John Martin, Jr., and Perry Sellars made good speeches. We are working hard." [39] In the midst of the campaign he wrote short notes. "Walk, drink water, eat lightly, sleep a lot, but not to the extent Van Winkle did," he advised. The next day he told her of "a beautiful purple Morning-Glory on the fence in the rear of the back lot—it is simply gorgeous." [40]

On November 5 Roosevelt won his third term. In Shelby County his victory was impressive but not as decisive at it had been in 1936. Willkie got eight times the vote that Landon had, but he still lost eight to one.[41]

After the election Crump was able to concentrate more fully on Tennessee's winning football team. The closest he ever came to requesting official favor in his own personal interest was in the matter of football tickets. "Mr. Crump asked me to mail to you the enclosed check . . . to cover the four tickets for the Alabama . . . game," wrote Mrs. Humphreys to Governor Cooper. "He thanks you so much for your trouble in securing these very desirable tickets for him." [42]

Later Cooper sent Crump a very special invitation to the Tennessee–Vanderbilt game. "Dear Mr. Crump," he very courteously began: "Mother joins me [the governor was unmarried] in hoping that you and Mrs. Crump, and any member of your family that you may bring with you, will be our guests out at the Mansion for the . . . game. I am expecting to sit with you at the game, since I have a ticket reserved with yours." The governor hoped that "the slight indisposition of which Mrs. Humphreys wrote" would be "entirely gone before your Nashville visit." [43]

Perhaps Crump felt that he was placing himself too conspicuously in the governor's favor, or possibly his "slight indisposition" was still with him, for he declined the invitation. Mr. Crump "regrets his inability to attend the game," wrote Mrs. Humphreys. "Mr. Crump has really been working too hard—he goes into these campaigns with hammer and tongs, never overlooking anything, even in the smallest way. . . . He was the faculty of influencing those

39 Crump to Bessie Crump, October 23, 1940. Crump Papers.
40 Crump to Bessie Crump, October 16, October 17, 1940. Crump Papers.
41 *Press Scimitar,* November 6, 1940.
42 Evelyn Humphreys to Cooper, October 15, 1940. Crump Papers.
43 Cooper to Crump, November 25, 1940. Crump Papers.

associated with him to work in like manner, seeing the good results he obtains." [44] Faithful and devoted, Mrs. Humphreys, when left to her own resources, employed phrases that Crump himself would have used.

In 1941 the war's maelstrom swept wider, but it did not yet include Memphis. There was in fact only one small occasion when those in authority failed to notice certain eccentricities developing in the machinery, making it necessary for Crump to adjust it.

There was too much stringency in the enforcement of traffic laws, and he made public mention of it. Traffic court fines were too heavy. Further, he hoped that the police department "will finally come to the realization that it is a great hardship for people, good people, to put up cash forfeits for traffic violations at the time of their arrest. Frequently they haven't the money with them. If a check is given and it is no good they know who the owner is and can attach the car. In many large cities, the arresting officer merely gives the violator a ticket which orders him to appear at a certain time in court. This seems to be the best course after all."

"Do you mean to convey the impression that Commissioner Boyle has been too severe?" a reporter asked. "No," said Crump, "I have high praise for Joe Boyle." It was just that "sometimes the police force can be geared up too high."

Those touched by Crump's statement were asked what they thought about it. The city court judge declared that he was "heartily in accord with Mr. Crump's statement. . . ." He had already "been giving the subject consideration and have been intending to take some sort of action in this regard."

Said Commissioner Boyle: "Mr. Crump has been dealing with the public for 35 years. I have been following his leadership for at least 30 years and will continue to do so in this case."

Said Mayor Chandler: "Mr. Crump's suggestions are fine and will have prompt and earnest consideration. . . . We of the City Commission have regretted every instance where there has been a hardship, but in the enforcement of traffic laws it is exceedingly difficult and almost impossible to avoid unfortunate experiences." [45]

In another difference of opinion, Crump did not so readily have his way. Because of expanding defense work, the federal govern-

44   Evelyn Humphreys to Cooper, November 26, 1940.
45   *Press Scimitar,* October 10. 1941.

ment's Office of Production Management issued a decree in November outlawing night football as "nonessential and impractical." Crump thought the order pointless. "I am most certainly for defense in any and every way to advance, promote and save," he told a reporter. "I would only burn one light in my home if that would help—use candles or pine knots without a murmur if that is the thing to do." But anyone could easily "figure it out themselves that there is more electrical current used when people stay at home with lights and radio than if they are away at the football games, with lights and radio turned off during their absence." [46]

He briefly discussed the OPM dispute in a letter to Mrs. Crump, then turned to the daily happenings of his life that he thought would interest her. "I didn't feel like making the trip to Nashville last Saturday to see Vanderbilt and Tulane," but he might see the game in New Orleans. "Am particularly anxious to see the magnificent, gorgeous drive they have built around Lake Pontchartrain. Have something like that in mind for Riverside Drive into Shelby Forest that we looked at." [47] Several days later he wrote to tell her he had gotten tickets to Robert Sherwood's *There Shall Be No Night,* as she had requested. "The cemetery looks awfully sweet—the winter grass is perfectly planted and no ragged edge to it. Flowers were beautiful." He had seen the Armistice Day parade that morning, which was "longer than usual—several hundred regular soldiers were in the march with a lot of equipment." He and Edward, Jr., had just returned to the office "after a nice walk down Main Street and back to the Tennessee Club where we had lunch." [48]

The quarrel with OPM smoldered and then abruptly died. Pearl Harbor ended it. Crump cancelled his planned trip to the Rose Bowl. "Now is no time to go gadding about the country," he declared.[49]

46 *Ibid.,* November 4, 1941.
47 Crump to Bessie Crump, November 5, 1941. Crump Papers.
48 Crump to Bessie Crump, November 11, 1941. Crump Papers.
49 *Commercial Appeal,* December 12, 1941.

⊠ ☐

Chapter XII

THE WAR YEARS

FOR SOME people the war offered an opportunity to elevate the scope of their activities to a participation in the drama of a great struggle, but not for Crump. He was aware of what was at stake in the war, but he was confident that it would be won, and that in the meantime he could do no better than to go on as usual working for Memphis and Tennessee. He saw the war as an occasion of transition for the South. After it was over Memphis would "flourish over . . . any other city in the South." The region was "destined to become a great beef cattle, dairy products, mule, hog, poultry and vegetable raising country, in addition to our cotton, corn, wheat and alfalfa." But before this could happen, there was a problem the South had to resolve. It was the discrimination in railroad rates "in favor of the Eastern and Northern cities. . . . When this is corrected, manufacturing plants will swarm to the South." [1]

His main interest in the home front phase of the war was victory gardens. Mayor Chandler frequently urged Memphians to grow gardens, and Crump was right behind him. Hundreds of people, he said, had taken Chandler's advice "and have profited by it." The war had forced England away from "big, juicy roast beef," and

---

[1] *Commercial Appeal,* January 3, 1942.

the English were "healthier and better off than ever before due to vegetables." He thought it likely that "more people in America die from overeating than undereating. There is more waste in America than in any country in the world." He added his usual homily on the subject. "John the Baptist lived on wild honey and locusts. . . . The ox, horse and elephant are the strongest animals in the world and yet they eat no meat." [2]

The war interrupted the largest project for Memphis on which he was currently working. The subject of a new Arkansas–Memphis bridge, said Crump, had been on his mind since 1937, when he realized "that the Harahan Bridge was obsolete and not in keeping with a great and growing city." The project was discussed for two years, with the first significant step taken in 1939. On March 14, the city commission adopted Commissioner Boyle's resolution establishing a Memphis and Arkansas Bridge committee, with a membership that included Senator McKellar, Congressman Chandler, Commissioner Davis, county board chairman E. W. Hale, and the editor of the *Commercial Appeal,* Frank Algren. Crump was elected chairman of the group.

Two hours after the committee's first meeting the chairman was on the job, making an initial survey of places where the bridge might cross. Earlier, he had favored a north Memphis crossing, but the advice of engineers convinced him that the best place was south of the two bridges already spanning the river.

"There's just no doubt about it," said Crump, standing on the bluff, "the engineers who built these railroad bridges knew what they were doing. They picked the best sites. Look at this point, it is the highest point on this side and at the narrowest part of the river." Joe Boyle stood listening as Crump expounded the engineering phase of the work. But "where are we going to get the money?" Crump asked.[3]

The answer to that question was the responsibility of the bridge committee, and that was where Senator McKellar could be useful. In the summer of 1940, congressional legislation authorized the establishment of a bridge commission with the power to enter into contracts for right-of-ways and bridge construction. The new commission was enlarged to include representatives from Arkansas. Again, Crump was chosen chairman.

2 *Ibid.,* March 21, 1943.   3 *Press Scimitar,* March 15, 1939.

Financing seemed assured when in the summer of 1941 Congress appropriated $125,000,000 for national defense highways and strategic bridges. But Roosevelt vetoed the bill because of an objection to the manner in which funds would be disbursed. "The President has just vetoed our roads and bridges bill," wired McKellar to Crump. Crump was not downcast. "Love's labor is not lost. We will get the bridge eventually." [4]

Three days after the veto, McKellar introduced a compromise bill which in due course became law. But it was not until February 12, 1944, that the project was approved by the U. S. Public Roads Administration. On March 2, the day American planes were pounding Truk Island, the War Department granted the necessary permit for construction. Material shortages deferred the actual building until the end of the war.

By the spring of 1942 the public mind had become sufficiently adjusted to the excitement of war to react again to politics. In March Crump announced that he would support Cooper again for governor, and that Will Gerber was his choice for Shelby County attorney general. Gerber already held the office by virtue of an appointment from Governor Cooper, made to fill the unexpired term of Marion Boyd who had been appointed to a federal judicial post. "I have never heard one word of criticism of Atty. Gen. Will Gerber," said Crump when he made the announcement.[5]

The arrival of spring usually found Crump off to the Hot Springs races, but in 1942 he joined McKellar in a tour of some of the historic spots of Virginia. Crump made it an occasion of ancestral communion, visiting places where his forebears had lived. "I do not think I ever saw a man enjoy a town more than you did Fredericksburg," McKellar wrote from Washington. "It was a great visit." [6]

By mid-summer the governor's race was developing momentum. At McKenzie, J. Ridley Mitchell, Cooper's primary opponent, attacked the governor as "a stooge for Crump." As long as "Charlie McCarthy Cooper is on Capitol Hill Crump and his political outfit will not repeal the poll tax. . . . There are many fine people in Memphis. What they need is to get rid of their Hitlers. . . . Pardon me if I remove my coat," said the would-be governor as he warmed to his work. "Take it off," somebody yelled from the crowd.

4 *Commercial Appeal*, August 5, 1941.   5 *Ibid.*, March 9, 1942.
6 McKellar to Crump, April 14, 1942. Crump Papers.

Browning was at the rally to help out. If everyone voted who favored Mitchell, said Browning, Mitchell would be elected. But there were some people in Tennessee who were not concerned about political intimidation. They were "in the class with the Quislings of Norway and the Lavals of France, willing to be the instrument for enslavement of their own people to gain the temporary favor of their ruthless oppressors. I can name you a few people who would meet Hitler at the docks if he should land in New York and say 'we have been with you all the time.' " [7]

Likening Crump to the enemies of democracy did not produce an important campaign issue. In August Cooper won in Tennessee and Gerber won in Memphis.

It was the governor's third term, yet he was still to be reminded that Crump was keeping a close watch on the state's affairs. Six weeks after the inauguration, Crump wrote Cooper about a *Press Scimitar* editorial that charged "Reckless Waste" at the capitol because of the large number of engrossing clerks, sergeants-at-arms, and doorkeepers being employed.[8] "I had practically a break with Scott Fitzhugh, Speaker of the Senate and Pete Haynes, Speaker of the House when they put on so many after promising they would not," warned Crump. It was surprising, for "you seem to have handled everything else so well." [9]

Later Cooper had his knuckles rapped again. "Understand recently two unworthy men have been paroled. Attorney General Gerber protested. . . . Realize you haven't the time to go into all those details, at the same time it is very, very important. . . . Please ascertain what lawyers—who asked for those paroles. . . . We are sure, very sure that you want these things done correctly." [10]

Cooper did want things done correctly, and in this instance "of course . . . a mistake was made." The secretary of the parole board "apparently overlooked standing instructions from me to grant no parole without the consultation and approval of the Trial Judge and prosecuting attorney." The secretary had offered to resign, "but I did not accept his resignation because he is really a very good man. . . ." [11]

7 *Press Scimitar,* June 22, 1942.   8 *Ibid.,* February 15, 1943.
9 Crump to Cooper, February 16, 1943. Crump Papers.
10 Crump to Cooper, November 12, 1943. Crump Papers.
11 Cooper to Crump, November 13, 1943. Crump Papers.

Crump was concerned about charges of freight rate discrimination against the South by the railroads, and he pressed this subject on the governor. "Mr. Crump is under the impression that you said the western states are discriminated against on railroad rates like the southern states," wrote Mrs. Humphreys to Cooper. Could the governor give her a list of the western and southern states that were affected?[12] Shortly afterwards Crump was suggesting that Cooper line up the western governors with those of the South on the freight discrimination issue. "I will be glad to follow your suggestion," Cooper responded.[13]

McKellar was enlisted. Would he please send Crump biographies of the members of the Interstate Commerce Commission. "Will get up information . . . at once and send it along to you shortly," wired McKellar.[14]

The issue sputtered along for a year. Crump was sure "some Wall Street Holding Company" was behind it all, for it was "very easy" for it to tell the railroads "what to do about rates in the different parts of the country." [15]

He was the old progressive, still on the attack. But World War II was provoking new questions of social relationships that old-fashioned progressivism had not thought to answer. "Mighty, wicked Wall Street" was no longer among the most important problems in the world. Totalitarianism and racism abroad did their part to induce a redefinition of the basic issues that confronted the Western world; so also did new research in psychology and sociology. Hitler's assaults on the Jews caused a few to take a second glance at racism at home. So did Gunnar Myrdal's *An American Dilemma,* published in 1944, and studied in Howard Odom's sociology classes at the University of North Carolina. For a few young Southerners, but nonetheless a growing few, traditional Southern racism was an abomination. The grossness of its inequity was something that could not be made right by the most expansive form of *noblesse oblige.*

A reappraisal of old racial values represented only part of the outlook of the avant-garde in the South. It included the desire for a society more broadly expressive of human values—a society less

12 Evelyn Humphreys to Cooper, March 8, 1943. Crump Papers.
13 Crump to Cooper, March 22, 1943. Cooper to Crump, March 22, 1943. Telegrams. Crump Papers.
14 McKellar to Crump, April 2, 1943. Crump Papers.
15 Evelyn Humphreys to Cooper, March 17, 1943. Crump Papers.

provincial, less suspicious of new ideas, less insistent on a conformity to outmoded and increasingly meaningless symbols.

Crump knew what was at work in the world. He read widely, but his judgments were made on the basis of traditional values. Those who would overthrow the "truth" had no right to the goodwill or even the tolerance of the community. To the young rebels of the Second World War era—challengers of the ancestral order—it seemed that Memphis and Crump stood together, hostile and impenetrable.

Crump gave clear evidence that he did not approve of some of the exceedingly liberal ideas of the times. In June, 1940, during the Presidential campaign, he publicly declared that he would "guarantee" that Earl Browder, the Communist presidential candidate, would not speak in Memphis. "The time has arrived in our country when every man and woman should stand up and be counted if they are for our government." [16]

From Battle Creek he wired Cooper, instructing him: "Please read chapter seventy two public acts of nineteen hundred thirty five regarding those seeking office who belong to a party whose sole purpose is to overthrow the government by force. . . . I suggest that you ask the state election commissioners to instruct all county election boards not to permit Browder and his Communist ticket or any other communists seeking office to be placed on the ballot. Suggest you tell newspapers what you propose to do." [17]

Meanwhile, he informed reporters that if there were any well-known Communists in Memphis, "they will be shown the highways. The Communists are responsible for France's slaughter. That country will never rise again. If we deal with them in a pussy-footing half-hearted way, like 'Yes, We Have No Bananas'—Were you pushed or shoved—Did the house burn up or down—we will get nowhere." [18]

The Communists, CIO organizers, agitators of the race question and of the tenant farm problem were all lumped together. When the *Press Scimitar* reported that a U. S. investigator was looking into the charge that Memphis Negroes were being intimidated, Crump declared the report was a "manufactured lie." The basis of the story, he said, was a letter to President Roosevelt from the Southern

16 *Press Scimitar,* June 11, 1940.
17 Crump to Cooper, August 22, 1940. Crump Papers.
18 *Commercial Appeal,* August 23, 1940.

Conference for Human Welfare charging that the Crump organization intimidated Negroes.

The Southern Conference, organized in 1929 to pursue a more redical approach to the abolition of racial and economic injustice in the South, would do more harm than good, Crump thought. "We have known the negroes always—know their problems, and are going to defend the right-thinking, working, honest negro, and they are ninety-five percent in majority; and at the same time we want them to keep their race together in peace, faith and confidence. We are not going to let the Press-Scimitar, or any New York or other foreign influence interfere with us. . . . The agitators and saboteurs under the guise of teachers, lecturers, farm and industrial workers with their vicious propaganda, will not be tolerated by the officials of this community. I am . . . certain of that." [19]

The *Press Scimitar* printed Crump's statement and admitted that he was correct in stating that a U. S. investigator had not called on him, inasmuch as this was information that "conforms to The Press-Scimitar's latest information from Washington."

Three weeks later Crump wrote to McKellar, asking for information about Dr. Will W. Alexander, executive secretary of the National Commission for Interracial Co-operation and a former administrator of the Farm Security Administration. "Some of these preachers are planning to invite Dr. Will W. Alexander . . . to address a interracial meeting here. What is Alexander's record? Someone told me he is terribly 'red.' " [20]

McKellar was just full of important information. "From what I have learned about him," he wrote, "he has been daft on the subject of interracial relations for a long time, having written a book about it." The senator added a *non sequitur* in the form of a gratuitous insult to the character of the high-minded Dr. Alexander, "I have long thought he was utterly unworthy and disreputable. I would not believe him on oath." [21]

Crump was disturbed, for there was growing evidence that some Memphis Negroes were interested in equalitarian ideas. In November, 1943, A. Philip Randolph, president of the International Brotherhood of Sleeping Car Porters, was invited to speak at the Memphis

19 *Press Scimitar,* January 10, 1940.
20 Crump to McKellar, January 31, 1941. McKellar Papers.
21 McKellar to Crump, February 3, 1941. McKellar Papers.

Mt. Nebo Baptist Church. But the talk was cancelled. Since Randolph's "radical" equalitarian views would doubtless be aired, Attorney General Gerber conferred with Negro leaders and successfully convinced them of the imprudence of having Randolph speak.

Crump had something to say on the subject. There was "friendly cooperation" between Negroes and whites in Memphis, but if there were race trouble "it would take us 25 years to recover." He did not want "imported" Negroes "to make unnecessary fire-brand speeches. . . . About 1 per cent of the negroes will never be satisfied no matter what is done for them unless there is complete social equality. The few in this part of the country who want that had better give the matter serious thought as long as they live in this section. That unhappy 1 per cent, with a mistaken sense of their own wrongs, usually pass down unwise thoughts to those further down the ladder and then there is mischief." [22]

Five months later Randolph slipped into town and made his talk. Sheriff Oliver H. Perry was apparently caught off balance. "Had I known the negro Randolph . . . and those he brought with him, were to make blackguarding speeches defaming this community and speaking ill of my friends, Mr. Hale and Mr. Crump, I would have pulled them out of the pulpit in Preacher Long's Beale St. Church. . . . I will be on hand at the next meeting." [23]

Crump had no patience with equalitarian doctrines, but his concern was not so much an expression of his personal feelings as it was of fear that a sudden assault on traditional racial values might cause violence. He had read in the Pittsburgh *Courier,* a Negro newspaper, that Memphis was one of the places in the United States where a race riot was possible. "Many of us would actually walk from here to Chicago, if that would prevent any serious race trouble in Memphis," he said. But he was also "sure we would . . . walk that distance to deal with any man or set of men if they were trying to stir up trouble." [24]

This tendency to suppress any outspoken opinions that challenged Southern traditionalism brought Crump into opposition with the advanced liberal ideas of the closing war years. The latter-day image of the Memphis boss was in the making. To many, he was already

22 *Commercial Appeal,* November 14, 1943.
23 *Press Scimitar,* April 3, 1944.
24 *Commercial Appeal,* November 14, 1943.

"Mr. Crump," the dandified reincarnation of a nineteenth-century Southern colonel who provided Memphis with shrewd and honest management. To the liberal, "Mr. Crump" was the Memphis boss whose totalitarian rule was used to preserve the dead and decaying past. Increasingly, he was made the object of attack by the liberal press. In response, Crump did what he thought a man of principle should do—he fought back. In doing so, he played the newspaper's game, producing headlines and excitement. In the case of the Nashville *Tennessean,* the battle was almost Homeric.

The campaign that Silliman Evans, the *Tennessean*'s owner and publisher, directed against Crump was centered on the latter's supposed opposition to the repeal of the state poll tax law and to the way in which he used Governor Cooper to control state politics. The break between Crump and Evans was reportedly intimated in the spring of 1940, when Evans entertained Postmaster General Farley and leading state Democrats at a barbecue at his home. Crump was invited, but he did not attend—as might have been expected—but neither did any of his lieutenants, most of whom were more flexible socially than Crump.

Shortly after the Evans barbecue, the *Tennessean* began taking the lead in promoting the repeal of the state poll tax law, which Tennessee had adopted in 1890. In the spring of 1941 a poll tax repeal bill was introduced in the legislature but was not passed. The day following, the *Tennessean* ran an editorial blaming Crump for the failure of the repeal. Immediately Crump wired Evans: "Have you got the courage to print word for word a reply from me on the front page of your paper in answer to your cowardly editorial?" [25] Yes, said Evans, Crump could say anything he wished, "subject of course to the general newspaper rules relative to space limitations, libelous matter, personal abuse, etc." [26]

The statement of conditions which had been imposed, Crump wrote back to Evans, "forces me to cut down my statement answering your unwarranted attack on me . . . to a very mild expression of my real feelings." Crump's "very mild expression" consisted of harsh name-calling and personal abuse. "You accidentally blew into Tennessee on a money making scheme three or four years ago and you will probably blow out the same way." Evans was trying to "bull whip and blackguard everybody who doesn't look your way.

25 Nashville *Tennessean,* January 22, 1941.   26 *Ibid.*

. . . Only a puffed up foreign frog who didn't know the people of this State would assume such arrogance." Crump's feelings also included "old . . . lying, political reporter, Joe Hatcher" who "wrote lying stories about us last Spring and he continues."

Having vented his feelings, Crump gave a statement of his position on the poll tax. He was against repeal until there was a provision for the permanent registration of voters. There were ninety-five counties in the state, he said, and in only six was there a provision for registration. "If the poll tax is removed . . . there is no way of identifying any voter. Talk about purifying elections by the repeal of the poll tax, look at what has happened in recent elections in Kansas City, Philadelphia, Chicago, Pittsburgh, St. Louis and New York where there has been no poll tax for many years. We would never be in favor of . . . repeal . . . unless there is registration everywhere." [27]

However sound Crump's justification of the poll tax, his critics could point out that he profited politically from it. In Shelby County the organization saw to it that the poll taxes of the vast majority of voters were, in one way or another, paid. But outside Shelby, where political organizations were not so efficiently managed, a far greater proportion of those eligible to vote did not. Anti-Crump opinion held that if the poll tax law were repealed, the number who voted outside of Shelby County would be considerably increased, and Crump's majorities would be nullified. The "Poll Tax Has Helped Crump, But it Won't Much Longer," was the headline that Jennings Perry of the *Tennessean* used to introduce an article on Crump in Marshall Field's ultra-liberal *PM*. "He has 'made the trains run on time' in his city," wrote Perry, but there was a large question about whether or not Crump believed in democracy. Possibly he thought he did, since "he makes the profession of faith, like so many others of our gentlemen down here, with a straight face." [28]

The *Tennessean* pursued an irreverent policy of needling Crump. On Christmas Eve, 1941, Joe Hatcher gave his column, "Politics," over to a fanciful letter from Governor Cooper to Santa Claus, "c/o E. H. Crump and Co.":

I have hung up my stocking over the fireplace, Dear Santa, and I do hope you will not forget me this year of all times.

27 Crump to Evans, January 20, 1941. Crump Papers.
28 *PM*, March 21, 1941.

I want a great big ballot box stuffed full of those Memphis ballots all marked one way, and a long letter saying what a swell little fellow I've been and how the people should put up with my Hollywood temperament so long as I do just as you say. . . .

I am going to light my Christmas Tree anyhow, and I would like to have it in Crump Stadium all lighted up just to show the OPM. Let's send the President a little toy Douglas Dam and tell him we want a new bridge across the Mississippi and nothing else. We'll name it the E. H. Crump bridge and say its for defense . . . .

> Yours, alone
> Prinky

Crump found nothing funny about the letter. "I have read the column in your paper which appeared on Christmas Eve in which you undertake to satirize me as Santa Claus and the Governor of the State as a little boy," he wrote to the *Tennessean*. "To parody the Holy Christmas Season for political calumny would occur only to a mind diseased and blasphemous. But the muckraker in the pond of the goo-goo eyed frog must *hatch* the foul eggs of his baseless falsehoods and irresponsible innuendoes, no matter what may be the criterion of good taste or the dictate of decency." The *Tennessean* ought to look at the realities of Tennessee politics, Crump advised. "The people of Tennessee have never seen the day when there has been less graft, and less special privilege. There has [*sic*] been no sales of pardons that has existed heretofore, and the conduct of the government for the benefit of every section of the State and value received for every dollar have been given under Governor Cooper's leadership." [29]

Crump could just as well have let the "Dear Santa" letter pass, or he might at least have confined it to his positive comments on the manner in which the state government was being conducted. The attack on Hatcher was strident.

Crump waited eight days for Evans to print his letter. When it did not appear, he wrote a follow-up note to the *Tennessean:* "If you had the courage of a yellow cur, egg-sucking dog you would print this letter." [30] In a previous era, Crump's words would have led to a duel with the editor, and in a sense that is what they were intended to do. He wanted satisfaction—a personal confrontation with Evans. But Evans chose to be civilized and not to deal with the

29 Crump to the *Tennessean*, December 29, 1941. Crump Papers.
30 Crump to the *Tennessean*, January 7, 1942. Crump Papers.

issue in an old-fashioned and possibly messy way. He dropped the matter.

Nevertheless, the *Tennessean* continued to represent Crump as the enemy of democracy in Tennessee. He was made into a whipping boy for the poll tax abolition crusade, and his insults and challenges to Evans were useful in creating the kind of image of himself that the *Tennessean* was constructing for its readers.

In 1943 the legislature finally repealed the poll tax law, but the action only precipitated a new phase of the controversy. On July 3 the state supreme court invalidated the legislative action on the grounds that the statute providing for poll tax collections was so basic to the constitution mandate behind the poll tax that the legislature could not repeal the statute without essentially altering the constitution.[31]

The decision brought a great outcry from the *Tennessean*. "The People Be Crumped," it proclaimed in a front-page editorial.[32] The onus for the defeat of the poll tax repeal was laid at Crump's feet because in a three-to-two decision, supreme court judge Frank Gailor, a Crump stalwart appointed to the bench just in time to participate in the making of the decision, voted with the majority.

Gailor most certainly had not been "instructed" by Crump in rendering his decision, but on the other hand, his judicial logic could have been influenced by his association with the organization. Yet he was no political hack; to the contrary, his rearing in a highly cultured family and his academic accomplishments as a Rhodes Scholar, made him a seemingly distinguished appointee to the court. Intellectual integrity and the immunities traditionally surrounding the office of justice should have enabled him to make an objective analysis of the issue despite his Shelby background.

Even if the *Tennessean* was correct in its assumption that Gailor had voted to please Crump, it missed the mark when it gave the impression that Crump opposed poll tax repeal out of a fear of "democracy." Crump had publicly stated his opposition to the poll tax in March, 1938, although he insisted then, as he did later, that repeal be coupled with a permanent registration of voters.[33] He could

31 Stetson Kennedy, *Southern Exposure* (New York, 1946), 100.
32 Jennings Perry, *Democracy Begins at Home, The Tennessee Fight on the Poll Tax* (New York, 1944), 239.
33 *Press Scimitar,* March 16, 1938.

not help but see that the system of collecting poll taxes was inefficient and wasteful. But neither would he forego the political benefits that he could derive from the existing situation. He would use it as long as he could.

Bad blood between the *Tennessean* and Crump reached its peak late in 1944, when Jennings Perry of the *Tennessean* published an attack on Crump entitled *Democracy Begins at Home, The Tennessee Fight on the Poll Tax.* It was a carelessly assembled work of pompous verbosity, but it created a stir in Tennessee and brought Crump out of his corner swinging hard.

On January 29, 1945, Crump mailed his "3 Slimy, Mangy Bubonic Rats" letter to the *Tennessean.* Copies printed on Crump Company stationery were distributed by the Shelby delegation to all members of the legislature. It was a letter on which Crump obviously worked for some time, going back over his notes to extract a striking phrase that he had heard or read somewhere, and looking through the dictionary for an especially apt and seldom used word.

"If the city of Nashville should ever follow the lead of the progressive city of Memphis and inaugurate a campaign for the extermination of rodents," he began, "Silliman Evans, Jennings Perry, and Joe Hatcher will undoubtedly take to the tall timbers. This trio of mangy bubonic rats are conscienceless liars who would stop at nothing in their unholy efforts to prejudice the good people of Tennessee against Memphis and Shelby County." He believed in freedom of the press, Crump said, "but not for a lying press," and "these rats enjoy the cowardly privilege of writing behind the lying sheets of the Tennessean. They are without virtues who write lies for their own profit. . . . It was easy for Father Adam to name the hog, snake, elephant, skunk, and the hound dog, but when it came to the bubonic rat he evidently had a mental preview of Evans, Perry, and Hatcher."

He was especially incensed at Perry. "Rat Jennings Perry is full of trickery, has a taste for low intrigue, and is mortgaged to the devil. . . . He wrote a book, *Democracy Begins at Home,* filled with lies, sent it free of charge to the legislators. He will not sell enough copies to get back the cost of the cover. . . . The insipid ass," Crump continued, "the moron. . . . He would like to deal in Greek philosophy, without knowing what he is talking about. He is the perfect example of the type of man who travels from cradle to the grave without having been aroused from the state of invincible ignorance. Only a low filthy scoundrel, pervert, degenerate, would write lies for profit."

Crump demonstrated that he knew some Greek history. "The next time Perry delves into Greek history, someone should tell him that Socrates taught Plato, Plato taught Aristotle, and Aristotle taught the world—he had perhaps the most amazing mind—the greatest capacity for obtaining and retaining knowledge than any man who has ever lived. Perry, to date, hasn't displayed enough knowledge of Greek to qualify him to open a restaurant."

"Now we come to slimy rat, Joe Hatcher," said Crump. Hatcher had written many lies about him. He had written that Crump "had people going through the department stores in Memphis, asking them to send me congratulatory birthday telegrams. That was a low, contemptible, lying statement. . . . Hatcher . . . is full of ululation."

After scurrying to the dictionary to find the meaning of "ululation" ("howling like a wolf"), the reader might go on to Silliman Evans. "Rat Evans would give his right arm if he could lure Capitol Hill and the whole legislature into his luxurious quarters in the Hermitage Hotel, his laboratory in which fake schemes could be concocted and put into effect for his personal aggrandizement. He has the gall, loves glamor, gusto, immodest display of gaudiness, money and everything that goes with a foul mind and wicked heart."

He concluded his letter with an extended recitation of the advantages that Memphis had over other cities—its comprehensive park system, good streets, efficient fire and police departments, low tax and utility rates.

So that a record of his letter would be preserved for history, he had McKellar insert a copy of it into the *Congressional Record*.[34]

The letter was toned to a level that Crump thought befitting the character of his attackers. It was old-fashioned, direct, and highly personal. The use of epithets was deliberate, for if there were any conscience, any manhood, to those whom he attacked, they would move out from behind their impersonal, impalpable journalistic anonymity and respond to the challenge. It irked him to his soul that journalists by innuendo, distortion, and rumor-mongering could

34 *Congressional Record,* Seventieth Congress, first session, Vol. XCI, Pt. 1, 1351–52.

create a gross caricature of him and that he could not give back the lie face-to-face.

The great Crump–*Tennessean* battle had its Memphis reverberations. In January, 1945, a bill came before the legislature to abolish blind Vernon Berg's refreshment concession in the Shelby County courthouse. The action was interpreted by the *Press Scimitar* as a Crump reprisal against Berg for having bought a copy of *Democracy Begins at Home.*

The abolition of the concession stand had nothing to do with the book, Crump wrote to the *Press Scimitar.* "Your Press-Scimitar has concocted a charge against me which you hope will receive public sympathy. I would be among the first to agree if there was one word of truth in it." But "you low contemptible fakers . . . are endeavoring to make much over the removal of Mr. Berg's stand, when Mr. Hale is planning to permit several blind persons, including Mr. Berg . . . to sell refreshments . . . from baskets around the courthouse." Berg "most certainly . . . had a perfect right" to buy *Democracy Begins at Home*" and it is fantastic to charge that any of us would protest and seek to punish him. . . . I have asked you several times to stop lying about me. You have a paper— I have none." [35]

The most sensational attack on Crump as an enemy of democracy came from London, in an article in the *Economist.* It was entitled "Manipulation in Memphis," and was written by "a Correspondent in Tennessee." Who the "correspondent" was has never been publicly declared, but it was alleged by Crump sources that he was a young *Press Scimitar* employee who had done military service in England. Whoever he was, his position was marred by gross oversimplifications and an apparent confusion as to the values that underlie the cause of democracy, since he appeared to support his position with an appeal to nineteenth-century racist dogmas.

Memphis was the scene of a defeat, the article began, "defeat of the cause in which the United Nations fight, the cause of liberty and democracy. For Memphis has a totalitarian government. When the oncoming war made the people of Memphis conscious of the preciousness of liberty and democracy, they were disturbed to see how similar in character their own local government was to that of

35 *Press Scimitar,* January 20, 1945.

Mussolini and Hitler—though, so far, not disturbed enough to rebel or even form an underground."

The Memphis situation, continued the "correspondent," should disturb liberals everywhere because it showed that a susceptibility to dictatorship was not "a peculiarity" of Germans, Italians, and "other lesser breeds," but could even infect "sturdy Anglo-Saxons." In Memphis " 'Ja' " elections were held "to ratify decisions made by the Leader," and Memphians lived in an atmosphere of fear.

What hope was there for the overthrow of this tyranny? Only the *Press Scimitar,* which was "aggressively opposed to the machine. Crump taunts the *Press-Scimitar* with having no political influence. But it has a good deal of influence with Crump." The *Press-Scimitar* had "demanded" that TVA power be brought to Memphis; the *Press Scimitar* had called for a safety campaign, and Memphis was one of the safest cities in the country; the *Press Scimitar* had called for an anti-noise ordinance, and Memphis was the quietest city in the world. The ironical conclusion was that "the *Press-Scimitar* may have helped prolong the life of the machine it fights. Its criticisms have held the machine in check, corrected many of its abuses, and prevented it from becoming intolerable." [36]

Aside from the *Press Scimitar* and the *Tennessean,* other newspapers viewed Crump with less alarm and covered the news he made with some degree of objectivity. The *Commercial Appeal* sometimes ran afoul of Crump's good humor, but it never took on the role of a St. George who would slay the dragon. One of its reporters, Harry Woodbury, was a favorite of Crump's and customarily got first chance at the news emanating from Crump's office. There were many times, said Woodbury, when he would hear Crump's rapid voice on the telephone: "Harry, this is Crump, I think you'd be interested in this. . . ." Fred Hixson, of the Chattanooga *Times,* wrote articles about Crump and the organization that were objective.

The smaller newspapers usually treated Crump favorably. One, the *Parisian* of Henry County, appeared puzzled at the way one Memphis newspaper handled Crump as a subject. "Up here in the sticks it looks like the paper is not backing up its home town, always going off on a Crump tangent. It goes under a fault finding complex. Now constructive criticism is mighty good to help a town erase any ills existing and newspapers are supposed to do that. But a constant

36 *Economist* (London), August 21, 1943.

blowing into just one ear doesn't appeal to the folks up here who are planning, as they grow up, to move to Memphis and settle down in the valley." Concerning Crump "and his newpaper opponent, we might conclude that there are still some newspapers of the sensational type. They sell to the emotional in the peanut gallery." [37]

Crump's loud protests to the newspapers showed that he possessed a human trait: he wanted to be appreciated. He never rose to the plane where philosophical consolations were a sufficient reward for his work in the face of misrepresentations about it. He remained almost boyishly proud of what he had accomplished and anxious that it be appreciated. As he moved into later years of his life, he would recite like a litany all of the reforms and improvements that had come to Memphis as a result of his effort. With the city as a model of progressive urban administration, how could he be so bad or the people so wrong who supported him?

Crump and his organization might affront the sensibilities of liberal journalists, but there were times when his politics appeared more liberal than some of the papers that opposed him. This was apparent in the election of 1944.

To be sure, neither he nor any important Tennessee newspaper supported country music artist Roy Acuff when he announced for governor in the spring of 1944. "There have been many singing and yodeling men elected to public office," Crump commented, but "I can't believe something unbelievable; that the people of Tennessee want a man for governor who knows nothing whatsoever about governmental affairs." [38] He joined McKellar and the *Tennessean* in supporting Jim McCord, an experienced state legislator. He would not support Cooper again, for Cooper, he thought, had been too temperamental. His public relations had not been good.

In July he announced that he would not go to the Democratic convention. He had been to two Chicago conventions, and the hall was a "broiler." But when Roosevelt was nominated for a fourth term Crump announced that he would go "all out" for him, and "it won't be a half-hearted pussy-footing fight." Roosevelt had made mistakes, but "I can easily hang my hat on Roosevelt's war work. . . . His cool head and wise thinking saved this country after Pearl Harbor. . . . Roosevelt wants a better and kinder world." The

37 *Parisian* (Henry County, Tennessee), April 10, 1944.
38 *Commercial Appeal,* January 23, 1944.

Republicans were "hungry." When "a horse has been feeding on roadside weeds for 12 long years, he gets to have a terrific craving for oats." [39]

The two Memphis newspapers, not unexpectedly, supported Thomas E. Dewey. So did Robert B. Snowden, a wealthy Arkansas planter, who styled himself a "Fighting Democrat," and made a speech on a Memphis radio station supporting the Republican candidate. So did L. E. Farley, a local lawyer, who charged that Roosevelt was a communist.

Crump responded with a large political advertisement in the *Commercial Appeal*. "Who Killed Cock-Robin?" he asked in large type. Farley "tried to kill Roosevelt, but his tiny bow and arrow failed him." Farley's anti-Roosevelt campaign was ridiculed. "We started to write the President today to withdraw because we felt he couldn't be elected, as Farley is against him. But when we reflected that Farley didn't vote for Roosevelt four years ago, that gave us a little comfort, and when we know positively the President was elected without his help, that gave us additional comfort. . . . Woe unto them who are pompous, for they will sooner or later be ridiculous."

He turned to the "alleged 'Fighting Democrats' " who were "getting tremendous publicity. We know that bugs swarm around small lights." If some of the "Fighting Democrats" were running for office in Memphis—speaking in the parks or on the street corner cracker boxes—putting out this old rehashed, canned Republican stuff, trying to brand Roosevelt as a Communist, their crowds would fall away from them just like a man climbing a ladder with an armful of eels."

"A lot of us are terribly ashamed that both Memphis papers are fighting our great President—endeavoring to make him out a Communist." When "the Republican papers . . . brand Roosevelt as a Communist, they should be nominated for the Hall of Fame as America's No. 1. Ananias." [40]

The same day the *Press Scimitar* gave space to Farley to reply. He was grateful for "allowing me all the space I need without charge to reply to Mr. Crump's paid advertisement." Because of their long term in office "the New Dealers and Crumpets now consider themselves the aristocracy and look down sneeringly on us common folks and our rights." It was "hard to believe that Mr. Roosevelt, born in

39 *Ibid.*, August 8, 1944.   40 *Ibid.*, October 26, 1944.

the lap of luxury, is a Communist. But as a lawyer . . . I know evidence when I see it—and the evidence proves the case." [41]

Three days later, Crump ran another statement, attacking Dewey for being hostile to the South and taking issue with those who said that Roosevelt was too friendly toward Russia. "Thank God for Russia. Every American should get on his knees every night and thank God for those Russians, for had it not been for them Hitler would have had every country in Europe and England on the ground, and he might have bombed New York." The Dewey speakers were "endeavoring to make the President out a Communist—how ridiculous—so unfair." [42]

On the Saturday before Tuesday's election, the *Press Scimitar* printed as a news item a Snowden statement attacking the New Deal, much of which was addressed to "Mr. Crump." Crump had already written an advertisement dealing with Snowden for Sunday's *Commercial Appeal,* and it was unnecessary to change a word of it to take care of all that Snowden said, or anything he might have said. "Lay That Pistol Down, Bob, Lay that Pistol Down," Crump head-lined his statement. He added a subtitle, "A Case for Old Doctor Bozo":

> I realize anyone is making an error when they argue with people whose opinion they do not take seriously.
>
> Of course, I could easily end this discussion, when it is known that Old Doc Bozo of Poplar Bluff, Missouri, who has been extracting the bray from jackasses, is headed this way, and he would very naturally take care of Bob among the first, and that would end everything. But I will not say that for I realize it is a coarse expression, and I now with-draw it and go on to something else. . . .
>
> A critic must have no cracks in his armor. I might tell Bob that a pot must shine before it calls the kettle black. Some who know Bob will say he has admirable capacity for indignation; but they also say you have to seine with a small mesh to catch him. No one would be surprised if Bob would come out with a quack cure-all to put hair the length of that of the Seven Sutherland Sisters on every bald head, and advertise himself as the great and only living two medicine man in captivity. His ideas on governmental affairs are equally impractical. . . .
>
> I suggest to Col. Bob, and this is no flash stuff, that on next Wednesday he retire to his palatial Arkansas plantation on Horseshoe Lake and finish getting in his 23¢ cotton which Roosevelt made possible.

41 *Press Scimitar,* October 26, 1944.
42 *Commercial Appeal,* October 29, 1944.

P.S.—Since the above ad was prepared, I note the Republican Press-Scimitar has carried a long harangue by Snowden on me. [43]

It was a masterpiece of political persuasion. To most Memphians the satire of the "old Doc Bozo" reference would be irresistible, and some of the oldtimers remembered the advertisements featuring the Seven Sutherland Sisters with their hair streaming to the ground. What humorous satire did not accomplish, the reference to Snowden's "palatial Arkansas plantation on Horseshoe Lake and his acres of 23 ¢ cotton" would.

On the morning of election day Crump delivered a parting shot: "Two Newspapers—One Cash Register" was the headline of his advertisement in the *Commercial Appeal.* "The *Press-Scimitar,* which operates under the same roof with *The Commercial Appeal* and does business out of the same cash register—prints its paper on the same press—owned by the same people in New York, has tried in every conceivable way to make Roosevelt out a Communist. They have published amazing and extraordinary stories—hit the low water mark in Journalism." [44]

In the voting that day the voters of Shelby County went for Roosevelt five to one, but the Democrats missed by ten thousand the high of sixty thousand votes that they had hoped to get. Thirty-three souls gave their vote to Norman Thomas, the perennial Socialist party candidate. In the governor's race McCord won with no trouble at all.

The election of 1944 was the last great fight Crump made for the Presidential nominee of the Democratic party. He had fought for them all—from Wilson through Roosevelt, but it was Roosevelt who laid the greatest claim on his allegiance. It was not only that Roosevelt and the New Deal had given Memphis TVA; it was that Roosevelt spoke powerfully for the common man and spoke with certainty; it was that Roosevelt, dragging his withered limbs in steel braces, moved so positively and confidently through the history of that troubled era that one seldom thought of him as afflicted. Crump admired the President and stood by him through his last campaign.

On March 13, 1945, Crump received a telegram from William D. Hassett, Roosevelt's secretary: "The president is desirous of seeing you and would greatly appreciate it if you could come to Washington the first of next week. Will you kindly advise if this is convenient

43 *Ibid.,* November 5, 1944.   44 *Ibid.,* November 7, 1944.

and I will arrange an appointment." The reply went out immediately: "Beg to acknowledge receipt of your telegram. Inasmuch as I have made all plans to accompany Mrs. Crump to Battle Creek I will arrange to be in Washington the twenty-first if that will suit the president." [45]

When he returned to Memphis, Crump had an account of his meeting with Roosevelt typed up by Mrs. Humphreys: "I went and my engagement was for 12:30. Basil O'Conner, head of the Red Cross was there, also Claude Pepper of Florida. Some soldiers, who looked like French and English by their uniforms. They went in and stayed 5 or 6 minutes. The two other men went in and stayed a few minutes. I went in and the President talked to me one hour. . . . I was the last person to see him that day, March 21st. That afternoon he went to Hyde Park, returned on the 29th. He didn't see anyone in Washington as he was only there two or three hours before leaving for Warm Springs, Ga., where he died. . . . I went up to the capitol and told Senator McKellar, Senator Barkley and Senator Hill that the president looked badly. I went on back to Battle Creek." [46]

What had Roosevelt wanted to see Crump about? The subject was McKellar and his plans to run again in 1946. Roosevelt wanted Crump to withdraw his support from McKellar and said that "McKellar was making a big mistake and wouldn't be reelected." Crump replied, "I told him he was wrong about that, he would be reelected."

There were good reasons for wanting McKellar retired. He was betraying signs of the irascibility of old age. His long years in the Senate made him a powerful figure, but he was no longer the progressive he once had been. The crest of the wave had passed him by, and the country would soon be faced with the issues of postwar reconstruction. Roosevelt wanted more flexible, up-to-date minds in the Congress. Crump may have agreed with Roosevelt on certain aspects of the problem, but agree to ditch McKellar, he would not.

Yet on V-E day Crump thought of Roosevelt. Memphians, he said, should make the day "an occasion for thankfulness and prayer, rather than hilarity and revelry." Roosevelt had "stepped into the

---

45 William D. Hassett to Crump, March 13, 1945. Crump to Hassett, March 13, 1945. Telegrams. Crump Papers.
46 Memorandum. Crump Papers.

lives of millions throughout the world when he began to do something toward preventing future wars. He has sown the seed for a peaceful world, and it looks as if the world will reap the benefit of his far-sightedness. The great Roosevelt has gone." [47]

47 *Commercial Appeal*, May 8, 1945.

⊠ ☐

Chapter XIII

THE 1948 DEFEAT

CRUMP was seventy-one years old when the war ended. Had he been willing, he might have retired and left the city to a new generation of leadership, anxious to prove itself in the postwar years. In the time that remained to him he could scarcely have fixed more rigidly the mold that he had cast for Memphis. It was a city metamorphosed from what it had been in 1905, when he had entered the city council. From 100,000 it had grown to nearly 400,000, sweeping eastward along avenues that radiated miles beyond the encircling parkway system, considered in 1900 as the farthest limits of the city's potential growth. In those days Memphis had been dirty and ill-kempt. Now there were places where it seemed to sparkle. A "City Beautiful Commission" promoted a continuing campaign to clean and beautify, and Crump, as in the old days, was frequently abroad at night, noting eyesores and planning their removal.

Back then, Memphis had had its streak of scarlet—dives and bordellos, and an easy-going political leadership that usually had the good sense not to kick at the pricks. Now, publicly at least, Memphis was pure—a "Sunday-school town," as a few of the oldtimers called it. During the war years police commissioner Boyle had been an unyielding purist on law enforcement. Memphians referred to him as "Holy Joe," and thought of him as a Puritan, humorless and dour.

Almost every year Memphis could boast of some honor it had received. It was the "cleanest" city; it was the "healthiest"; it had the least noise, and its fire department was the most efficient. Out Union Avenue blocks of hospitals clustered. A magnificent new hospital for tuberculosis was under construction, promising practically to eliminate the disease which fifty years before was feared more than any other, having taken the lives of so many of every class.

Even that damning statistic, the murder rate, could no longer brand Memphis as the most sinful. In the last six months of 1946, fewer murders were committed in Memphis than in New Orleans, Atlanta, Birmingham, Nashville, or Jacksonville. Indeed, when compared with Atlanta, the number of murders committed in Memphis for the period was less than one-half, Atlanta having 97 and Memphis 44.[1] The trend toward less violence was well established. By 1960 the Memphis murder rate (murders per 100,000 population) was the lowest of any major Southern city—7.8—followed by New Orleans, Richmond, Atlanta, Jacksonville, Nashville, and Birmingham, with rates of 8.5, 9.3, 10.7, 11.2, 11.5, and 17.5, respectively.[2] What a contrast to the year 1916, when the Prudential Insurance Company statistician, Frederick Hoffman, assigned to Memphis a murder rate of 89.9, then double the rate of its nearest rival—Atlanta!

As remarkable as anything else, the changes that had occurred in forty years had been brought about with such efficiency of financial management that by the end of the war the Memphis tax rate, always low, was reduced from the figure of $2.13 per $1,000 of assessed valuation of the Overton period to $1.80 in 1946. Indeed, the financial picture for the city looked so rosy that Mayor Chandler had used surpluses of the war years to set up a "Pay-As-You-Go" plan with a "Permanent Improvement Fund" so as to avoid future borrowing in the form of bond issues.

For many of its inhabitants, Memphis had fulfilled the promise of its name. It was a place of "good abode," a place where inhabitants were relieved of the disabilities of a half-century past: the curse of sickness, squalor, and brutishness. More people could arise in the morning and face the day with the confidence and optimism that

1 Federal Bureau of Investigation, *Uniform Crime Reports for the United States and Its Possessions,* XVII, No. 2, 1946, pp. 100–103.
2 U. S. Department of Justice, *Crime in the United States* (Washington, 1961), 53–77.

come from physical well-being they could work in an economic climate that gave the assurance that they could improve their lot and fewer would have their lives terminated by violence.

That more people were freer of disease, of poverty, and of a drab gracelessness of life, did indeed make them freer beings. Yet Memphis had sold its soul to Crump and lost its freedom, the critics declared. The average citizen could understand nothing of this charge, but a few, aware that the highest and purest form of freedom involved faculties of the mind and spirit, depressingly sensed that there was something basically hostile in Memphis to their aspirations. And they concluded that it must be that Memphis had really sold its soul to Crump for a mess of pottage. To be sure, Crump did, in the years of the New Deal and after, comment more frequently on what he considered the radical and unsettling trends of the times. But the wall of hostility in Memphis that prevented some intellectuals from finding a comfortable place in its society was not Crump's creation. It was still the persistence of an anti-intellectual agrarian and religious traditionalism. And this could be altered only by time and through the operation of the simpler and vital kinds of freedom that Crump was so instrumental in bringing to Memphis.

Crump might have retired from public leadership in 1946, and perhaps his image would have come off better for it. There were instances when his ability to gauge the temper of the electorate lost its finesse. There were times when he seemed querulous and intemperate. But that Crump should have voluntarily removed himself from the political picture at the end of the war would have been unthinkable. Memphis was a part of him. Expecting him to leave politics would be like asking him to nullify his being. Francis Andrews, a member of the organization and one of Crump's most devoted supporters in the last years, stated that in the summer before Crump's death, the two of them sat in Crump's side yard one evening where Crump told him with deep feeling that he would never surrender his role in the affairs of the city, that he loved Memphis and could never stand to see it taken over by someone else who might do it harm.[3] Two years before he died, Crump got a copy of *Winston S. Churchill's Maxims and Reflections*. A line from Churchill's broadcast to the French on October 21, 1940, caught his eye: "Frenchmen!

3 Interview with Francis Andrews, January 7, 1958.

For more than thirty years in peace and war I have marched with you, and I am marching still along the same road." In the margin, Crump wrote "Mphs." [4]

The end of the war did not find him lacking in either energy or ideas for pushing the development of the city. For some time he had been thinking that a large barren island off the south Memphis shore would be an excellent industrial site if some kind of causeway could be built to connect it with the mainland. In March, 1946, he and U. S. Engineers invaded President's Island, as it was called, with an amphibious landing of thirteen jeeps to study its suitability as an industrial site. Memphis had had a considerable impetus toward industrialization during the war; Crump wanted more. If the city was to keep up with its rivals, he said, "it behooves us to take that rubber band off our civic wallet and go after the things that contribute to growth and progress. . . . Let's not wait for the cow to back up to be milked, but let's go into the pasture and get her." [5]

He pushed for more beautification of the city, even suggesting that it would be "a wonderful thing if a day could be set aside each Spring upon which every car owner would give his automobile . . . a good bath." He wanted the City Beautiful Commission to encourage "a large committee among the colored people" to work in the beautifying campaign. "Let it never be said in Memphis that any section . . . is too poor to paint and too proud to whitewash, and dog-fennel and Jimson weed makes a more beautiful lawn than Bermuda grass." [6]

Some of his actions, though, produced suspicion and even resentment among a very small but definable class of Memphis liberals that made its appearance in the postwar era. One issue was censorship. Following the war, Crump became quite concerned about the state of popular reading. "Books portraying lewdness and perversion should be suppressed. . . . Indecent literature poisons and kills the good in the hearts of children and is dangerous to American home life." He had come to the conclusion that "never in the history of America have books been sold so indiscriminately on the open market which are so saturated with obscenity and degeneracy." In some manner, he felt that the blame lay with "the intellectual kind" who

4   Colin Coote (ed.), *Winston S. Churchill's Maxims and Reflections* (Boston, 1949).
5   *Commercial Appeal*, September 25, 1945.
6   *Ibid.*, November 20, 1946.

"feel they must praise—especially those who claim to be very broad-minded—pretentious fakers." It reminded him of the "old days when . . . if someone well known wrote a play, even if it wasn't worthwhile, many felt compelled to whisper that the play was great stuff, when it was utterly unworthy." However, he concluded, "Joe Boyle, who had done a fine job in making Memphis the cleanest city in America, has stated he will go into the matter fully. He may ask for a committee of three or five to supervise and censor literature the year around." [7]

The censorship that evoked the most anguished outcries from "the intellectual kind" came from Lloyd Binford, who watched over theatrical entertainment. Binford, who was nearing eighty, was most concerned that Memphians be spared heresy regarding the racial theme. In the fall of 1947, he banned Mary Martin and "Annie Get Your Gun." "Of course, I said it can't show here," he was reported to have said. "It's social equality in action. It has been turned down in other Southern cities." He objected to Negroes in the cast being portrayed as a railroad conductor, a waiter, and a porter. "We don't have any negro conductors in the South." [8]

Back during the war, Crump had expressed an appreciation of Russia, but he quickly lost it. "Personally I detest red," he said, "not only Soviet Russia's greed, hate and jealousy, but I dislike red for my hair was red for many years. I was kind to it, kept it trimmed and perfumed, slept with it, always had it on top. Yet, with all my kindness, love and affection it deserted me—turned out to be a traitor. It is now as white as the peaks of Mt. McKinley." All of this was good humor, but he went on to label others with the perfidy he ascribed to his hair—the Memphis League of Women Voters, "hatched by the C.I.O. sympathisers." He was also critical of the Americans for Democratic Action. "There's one word behind the scenes that's agreed on—Red." [9] His willingness to use the term "Red," as it became increasingly a sensitive issue in national life, irritated some people.

In November, 1947, a situation arose that dismayed a few of the city's white residents and many of the colored. The American Heritage Foundation, sponsor of the Freedom Train, took Memphis off the train's scheduled stop for January, 1948, because city officials insisted

7 *Ibid.,* October 22, 1946.
8 *Press Scimitar,* September 29, 1947.
9 *Commercial Appeal,* August 14, 1947.

that riders be segregated. Crump called the situation as he saw it: "A custom of 150 years can't be sidetracked in a day or year and made workable. . . . Yes, Memphis would like to have the Freedom Train. The whites and colored would like to see it," but it was regrettable that "there are many whites and colored who hate one another viciously, and there is no patent medicine overnight cure for it." [10]

Among the issues that encircled him, one, manufactured by the *Press Scimitar,* swirled heavily. On October 6, 1947, the paper gave nearly a whole page to an article by two reporters, Alfred Anderson and Richard Wallace. "They don't treat everybody alike at City Hall," was the opening announcement. "They don't even treat all sections of the city alike." The organization not only discriminated against some to favor others, but it discriminated against one section of the city to favor another. "Did you ever wonder why Memphis grows East so easily? Did you ever wonder why it had such a hard time growing north or south?"

The article was cast in such a way as to suggest an important revelation, but there was no mystery why Memphis grew eastward. Industry and lowland areas rimmed the city at its northern and southern edge; the only suitable land for residential construction was to the east.

Crump was irritated, and presumably as a reflection of his irritation the Shelby County Grand Jury cited the article as the basis for an investigation. The *Press Scimitar* hurriedly pointed out that the Grand Jury's allusion to "charges of law violations contained in the article" was wrong. "For the record we wish to point out that we made no charges of law violations in that article." [11]

Nevertheless, associate editor Meeman and the article's two authors were subpoenaed to testify as to what they knew. The next day Crump bought space for a statement in the *Commercial Appeal* to make his own announcement of the grand jury's findings: "None of the witnesses could give any evidence that would tend to show that any City Official had, during the past twenty-five years, given the 'nod' to any politician as to where any stores, parks, or schools were to be located, or that any 'pipeline' existed from City Hall to any politician or individual." Crump provided his own editorializing: "The *Press-*

10 *Ibid.,* November 24, 1947. 11 *Press Scimitar,* October 15, 1947.

Scimitar with all its shamelessness and stupidity makes statements destitute of the truth in a full page write-up, yet calls no names. Oh! how that paper would dearly love to be able to say that E. H. Crump & Company had the nod—had a pipe line to the City Hall and has received special favors, whereas the truth is far otherwise. . . . The Press-Scimitar should be punished for spreading unfair, untruthful, scurrilous propaganda about this wonderful city—a great city to live in—a cheerful city—a healthy city—a growing city in spite of Meeman's Press-Scimitar. We all know individuals perish, but the truth is eternal." [12]

There was one subject, however, on which Crump and the *Press Scimitar* might have agreed—birds. On April 15, Crump sent similar letters on the subject to Ernest C. Ball and Miss Sue Powers, super-intendents of the city and county schools respectively. "As you know," he began, "springtime is 'nesting time' for all of our birds, and by the same token it is 'testing time' for the loyalty of our Memphis boys and girls in seeing that bird's nests are unmolested. I hope you will ask all of your principals and teachers . . . white and colored, to impress upon their pupils the importance of conserving our bird life." Then he went on to explain why it was so important to be "champions rather than foes" of "our feather friends." Birds ate the bad insects. Finally, he coined a slogan for the kiddies which he put in capital letters, then underlined: "LETS FIGHT OFF THE CATS WHICH EAT THE EGGS AND DESTROY THE YOUNG IN THE NESTS, ON THE GROUND AND IN THE BUSHES.[13]

The letter definitely marked Crump as anti-cat and doubtless produced rebellious mutterings among parents who where cat fanciers. He was also anti-pigeon, especially toward those that waddled around Court Square. The only thing they did was to glut themselves "by children feeding them peanuts so they'll have strength to fly around and mess up the city." [14]

Two well-publicized threats were made on Crump's life in this period. On May 17, 1946, and again on January 12, 1948, he received anonymous letters apparently from the same person, demand-ing money or else he or his wife would be killed. He did not seem

12 *Commercial Appeal*, October 16, 1947.
13 Crump to Sue Powers; Crump to Ernest C. Ball, April 15, 1947. Crump Papers.
14 *Commercial Appeal*, March 14, 1947.

to be worried about the extortion demands, sent by "Revised Capone, Inc." Following instructions, in the second demand, he deposited a case at the appointed place, but it was not taken. It was just as well. All that was inside was a note. It was addressed to "the coward perpetrating this dastardly thing. Anyone could take a white mouse with baby teeth and run you into the Mississippi River." [15]

The first extortion demand set Crump to reminiscing about previous occasions when his life had been threatened. He recalled a letter he had received a year before demanding that he put some money in a tree in West Memphis, Arkansas. "Mrs. Crump and I drove over and looked at the tree. I decided it would be much more dangerous for me to climb up the tree . . . than to disobey the order," he said.

He brought to light a reported threat to his life and that of Attorney General Gerber's back in 1940. According to the secretaries' notes, the murder plot was revealed in the confession of a prisoner in the Davidson County jail, who thought that by making the confession he would influence Crump to intercede with Governor Cooper to prevent his extradition to Louisiana where he was wanted for murder.

According to the prisoner's story, he had agreed to murder Crump and Gerber for money to be paid by hoodlums who had run Memphis gambling interests before the 1940 clean-up. The prisoner related that he had even gone to Crump's home and had hidden in the shrubbery to look over the situation. Then he went to Holly Springs and spent two days there registered in the Van Dorn Hotel under an assumed name, hoping to find an easier chance of getting a shot at Crump.

But his employers were slow in raising the money, so the assassin, fearing that news of the plot had leaked, gave up the job. Later, realizing that he was going to be extradited to Louisiana, he hanged himself in his cell.

The story, taken first-hand from the prisoner by the Memphis assistant attorney general, James E. Pleasants, is altogether plausible. Not only did the prisoner's recitation of circumstances conform to actuality, but the whole concept was typically that of a hoodlum whose empire was threatened. Crump was certain that it was true; in fact, he could name all of the principals in the plot and assign various degrees of complicity to them.[16]

15 Secretaries' notes.
16 The Secretaries' notes contain a full account of the assassination plot.

In October, 1947, Crump was approached by a man who he shortly decided was an assassin of a different character. He was an eastern newspaperman, introduced to Crump by Judge Camille Kelley. "He said he wanted to write a fair book about me," Crump later noted— "one that had never been written." Crump was immediately suspicious of his would-be biographer's purpose. "He asked me to get tickets for him for the football game which I did, but he left the city before the game. It was perfectly apparent from his demeanor that he had an insidious purpose in mind. I discovered that in the beginning and finally told him he was here for no good purpose. He had sought every person who had opposed me trying to get something." He had even told Judge Kelley that "he and his wife had been neglected—hadn't been invited around to card parties, out to the clubs, dinners, etc. He was not only playing the game of snake in the grass . . . but wanted to invade my home—go around socially, pick up any crumbs here and there." [17]

It was a time for Crump when the passing of years brought a closing circle of events that had begun in his early years in Memphis. One day in January, 1947, Galen Tate came to his office. He had been Crump's friend of the early years, an usher at his wedding. Later, politics broke the friendship, and Tate turned on Crump. For years they were enemies, with Tate's name high on Crump's list of the excommunicated. Now Tate was old, without a job, and in need. Could Crump, out of a respect for the friendship they had once shared, now assist him? "They never come back" was a saying Memphians had for those who had been dropped. Perhaps time had mellowed Crump, but more likely he recognized that Tate was truly in need. He was given a job in the County Clerk's office, helping with the sale of license tags.

The surprise felt by those who knew the history of the Crump–Tate feud was compounded a month later when Crump invited Overton back into the fold. "We have asked Watkins Overton to run for president of the City Board of Education, which needs truing up," he stated in a letter to the *Press Scimitar*.[18]

Why had he taken this step? He simply decided, apparently, that

---

Crump himself related the story to a *Press Scimitar* reporter, May 22, 1946.

17   Memorandum. Crump Papers.   18   *Press Scimitar*, April 2, 1947.

Overton was the man for the job, and he thought it was something Overton would like to do. "The only disagreement between us was over the city purchasing the gas plant," explained Crump. "There was merely a matter of opinion. We agreed all the way through on the city taking over the electric light plant." [19] Crump preferred to forget the "poison pen" letter and to think of the fruitful association that he and Overton had had for over a decade.

Later on in the summer of that year Crump went to Battle Creek for a month of health-building. He returned in August to find a rumor circulating that he had died. There was not a word of truth in it, he said. He did not mind people inquiring if he were dead "so long as it's not true. . . . But it would hurt my feelings if it were so." He said he was feeling fine, had a "lot of vitamins and would be around for many, many years." [20]

The next year the circle closed in the life of Crump's longtime assistant and secretary, Marvin Pope. He died alone, in his apartment. In recent years he had served as Chandler's secretary when Chandler was in Congress, and when Chandler came to Memphis to become mayor, Pope came with him. Pope was an amiable man, with an old-fashioned courtliness, who gave his best to Crump and combined with it a loyalty that was almost worshipful. Over the years, Crump stuck by his friend, assisting him when misfortune was his lot. "He was intelligent, faithful, always considerate, and absolutely honest in spirit and deed," said Crump in final tribute.[21]

Politics went on as usual. In the spring of 1946, Crump reshuffled the organization and added five war veterans to the list of candidates up for election that year. The principal contest was the senatorial race, and Crump stuck with McKellar. Running against him was E. W. (Ned) Carmack, a Knoxville newspaper editor and son of the famous Edward Ward Carmack, Tennessee's "peerless statesman," who had deserted the *Commercial Appeal* to serve Bryan and free silver. Crump attacked Carmack in his usual slashing manner, accusing him of being the *Tennessean*'s candidate only after the Nashvillepaper failed to get first Gordon Browning and then Congressman Estes Kefauver to run against McKellar. Carmack, continued Crump, was "a failure as a lawyer, failure as a newspaper man; too heavy for light work, and too light for heavy work."

19 *Commercial Appeal*, February 24, 1947.
20 *Ibid.*, August 11, 1947.   21 *Ibid.*, September 20, 1948.

An issue in the election was McKellar's advancing age, and Carmack wanted to know why it was that Crump was having to do the campaigning for McKellar. "Has the cat got Senator McKellar's tongue?" he asked. Further: "Who made Mr. Crump a judge in Israel anyhow, to decide finally and forever who is and who is not a failure? All men I know are failures in some part of their lives. I am conscious of some in mine. I expect this equips me better to serve the general run of my fellowmen than some proud strutter who supposes himself a 100 per cent success. I wasn't brought up to condemn men who have failed—only those who haven't tried." [22]

In July, to the astonishment of many, the *Press Scimitar* announced that "We Are For McKellar." The Senator had worked for many progressive measures for Tennessee and had never quit a fight.[23]

Crump could not forebear derisive comment. "Our home man, Senator Kenneth McKellar, is doing so well," he wrote to the *Press Scimitar,* "I hope Editor Meeman's endorsement . . . won't set him back." He could not understand why the *Press Scimitar* would endorse McKellar, "and on the same page, immediately under your puerile endorsement, you print a scurrilous article designed to injure Senator McKellar, written by Thomas Stokes, a rank outsider, a notorious 'smear writer' who does not live in this state." Crump concluded with a homily which he had at hand. "Mr. Meeman evidently believes in the doctrine that he may do evil that good may come. No fountain at the same time yields fresh and salt water." [24]

In the election on August 1, McKellar won an easy victory. As was expected, Governor McCord won over Gordon Browning, who was still overseas in the Army and who did not press a serious campaign. The surprise in Shelby was the nearly 6,000 votes that Browning received, nearly twice the number that Carmack got in the county.[25] Browning, most assuredly, would be back in strength for the election two years hence.

Crump regarded the election as a victory over the CIO political action committee that had taken an active role in the election. "It was a great vindication for Senator McKellar and Governor McCord," he said.[26]

22 *Press Scimitar,* April 4, 1946.
23 *Ibid.,* July 12, 1946.
24 *Ibid.,* July 30, 1946.
25 *Commercial Appeal,* August 2, 1946.
26 *Ibid.,* August 2, 1946.

The day after the election, Thomas L. Stokes gave his view of it in his syndicated column in the *Press Scimitar*. "That Crump Election Was a Sight to See'.: It Wasn't Democracy." The CIO trained poll watchers were not normally molested, he said. On the other hand, voters had no privacy in casting their ballots, voting "at little shelves along the wall with a small partition between one place and the next, open to view. . . . Workers for the Crump ticket stood right at the door of the polling places, with the air of being completely in charge, handing out Crump sample ballots in violation of the law that requires them to stand at least 50 feet away." [27]

Crump circled the part about the violation of the fifty-foot law, indicating that he disagreed with Stokes's statement.

The victories of McCord and McKellar were confirmed more emphatically in the November election against the Republican opposition, giving Crump the occasion to denounce those who had questioned McKellar's mental and physical fitness to continue in office, and who, indeed, had declared that his absence from the campaign could mean only that he was dead. It was the "hungry vultures" who had put it out that McKellar was dead. "It is all over town that they have been watching the dead wagon from the hospital, the undertaking parlors, the cemeteries. . . . These buzzards have prayed they would be able to pluck something from his honored hand but again and again, how disappointed they are." [28]

McKellar may have been failing, but he was not dead, and to one woman, at least, the senator was still a very attractive man. Would Crump intercede for her with McKellar, the lady wrote. "No need to stall. I want you to play the role of cupid for me. . . . If you don't I promise you I'll *never* vote again." She had "much to offer him the rest of his personal life." He had "worked hard, long and earnestly— should he not then be properly and completely rewarded for his integrity and devotion? Mr. Ed., I'll wager that if he gave himself a fair chance to know me he might find appealing qualities in my nature. . . . Remember, if you want any future votes—get busy, please." [29]

It was a too delicate matter for Crump to attempt to cool the

27 *Press Scimitar,* August 2, 1946.
28 *Commercial Appeal,* November 6, 1946.
29 Crump Papers.

woman's passion with a written reply. On her letter there is the note:
"Mr. Crump talked to . . . [her]."

The day after the August primary election, Mayor Walter Chandler
took an action that had been anticipated for six months. He would
soon resign as mayor, leaving over a year of an unexpired term. Had
there been a break with Crump? Both emphatically denied it. "I'm
sorry to see Mayor Chandler leave," said Crump. "I had hoped he
could serve out the rest of his term." [30]

Why had Chandler resigned? Several reasons, possibly. He was a
sensitive and scholarly man, with no great taste for the raw combat of
politics. Behind the wall of Crump's strength, he was free to administer Memphis without having to fight the daily battle of politics.
There were no daily conferences with Crump; indeed, months might
pass without an exchange between them, but nonetheless the mayor
was free to operate only within Crump's line. While they were broad
lines, Chandler in one instance crossed over. It involved his "pay-as-
you-go" plan of city financing, the concept that some tax money each
year would be put into a special fund from which money could be
drawn for major capital improvements.

After Chandler left office the disagreement was revealed. "Pay-as-
you-go?" asked Crump. "How many hospitals, hotels . . . and parks
would we have today if the pay-as-you-go plan was the only plan
pursued? During the war years and since, with business good and
everyone paying taxes, cities have been able to save a few hundred
thousand dollars, but an inconsequential amount compared to their
needs, if they are to hold their gains in the way of increased population and expanding industries. Pay-as-you-go travels the road to
nowhere. . . . Pay-as-you-go is weak in theory and utterly impossible
in practice if the community is to advance." He concluded, as usual,
with aphoristic counsel: "We are not living in the Middle Ages, nor
do we want to go back to the camel, the ox cart, the mule drawn
street cars, the razor back hog and the long horned cow." [31]

He was undoubtedly correct, but some—Chandler especially—
might have felt that he expressed himself rather bluntly. Possibly,
too, Chandler was tired of the job and longed for the freedom that

30 *Press Scimitar,* August 7, 1946.
31 *Commercial Appeal,* March 27, 1947.

Washington would afford. Why had Crump not done as Roosevelt suggested—urge McKellar to retire gracefully? Then Chandler could climax his public career in the United States Senate. When Crump insisted on supporting McKellar, Chandler was dispirited. A promotion that he thought he deserved was denied him.

After Chandler resigned, the city commission elected Sylvanus Polk as an interim mayor until a special election could be held in March, 1947. James E. Pleasants was chosen to run, and there was, of course, no opposition. Pleasants, from Clarksdale, Mississippi, had gotten a law degree from the University of Mississippi in 1930, entering the city service in 1939 as an assistant city attorney. In September, 1942, he was elected judge of the criminal court, but took a leave of absence in June, 1943, to enter the Navy. After the war, he was one of the contingent of Crump's "veterans" that were pushed ahead in politics. Pleasants was not a happy choice. He was ill and insecure and shortly would resign.

Late in December, 1946, Crump went to New Orleans to see the Sugar Bowl game. A newspaperman caught him in the hotel lobby. What did he think of his fellow Democrat in the neighboring state of Mississippi, Senator Theodore Bilbo? Crump said nothing for a moment, but "stared at a chandelier" as he thought over what he would say. "I've always been a Democrat. . . . I'll live and die one . . . but I think that everyone knows that there have been some times when I've had opinions of my own . . . let's just let it go at that." Then he quickly took over the interview. "When you get to Memphis," he told the reporter, "look me up. . . . I've got a farming business . . . cotton . . . peanuts . . . a real estate firm . . . a Coca-Cola business and an investment banking business . . . you can't miss it." [32]

Crump had no use for the shenanigans and crudities of a person like Bilbo. It is almost plausible to suspect him of indulging in the recitation of his holdings so as to indicate that he could not be identified with the fraternity of Southern politicians whose demagoguery was sometimes associated with a poor white origin.

He was equally concerned that he not be thought of as one of the same stripe as Curley of Boston, Hague of Jersey City, or Pendergast of Kansas City. Harry S. Truman, President of the United States,

32 New Orleans *Item,* December 28, 1946.

suffered his greatest disability in Crump's estimation because he had been nurtured in the Pendergast organization. Crump "abhorred the appearance of evil," said Walter Chandler.[33]

There were also other reasons why Crump disliked Truman, and he stated them in March, 1948. "I will vote for a democrat next November, but it will not be for Truman. If Truman is nominated in Philadelphia, Senator Harry Byrd of Virginia, or some other fine Democrat of his high calibre, and another good Southerner . . . would undoubtedly sweep the Southern states. Truman had made a "scheming, cold-blooded effort to outdo Henry Wallace and Governor Dewey . . . for the negro vote, he has endeavored to reduce the South to a country of crawling cowards." He was "very happy we didn't vote for Truman for vice president. We thought he was the type of man who would pardon Jim Curley. . . . Memphis and Shelby County didn't acquiesce in his political Freedom Train."

Crump turned his fire on Mrs. Roosevelt. The South had had enough of her "frogging around with her Communist associates in America." She had "practically been Truman's mentor. The time has come for a showdown in the South." [34]

The vehemence of his words left no doubt that they were expressions of his true feeling. They hint that something had gone out of him. In the minds of many, the New Deal had introduced radical departures in American social and political values, yet Crump had ridden the wave of New Deal liberalism with a kind of exuberance. Roosevelt slew dragons, and Crump was excited by the spectacle. There were things about Truman that Crump might have admired. How many times had he overlooked faults because the man in question had risen from humble origins? But Truman produced no excitement, only a brown distaste, and civil rights were a false doctrine. The time had come to take a stand against it, against the CIO, against a liberalism that moved so far left that it was tinged with red. Perhaps the times had passed him by; he was an old man and could no longer ride abreast the wave. He must take a stand if any of the eternal values for which he stood were to be preserved.

He girded for battle in August, 1947, when Shelby County voters

33 Interview with Walter Chandler, July 10, 1957.
34 *Commercial Appeal,* March 2, 1948.

were being registered. The 1948 elections were going to be "a brick-bat throwing fight against Communist front organizations," he warned. "All Memphians should prepare themselves to vote." [35]

The lines began to form early. As the registration proceeded, McKellar wrote Crump: "I am not for Browning for Governor. I imagine you are for McCord and he will be satisfactory to me." [36] Now who would McKellar and Crump agree on as a suitable can-didate for the Senate? There was Congressman Estes Kefauver, certain to make the race. Whether McKellar had seen Kefauver as a future challenge to his position, or whether there was some other reason, McKellar did not like the congressman. Back in July, 1944, when he was attending the Democratic convention in Chicago, McKellar had written Crump about some of the actions he had taken. He thought that Truman was all right for vice-president, but he "would have very much preferred Bankhead or Byrd to Bark-ley. . . ." The Tennessee delegation "was very harmonious except for alternate Kefauver. He was present at each meeting of the delegation and . . . objected to everything." The convention "did not pay him a particle of attention. He caused some laughter when he claimed Jefferson as a Tennessee President. He is about as stupid as they make them." [37]

Crump and McKellar would stand together against Kefauver, but the incumbent, ineffectual Tom Stewart was not the man to make the race against him. In September, Crump told Stewart that he would not have Shelby's support in the following year's race. "We told . . . [him] that we couldn't vote for him again. We gave reasons. . . ." [38]

In January, 1948, Kefauver announced for the Senate. Soon Crump began to gather the "brickbats" to which he had alluded in the previous August. Will Gerber mapped strategy. A letter from the attorney general to McKellar indicated the line of attack. "We are very anxious to get everything we possibly can to show that Kefauver has been voting right along with Marc Antonio [Vito Marcantonio]. Would you be kind enough to get someone to check the record as far back as possible and get us a list of Bills passed in the House in which

35 *Ibid.*, August 11, 1947.
36 McKellar to Crump, August 15, 1947. McKellar Papers.
37 McKellar to Crump, July 26, 1944. Crump Papers.
38 Scrapbook news clipping.

Mr. Crump of Memphis

Kefauver and Marc Antonio's votes were identical. Also any other information you can give us that can be used in the ensuing campaign on Kefauver." [39]

Then surprise—Stewart did not lie down and play dead. He would run too, because "I am so deeply interested in so many matters of government that I hope for a chance to continue to serve my people." [40]

In April Crump revealed that he would support Judge John Mitchell of Cookeville for the Senate. "We have never seen him, never met him," said Crump, but "we understand that he is a very fine man. Col. Roane Waring, who served in the Army with him, says there is no better." [41]

Who was Colonel Waring, on whose recommendation Crump placed so much weight? Surprisingly, he was the president of the Memphis Street Railway Company, an institution that in Crump's catalogue of wicked corporations came second only to the utilities. In former times, when Crump had leveled a verbal blast at the company he added the observation that its president was a "good citizen." But Waring's conservative politics had not been Crump's, and now it seemed almost unnatural that the fire-eating progressive of yesteryear should be making common cause with the president of the traction company.

Truman and civil rights had brought them together, and when the Shelby County Democrats went to the state convention at Nashville, Colonel Waring was their spokesman. Governor McCord made the keynote address, attacking the civil rights program as "a grave danger to the southland" and declaring that "the honor and integrity of the South shall not be bartered for votes in Harlem."

Colonel Waring introduced the Shelby resolution that would have had the Tennessee delegation walk out of the national convention to be held at Philadelphia if Truman were nominated. It was defeated, but not before Waring gave it his best oratorical support: "Never has there been a more brazen invasion of states' rights. . . . We have been sold down the river. . . . We owe it to ourselves and to the South to rebuke the perpetrator of this vicious legislation."

The defeat of the resolution nettled Crump: "It would have been

39 Will Gerber to McKellar, February 19, 1948. McKellar Papers.
40 Scrapbook news clipping.
41 *Commercial Appeal,* April 16, 1948.

another story if there had been a roll call. . . . We down this way will never vote for Truman in the Philadelphia Convention. In fact, I will personally never vote for him at the convention or election." [42] The South stood at Armageddon, as Crump had already warned: "I say again in a most positive way . . . we are at the cross-roads— when people will have to stand up and be counted." [43]

He himself was certainly going to stand up and be counted. If it were not for the election "Mrs. Crump and I would have pulled up January 1st for a long vacation—South American trip. After 45 years in politics we both need it." [44] He gave up something infinitely more important to him than a pleasure trip. For thirty-six years he had been going to Battle Creek for an annual check-up and rest. There was no restorative rest and diet for him at Battle Creek that summer.

The attack on Kefauver was based on the information supplied to Gerber by McKellar's office. Crump pressed his attack in large full-page political advertisements that were carried in the principal newspapers throughout the state. Kefauver was a Communist sympathizer proven by the several occasions on which he had voted with Vito Marcantonio, the New York congressman who was regarded by many as a leftist extremist. Crump recited his evidence:

1. That Kefauver voted with Vito Marcantonio, the oxblood red Communist of New York City, on Feb. 10, 1943, to abolish the Un-American Activities Committee. . . . Congressman Clifford Davis voted against abolishing the committee.
2. That Kefauver voted with Marcantonio on Jan. 5, 1945, against an appropriation for the Committee. Congressman Clifford Davis voted for the appropriation.
3. That Kefauver voted with Marcantonio on Jan. 5, 1945, against a Resolution to make the Un-American Activities Committee a permanent committee of the House. Congressman Clifford Davis voted for the Resolution.
4. That Kefauver voted with Marcantonio on May 17, 1946, against a resolution to cite for contempt 16 Communist witnesses who had refused to give information to the Un-American Committee; furthermore, that he was the only Southerner and, of course, the only Tennessee Congressman, to vote against their cases sustained only a few days ago, Monday, June 14, by the Supreme Court of the United States. . . . Congressman Clifford Davis voted to cite these Communists for contempt.

42 *Ibid.*
43 *Press Scimitar,* March 24, 1948.
44 Memorandum. Crump Papers.

In addition to Kefauver's voting against the Un-American Activities Committee, he had accepted an invitation to speak before "the Independent Citizens' Committee of Arts, Sciences and Professions in New York City, a notorious left-wing organization and unquestionably sympathetic with Communism"; he was against the filibuster; and he had voted with Marcantonio against a resolution to bring up for consideration a measure known as the "loyalty Bill," which "provided for the removal and prevention of appointments in the Executive branch of the government of communists." [45]

All of this, Crump insisted, proved Kefauver's leftist sympathies. On July 8, Mayor Pleasants took to the air on eleven west Tennessee radio stations to deliver a challenge. A "non-partisan committee" would be appointed, before which Editor Meeman should appear to try to disprove Crump's charges that Kefauver's Congressional record showed sympathy toward the Communists. If Meeman did not convince the committee that the charges were false, then Meeman would leave town. If Meeman did convince the committee, then Crump would leave town.

It was all very tense and exciting. Kefauver, perhaps sensing that a stage had been set where he might pick up a few votes, offered to appear before the committee himself if Judge Mitchell would also appear. Each would argue his position and let the committee make a decision.

The question of the committee quickly became wearying. Said Crump: "No committee is necessary to determine whether Kefauver is a Communist sympathizer. His record speaks for itself. The people will decide that issue on August 5." [46]

It was after the flurry of the "committee" challenge that John Gorman, a Memphis labor leader traditionally friendly to Crump, visited Crump in his office to "request that he tone down the virulence of Gerber's attacks on Kefauver." Crump "admitted that the newspaper ads were raw, but said that the thing had gone too far to change the policy at that time." Besides, he did not like Kefauver. He thought him a radical. Then Gorman, who had known the Crump of earlier years, asked a question: "Mr. Crump, can't you remember back in the early days of your political career that people were calling you a radical—the 'red-snapper.' " Crump suddenly leaned back in his

45 *Commercial Appeal,* July 9, 1948.
46 *Ibid.*

chair, and peered fixedly at Gorman through his glasses, "You're right," he said with emphasis.[47]

Gorman later said that he had felt that Crump's ads were too strident and abusive to be convincing to an overwhelming majority of the Memphis electorate in 1946. Crump had misfired.

He misfired on another ad. It employed the folksy kind of allegory that he had used so effectively in the past. Kefauver reminded him of "the pet coon that puts its foot in an open drawer in your room, but invariably turns its head while its foot is feeling around in the drawer. The coon hopes, through its cunning by turning its head, he will deceive any onlookers as to where his foot is and what it is into. If the coon could talk, he would say: 'You have me wrong—I have made a mistake, look at my turned head. I am sorry about my foot. I couldn't see what I was doing." In other words, Kefauver had a foot in the Communist camp but could pretend it was all very coincidental.[48]

Kefauver saw an opening. He began to wear a coonskin cap, saying that he was not "Mr. Crump's pet coon." The cap came from a "genuine Tennessee coon, whose rings were in its tail, not in its nose." [49]

Crump fought as hard against Browning. The battle of a decade past was still fresh in his mind. If Browning had not been in the picture, he would have stayed out of the state election in 1948. "It would have been my very great pleasure to say I am through with anything in the State—my activities will only be in Shelby County where there will be but little trouble," [50] he wrote in a roughed-out letter to an unnamed Northern correspondent. He added a word of caution. "Should they ask about the vote down here, merely reply the people are with us if they think the issue is right. As to number, not suggest anything—never have. A lot of fellows would like to know that—like to make a bet—we never tell."

He made a brief memorandum of his campaign plans against Browning. "He did it before and he will do it again if given a chance. . . . Name everything he did before—enumerate. . . . Talk about

47 Interview with John R. Gorman, September 22, 1957.
48 Allen Hampton Kitchens, "Political Upheaval in Tennessee, Boss Crump and the Senatorial Election of 1948" (M. A. thesis, George Washington University, 1962), 16.
49 *Ibid.*   50 Memorandum. Crump Papers.

the number of Governors—Brownlow the worst—Gordon Browning was next. . . . Capitol—Sodom and Gomorrah. . . . List what he had to say about me." [51]

In July, the full-page anti-Browning ads began to appear in the state newspapers. "Browning, as governor for one term, converted the proud capital of Tennessee into a regular Sodom and Gomorrah, a wicked capital, reeking with sordid, vicious infamy. His handy vultures were also there. One may re-brand a hog with a smooth crop, a fork in the end of its ear, or a bit out of the bottom of its ear, yet it remains the same hog." Then as he customarily did in anti-Browning statements, he reviewed the causes of the break a decade earlier.[52]

When some objected to the extreme language of Crump's ads, he replied with more accusations. To Alfred Mynders, who wrote "Next to the News" in the Chattanooga *Times* Crump declared that he still wanted to know what had gone on in 1938 at the state capital. "What was the payoff on all those murderers, rapists, bank robbers, burglars whom Browning pardoned without a recommendation from the judge, jury or prosecutor? More than 50 of those convicts were subsequently returned to the penitentiary for additional crimes after a brief period of freedom. There is documentary proof of this. I realize Browning and his supporters are very touchous about these . . . things. Shakespeare said, 'Few people love to hear the sins they love to act.' Yes, I say again and again Browning would milk his neighbor's cow through a crack in the fence." [53]

Mynders professed to be shocked by Crump's charge. "No one in Tennessee would connect Gordon Browning with any payoff except Mr. Crump. And he would not do it except in desperate anger. . . . The violent language he has used about Col. Browning has angered Tennesseans as nothing in recent years. It is one of the things which brought Congressman Albert Gore back to Tennessee to stump the state for Col. Browning." Mynders did not, however, reply to the charge that Crump had been making since 1938, that Browning's pardons were excessive.[54]

Where Crump was concerned, Browning played upon a theme

51 Memorandum. Crump Papers.
52 *Press Scimitar,* July 21, 1948.
53 Chattanooga *Times,* July 30, 1948.
54 *Ibid.*

that was certain to get votes: the dark, relentless, and vaguely sinister figure of Will Gerber. At Johnson City, Browning said that "Crump uses Gerber to ride herd over the Legislature like a straw boss. . . . If Willie tries anything like that when I'm governor, I'll personally kick him off Capitol Hill." [55]

Later, Browning satirized Gerber's position with Crump in a fanciful tale that Crump found objectionable. Browning told the story to a west Tennessee audience five days before the election:

A fellow from Shelby County was talking to me the other day and told me he lived near the cemetery. He said he saw a light flashing out among the tombstones one night, and, E. H. Crump with a notebook and pen, and down on knees was little Willie Gerber, reading off the names. He came to one he couldn't read because the moss had grown up all over it. "Just put down any name," he said, "I know there's a name here, but I just can't read it."

"No Willie," replied Mr. Crump, "you've got to read it. We've got to have the right name. This has got to be an honest election." [56]

Browning's recitation was reported in the *Press Scimitar,* and Crump responded with an indignant ad. "A Ghoulish Example of Browning's Idea of Fair Play," he said. "I am sure that no one can imagine me or Will Gerber in Elmwood Cemetery, where my dear son is buried and where so many of my dear relatives and friends rest, at night, with a dark lantern, getting names to use fraudulently in an election." [57]

The *Press Scimitar* editorialized on Crump's outcry. "Mr. Crump is not simple-minded and he should know that Browning told this anecdote not as a statement of a real incident but as a humorous satire on methods which have been used in Shelby elections of the past." [58]

The *Press Scimitar* was wrong. The newspaper and many others were always wrong when they attributed to Crump a mode of sophisticated thinking he did not employ. Crump's mind was simple and direct, as simple and direct as the maxims and aphorisms on which he patterned his thinking and conduct. The subject of the departed was not, in his view, one that should be introduced into politics to get votes. He had such a strait-laced reverence for the dead that most people would have found it extreme. When he was congressman,

55 *Commercial Appeal,* July 24, 1948.
56 *Press Scimitar,* August 3, 1948.
57 *Ibid.*
58 *Ibid.*

he had gotten a letter from a woman requesting his assistance in prosecuting a suit against the estate of a man whom he had known and who had been very hostile toward Crump. Crump had quite a dossier of unsavory facts about him. Would he make a statement about the man's character to help the woman in her suit? No, said Crump, for "when the Lord lays His hands on a man, I take mine off." [59]

This feeling of reverence for the dead was his own rationalization for objecting to Browning's tale. Because in the story he was the butt of the joke and because his age was making him querulous, the enormity of Browning's sin was compounded by having the cemetery episode occur in Elmwood "where my dear son is buried."

Part of it was that Crump sensed a defeat in a state election. It had been a long time since that had happened to him—back in 1928 when he supported McAlister against Horton. For the *Press Scimitar* it had been a long time, too, waiting for an election that would offer even slight evidence that its crusade had borne fruit. It savored victory early. On the evening before the election it ran a large, front-page editorial: "Let the Flag Fly in Our Hearts As We Go to the Polls Tomorrow." It had been "the first campaign in the American spirit . . . in many years." The "old morbid fear has gone from Shelby County. No longer are men afraid to do right. They speak the truth that is in them. . . . 'Perfect love casteth out fear.' " [60]

Kefauver was confident, too. On the day before the election he came to Memphis. "Do not fear the result. . . . We are going to win," he said.[61]

The next day the Tennessee electorate made Kefauver a senator and Browning a governor again. Over the state Kefauver had gotten roughly 150,000 votes; Stewart, 118,000; and Mitchell, 79,000. In Shelby County, Kefauver's vote was approximately 28,000; Mitchell's 38,000; and Stewart 3,000. In the governor's race, Browning got a state vote of approximately 215,000, and McCord just over 160,000. In Shelby it was over 20,000 for Browning and 48,000 for McCord.

Two things were immediately obvious: that a vote split between Stewart and Mitchell over the state had probably elected Kefauver; and that Shelby County had failed to turn the tide in the governor's

59 Secretaries' notes.
60 *Press Scimitar*, August 4, 1948.
61 *Commercial Appeal*, August 5, 1948.

race. Obviously, Crump knew that from the time that Stewart announced, he was on thin ice. He could have backed out of the fight. He had pulled out of the city elections in 1924 when he saw that running his own candidates might result in a Klan victory over Rowlett Paine. Walter Chandler had been withdrawn from the governor's race in 1940, when it appeared that he could not be elected. Conceivably, Crump might have supported Kefauver. Kefauver's record was progressive; he was honest; and he unequivocally favored TVA. Crump had supported Leon Jourolmon for the state utilities commission in the thirties during the TVA fight, and Jourolmon had been called a "red."

How had he put himself in the position of backing a weak candidate, chosen by a Memphis Street Railway Company magnate in 1948? Possibly McKellar had communicated his unreasoning dislike of Kefauver to Crump. After the Roosevelt conference, Crump seemed to stand more solidly with McKellar. Perhaps he felt that the subject of McKellar's age, so frequently invoked, was all the more reason to stand with him. Both were old; they had worked together a long time. Age and sentimentality bound them.

Fighting with his back to the wall, Crump put huge sums in a statewide campaign of newspaper advertisements, emphasizing the "red" theme which he thought the record revealed.

It would have taken a lot of Shelby magic to save the governor's office for McCord in 1948, and the magic was not there. How did it happen that the man who above all others was anathema to Crump could get 20,000 votes? There were many reasons. Harry Woodbury, close to Crump and the temper of the Memphis electorate of that period, has provided good reasons. There were, he says, several areas of disaffection in the Memphis electorate. "One was when Sam Pharr was appointed to fill a vacancy on the state utilities commission. Sam made a lot of enemies and antagonized the railroads. He made all the people on the commission turn in their passes. He came back to Memphis with a display of passes he had collected." The Memphis police force was disgruntled. Members wanted better pay. Some of the organization lieutenants were "getting too high-handed." The railroads were antagonized by the decision to enforce the anti-smoke ordinance. "Henry Buck, the terminal superintendent for the Illinois Central Railroad, was arrested and jailed."

Of greater significance, "the war was over and there were a lot of new families in Memphis. They needed homes; streets were in bad repair, and while the city was anxious to meet the needs, there were material shortages. Returning veterans were willing to speak their piece and did. The organization tried to recognize the veteran's claims. Many city and county jobs were turned over to veterans." Some irresponsible elements of the organization had waged a campaign of scurrility against editor Meeman. Fair-minded people resented that.

Finally, "Crump's style of campaigning" did not go over in '48. The war had stirred the city's population—new elements. Crump's old-fashioned slambang newspaper campaign was not appreciated by a newer and more sophisticated electorate.[62]

Crump gave his reasons for the defeat: "Analyzing the returns from the labor wards it is obvious that labor had a field day in Memphis. . . . Kefauver voted against the Taft–Hartley Bill. That suited labor. Governor McCord had signed the Open Shop Bill. That displeased labor."

He thought the McCord sales tax might have had something to do with the voting. When "McCord talked to us about a sales tax in the Fall of 1946, he said the schools would have to close, that the teachers were underpaid and that the state had no money. He further said that the only solution lay in the enactment of a sales tax. We told him in view of what he had said, we would not oppose it notwithstanding we had always been against a sales tax."

Crump said he was "absolutely not" retiring from politics. "As long as I live I propose to always lend a helping hand where I can be of any assistance to this great and beautiful city—Memphis, Shelby County and the State of Tennessee in the interest of good government and honest public officials which we have had for years." [63] He had stated his political credo—honest government—and he would stick by it to the end.

In Boston on November 22, editor Meeman gave his view of the election in an address to the National Conference on Government, sponsored by the National Municipal League. It had been the triumph of democracy. The editor mentioned his personal role in breaking the boss's hold on the city. "Kefauver came to Memphis. Charlie and I

62 Interview with Harry Woodbury, October 29, 1957.
63 *Commercial Appeal,* August 8, 1948.

invited about 100 people to come to his hotel suite to meet him. Forty came. . . . In that first meeting were four men who became the nucleus of the Kefauver committee."

The address sounded as if some of the ideas had been borrowed from the London *Economist* article of 1943 on Memphis: "It has often been said of peoples who succumb to dictatorship in explanation or extenuation of their passivity that they were not of the Anglo-Saxon blood and tradition," but that was not true of Memphis. "Except for its negro population, Memphis was predominantly Anglo-Saxon. . . ."

The election had brought exhilarating changes: "To hear merchants in a community, standing out in front of their stores, talking politics freely and discussing community and city affairs . . . would not be unusual in almost any part of America. But it was so unusual in Memphis on the morning of August 6 . . . that people began to talk about this new freedom which had always been assured them. . . ." Meeman had a prediction: "We Memphians never do things by halves. We have been pronounced at one time the safest city in the country, the cleanest city, the healthiest city, and the city freest from fire, the city with the least noise." Now Memphis "will have the best non-political council-manager government in the nation. I predict we will have the most active citizen's movement, city officials who are appointed on the strictest merit system and most brilliantly qualified . . . of any city in the country." [64]

Shortly after the election Will Gerber announced that he would retire before January 1, "to enter private law practice." He was guided "by a pledge to his son." The election had nothing to do with his decision, he maintained, but others said that his abusive speeches against the opposition were resented by some of the electorate.[65]

Gerber was stepping down, the Jewish immigrant boy who had sold papers on the streets of Memphis and who, because Crump admired his fierce struggle to improve his lot, had been taken into the city government and watched over to see that he got the promotions he merited. Though Gerber left the bruised sensibilities of those scalded by his invective, he also left a city completely clear of racketeering, loan sharks, medical quacks, and soothsayers. His objective

64   Address given in Boston by Edward J. Meeman at the National Conference on Government, November 22, 1948. Typewritten manuscript.
65   *Commercial Appeal*, August 26, 1948.

was a clean city, and he worked indefatigably to get it. The gamblers and confidence men who fixed an eye on Memphis always found Gerber way ahead of them. He had a genuine devotion to Crump, and when it appeared that he had become a political liability, he stepped down.

After the primary there remained the general election. Crump would support the Democratic nominees in the state, but he would not support Truman. In October he announced that "after conferring with Mayor Pleasants, Chairman E. W. Hale . . . and many of our friends . . . we have decided to go for the States' Rights ticket." [66]

In November Memphis gave Strom Thurmond, the States' Rights candidate, 2500 votes more than Truman, but otherwise supported Browning and Kefauver with heavy majorities over their Republican rivals.

The election left in its wake a number of issues of concern to Crump. Mayor Pleasants, increasingly ill, involved his office in a widening swath of accusation and controversy. There had been discontent in the police department where higher wages were sought. On November 8 he ordered the police to report to their assembly hall where he supposedly read to them an intemperate statement, declaring that whatever the force had been led to believe, the organization was not on its way out." [67]

On Christmas Eve Pleasants announced that he would resign on January 15 because of his health which had "not been good since I returned from the service." Watkins Overton would be mayor again. Crump was hopeful that the harmony of nearly two decades past could be restored.

The election produced the nucleus of a political organization to oppose Crump. Organized to assist Kefauver and Browning, the Meeman-inspired "Citizens Committee" pressed for changes in the operation of the city government. The committee had among its membership a prominent Memphis physician and a Memphis businessman, young and progressive Edmund Orgill. There were also young lawyers like Lucius Burch and veteran Bill McTighe, who wore his combat boots to poll-watch in the election. Some of the things that the committee wanted had been under consideration by the organization—like a "little Hatch Act"—but on one issue Crump and the

66 *Ibid.*, October 7, 1948.   67 *Press Scimitar*, December 24, 1948.

committee stood poles apart. It was on Meeman's pet idea: a city manager form of government. Crump realized there was no popular demand for a change in the city's charter. He would welcome an election on the subject, he said.

His assurance was realistic. There was no real challenge to his supremacy in Memphis. But it was realism for the moment, for even Memphis was beginning to outgrow the conditions that had produced the Crump era.

☒ ☐

Chapter XIV

REST AT LAST

ON OCTOBER 2, 1949, Crump celebrated his seventy-fifth birthday. "It was a wonderful day," he told Harry Woodbury. He had spent the day in Holly Springs, going to the quiet cemetery there, with the old cedars and iron picket fence, to place wreaths on the graves of his parents, "as I always do." Fifty-two of his relatives were buried there, he said. He had toured the places where he had lived as a boy, "with my sons, Edward and Robert." He had thought of many things as he rode about the little town. "When I first got into politics, they used to say around here, 'Let's run this country gig back to Holly Springs.' I always told them if I left Memphis, I knew no place I'd rather go. I love life. I love people." Yes, said Crump, "it was a wonderful day." [1]

Through the vicissitudes of politics, he always had his family as a harbor of peace in his life, and it never meant more to him than it did in his old age. His sons managed the business with outstanding capability and were rearing families of their own in which they tried to inculcate the same tradition of family closeness in which they had been reared. Crump told his grandchildren the hero-tales of the past in which his forebears had had a part. Every Friday night Edward, Jr., and Robert took their children to the grand-

[1] *Commercial Appeal,* October 3, 1949.

parents' home for dinner, and every Sunday morning the grandparents visited their sons and their families.

In the spring of 1947 Crump's granddaughter, Betty Crump, was
elected queen of the Memphis Cotton Carnival. It was an occasion
of ceremonial pomp and revelry, climaxed by the king and queen
of the carnival coming down the Mississippi on a barge where they
could be seen by all their Memphis "subjects." Betty Crump soon
set herself to more important matters, for the carnival was scarcely
over before she married a young Memphis businessman, Frank
Pidgeon, Jr.

To his grandchildren away from home Crump wrote letters of
counsel. To grandson, Robert Crump, Jr., attending school in Virginia, he wrote to urge him to read. "We must look upon books as
living things, undying in their influence over our own thoughts and
actions. A man's reading gives a clear picture of his character." [2]
To granddaughter Betty, he philosophized on adversity. "Misfortune, adversity and sorrow came to us all in time. Our cure, then,
is not to quit, mourn our misfortunes, but to take heart and always
go on. Experience has so often taught us happier and better days
are ahead." [3]

Christmas was always a big event in his life, not only for the
occasion of communion it offered the family, but because it gave
him the opportunity to remember the "worthy" people he admired.
"He was Santy Claus himself around Christmas," said Tom Phillips.
"He had the whole back of his office stacked with presents for
people likely to be forgotten by others and from whom he neither
got nor wanted a return present." [4] The year he died, he already
had his list made up for a Christmas he would never see. Each
house servant got $50; the garbage man, $40. Every charitable institution of the city was given $40. There were over two hundred
people on his list, receiving variously cheeses, fruit, cakes, ties,
candy, flowers, and whiskey. Wreaths were put on the graves of his
family and relatives in Holly Springs, even on the graves of close
relatives of his friends and employees.

Christmas aside, his private charity found its way to particularly
needy persons about the city. "Yours received on yestidy," came a

2 Crump to Robert Crump, Jr., October 19, 1951. Crump Papers.
3 Crump to Betty Crump, undated. Crump Papers.
4 Interview with Tom Phillips, August 15, 1957.

letter from an old man. "Found me up—about. I sure was glad to get your check it come just in Time of Need. I thank you tonge can not tel. My Dear Friend I pray that The Good Lord will Bless you and your whole family. . . . I ben a christin 66 years I will be 80 on the 22 of March so good nite sir." [5]

This extensive off-hand charity continued into old age. Phillips tells of an incident that occurred in the spring of the year Crump died. They had just left a barbershop and were walking through an alley toward Crump's office. "At Tony's restaurant, four Court House officials stopped to chat when one of the most repelling look-ing bums I have ever seen called to him asking for a moment of his time." Crump excused himself, went over, and handed the man a bill. When he returned, one of the group chided him for his act, stating that the beggar was a professional bum and spent half his time in the workhouse. "I know," said Crump, "but even a bum can get hungry." He explained that "there was a deep underlying pri-mary cause for such cases, and if we could reach back and obliterate that cause many now hopeless cases could be restored to society." [6]

A sense of time and the fullness of age was upon him. After the war there was only one man left in Memphis who had run for a public office back in 1904, when Crump began his career. It was C. C. Ogilvie, who had stood for a place on the board of education. When Crump met him on the street, he would stop and hold up two fingers—"we are the only two left," was the meaning of this gesture. Ogilvie would nod, smile, and return the salute.

He continued to make pages of notes of his beloved aphorisms, typed up by Mrs. Humphreys. "I do not believe in the doctrine that we may do evil that good may come. . . . The highest joy in life is to be dedicated to some cause, some service beyond personal suc-cess. . . . Many good horses have to plow—never given a chance to run."

He jotted his thoughts on notepads with his large scrawl. "I am no accidental character in the game of politics, if I were I would be quickly disposed of . . . God might have made a better berry than the strawberry, but doubtless he never did. There might be a better place to live than Memphis but no such place."

"What Will Happen When Crump is Out of the Picture?" asked

5   Paul Crump to Crump, December 20, 1951. Crump Papers.
6   Phillips, "Edward Hull Crump, An Appreciation."

the *Press Scimitar*. Such a question could have evoked Crump's notepad comment, "Meeman Rat," scrawled full across a page.

One of Crump's greatest personal satisfactions in the post-war years was the completion of the Memphis–Arkansas Bridge. It had taken eleven years to bring the project to reality. With all the planning and concern he had put into it, the bridge opening had discordant overtones for him.

There was first the question of its name. In April, 1949, with completion in sight, the bridge commission members with whom Crump had worked so closely, met at the call of the vice-chairman and unanimously decided that the bridge should be named for Crump. One member declared that Crump had "done everything except pay for it," and that there was no one else who could more deserve the honor.[7]

When asked what he thought about it, Crump said he had "never suggested to anyone" that the bridge be named for him, "nor have I coveted the glory attached to it. It is sufficient to know that we have done a good job and to realize that our bridge is nearly ready." He thought it should be named the "Memphis and Arkansas Free Bridge." That there were no tolls on it represented a significant accomplishment, in his view.

But Governor Browning objected. It would be named "Memorial Bridge—just like the veterans of the state have asked." [8] The commission did not have the right to name the bridge, he said. That was the prerogative of the state highway department.

In November, when the bridge commission met to conclude its business, Crump insisted that his name be dropped and that the bridge be called the "Memphis and Arkansas Bridge." It was by this name that it was formally dedicated.

Then followed the controversy over a proposed celebration for the bridge opening. The Memphis chamber of commerce, seeing a celebration as something it could promote, appointed a committee to handle the affair and named an executive secretary to coordinate planning. Crump was sharply critical of the idea. It seemed to him that the committee was bypassing most of the people who had done the real work on the project. "Now after all these eleven years of laborious work," he wrote to the president of the chamber of com-

7 *Commercial Appeal*, April 17, 1949.
8 *Ibid.*, November 12, 1949.

merce, the people who really made the bridge possible, "were asked to play a part about like bat boys on baseball teams. I would hate to think this was a calculated plan."

He was against any celebration. "There was no hurrah when the bridge over the Southern Railroad . . . was recently opened . . . No drum beating when the city . . opened up the River Front Drive. Nothing when the light and gas plants were acquired for the people of Memphis. . . . It may be the wiser solution when the bridge is completed to pull down the bars and let the traffic flow." Further (and this was the kernel of the matter), "you selected a man as Executive Secretary to act as Publicity Promoter—one who has lately come to this section from New York for the sole purpose, I am informed, to sling mud at one of the members of the Bridge Commission. . . . The building of this bridge has been a very serious matter with many of us and should not be toyed with." [9]

The letter put an end to the plans for a celebration. For Crump, it was a move toward blocking the galling possibility that Browning would come to Memphis and be cutting ribbons and making speeches when the governor had done relatively little on the bridge project.

But Browning was not to be shunted aside. With singular gracelessness, he appointed Crump's most vehement latter-day critic, Lovick Miles, as his representative to plan an opening celebration. Forthwith, Miles and the Arkansas governor's representative wrote Crump urging him to delay the opening of the bridge until the proper ceremonies could be held. The affair would be "patriotic, religious, non-political and nonpartisan" and would be climaxed by Governor Browning shaking hands with Governor Sid McMath of Arkansas.[10]

But Crump was not going to fall in with any plans that Lovick Miles might be making. On January 18, 1950, shortly after 6 P.M., the last load of hot asphalt was dumped, and the bridge was finished. Just after midnight, when the asphalt had sufficiently cooled, Crump, Chandler, and Will Fowler, the city engineer, watched the barricades come down and then they drove across. The bridge was then officially open.

Crump would like to have had the bridge named after him, but when Browning opposed it, that ended it. He had no intention of

9 Crump to Caffrey Robertson, November 18, 1949. Crump Papers.
10 *Commercial Appeal,* December 6, 1949.

letting the governor make it appear that his work on the bridge had been motivated by a vainglorious expectation of its being named for him. At the suggestion of Mayor Overton, the city commission did rename the old streets, Iowa and Iowa Extended, out of which the Memphis approach to the bridge had been made, the "E. H. Crump Boulevard."

Ten months after the bridge opening, another Crump-conceived project was realized. A dam had been built across the lower end of the Tennessee Chute, the strip of water that separated the mainland from Presidents Island. The project provided a harbor about four-and-one-half miles long and 2000 feet wide, and made 7800 acres available for industrial development. The one remaining island off the Memphis shore was Mud Island, presenting an unpleasant prospect of mud and marsh for the scholars who worked from the second-floor reference room of Cossitt Library. This, said Crump, should be beautified to make it a "picture card" riverfront.

Ideally, Crump should have spent this remaining years in an atmosphere of political serenity. The old zest for attack seemed to have left him. He shortened his political lines to Memphis and Shelby County, where he seemed to be as strong as ever. In the Democratic primary of 1950, tickets offered by the Citizens Committee group for local and state offices were soundly beaten.[11] With Overton back in the mayor's office, there was hope that the turbulence of local politics could be stilled.

The hope that there would be peace in the mayor's office was soon shattered. In October, 1950, Commissioner Boyle accused Overton of trying to build up a personal political machine with the assistance of Overton's close friend Bert Bates, a local Legion commander and automobile sales executive. When Bates's son Guy had his salary increased by $100 monthly as Overton's secretary, Boyle, commissioner of finances, refused to sign the check. There were other irritations.

The trouble was that Overton felt himself hemmed in, with all of the commissioners apparently reporting to Crump and taking his lead on issues that arose. There was Boyle, undeviatingly loyal to Crump and unwilling to follow any policy except one approved by Crump. The same was true of young Claude Armour, police

11   The author poll-watched for the Citizens group in this election.

commissioner and Boyle's protégé. The other two commissioners, Oscar Williams and R. S. Fredericks, were Crump-chosen.

Squirming in what he regarded as his anomalous position, Overton recommended what he called a "strong mayor" form of government. He wanted an expansion of the appointive power, a veto over the actions of the commission, definite financial control, and a further definition of the powers of the mayor. Crump had a comment on the strong mayor plan: "No good man would want that authority and no bad man should have it." [12]

Crump, however, did not want another rupture, and Overton was placated, although the mayor's sensibilities remained obviously bruised. Just how estranged Overton had become was indicated in June, 1951, when Browning visited the mayor's office. Browning explained that he was there just to talk about the $1,500,000 Negro hospital to be built in Memphis. There had seldom been a visit "that caused quite so much talk by Courthouse employees," commented the *Commercial Appeal*.[13]

Was Overton seeking aid and comfort from Browning? Not outwardly, at least, for two weeks after the visit he and Crump made an adjustment in the situation he found so intolerable. Harry Woodbury, fresh from Crump's office, no doubt, informed the public as to what was going on. "We are supposed to elect a mayor and some city commissioners this Fall, remember?" he asked in his *Commercial Appeal* article. Overton wanted to run again and had called on Crump saying he would appreciate Crump's support. He would, however, like to have something to say about the commissioner's race.[14] The "talk was," Woodbury later reported, that Boyle and Fredericks would not run again and that their place would be filled by two men agreeable to both Overton and Crump.

Thus was born the "peace ticket," with Overton announcing on July 12, 1951, that he would run with Crump's blessing along with Frank Tobey and John Dwyer for the commission. Overton remained in office a year-and-a-half. It was not a pleasant time for him. Where his gadfly had once been Boyle, it was now Claude Armour, repeatedly critical and charging the mayor with "underhanded, two-faced methods" in conducting city affairs.[15] Finally in February, 1953, after the four commissioners fired the city personnel

12 *Commercial Appeal,* February 11, 1951.   14 *Ibid.,* June 24, 1951.
13 *Ibid.,* June 15, 1951.   15 *Ibid.,* December 5, 1952.

director over his protest, Overton announced that he would resign on March 1. He said he was leaving because "no man could continue to serve as Mayor and maintain his self-respect." [16] After his statement the commissioners got together and announced that the new mayor would be Frank Tobey, the man whom Overton had made commissioner. When Overton heard the news, he was moved to acid comment: "I am not surprised. The plot has been clear for some time. If I may, as a humble citizen, quote the immortal Shakespeare, I would say, 'Et tu, Brute.' " [17]

But Overton did not carry his bitterness to his grave with him. When asked, shortly before his death, to discuss his differences with Crump, he simply said that they "were largely a matter of temperament between two people, both of whom could often be stubborn and had minds of their own, but who were equally devoted in their own ways to the best interests of Memphis." He attributed to Crump the possession of "a great understanding of human nature and politics." Crump, he said, had done many fine things for Memphis.[18]

Crump regretted that there had to be another break with Overton. Overton, like Chandler, had been intelligent, high-minded, and capable. Crump could bring a grinding, wearing pressure on a man, as was the case with Overton, but he was also a sentimentalist who liked to reflect on the bright moments of the past, and with Overton there had been such moments.

The Overton incident was not the only unhappy one in the politics of Crump's last years. Early in February, 1952, McKellar announced that he would run again for the Senate, "God willing." He was announcing early because he wanted no one to mistake his intentions. Three weeks later he telegraphed Crump a message that could be taken as a pathetic expression of appreciation that he had finally gotten Crump's support. "For more than 50 years we have been friends. You have managed my matters in a most marvelously successful way. I am under everlasting obligation to you, and I thank you with all my heart and soul. I know you had the backing of your lovely wife. . . . I am under obligation to you that words cannot express, and I believe you know my heart." [19]

16 *Ibid.,* February 7, 1953.
17 *Press Scimitar,* February 20, 1953.
18 Overton to the author, June 19, 1958.
19 McKellar to Crump, March 27, 1952. Telegram. Crump Papers.

Crump took no active open part in the campaign, except to issue a brief statement in March that he would support McKellar and young Frank Clement against Browning in the governor's race. Clement looked "like a winner." [20] It was a new experience for many Memphians, no full-page advertisements, no harsh charges. McKellar himself made only two major speeches during the campaign.

To Crump's Memphis opposition it seemed that the time had come to make a concerted attack on his unchallenged hold over the city, which had lasted nearly a quarter of a century. Not only did it seem that he was retiring from the field, but one of the principal factors which his critics had declared was responsible for his success was altered. For years it was charged that Crump's control of the election machinery went far to explain his lop-sided victories. But in June, 1951, Gilmer Richardson, Browning's principal Memphis supporter, moved into the courthouse to supervise the permanent registration of voters, something that Crump had been advocating for over a decade. For the first time in over half a century, the Memphis voters faced an election for which they would not have to pay a poll tax. Thus, the Citizens group was led to hope that they might undermine Crump's strength at home.

The election withered their expectations. Crump seemed as strong as ever. Not only was the slate of opposition candidates for all local offices easily defeated, but Frank Clement defeated Browning. Crump was "back in the saddle" in Tennessee, the political experts were saying. But Crump was not buoyed up by such pronouncements. "I definitely have no desire to be in the saddle if I could," he remarked.[21] All he expected of Clement was that Memphis be treated fairly in appropriation outlays. He had already said the change in control of the election machinery would make no difference. He hoped that voting machines would be acquired quickly. "Personally, I'm sorry we didn't have voting machines 40 years ago. We'd have won the elections just the same." [22]

In the case of McKellar, the expected occurred. Gore won easily; indeed, McKellar came close to defeat in Shelby County. Crump had anticipated the results, and after the primary he revealed that

20 *Commercial Appeal,* March 7, 1952.
21 *Ibid.,* August 10, 1952.
22 *Ibid.,* March 20, 1952.

he had urged McKellar not to make the race. "I told him he hadn't been over the state for 10 years. . . . I thought he had done enough for the people of Tennessee, and could so easily, so gracefully retire." He went on to say he would "absolutely" give Gore his full support in the November election. Gore was hardworking and had fought his campaign "on a high plane." [23] Likewise, he would vote for Stevenson against General Eisenhower. He would always be a Democrat, and besides, he did not like Eisenhower's anti-TVA position.

Yet he could not help but feel a sadness at McKellar's defeat. His mind ranged back over the many years of their association and the innumerable services that McKellar had rendered him in obtaining some of the important goals he had set for Tennessee and Memphis. They had worked together for years to get TVA; then for the bridge and the Memphis harbor site for industrial development. They had shared many pleasurable, relaxing moments together at horse races and on the historic tours that both were so fond of. "Tennessee has lost a wonderful friend," Crump noted on his memorandum pad. "Senator McKellar had great energy, courage, was always available and always so reliable. His record is that of accumulative achievements over the years." [24]

McKellar's retirement certainly must have caused Crump to reflect on the fact that his own days were numbered. What thought had he given to the city's future when he would no longer be around? Crump was pretty certain he would be around a while yet, but if he was not, he doubted that anything drastic would occur. Writing to the editor of the Dallas *News* to thank him for an editorial comment on Memphis and Crump which he thought was fair, Crump said that he felt "that Memphis could move right along should I decide to 'kick the bucket.' " But he was not thinking of that at the moment. Fortunately, "for me at my age I feel like a colt in clover. Of course, there is no indispensible person." [25]

But the years left to him were few, and in the winter of 1951, there was almost a symbolic foreshadowing of Crump's own end. In the early morning of February 6 Crump got a telephone call from his nephew Ed Rather, president of a Holly Springs bank.

23 *Ibid.*, October 1, 1952.
24 Memorandum. Crump Papers.
25 Crump to William B. Ruggles, editor, Dallas *News*, March 19, 1952.

"Uncle Ed," he said, "you'd better come down if you want to see anything of Holly Springs, because it looks like it's going to burn up." Rather said he had called the Memphis fire department for help, but had been turned down.[26] Could Crump help? Crump could, and at 6:58 A.M., the Memphis fire department sent two pumpers racing down Highway 78 to help fight the fire that was eating up the town's central business district. Crump himself, riding in a chief's car, went with the screaming procession.

At Holly Springs, he stood amidst the equipment, gesticulating with his cane and offering suggestions on how to organize the fight against spreading flames. As the Masonic building collapsed, he turned to his nephew and observed sadly: "I've danced many a mile in that old building." By afternoon, the fire was under control, but not before it had gutted much of the historic center of the old town.

Later, the *Press Scimitar* reported "some quiet criticism" of Crump's action in having pumpers sent to Holly Springs. It weakened the Memphis force. Moreover, the fire department charged for its services outside Memphis.[27]

The criticism was mean. The Memphis firemen who went had just come off the night shift of duty and had volunteered for the job. The neighboring towns of New Albany and Oxford sent nearly all of their equipment to help, and Crump personally paid $469.46 into the city treasury to cover the expense of the effort. Later, he explained that he had overridden no one in instituting the operation. "I asked Commissioner Armour if he could send equipment. . . . I asked Mrs. Evelyn Humphreys, my secretary, to call the Mayor for his sanction. . . . I have never presumed anything. . . . I have never used the city or county governments in any way. It is up to those who are duly elected by the people to run the affairs of the city and county." [28] Overton defended the action. "I don't remember when we ever charged another town for the service of our fire department. . . . We always try to be good neighbors." He would, though, accept Crump's check.[29]

Holly Springs was grateful. Crump's cousin, Mrs. Ann Craft,

26 Interview with Ed Rather, June 24, 1957.
27 *Press Scimitar,* February 7, 1951.
28 *Commercial Appeal,* February 12, 1951.
29 *Press Scimitar,* February 7, 1951.

wrote him of the town's appreciation. "Without any doubt, dear Edward, you are the most generous, most loyal man I have ever known, and I am proud of being your cousin! You saved us and everyone in town knows it and is most appreciative." [30] Crump answered her note, and revealed the depth of his feeling for the town of his boyhood years. "It has been fifty-nine years since I departed from Holly Springs, but my heart has never left it. In the destroyed old Masonic Hall dwelt thoughts of the care-free days of unworried youth, where every conceivable form of entertainment known in those days was presented. . . . And binding memory still closer is the beautiful cemetery where lie awaiting the Last Trump call of my paternal family save me—mother, father, sister, brother—as well as forty-eight other relatives. My heart will ever be with Holly Springs and it was my melancholy privilege to secure the utmost aid in saving that lovely city from a worse devastation." [31]

Later, Crump got a reminder of his early days in Memphis. A letter came from San Francisco: "There isn't the slightest chance that you will recall Bob Handy, a callow youth of the gay 90's in Memphis?" Crump was asked. "Anyhow, Edward, I remember you as one of our gang who frequented Luehrman's quaffing Anheuser-Busch at the oak-round tables. . . . One of my good friends who did not often hoist the old stein was Dabney Crump. I recall you stalking in occasionally from some harness and saddlery shop on 2nd Street. And it stands out in my memory that you married the beauteous Bessie McLean. . . . More power to you—Ed—we read a lot about you . . . but I for one know that you are 'Boss' only because the good people of Memphis made you so." [32]

The remembrances of the past were frequent now, but some were not pleasant. One of his last notepad comments harkened back to his ouster. "The most unsupported and fantastic accusations were freely made. Book out Bal 3 cents." The utilities had dredged to the bottom and found every penny accounted for except three cents.[33]

He was nearing eighty, but he continued to interest himself closely in the city's affairs. In 1953 he proposed that the old Bell Tavern be

30   Mrs. Ann Craft to Crump, undated. Crump Papers.
31   Crump to Mrs. Ann Craft, February 20, 1951. Crump Papers.
32   R. L. Handy to Crump, September 25, 1952. Crump Papers.
33   Memorandum. Crump Papers.

restored, the central feature of the city's wild river-town early history. In April, 1954, he was named chairman of the board of directors of the Oakville sanatorium. Persevering to the end, the *Press Scimitar* protested. "It is almost unbelievable that the man who has played a major role in keeping Oakville Sanatorium hamstrung for months has been named by the City Commission to head the Oakville Board." The paper hoped that Crump would "move swiftly to recommend the needed operating room and detention ward facilities" that the previous chairman had wanted and Commissioner Boyle had opposed.[34]

Crump approached his new job with his customary concern that he have concrete factual data on which to make his plans. Harry Woodbury was employed to make a survey of other state tuberculosis institutions and to determine what facilities they found necessary for successfully operating the plant. The issue that had prompted Crump's predecessor, Dr. Henry Rudner, to resign was, according to Woodbury, moving towards a resolution in favor of the position that Dr. Rudner had taken.

Crump was brought into another area in this period which in the past he had always deliberately shied away from. A group of progressive students at Memphis State College, led by Jim Brister, an ex-state legislator who decided he needed a college education, went to Crump to enlist his assistance in having the school's charter changed to elevate it to university status. Crump favored the idea, but thought former Mayor Rowlett Paine was the proper man to head the project because Paine had started the move to make the institution something more than a teacher's college. Crump said he had thought about Memphis State "time and time again all these years, but I've never attempted to make any move, realizing it would be mighty controversial, create a lot of feeling—probably unnecessarily so." [35]

Elevating Memphis State College to university status was a worthy project, and if substance could have followed the name, perhaps some of the humanizing changes could have been introduced into Memphis society that the city's critics claimed were needed. Crump was a political leader, not the arbiter of the city's intellectual standards, and except for his relatively few animadversions on oversophisticated intellectuals, he properly remained away from any

34 *Press Scimitar,* May 1, 1954.   35 *Ibid.,* April 9, 1952.

semblance of interference with the city's institutions of higher learning.

In March, 1954, Crump made his final statement on the Memphis Street Railway Company and its management. It sounded like the progressive of old. "I hear some of the coterie who want 15 cents fare are telling it around that I am too much of a dictator. They had better spend more time in giving the people first-class street car service which they promised to do when they got 12 cents than going around trying to smear me." [36]

The 1954 political campaign was his last. He kept a careful tab on what was developing. "Gordon Browning is in Memphis today at the Peabody Hotel, room 701, meeting with the following," wrote Mrs. Humphreys in a memo to Crump.[37]

Crump said he would support Clement again against Browning, although he "had made mistakes, but in the main he has tried to make a good governor." [38] Overton supported Browning. Browning's administration had spent $2,000,000 on Memphis streets when he had been mayor. "Browning is not a hypocrite. Personally, I shall cast my vote for Gordon Browning." [39]

The big issue in the campaign was Crump's position in the senatorial contest between Congressional representative Pat Sutton and Estes Kefauver. Sutton was the knight errant of a vocal class of Memphians looking for a local champion to stand alongside Senator Joseph McCarthy in his Great Crusade. County Chairman E. W. Hale announced he would support Sutton, but Crump refused to commit himself. He said that to "be honest and fair," he would have to give Kefauver credit for doing some good things. He had been a strong supporter of TVA "which means everything to Memphis . . . and further as chairman of that committee [Senate Crime Investigating Committee], he opened the door to some very ugly things in America. . . . Any assistance from anyone to curb corruption is desired by all right thinking people and most certainly very commendable." [40]

But toward the end of the campaign a frantic Sutton took it on himself to suggest strongly that Crump would "pass the word" for

36 *Commercial Appeal,* March 21, 1954.
37 Memorandum, August 17, 1953. Crump Papers.
38 *Press Scimitar,* February 1, 1954.
39 *Ibid.,* August 5, 1954.
40 *Commercial Appeal,* March 31, 1953.

him. Robert Snowden, the Arkansas planter, worked actively for Sutton, suggesting on one occasion that his man stood in such favor with the organization that it would supply a police escort to enable Sutton to make a hurried trip from one television station to another. But when a Sutton man telephoned the police department to make the arrangements, he was "turned down completely and quickly." [41]

In the election, Shelby County used voting machines for the first time, and they registered an outcome that tallied with the prediction of organization leaders. Shelby gave a 40,000 majority to the victorious Clement and 27,000 to Kefauver, likewise reelected. The returns "revealed that the influence of 'Mister' Crump in his home county appears greater than ever," said the Nashville *Banner*.[42]

Second to Battle Creek, Crump liked to go to Hot Springs for rest and relaxation at the races. He and Chandler went over in March, 1954, to take a vacation and to think about a slate of candidates for the coming election. As the two men discussed prospective candidates, Crump told Chandler that if he wished to run, he would support him for the United States Senate. That evening Chandler sat down in the lobby of the Arlington Hotel, after Crump had gone upstairs to retire, and wrote Crump a note. It was a document that bespoke Chandler's high character:

I wish to put in writing my appreciation of the high compliment which you paid me today by expressing your willingness to support me for the United States Senate.

With your confidence I would have a great incentive to win, and I believe that I could so, but I would be in my sixty-eighth year when I took office, and I feel that the best interests of Tennessee would be better served by a younger man there.

Whatever success I have had in public office has come through your sponsorship and leadership. I would have relished the chance to go to the Senate in 1947, when it was thought that Senator McKellar might retire, but everyone recognized the value of his seniority, and he should not have had opposition in 1946.

For fifty years your services to the people of Memphis have been unparalleled and your record has been nothing less than remarkable; and I hope that I can keep my health and find the time I can write that history for future generations.

If I do not get this cherished opportunity, I can write now for everyone to read that I think that to an extraordinary degree you have the

41 *Ibid.*, July 19, 1954.
42 Nashville *Banner*, August 12, 1954.

integrity and loyalty and the will of Andrew Jackson, the efficiency of James K. Polk, and the courage of Andrew Johnson; and that triumvirate would shed lustre on any State's history. I cannot define greatness, but I know that there is such a thing and that you have it. [43]

After the Arkansas trip Crump seemed to decline, Tom Phillips thought. The will that once had driven him to long hours of work could no longer push a body that was worn out. He would leave his office early, going home so exhausted that he retired immediately. Mrs. Crump would have a tray brought to his room, and they would have their evening meal together there. In June he ceased going to his office. Yet he continued to oversee his business and attend to the details of politics by using his bedside telephone and having Mrs. Humphreys bring work to him. On July 23 he visited his office for the last time. Some days later, at about 2 A.M., Clint Cleaves heard the buzzer in the servant's quarters summoning him. He found Crump in a profound sweat and vomiting.

Late in August he was put in the Baptist Hospital for a thorough physical examination. Visitors were prohibited, but one day Crump heard Joe Boyle's voice in the hall. Going to the door in his pajamas, he told Boyle that he was fine and would be out in a few days. Willie Thomas, Crump's gardner, came to see him. "Send up a prayer for me Willie," Crump said.[44] Monsignor Kearney, who was a friend of his, went to the hospital to bless him.

He went home on September 2 with no obvious cause for his wasting strength having been found. He had no fever, no infection; his mind was as lucid as ever, but his heart was just worn out.

Through September he rolled around the house in a wheel chair. Nurses attended him constantly. Occasionally he found the strength to make a telephone call. His last one was to Malcolm Adams at the *Commercial Appeal*'s city desk. "They have arrived," he said. The long-awaited black squirrels were at their new home among the trees at the Oakville sanatorium. He had watched them many times when he had been a patient at Battle Creek, and he wanted the Oakville patients to have the same pleasure.

He was eighty on October 2. Despite his weakness, he had himself carried downstairs to look at the many flowers that well-wishers had sent. Before returning to his bedroom, he rolled his wheelchair

43 Chandler to Crump, March 31, 1954. Crump Papers.
44 Interview with Willie Thomas, August 8, 1957.

to the door, opened it and took a long look at his yard, as if to register permanently on his mind a last impression of his flowers and shrubs. He was carried finally to his bed.

Five days later his condition became critical, and doctors placed him in an oxygen tent. He had been in a goldfish bowl much of his life, he said to his sons. It looked as if he were going out in one. Throughout all the last days of his illness, as he talked to Edward, Jr., and Robert about the details of carrying on the business and family affairs, his humor and spirit were unfailingly good. Edward, Jr., thought it was an "absolute front" to keep Mrs. Crump from worrying. "He literally faced death with a smile," his son said.

On October 14 he was reported much worse. His last coherent words before lapsing into a coma were to ask for Mrs. Crump. "Where is my Betty? I want her to hold my hand." [45]

The news that Crump was dying swept over Memphis. Tom Phillips, grief-stricken, went to the Crump Company office, wanting in some way to help. An office phone rang, and he answered it. It was Will Gerber. With a voice breaking with emotion he said he had heard that Crump was dead. Old Richard Borner, the fireman who had befriended Crump when he first arrived in Memphis, made his age-bent way to the Crump home where he said the prayers for the dying from his missal.

Death came at 4:53 P.M., October 16. Forty-five minutes later a hearse moved out of the driveway into the swelling evening traffic of Peabody Avenue, turning west into the bright orange sunset. Reporters, watching from their cars, sent the word that Crump was gone.

He was buried in Elmwood Cemetery according to the rite of the Episcopal church. On the evening before the funeral Father Kearney had gone to the Crump home where the body lay and had prayed for the repose of the soul of the man he admired so much.

"We start young, full of courage, confident . . . but as life races through the normal number of years we arrive at the other end, old, tired, trembling greatly that it is all welcoming death that brings rest at last." So Crump noted shortly before he died.

45   Interview with E. H. Crump, Jr., January 7, 1958.

CRITICAL ESSAY

ON AUTHORITIES

MANUSCRIPT COLLECTIONS

The papers of E. H. Crump constitute the most substantial and significant source of information about his life. When Crump died in 1954, the papers were placed in storage in the Crump Company office building. Since this material was not organized for research use, the significant had to be separated from the insignificant. Generally excluded was the correspondence that related to the day-by-day conduct of his business affairs, whereas that which pertained to his public life and a considerable amount of his private family correspondence was kept for investigation.

Crump was scrupulously careful to preserve the record, and there is scarcely a thought inscribed on a notepad that he did not save. A part of the job of research was to go through a large cardboard carton filled with notepads that had collected over a number of years. Crump also made elaborate memoranda covering the circumstances and significant facts of any controversial situation in which he was involved. The memoranda were customarily prepared at the time of the event or shortly thereafter.

The concern Crump showed for family history is witnessed by his preservation of documents and letters that fill in some of the story of his background. This material includes old contracts, inventories, and an interesting unsigned manuscript—"History of Marshall County" [Mississippi]—apparently written in the closing years of Reconstruction.

A very useful source is the Crump scrapbook collection. This consists of a number of large ledger books in which had been pasted newspaper clippings of articles that began with the early years of his public career. From the character of these clippings it appears that Crump tried to collect everything that was written about him whether it was favorable or not. The same is true of periodical material. Anything printed about him he preserved, and he customarily embellished it with marginal notations giving his own point of view.

There are two other highly useful sources in the Crump material. One is a loose-leaf notebook that contains about 150 pages of typed notes on Crump's life. These "Secretaries' Notes" were made principally by Marvin Pope, who planned to use them in a biography of Crump. Pope served as Crump's secretary for years and he frequently heard his employer relate anecdotal material about his youth and later life which Pope jotted down. Another source of similar character, but briefer, is Thomas Phillips, "Edward Hull Crump, An Appreciation." This is a typewritten statement of Phillips' own reminiscences covering some of the highlights of his association with Crump. Since Phillips knew Crump when the latter was a young man newly arrived in Memphis, his recollections provide some information on a relatively obscure phase of Crump's life.

Bessie Byrd McLean, who became Mrs. E. H. Crump in 1902, kept a scrapbook before her marriage. This is filled with letters from suitors, theater ticket stubs, invitations, announcements, and occasionally a flower pressed between the pages. This source reveals a happy girl enjoying life in the carefree era of the 1890's.

An important collection of manuscript materials that has a bearing on Crump's life is the K. D. McKellar Collection in the Memphis, Tennessee, public library. McKellar, like Crump, saved every scrap of written material that passed over his desk during his many years in the United States Congress. As a consequence, the ponderous character of this collection presents a problem for the researcher.

Mr. Joseph Griggs of the Memphis Public Library is currently ordering the material for research use.

Some of the manuscript material relating to the career of Frank Rice was made available to the author by the Rice family.

A new collection, available too late for the author's use, is the Ben W. Hooper Collection at the library of the University of Tennessee. Hooper was governor of Tennessee from 1910 to 1914 and was notable principally for the zeal with which he espoused the cause of prohibition.

GOVERNMENT DOCUMENTS: CITY, STATE, AND NATIONAL

The important documents relating to the history of Memphis are in the Memphis Collection of the Cossitt Library of Memphis. The most usable of these documents are the annual reports of the city government and the *Memphis Digest,* a compilation of city ordinances and city charter amendments by the state legislature. The *One Year and Eight Months Under Commission Government* (Memphis, 1911) is useful for an official view of the accomplishments of the first eighteen months of Crump's mayoralty.

The record of the legislation of the Tennessee state legislature is found in *Acts of the State of Tennessee* and *Public Acts of the State of Tennessee.*

The publications of the United States Bureau of the Census are basic sources for urban history. Two government documents contain information relevant to Crump's role in the electrical power issue. A detailed study of the structure and interconnections of utility corporations can be found in *Utility Corporations, Summary Report of the Federal Trade Commission to the Senate of the United States,* Document 92, Part 72-A (Washington, 1945). Issues relating to the writing of the Congressional bill creating the Tennessee Valley Authority are found in *Muscle Shoals, Hearings Before the Committee on Military Affairs,* House of Representatives, Seventy-Third Congress, First Session, April 11 to April 15, 1933 (Washington, 1933). The Federal Bureau of Investigation's Uniform Crime Reports For the United States and Its Possessions, XVII, No. 2 (Washington, 1946) contain tables of urban crime rates.

INTERVIEWS

The research for this biography began just three years after Crump's death. Some persons were still living who had known him for almost the whole of his lifetime. Mrs. Matt J. Coffey and Mrs. Helen Craft of Holly Springs, Mississippi, called up memories over the span of a half-century to furnish anecdotes about the young Crump. I spent a day at Hudsonville (an old store at a railroad crossing) going over the area where Crump was born. Miss Dora Boone, near ninety, still facile of mind, provided information about the Crump home and family. Mr. Mason Jones of Memphis had known Crump nearly three-quarters of a century. He had shared with him the boyhood pleasures of fishing and swimming, and both had attended the same school in Holly Springs. In their later years they lived on opposite sides of Peabody Avenue in Memphis and frequently met to exchange reminiscences about the days of their youth.

In Memphis, interviewing went on over most of the year 1957. I discussed the subject of Crump with anyone who had known him, but most of the pertinent information was derived from a limited number of interviews. Mr. E. H. Crump, Jr., was interviewed many times. He was an especially valuable source, not only because he was always careful to see that the information he provided was precisely correct, but because of his proximity to the subject. Miss Clara Muller, who was associated with the Crump Company for years, provided many insights into Crump's character. Important information was provided by one man, who perhaps more than anyone else outside the Crump family, knew the subject really well. Mr. Thomas Phillips' association with Crump began in the early years of Crump's residence in Memphis, when the two met in Luehrman's Restaurant. Later, when Crump became mayor, he made Phillips his first assistant. Their association lasted over the course of Crump's life. Phillips admired Crump very much and was utterly loyal to his memory. As a man of intelligence and integrity he provided reliable information on a number of controversial issues in which Crump had been involved. Phillips was always very concerned that what he said be true; he was equally concerned that it also be just. He tried to see an issue in its broad perspective, and if a person tended to appear badly in a situation, he was quick to give the extenuating circumstances.

An attempt was made to interview Senator McKellar. The senator was found in a room at the end of a long, dimly lit hall in Memphis' Hotel Gayoso. Attended by a practical nurse, he had slipped too far into the shadows to maintain a coherent thread of discussion. Repeatedly he said: "E. H. Crump was straight as a string."

Among those who had opposed Crump politically, the most important testimony came from interviews with Governor Gordon Browning and Mr. Gilmer Richardson of Memphis.

NEWSPAPERS

As a colorful, quotable, and controversial subject, Crump had a wide press coverage during the high years of his career. It was not a coverage that he always appreciated, and some of his epic battles were fought with newspapers. In Memphis his most vocal and persistent opposition came from the Memphis *Press Scimitar,* a paper that closely reflected the thought and journalistic techniques of its editor, Edward J. Meeman. Where the subject of Crump was concerned, editorial usages scarcely veiled the person of Meeman himself in defining *Press Scimitar* policy toward Crump. Even so, in conducting research, the *Press Scimitar*'s editorial position was taken as primary evidence in itself. It was thought better not to go behind the editorial to the person of the editor.

The newspaper that found Crump anathema in the early years of his political career was the Memphis *Commercial Appeal.* A widely influential paper in the mid-South, it was owned in the pre-World War I era by local capitalists who looked askance at Crump's progressivism. Its editor in that era, C. P. J. Mooney, made the *Commercial Appeal* into a highly vocal anti-Crump organ. In the Depression era the paper was absorbed into the Scripps-Howard system. After that, it avoided crusading editorial positions with respect to Crump.

The Nashville newspapers, the *Tennessean* and the *Banner,* were very useful. In the early forties the *Tennessean,* owned and edited by Silliman Evans, took a strong anti-Crump position, expressed in part by a Crump-baiting penchant by some of its writers. Fred Hixson of the Chattanooga *Times* found Crump an interesting subject, about whom he wrote descriptively and accurately. The Knoxville *News-Sentinel* usually echoed the *Press Scimitar*'s point of view.

The Holly Springs *Reporter,* filed in the Holly Springs courthouse, was covered for the period 1875–1895. This source contains bits of information about the activity of the young Crump as well as interesting material on Southern town life in that era.

PERIODICALS

Periodical material on Crump can be used to find out the popular national image of Crump in the thirties and forties. The following reveal this tendency: Jonathan Daniels, "He Suits Memphis," *Saturday Evening Post,* CCXI (June 10, 1939), 48; Hugh Russell Fraser, "The Memphis Machine," *Real America* (April, 1935), 36–37; William G. Shepherd, "O Say, Can You Hear?" *Collier's,* LXXXIX (May 7, 1932), 13; *Time,* XLVII (May 27, 1946), 22; and *Time,* XXVII (May 25, 1936), 56.

For an article that seems to have effectively underlined an image of Crump held by the liberal press of the war years see "Manipulation in Memphis," *Economist,* CXLV (London, England, August 21, 1943), 235–36.

Articles that have a bearing on Crump-involved issues in Memphis and Tennessee are: *Literary Digest,* XLV (October 19, 1912), 656–57; Andrew A. Bruce and Thomas S. Fitzgerald, "A Study of Crime in the City of Memphis, Tennessee," *Journal of the American Institute of Criminal Law and Criminology,* XIX (August, 1928), 14–26; Walter Davenport, "Tennessee for Hoover—Missouri for Smith," *Collier's,* LXXXII (September 29, 1928), 42–44; Ralph G. Hon, "The Memphis Power and Light Deal," *Southern Economic Journal,* VI (January, 1940), 347–65; and Hugh Russell Fraser, "Memphis Votes for Cheaper Power," *Nation,* CXXXIX (November 28, 1934), 615–16.

STUDIES IN MEMPHIS AND TENNESSEE HISTORY

The best brief history of Memphis is Gerald Capers, *The Biography of a River Town, Memphis, Its Heroic Age* (Chapel Hill, 1939). An older, more voluminous work is J. P. Young, *Standard History of Memphis, Tennessee* (Knoxville, 1912). A study of a particular era of Memphis history is William D. Miller, *Memphis During the Progressive Era.* Shields McIlwaine, *Memphis Down in Dixie* (New York, 1948), has several episodes dealing with Crump's early political career.

Two works in particular have an important relationship to Crump's public life. Everett Robert Boyce (ed.), *The Unwanted Boy: The Autobiography of Governor Ben W. Hooper* (Knoxville, 1963) is a valuable study of the political ramifications of the Tennessee Prohibition movement. John Berry McFerrin, *Caldwell and Company* (Chapel Hill, 1939) is an excellent and absorbing study of a Tennessee-based financial structure that expanded its operations into state politics.

Two works have Crump as their subject. Jennings Perry, *Democracy Begins at Home, The Tennessee Fight on the Poll Tax* (New York, 1944) is a source of some of the anti-Crump legends circulated by Crump's Tennessee opponents. Gerald Capers, "Memphis, Satrapy of a Benevolent Despot," in *Our Fair City,* ed. Robert S. Allen (New York, 1947), is critical of Crump and makes perceptive observations about the Crump–Memphis phenomenon.

Helpful unpublished studies are James Curry, "Memphis in the First World War" (paper read before the West Tennessee Historical Society, May 5, 1951); Virginia Phillips, "Rowlett Paine's First Term as Mayor of Memphis, 1920–1924" (M.A. thesis, Memphis State University, 1958); and Allen Hampton Kitchens, "Political Upheaval in Tennessee, Boss Crump and the Senatorial Election of 1948" (M.A. thesis, George Washington University, 1962).

MONOGRAPHS

Works dealing with Crump-related subjects are Lucy Randolph Mason, *To Win These Rights, A Personal Story of the CIO in the South* (New York, 1952); Merah Steven Stuart, *An Economic Detour: A History of Insurance in the Lives of American Negroes* (New York, 1940); and Herold Zink, *City Bosses in the United States* (Durham, 1930). Superficially critical of Crump is Charles W. Van Devander, *The Big Bosses* (New York, 1944).

To understand Crump's mind it is necessary to understand something of the mind of the South. On this there is still no work of more penetrating perception than Wilbur J. Cash, *The Mind of the South* (New York, 1941). Some parts of Twelve Southerners, *I'll Take My Stand: The South and the Agrarian Tradition* (New York, 1930) have good insights into the Southern mentality.

INDEX

Acuff, Roy, 302
Adams, Malcolm: quoted, 210; mentioned, 351
Adams, Null, 228
Agricultural Adjustment Act: Crump's vote for, 179
Airplane: first flight over Memphis, 78
Alexander, Dr. Will W., 292
Alger, Horatio, Jr., 45
Algren, Frank, 287
Allen, Thomas H.: signs TVA contract, 230; and utility purchase negotiations, 261
Alley, J. P., 127
American Civil Liberties Union: in Norman Smith case, 215
American Heritage Foundation: freedom train and segregation issue, 312

Americans for Democratic Action, 312
Anderson, Albert, 17
Anderson, Alfred, 313
Anderson, Harry R., 130
Anderson-Wallace article: in *Press Scimitar,* 313
Andrews, Francis: quoted, 310
Anti-semitism: Crump's opposition to, 198–99
Armour, Claude: and Holly Springs fire, 346; mentioned, 341–42
Army training camps: effect on Memphis, 276
Ashcroft, Thomas C.: elected mayor, 113; quoted, 117–18; in McLain ouster suit, 119; resignation of, 120; accused by Crump, 122; disclaimer, 124; vice control, 127; mentioned, 214, 216

361